Springer Proceedings in Business and Economics

Springer Proceedings in Business and Economics brings the most current research presented at conferences and workshops to a global readership. The series features volumes (in electronic and print formats) of selected contributions from conferences in all areas of economics, business, management, and finance. In addition to an overall evaluation by the publisher of the topical interest, scientific quality, and timeliness of each volume, each contribution is refereed to standards comparable to those of leading journals, resulting in authoritative contributions to the respective fields. Springer's production and distribution infrastructure ensures rapid publication and wide circulation of the latest developments in the most compelling and promising areas of research today.

The editorial development of volumes may be managed using Springer Nature's innovative EquinOCS, a proven online conference proceedings submission, management and review system. This system is designed to ensure an efficient timeline for your publication, making Springer Proceedings in Business and Economics the premier series to publish your workshop or conference volume.

This book series is indexed in SCOPUS.

Samuel O. Idowu · Cătălina Sitnikov ·
Anca Băndoi · Ercan Özen
Editors

Competitiveness and Sustainability in the Digitization Era

Proceedings of the 16th International Conference on Competitiveness and Stability in the Knowledge Base Society (iCOnEc), Romania, October 25–26, 2024

Springer

Editors
Samuel O. Idowu
Guildhall School of Business & Law
London Metropolitan University
London, UK

Cătălina Sitnikov
Faculty of Economics and Business
Administration
University of Craiova
Craiova, Romania

Anca Băndoi
Faculty of Economics and Business
Administration
University of Craiova
Craiova, Romania

Ercan Özen
Faculty of Applied Sciences
Usak University
Usak, Türkiye

ISSN 2198-7246 ISSN 2198-7254 (electronic)
Springer Proceedings in Business and Economics
ISBN 978-3-031-91777-6 ISBN 978-3-031-91778-3 (eBook)
https://doi.org/10.1007/978-3-031-91778-3

This Springer imprint is published by the registered company Springer Nature Switzerland AG
The registered company address is: Gewerbestrasse 11, 6330 Cham, Switzerland

Contents

Digital Metamorphosis: Harnessing Transformation in the Public Sector for Sustainable Governance and Resilience

Andreea-Florentina Crăciun, Muhammad Umar, Meng Qin, Ana-Cristina Nicolescu, and Oana-Ramona Lobonț

Abstract In an era where digital transformation is a defining characteristic of organisational evolution, the public sector is shifting profoundly toward modernisation through digitalisation. This chapter examines the opportunities for integrating digital technologies within public administration, focusing on sustainable governance and the sector's ability to adapt to rapid technological changes. Digital transformation (DT) is positioned as a continuation of the technological progress that began with the First Industrial Revolution and has since evolved through subsequent phases. With DT now aligning with Industry 4.0 and the emergence of Industry 5.0 concepts, public institutions are under increasing pressure to transform to meet the expectations of a digitally empowered citizenry. A complex bibliometric analysis, complemented by insights from the Digital Economy and Society Index (DESI), underpins this study, allowing for a comprehensive view of digital transformation's trajectory within the public sector. Applying the k-means++ clustering method in Orange analysis software has provided a robust framework for categorising EU Member States based on their digitalisation, good governance, and characteristics of government effectiveness. The findings highlight vital dimensions influencing digital adoption, including

A.-F. Crăciun
Faculty of Economics and Business Administration, Doctoral School of Economics and Business Administration, West University of Timisoara, Timisoara, Romania
e-mail: andreea.craciun97@e-uvt.ro

M. Umar
Adnan Kassar School of Business, Lebanese American University, Beirut, Lebanon
e-mail: muhammad.umar@lau.edu.lb

M. Qin
School of Marxism, Qingdao University, Qingdao, China

A.-C. Nicolescu (✉) · O.-R. Lobonț
Faculty of Economics and Business Administration, Department of Finance, Information Systems, and Business Modelling, West University of Timisoara, Timisoara, Romania
e-mail: cristina.nicolescu@e-uvt.ro

O.-R. Lobonț
e-mail: oana.lobont@e-uvt.ro

S. O. Idowu et al. (eds.), *Competitiveness and Sustainability in the Digitization Era*, Springer Proceedings in Business and Economics,
https://doi.org/10.1007/978-3-031-91778-3_1

human capital, infrastructure, and governance. The analysis underscores the central role of skilled personnel and dynamic capabilities within public institutions, where effective management and adaptive digital strategies prove essential for sustainably embedding DT. Moreover, the chapter explores the public sector's response to digitalisation challenges, such as ensuring data security, fostering interagency collaboration, and cultivating resilience against disruptions. This chapter underscores the need for a coordinated approach in the digital transformation process, making the audience feel the urgency and importance of collaboration. The results of this exploration underscore that while digital transformation offers immense potential for enhanced efficiency and service delivery, achieving these goals requires a coordinated approach that balances technological innovation with robust governance frameworks. This chapter contributes to the ongoing discourse on digital public governance by elucidating the multidimensional impacts of digital transformation and outlining strategic pathways to foster an adaptable, resilient, and digitally advanced public sector, instilling a sense of hope and optimism about the benefits of digital transformation.

1 Introduction

The public sector's digital transformation (DT) represents one of modern history's most significant governance and public administration shifts. While "digital transformation" has become widely used, its far-reaching implications extend beyond simply digitising processes or services. Digital transformation is a holistic and fundamental overhaul that redefines how public institutions operate, interact with citizens, and address societal challenges. It builds upon technological advancements that began with the First Industrial Revolution, where mechanisation reshaped production. It has evolved through successive revolutions, each marked by increasing technological sophistication and connectivity. The current phase, often associated with Industry 4.0, introduces a highly interconnected digital environment characterised by artificial intelligence, data analytics, automation, and the Internet of Things (IoT), placing the public sector in a position to harness unprecedented operational efficiencies and citizen engagement opportunities.

Unlike previous industrial advancements primarily focused on private sector productivity and industrial growth, digital transformation in the public sector brings unique challenges and responsibilities. Public institutions must not only adopt and integrate advanced technologies but must do so in ways that prioritise transparency, inclusivity, and security. Additionally, introducing these technologies comes with complex requirements, from upgrading legacy systems and fostering digital literacy among public servants to ensuring data privacy and addressing cybersecurity threats. The public sector, therefore, must navigate the intersection of technological change and public accountability, with a heightened focus on building trust and fostering resilience among citizens. It is important to note that while digital transformation offers significant benefits, it also poses potential risks, such as data breaches, privacy concerns, and the digital divide. Addressing these risks is crucial for successfully implementing digital transformation in the public sector.

In this context, digital transformation goes beyond technology; it encompasses organisational culture shifts, leadership development, and the reshaping of processes to foster innovation and responsiveness. Many public services, such as tax administration, health care, and education, have been restructured to incorporate digital processes that streamline operations and enhance accessibility. For example, e-government initiatives aim to make services available online, reducing bureaucratic delays and allowing for greater transparency. However, the successful implementation of such initiatives hinges on a workforce equipped with digital competencies and leadership that is agile and proactive in addressing the challenges of a rapidly changing digital landscape.

The contribution of this chapter is significant, as it provides a well-rounded exploration of digital transformation by employing a multidimensional approach. The chapter offers several key insights by combining a comprehensive literature review with bibliometric analysis and incorporating data from the Digital Economy and Society Index (DESI). First, a comprehensive context of literature review provides a thorough background on digital transformation, summarising existing research, identifying core themes, and highlighting gaps that enable readers to understand the evolution of digital transformation theories and practices. Second, the quantitative insights of bibliometric analysis give a data-driven perspective, identifying influential authors, articles, and trends within the field and offering a visual map of how digital transformation research has evolved. Third, this analytical framework allows us to examine how digital transformation has progressed in public administration and assess the maturity of digital adoption across various European Union countries.

With its multidimensional approach, the chapter is positioned to inform policymakers and practitioners by presenting a balanced view of theoretical underpinnings and practical data, making available resources for formulating strategies to enhance digital transformation efforts effectively. Key elements of digital transformation in the public sector—including human capital development, technological infrastructure, and governance effectiveness—are identified as critical for sustainable digital progress. The public sector's journey through digital transformation reflects broader societal shifts and specific institutional adaptations. Digital transformation demands that public institutions become agile and responsive, integrating digital tools that promote efficiency, responsiveness, and citizen-centric governance. However, adopting these tools is often uneven, revealing disparities in digital maturity across regions and countries. These disparities can be attributed to factors such as varying levels of investment in digital infrastructure, differences in the availability of skilled workforce, and the effectiveness of governance frameworks. This chapter examines these disparities and assesses the factors contributing to successful digital transformation, such as robust governance frameworks, strategic investments in digital infrastructure, and a skilled workforce.

As the public sector progresses through this transformation, it faces a dual mandate: modernising operations to meet contemporary needs while preserving public trust and ethical standards. This chapter's discussion ultimately seeks to provide a nuanced understanding of the digital transformation process, its multifaceted challenges, and its potential to redefine public service delivery for a digital future. This examination underscores the need for a strategic and adaptive approach to digital transformation, ensuring that public institutions remain resilient and responsive in an increasingly digitalised world.

The chapter's structured overview is as follows: after introducing the main focus of the chapter, on understanding digital transformation within the public sector, outlining the objectives, methods and significance of studying digital transformation's impact on public governance, Sect. 2 defines and frames digital transformation, examining theoretical models and identifying common challenges, such as technological limitations and cultural resistance within public organisations. Also, a dual-method approach, by applying various types of bibliometric analysis through Rstudio's Bibliometrix and a targeted literature review, provided both quantitative insights into publication trends, influential works, and key thematic clusters, as well as qualitative insights into the broader context and depth of current research. Section 3 effectively highlights the dynamic interplay between digitalisation, good governance, and government effectiveness across EU Member States from 2017 to 2022. By leveraging data from the DESI and SGI databases, the analysis provides valuable insights into the trends and correlations among these critical indicators and underscores the importance of a coherent approach to digital transformation within public institutions, revealing that advancements in digital capabilities are closely linked to improvements in governance and effectiveness. The clustering analysis further identifies distinct groupings of countries, allowing for a nuanced understanding of how different nations are progressing in their digital journeys. Finally, the last section concludes the chapter findings, contributing to a deeper understanding of the role of digital technologies in enhancing institutional performance and offering a foundation for future research and policy development aimed at fostering sustainable governance in the digital age.

2 Implications of Digital Transformation in the Public Sector

2.1 Conceptualizing Digital Transformation

Digital transformation (DT) is a standard process today, part of a chain of change that began with the first Industrial Revolution (IR) in 1765. This transformation, while challenging, promises significant benefits for the public sector. Thus, digital transformation is just one stage before a future industrial revolution. Regarding timing, TD overlaps with two revolutions: Industry 4.0 and Society 4.0. Technology was the driving factor of change in all revolutions (Almusaed et al. 2023), and the goal was evolution. As shown in Fig. 1, 7 stages in industrial evolution have been identified, two of which are located on the time axis in the appropriate future (Estrada and Arturo 2024). Each industrial revolution (IR) had its characteristics as follows:

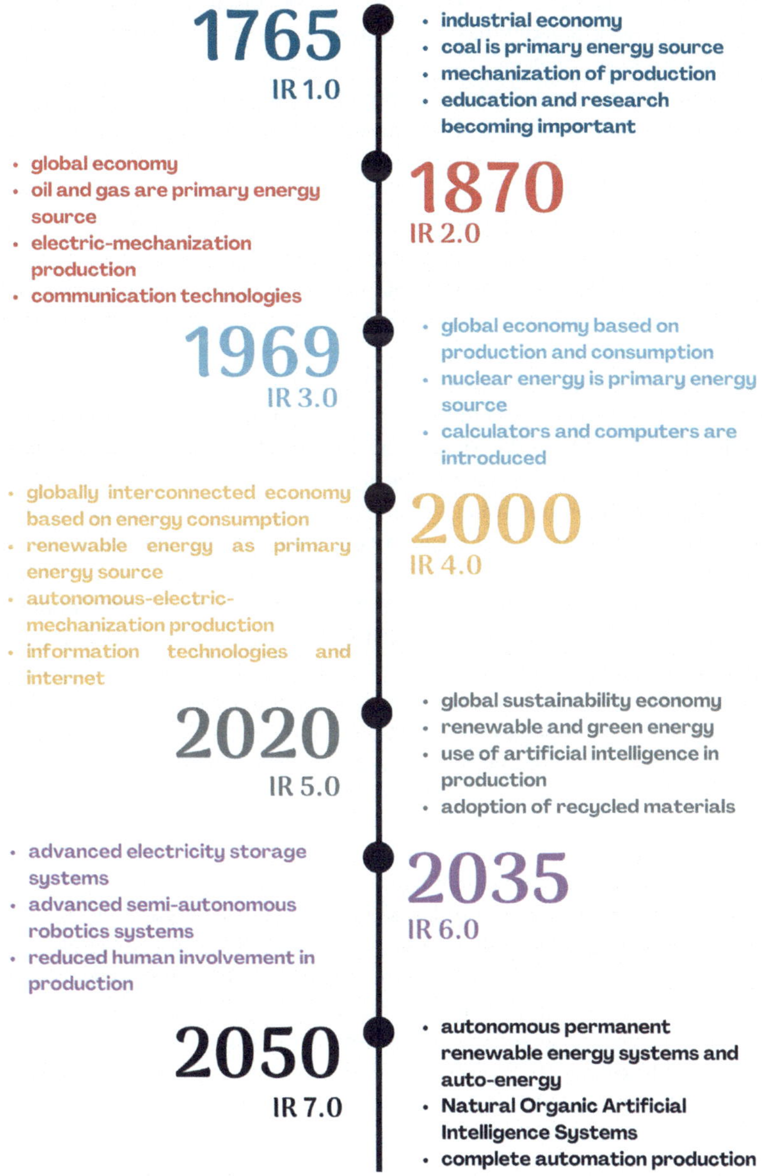

Fig. 1 The period and characteristics of the Industrial Revolution. *Source* Authors' processing based on Estrada and Arturo (2024)

- IR 1.0: This shifted from manual to mechanised production, with coal as the primary energy source;
- IR 2.0: Distinguished by using oil as the primary energy source in electro-mechanised production. The increase in production capacity generated by technological development has also transformed the economy into a global economy;
- IR 3.0: Nuclear power has significantly changed production power, creating a consumption-based economy. The introduction of the first elements of digital technology, such as computers, led to a faster pace of development;
- IR 4.0: Renewable energy sources have been developed to reduce the environmental impact, which started with the first revolution. Autonomous electric technologies were introduced in production, and a heavy transportation network was created. The economy reached its highest level of global interconnectedness ever, emphasising the global impact and shared responsibility of the digital transformation;
- IR 5.0: Represents today's industrial revolution, where artificial intelligence enters many areas. This revolution significantly affects the entire population's education, lifestyle and living standards. At the same time, it is beginning to increase the range of sustainable solutions for manufacturing;
- IR 6.0: Semi-autonomous robot systems will significantly reduce human intervention in most economic processes. Also notable will be new renewable energy storage capabilities;
- IR 7.0: The latest industrial revolution, the characteristics of which are already being defined today, promises the identification and use of self-energy generating systems, taking the whole economy to the next level. Moreover, concepts of advanced technologies are emerging, such as natural organic artificial intelligence systems, microchips, mega-computers and humanoid robots that will eliminate human activity from many fields (Estrada and Arturo 2024).

The IR stages approach aims to outline the framework associated with the research topic, translate it into the paper, and correctly use all the terms interconnected with the digital transformation process. Because, for the most part, the evolution from one revolution to another is mainly based on technology, researching it requires a high level of knowledge of specific terms (Noble et al. 2022). Moreover, because the future involves the technologisation and robotisation of many processes, all changes in the present need to consider the big picture of the future, especially in terms of changes in the public sector where implementation requires an extended period (Bousdekis and Kardaras 2020). Keeping all these aspects in mind and analysing the most important articles in the literature, we consider that the first step in the further literature review is to identify the definitions of keywords related to the subject of analysis, a step that we followed in the first research report for terms specific to the phenomena of tax evasion and the shadow economy.

According to the authors Lanzolla et al. (2020), the literature has developed on an inconclusive theoretical basis, which has led to the use of unsubstitutable concepts in the same context. Digitisation and digitalisation belong to this category. Successive stages of change have taken place by integrating digital technologies into human activity, with digitisation as the starting point. Digital technologies refer to software, automated information processing systems, digital services, data visualisation and others (Sanina et al. 2021). Digitisation makes physical products programmable, addressable, communicable, memorable, trackable, and associable (Yoo et al. 2010). However, the Organisation for Economic Co-operation and Development (OECD) perceives digitisation as converting analogue data into digital format, thus replacing paper-based processes with digital applications that quickly process information to achieve higher efficiency (OECD 2022). In the field literature, digitisation is also recognised as an aid for management structures to perform their functions better (Sanina et al. 2021). Gradillas and Thomas (2022) systematically reviewed the literature on digitisation and digitalisation in innovation, analysing 26 different definitions of the two concepts. After comparing and delimiting them into seven categories, they concluded that there is a clear difference between digitisation and digitisation. Digitisation is "the creation of digital artefacts by transforming analogue information into digital information using conversion, representation and enhancement processes". Conversely, digitisation is "the transformation of the socio-economic environment through the adoption, application and use of digital artefacts". Specifically, digitisation is a stage that precedes digitisation and uses the results of digitisation to create new economic and business opportunities and improve quality of life.

In terms of digital transformation, the OECD considers this to be the effects of digitisation on the economy and society, changing the way people communicate, the labour market, the skills required, the level of privacy, and even security. Likewise, education and health or politics are affected (OECD 2022). Digital transformation also entails a radical overhaul of management structures (Sanina et al. 2021). The first changes are the strategic renewal of the business model, the collaborative approach of the institution and organisational culture, and the constant use of digital technologies in operational processes. Moreover, the entire change driven by this process is based on agility (Warner and Wäger 2019).

Using the concept of research circles as defined by Hevner (2007), Aghakhani et al. (2024) developed a generic (conceptual) goal model adaptable to any organisation that can be guidelines for developing a digital transformation strategy. In order to identify the suitability of the model, they distributed semi-structured questionnaires, and to prove its applicability, the generic conceptual model was applied at Saint-Romain Hospital. The authors' results showed that the objectives of TD can be categorised into four broad categories, namely (i) developing a digital journey, (ii) identifying structural changes, (iii) assessing financial capability, and (iv) identifying changes in value creation. The goal of digital transformation boils down to building capabilities to innovate or replace a business model, relying on collaboration and organisational culture change (Warner and Wäger 2019).

Along with a documented digital transformation strategy tailored to the entity's needs, the successful implementation of this process is also linked to the entity's dynamic capabilities, found in the organisation's ability to recognise changes in the environment, identify and use future opportunities, and reshape its current resources as required (Konopik et al. 2022). Teece (2018) identified the interdependencies of the three dynamic capabilities that can guide organisational transformation in the context of digitisation as follows:

- sense—identifying opportunities by bringing technological possibilities and developing technology;
- capture/attract (seize)—defining and improving the business model and attracting sources to engage in TD by anticipating competitors' reaction and defending intellectual property, all outlined in a strategy;
- transform—realign structure and culture by adjusting existing capabilities and investing in additional capabilities.

In conclusion, conceptualising digital transformation involves understanding it as a complex, multi-dimensional process that extends beyond technology adoption. It encompasses shifts in organisational culture, operational models, and strategic thinking to effectively harness digital tools and data. Successful digital transformation requires technological upgrades, adaptive strategies, dynamic capabilities, and a forward-thinking mindset that can respond to evolving external conditions and emerging opportunities.

2.2 The Digital Transformation Waves in the Public Sector

In order to identify the implications of digital transformation in the public sector, we used several types of bibliometric analysis carried out in Rstudio software through Bibliometrix, followed by a literature review conducted based on the results obtained in the analysis. We used the Web of Science database and documents section to obtain the documents relevant to the secondary research objective targeted in this subchapter. We carried out the selection through the search engine. The search was based on the keywords "digital transformation", "public sector", and "tax administration". The criteria for including documents in the search result was that the title, abstract, keywords plus or authors' keywords contained the combination of digital transformation and public sector or tax administration. Their use was based on the transition from the general sphere—public sector—to the central topic—tax administration. We have also applied filters in the analysis, reducing the time to 2000-present day, corresponding to IR 4.0 and the beginning of IR 5.0.

Moreover, this filter helps us track the evolution of the literature relevant to this study in the recent period. In Table 1, we have centralised the main results of the literature metrics specific to the dataset we obtained from the data cleaning step. The information is structured in five groups and provides an overview of the research topic.

The publication trend identified by the annual scientific output (Fig. 2b) and the average number of citations per year (Fig. 2a) are determinants of scientific performance that indicate the evolution of the topic under analysis and the degree of maturity. Digital transformation is a process that is part of the field of information and systems technology, and its link to the public sector can be investigated independently

Table 1 Summary of the bibliographic metrics identified on the topic researched in WoS

Description	Results
Main data information	
Period	2000:2024
Source (Journals, Books)	877
Documents	1.574
Annual growth rate %	11.66
The average age of the document	6.33
Average citations per document	6.619
References	52.399
Content of documents	
Keywords Plus (ID)	1.266
Authors' keywords (DE)	3.985
Authors	
Authors	3.309
Authors of single-authored documents	500
Collaboration of authors	
Single-authored documents	575
Co-authors on the document	2.43
International co-authorship %	17.22
Type of documents	
Articles	1.077
Article; book chapter	31
Article; data paper	2
Article; early access	34
Article; proceedings paper	14
Biographical-article	1
Book review	15
Editorial material	24
Editorial material; book chapter	1
Meeting abstract	1
Proceedings paper	343
Review	30
Review; book chapter	1

Source Authors' processing by using Bibliometrix software

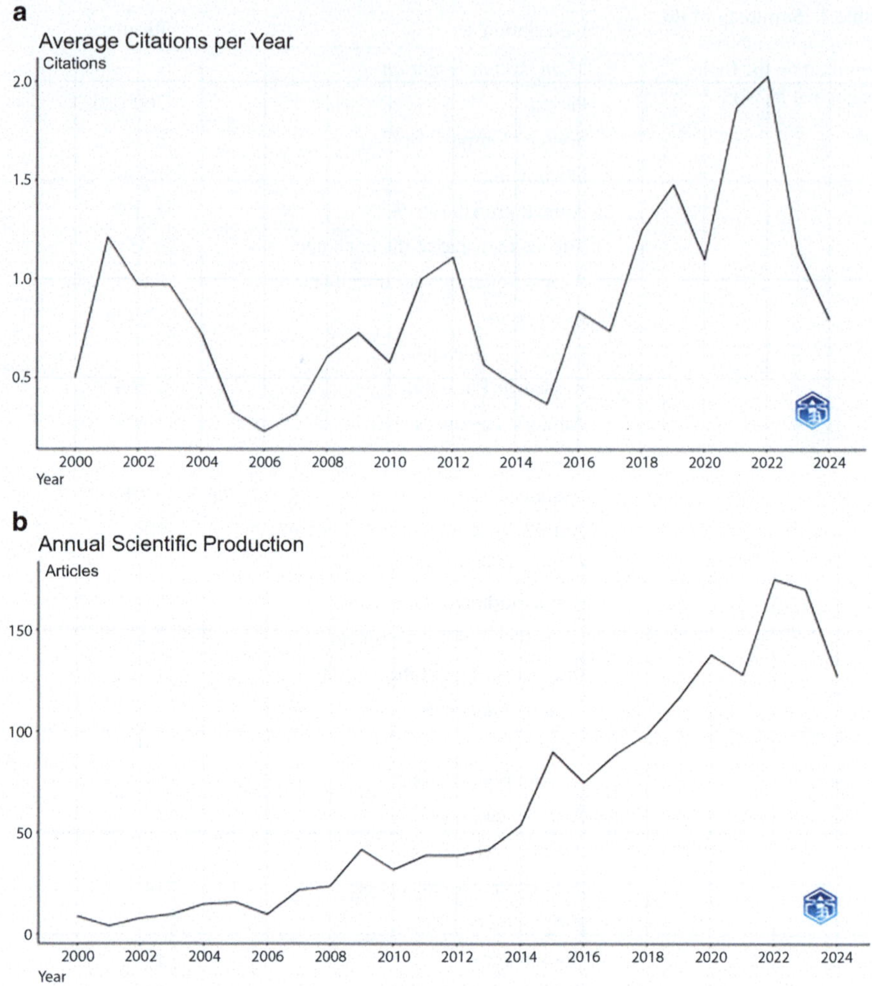

Fig. 2 **a** Average citations per year and **b** Annual scientific output. *Source* Authors' processing by using Bibliometrix software

of the economic sphere, which is why the trend of average citations per year (a) differs from the trend of scientific productivity (b) of the subject. Tracking the yearly scholarly output, we can say that the research on digital transformation in the public sector and especially in tax administration has not yet reached a maximum threshold of published papers, which means that the topic is still evolving and discoveries are still being made.

Over the 25 years of analysis, the topic has evolved considerably. In order to track this, we analysed the thematic evolution for the following timeframes: 2000–2010, 2011–2020 and 2021–2024. Figure 3 contains the graphical outline of the changes.

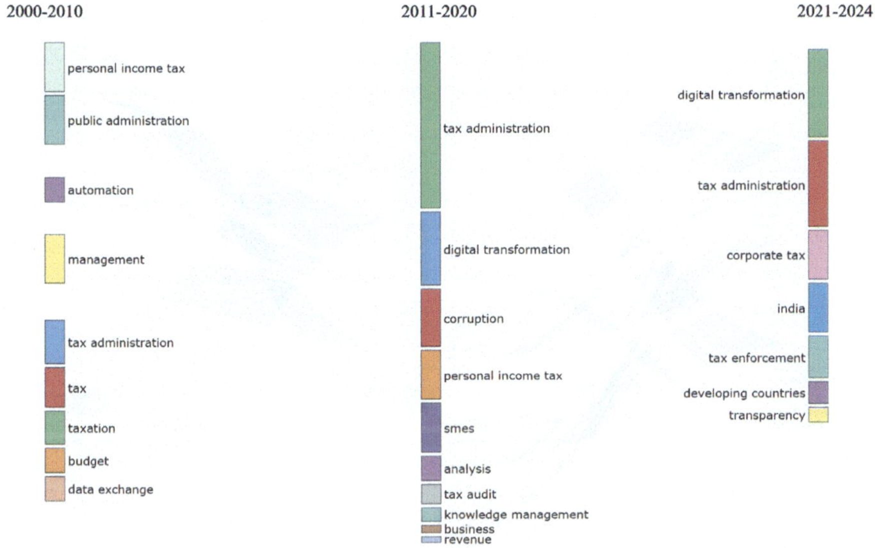

Fig. 3 Evolution of research themes 2000–2024. *Source* Authors' processing by using Bibliometrix software

In the first time interval analysed, corresponding to the first half of the Industrial Revolution 4.0, it is characteristic to research taxes, budget, tax administration and public administration in separate contexts. Also, themes specific to IR 4.0, such as automation or data exchange, emerge in this first timeframe.

The second interval analysed, i.e. 2011–2020, overlaps with the last half of RI 4.0 and the beginning of RI5.0. The beginning of 2020 also saw the COVID-19 pandemic crisis, which is why the adoption of digital technologies has accelerated. It is observed that the dominant theme during this period is tax administration, followed by digital transformation and corruption. Notably, management-related research on the analysed topic evolves into corruption research, public administration and automation are taken up in the digital transformation theme. In contrast, tax administration, taxation, taxation, budgeting and data exchange are grouped in the tax administration theme. Furthermore, analytics, tax audits, knowledge management, and business and revenue emerge in small and medium enterprises.

Finally, the third range of analysis already illustrates the popularity that digital transformation has gained at the expense of tax administration. In contrast to the previous period when tax administration centralised several approaches, it is divided into new themes such as tax enforcement, developing countries and transparency. In conclusion, digital transformation in the public sector and tax administration is a research topic of high interest among the authors. It is constantly evolving and updating with the evolution of the technology sector.

Figure 4 represents the evolution of the research topics included in the earlier themes based on the authors' keywords. As can be seen, the topic with the highest

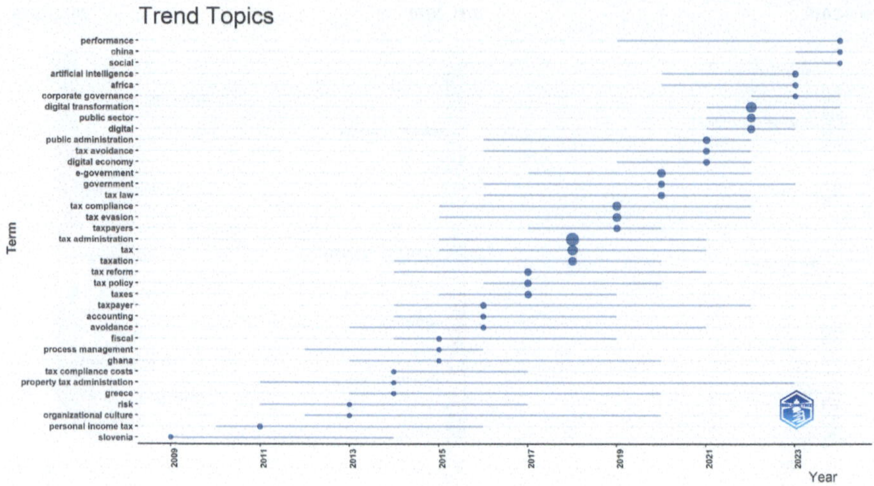

Fig. 4 Evolution of research topics by authors' keywords. *Source* Authors' processing by using Bibliometrix software

coverage over time is property tax administration. However, the highest frequency of use is attributed to tax administration, followed by tax and taxation. Also with high frequency are digital transformation, public sector, and digital.

Suppose the analysis is oriented towards the field dedicated to the content in the abstracts of the documents. In that case, we see a change in the structure regarding the evolution of research topics. The abstract is considered the essential part of the paper, which should provide relevant, correct and complete information about the content of the paper and should contain the keywords to be correctly indexed in databases and search engines (Tullu 2019). Not all researchers consider this aspect in practice, so the authors' keywords do not always correspond to the paper's content. Figure 5 shows a significant difference from the first analysis performed. Thus, if the topics with the highest frequency of use within the abstracts are analysed, also this time, tax administration is in the first place, followed by digital transformation, the public sector and the tax system. Among the most new topics are the digital sector, digital health, study contribution, artificial intelligence, tax enforcement and digital technologies.

Taking both results into account, we can say that the research topic for our theme has lately been addressing elements related to technologies and systems. This means that the studies are becoming more specific and contain more technical information related, in particular, to the adoption and integration of digital technologies in the public sector and tax administration.

In order to review only the most relevant papers in the literature, we used two types of analysis to highlight them: analysis of the most relevant authors according to the number of papers published and analysis of the most cited papers according to overall citations. The authors shape the topic's evolution through the number of papers published on the researched topic. In this sense, we can say that Magnusson,

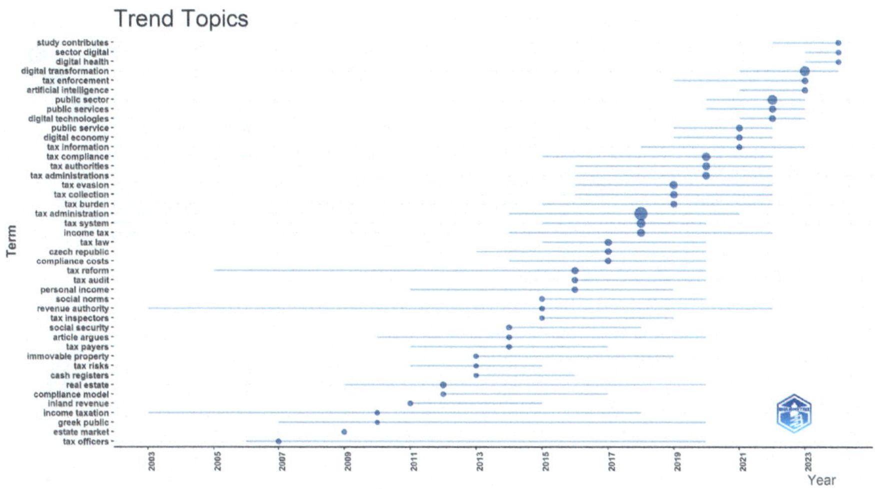

Fig. 5 Evolution of research topics by abstract content. *Source* Authors' processing by using Bibliometrix software

with 11 published papers, has influenced the analysed theme the most. Figure 6 indicates Delgado (with eight papers), Alm (with seven papers), Dobrovic (with seven papers), Edelmann (with seven papers), Mergel (with seven papers), Santoro (with seven papers) and Slemrod (with seven papers) as being among the authors with significant contributions.

However, the number of documents alone cannot identify real influence. By overlaying the previous analysis with that of the most relevant documents in terms of overall citation counts, we construct a complete framework that attributes the impact

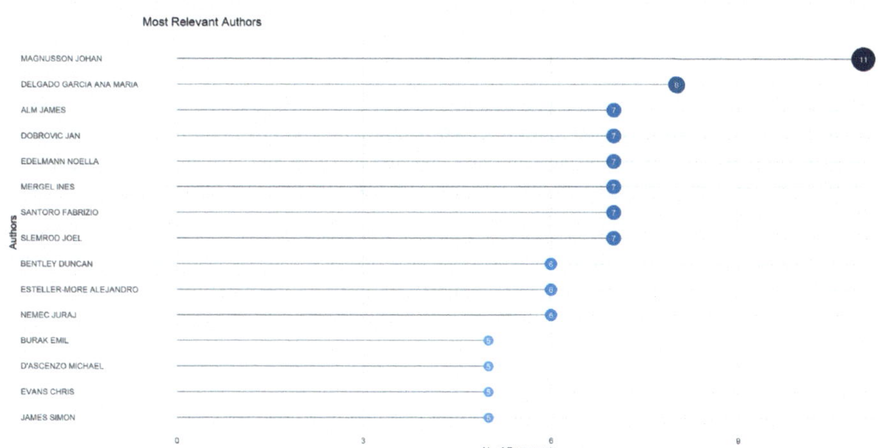

Fig. 6 Most relevant authors by scientific productivity. *Source* Authors' processing by using Bibliometrix software

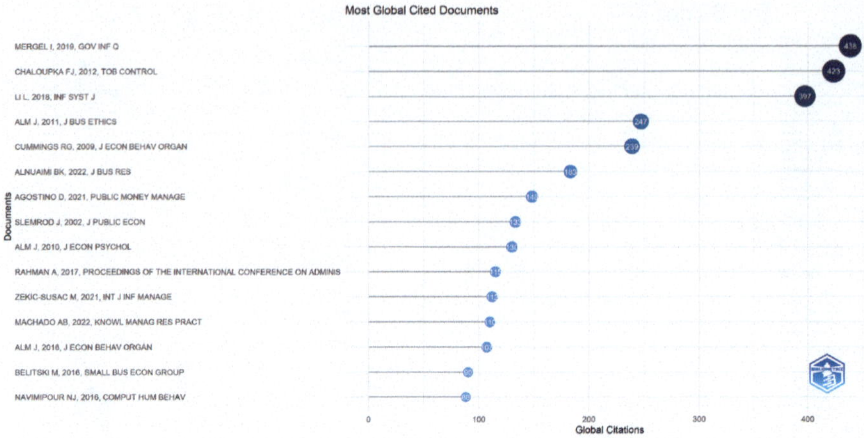

Fig. 7 Most relevant papers by the overall number of citations. *Source* Authors' processing by using Bibliometrix software

of authors on the topic under investigation. Figure 7 contains the results of the analysis. Among the 15 most cited papers globally, Alm holds 3 with 247, 148 and 130 citations. Mergel has only one document in the ranking but ranks first with 438 citations, followed by Chaloupka with 423 citations and Li with 397 citations. Chaloupka and Li were not among the 15 most productive authors. However, they made a significant impact in the field with one paper.

Considering all the results obtained from the bibliometric analysis, we can select the literature revealing the most essential implications of digital transformation in the public sector and tax administration. Mergel et al. (2019) provide the most comprehensive insights on the impact of digital transformation by structuring them into elements, motives, objects, processes and outcomes of digital transformation. The reasons why the public sector turns to TD can be internal or external, and the influence of external motives, such as pressure from citizens or businesses, is the greatest. Among the objects that are affected by TD, the authors list (i) processes, (ii) services, (ii) products, (iv) relationships, (v) technologies and (vi) operating models. The digital transformation processes that are taking place in the public sphere refer to digitisation of processes, digitisation of physical documents, digitisation of relationships, digitisation of services, use of new technologies and development of new competencies. Most important are the digitisation of processes and the use of new technologies. Finally, the TD outcomes outlined by the authors refer to outputs (new services, products, processes and skills), outcomes (improved services, processes and relationships, policies and digital environment) and impacts (added value, organisational change, digital society and democratic principles). The implications of TD for the public sector imply a significant change covering all the main aspects, seen as a reconstruction of what the public sector does and what it delivers.

Li et al. (2017) conducted a study regarding digital transformation implemented by entrepreneurs of SMEs. Although the study addresses the private environment, its results can be extrapolated to the public environment. Digital managerial capabilities can guarantee success in the TD process, which means that leaders of institutions are responsible for improving their capabilities to build and reconfigure organisational resources and competencies. Moreover, the leadership of institutions should emphasise adopting digital technologies only after ensuring qualified personnel lead the digital transformation process (AlNuaimi et al. 2022). In addition, the public sector should move towards agility and follow the best practices in the private sector. Agility implies the ability of a system to respond to changing needs cost-effectively and without affecting the quality of the products and services provided.

The most negligible implications of digital transformation in the public sector are still found in organisational structure, culture, mission, and people's responsibilities. However, the combination of factors influencing TD involves a sense of urgency, the need for change, defining a shared vision, and creating a collaborative environment, factors for which leaders in public institutions must be accountable (Tangi et al. 2021).

When discussing digital transformation in the public sector, sector-specific and process-specific technical terms also arise. To fully understand these, we provide their definitions as identified in the literature in Table 2.

An overview of the implications of digital transformation for public governance is outlined in the European Commission's 2023 report. According to the report, public

Table 2 Terms specific to digital transformation in the public sector

Term	Definition	Source
e-government (e-government/e-Gov)	"the Government's use of web-based Internet applications and other information technologies, combined with processes that implement those technologies, to a) improve access to and delivery of government information and services to the public, other agencies, and other governmental entities or b) make improvements in government operations that may include effectiveness, efficiency, quality of service, or transformation"	US Congress (2002)
e-governance	"involves making and implementing decisions, proper leadership, putting organisational arrangements in place, securing resources and funding, establishing accountability and measuring success"	Godse and Garg (2007)
Innovative governance	"governance through new approaches such as participatory government, open government or public-private partnerships"	Hartley (2005)
Digital services	"services that are obtained and/or provided through a digital transaction"	Williams et al. (2008)
e-public services	"public service mediated by electronic technologies and characterised by availability and accessibility"	Linggren and Jansson (2013)

Source Authors' processing

governance faces several strategic challenges in the context of the TD that it has to address and for which it has to find the most appropriate solutions in order to continue to operate at the highest standards. Specifically, the challenges are the following:

- Strategic Challenge 1—Living with turbulence: open strategic autonomy, security and risks, and societal resilience. Open strategic autonomy refers to the ability of a government to procure the most strategic goods and services for itself and those it needs to procure to come from trusted countries. Among the elements of risk and security, the European Commission cites risks to economic recovery, social and environmental concerns, threats to the continued provision of financial services, fiscal stability and the financial system's resilience, and cyber security;
- Strategic Challenge 2—Changing geographies: European and global geopolitics, reordering settlements and communities, turbo-charged localities and communities. These challenges relate to recent conflict situations and the trend of counter-urbanisation;
- Strategic Challenge 3—Hybrid human-centred relationships: preventive public services, community-based solutions, justice, fairness, and inclusion by design. This challenge is the most important from the citizens' point of view because how it is managed directly impacts their well-being. The state must take all necessary steps to adapt its range of public services and goods to the real needs of citizens;
- Strategic Challenge 4—People-planet systems: from sustainability to resilience to regeneration and dynamic systems. Public governance must identify the best ways to work with nature and promote human interaction as a source of innovation, including technological innovation (European Commission 2023b).

Also, the European Commission's 2023b report finds how the relationship between digital transformation and the public sector has changed since the 1990s. Thus, Table 3 provides a brief overview of public services, the role of people in their delivery, the technologies involved and examples from practice.

To summarise, all aspects of digital transformation in the public sector and tax administration that have been uncovered have been transformational, both for the way of working and the processes involved, as well as for the thinking of citizens and government leaders, forcing each of them to acquire a range of digital capabilities and skills to be able to use digital technologies for the purpose they were created, namely to deliver fast and accurate results, with broad availability, using the minimum of resources in their generation.

Table 3 The evolution of digital transformation in the public sector and its implications

	Digitally supported public services (since the early 1990s)	Digital-enabled public services (since 2000)	Digitally managed public services (since 2008)	Digital-only public services (from 2015)	New hybrid public services (from 2020, but especially in the future)
Description	People deliver services based on physical labour or physical goods, but processes are digitised	The potential to digitise public services is enormous, but digital technology is not being embraced to do so	Public services can be digitised to a large extent. Based on technology, they can run operations and functions in the background, providing personalised, non-material services	Artificial Intelligence (AI) analyses and delivers information and automatically intervenes to provide fully connected and predictive services	Platforms, web solutions, AI, etc. to enable people to regain control over their digital lives
The human role	Deliver the service using digital technology	People make all the decisions	Step in when needed	Defines the framework and conditions for delivering results	Physical and digital control, a hybrid of emotional, human and digital interactions
The role of digital technology and its generation	Supports people in delivering services Gov 1.0 and Web 1.0	Activate the service Gov 2.0 and Web 2.0	Generate and deliver the service Gov 3.0 and Web 3.0	Finds and analyses data and makes decisions within conditional limits Gov 4.0 and Web 4.0	Performs all tasks under conscious human control and/or predictive and benign intervention Gov 5.0 and Web 5.0

(continued)

Table 3 (continued)

	Digitally supported public services (since the early 1990s)	Digital-enabled public services (since 2000)	Digitally managed public services (since 2008)	Digital-only public services (from 2015)	New hybrid public services (from 2020, but especially in the future)
Examples of public services	Legislation, education, transportation, health	e-health e-medicine e-learning e-government	Making payments and fees, purchase of services, obtaining licenses, permits, authorisations	Risk identification and management systems, comprehensive services for individuals/legal entities	Fully hybrid services of all kinds, full virus support
Paradigms of public governance	(1) Traditional Weberian (2) New public management (3) Neo-Weberian	(4) In the network (5) Public value	(6) Poverty and austerity (7) Open governance: open, platform, participatory, inclusive, co-creative, behavioural and cultural (8) Sustainability governance: sustainability, circularity, nature-based (9) Local and community governance: local, civil society involvement, community		(10) Turbulence (11) Geographical change (12) Human-centered hybrid systems (13) Human-planet systems

Source European Commission Report (2023b)—adapted from European Digital Forum

3 Integrating Digital Technologies: Transforming Institutional Processes for Enhanced Efficiency and Innovation

In terms of how digital technologies have been adopted and integrated into the processes of institutions, this can be identified through the Digital Economy and Society Index (DESI), developed by the European Commission through 4 dimensions, namely human capital, connectivity, digital technology integration and digital public services and ten sub-dimensions, totalling 30 indicators that have been tracked from 2017 to date. However, in 2021, the European Commission decided to extend the target objectives for the Digital Decade by introducing more indicators to check the distance from the proposed targets (European Commission 2023a). Considering the issues related to the change in the DESI index construction methodology, we have analysed the evolution of this index only for the period 2017–2022 for comparability. We also analysed how Good Governance (GG-Good Governance) and Government Effectiveness (GEFF—Government Effectiveness) have evolved relative to DESI—furthermore, an ordinal correlation analysis and clustering via k-means++ to identify possible relationships within the dataset.

The data included in the analysis were collected from the European Commission's database (DESI) and the Sustainable Governance Indicators (SGI) database in a panel format, with annual frequency spread over 2017–2022. The sample of countries analysed in this chapter covers all EU Member States. Table 4 details the indicators, their abbreviations, and the unit of measurement.

The DESI index's dimensions are weighted equally, i.e., each dimension represents 25% of the index value. These dimensions have been outlined according to the four primary areas of interest of Digital Compass 2030, a program implemented at the European Union level. Constructing the dimensions is considered the pursuit of overall progress in digital development (European Commission 2022).

The statistical description of the dataset in Table 5 shows us an inequality in the number of observations across variables, with good governance and government effectiveness having missing records for 2021. The most significant variation between the minimum and maximum value of the indicator belongs to digital public services, which means that either at the period level or at the country level, there were significant differences between the two years included in the analysis. The standard deviation of DPS, CONNECT and RTD is higher, indicating a more extensive range for the values recorded. The skewness of the data, as represented by the Skewness coefficient, shows a favourable distribution, except for DPS. In identifying the distribution type of the data, the Kurtosis coefficient and the Jarque-Bera test confirm the existence of an almost normal distribution, with CONNECT and DPS being significant exceptions.

The evolution of the indicators throughout the analysis evidences the level of digitisation of the countries within the European Union, following all the essential domains, i.e., population, public sector, and business sector, and the connectivity between them. Figure 8 graphically illustrates this evolution, building a picture

Table 4 General information about the dataset

Name	Notation	Description	UM	Optimisation	Source
Connectivity	CONNECT	Dimension of the DESI containing broadband and mobile network information, including prices and coverage	Score 0–100	Maximum	European Commission
Digital Public Services	DPS	DESI dimension measuring the level of eGovernment	Score 0–100	Maximum	European Commission
Human Capital	HC	DESI dimension assessing the digital literacy of the population	Score 0–100	Maximum	European Commission
Digital Technology Implementation	RTD	DESI dimension that measures the level of digitisation in online trade and private business	Score 0–100	Maximum	European Commission
Good Governance	GG	Examine the governance capacities of a political system in terms of its executive capacity and accountability	Score 0–10	Maximum	SGI
Government effectiveness	GEFF	Assesses a government's implementation performance against the performance criteria set by the government for its work	Score 0–10	Maximum	SGI

Source Authors' processing

of the existing situation. Regarding connectivity levels, Italy, Greece, Austria and Cyprus have made significant progress, driven by the roll-out of broadband and mobile networks and a change in pricing policy for mobile and data subscriptions. Compared to the baseline period, all countries scored better in the final period. Regarding digital public services, the Netherlands, Malta, Finland, and Estonia have the highest ranking, with 21 and 22 points. At the other end of the scale, Romania scores just over 5 points, and together with Greece (9.8), Bulgaria (12.9) and Slovakia (12.9), complete the ranking of the least developed countries offering e-government services by the end of 2022. Even though the COVID-19 pandemic has accelerated

Table 5 Descriptive statistics of the data

	CONNECT	DPS	HC	RTD	GG	GEFF
Mean	9.403883	14.32554	11.41167	7.374540	6.465481	6.362963
Median	8.936715	14.61359	11.06852	7.167009	6.490000	6.000000
Maximum	19.27232	22.79479	17.84766	14.77164	8.930000	9.000000
Minimum	3.167988	1.853090	6.869039	2.529783	4.240000	3.000000
Std. Dev	3.205438	4.185998	2.354427	2.601790	1.160569	1.538595
Skewness	0.653414	-0.472549	0.357277	0.416285	0.303311	-0.042914
Kurtosis	3.103606	3.136695	2.664996	2.976242	2.696827	2.291754
Jarque-Bera	11.60009	6.155286	4.203994	4.682720	2.586956	2.863007
Probability	0.003027	0.046068	0.122212	0.096197	0.274315	0.238949
Sum	1523.429	2320.737	1848.690	1194.675	872.8400	859.0000
Sum Sq. Dev	1654.248	2821.135	892.4754	1089.859	180.4873	317.2148
Comments	162	162	162	162	135	135

Source Authors' processing in EViews

digitisation, these countries must align their strategies and targets with those that scored above average. The population's digital literacy level, as measured by the human capital indicator, is on an upward trend for analysis, except for Greece and Bulgaria, which at the end of the analysis period had lower scores than during the period. Referring to the timing of the decrease, in the case of Bulgaria, the difference can be explained by the adverse effects of the pandemic. However, in Greece's case, the trend change was generated after 2021, which is outside the scope of these effects.

The score for implementing digital technologies in the private business sector follows a moderate upward trend. Sweden, Italy, the Netherlands and Belgium mark a more significant increase. Again, in 2022, Romania, Bulgaria, and Hungary stood out with the lowest scores of 3.7, 3.8, and 5.3, respectively. As far as good governance is concerned, this index does not show a significant evolution over the period analysed, which means that an improvement in the level of digitisation of society and the economy does not implicitly lead to an improvement in the governance capacity of a political system. Moreover, Poland (−1.06), Hungary (−0.7), the Netherlands (−0.5), and Romania (−0.44), along with six other countries, have lower scores in 2022 compared to 2017. This emphasises the need for governments to develop their dynamic capabilities to deliver quality public services in the development context. The same is valid for government effectiveness, where only nine countries have better scores in 2022 compared to 2017. The results can be explained by the effects of adverse events in 2020–2022 but cannot be explained by them alone.

Before the exploratory analysis of the variables, we turned to Spearman correlation analysis to identify potential non-linear relationships between the variables, considering that they tend not to be normally distributed. In Table 6, the results generated using EViews software provide an overview of the general-order relationships for the variables in the dataset. The results reveal that digital public services

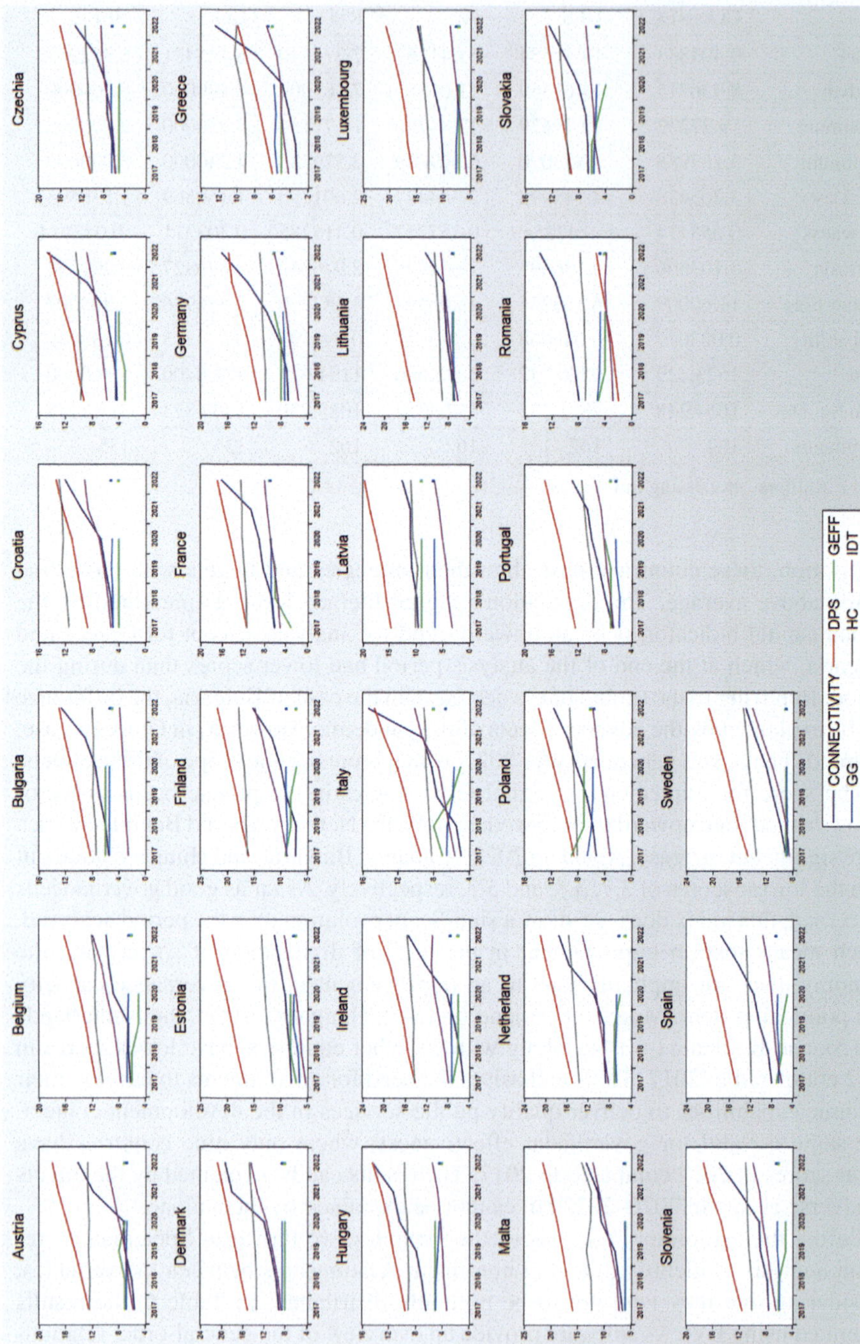

Fig. 8 Evolution of DESI dimensions, good governance and government effectiveness. *Source* Authors' processing in EViews

Table 6 Spearman rank correlation

	CONNECT	DPS	HC	RTD	GG	GEFF
CONNECT	1.000000	0.662472	0.362228	0.498971	0.307117	0.272131
DPS	0.662472	1.000000	0.767901	0.754580	0.677896	0.515291
HC	0.362228	**0.767901**	1.000000	0.764111	0.685181	0.345272
RTD	0.498971	**0.754580**	**0.764111**	1.000000	0.581172	0.275913
GG	0.307117	0.677896	0.685181	0.581172	1.000000	0.748427
GEFF	0.272131	0.515291	0.345272	0.275913	**0.748427**	1.000000

Source Authors' processing in EViews

and human capital have a robust positive correlation (0.76), which is in line with other studies that have analysed human capital as a factor in the success of digital public service provision (Kirilor and Kazakova 2022; Ringson and Matshabaphala 2023). A strong positive correlation has also been identified between digital public services and the deployment of digital technologies, with DPS being based on digital infrastructure (OECD 2022). Likewise, good governance and government effectiveness have a strong positive correlation, implying that the level of implementation of a government's performance criteria is directly related to the capacity of executive governance that leads to adopting a long-term vision that considers future generations' interests. The other variables also showed positive correlations but were of moderate intensity and less statistically relevant.

In the last stage of data analysis, we used Orange analysis software to cluster the countries according to the values of the indicators in the last year of analysis. This step aims to identify countries with the same characteristics of digitalisation, good governance and government effectiveness. Using the k-means++ clustering method, we obtain homogeneous and spherical distribution groups of countries. This algorithm is the improved version of the k-means method, the specific element of which is the selection of the initial centres. In order to obtain clusters of countries with similar characteristics, we selected to divide the countries into five homogeneous groups. In generating the analysis, we pre-processed the data by normalising them and set the maximum number of iterations to 300. The results are displayed in Fig. 9.

As displayed in the graphical representation, the Nordic countries Sweden, Denmark, and Finland have common characteristics that cannot be associated with other countries, forming cluster 4. Another group of countries with obvious similarities is Ireland, Malta, and the Netherlands, found in cluster 1. Lithuania, Latvia, Estonia, Estonia, Belgium and Portugal form cluster 3. The geographical location of the first three countries may explain the similarities and matches in the same cluster. Clusters 5 and 2 are the most numerous and contain countries with a high (cluster 5) or low (cluster 2) level of digitisation and public governance.

According to the results obtained in the exploratory analysis, we can say that the selected variables can be used in advanced models to capture the impact of digitisation on the public sector. The significant differences between countries in DESI, good governance, and government effectiveness may indicate significant deviations from

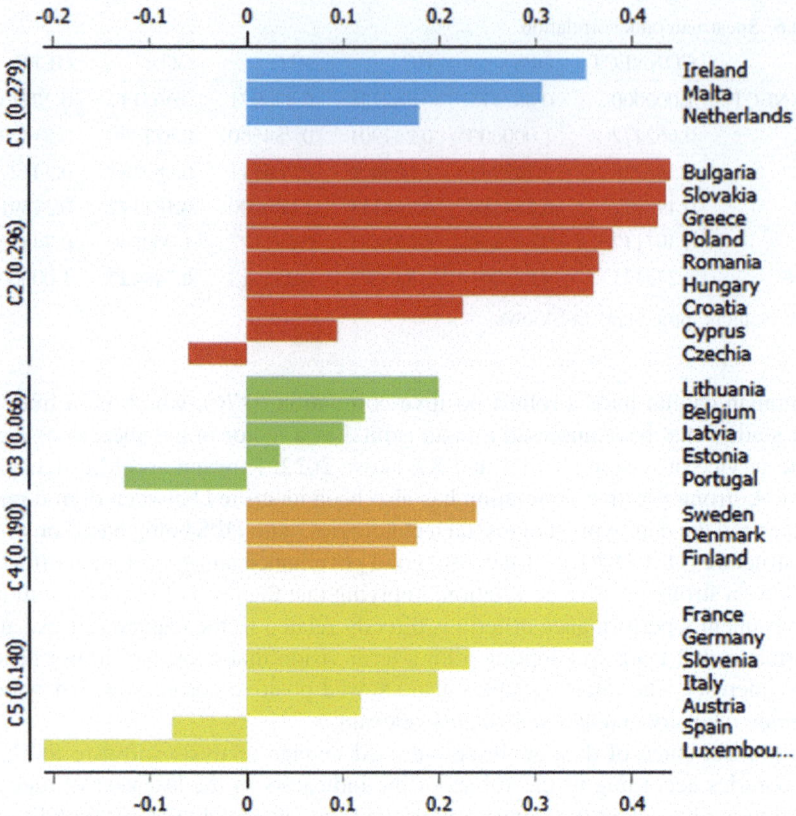

Fig. 9 Country composition of the clusters of the k-means++ analysis. *Source* Authors' processing via Orange

the targets set in the European Union's Digital Compass 2030, which can be corrected by implementing these targets in national digital transformation strategies. However, countries must focus on human capital for successful implementation, including reforming the education system to produce more information and systems technology specialists and digitally savvy citizens.

Another aspect to consider is the level of digital public services. Even if Romania has implemented in the last 2 years at the level of fiscal services the Virtual Public Space platform, the unified reporting SAF-T, e-invoice, e-transport and most recently, e-VAT, there are many other services in the public administration sphere that need digitisation. One example is identity cards, which express one's voting choice electronically. Regarding connectivity, Romania scores well, which means that the current digital infrastructure allows the implementation of digital technologies in all sectors.

4 Conclusion

This chapter effectively elucidates the implications of digital transformation in the public sector through a comprehensive approach that combines bibliometric analysis via Rstudio's Bibliometrix with a focused literature review. By systematically analysing existing research and identifying key trends, patterns, and themes, the chapter provides a nuanced understanding of how digital transformation reshapes public sector operations and governance. Investment in human capital development is fundamental for the success of this transformation. For technology-driven policies to succeed, public servants must be equipped with digital skills, including data literacy, cybersecurity awareness, and adaptive thinking. This calls for policies that institutionalise continuous learning and development programs, ensuring that the public workforce remains agile and capable of meeting the demands of an evolving digital environment. Future policy frameworks should prioritise funding and support for training programs that foster a digitally skilled and forward-thinking workforce, directly aligning human capital with the digital transformation goals of the public sector.

Also, our analysis effectively highlights the dynamic interplay between digitalisation, good governance, and government effectiveness across EU Member States from 2017 to 2022. The transformative journey toward a digitally empowered public sector requires an approach that integrates advanced technology, human capital, and robust governance frameworks, all underpinned by proactive policy-making. Digital transformation in the public sector transcends mere technological upgrades, including a redefinition of how public institutions operate, engage with citizens and address rapidly changing societal needs. By reshaping traditional workflows, service delivery mechanisms, and governance structures, digital transformation offers unprecedented opportunities to modernise and enhance public administration.

Applying the k-means++ clustering method in Orange analysis software has provided a robust framework for categorising EU Member States based on their digitalisation, good governance, and characteristics of government effectiveness. Our results established five distinct groups of countries with similar profiles within the EU. This systematic clustering enhances our understanding of the diverse landscape of digital transformation across the EU and highlights the varying levels of governance effectiveness among member states. The insights gained from this analysis can inform policymakers and stakeholders about best practices and potential areas for improvement, ultimately contributing to more effective strategies for fostering digital advancement and enhancing governance within public institutions. Governance structures also need to be redesigned to prioritise resilience and flexibility. Policies must be formulated with built-in adaptability to navigate emerging challenges such as cybersecurity threats, data privacy concerns, and ethical considerations surrounding AI usage. Policies should establish clear guidelines and regulatory frameworks that emphasise ethical data use, protect citizens' privacy, and mitigate cybersecurity risks.

The European Commission's framework for strategic digital challenges highlights policy directions, such as open strategic autonomy, which underscores the importance of securing domestic digital resources. This approach aligns to achieve resilience to supply chain disruptions and geopolitical uncertainties, particularly for sectors critical to public welfare, such as healthcare, education, and emergency services. Policy-makers should prioritise investments in these strategic sectors, ensuring they are resilient, adaptable, and capable of maintaining operations during crises. Policy emphasis on such resilience can lead to developing digital infrastructure that supports current needs and is robust enough to withstand future shocks.

Moreover, a human-centred approach to digital governance requires policies addressing digital transformation's ethical dimensions. Policies should mandate the inclusion of citizen feedback in the design and deployment of digital public services, ensuring that they meet diverse societal needs. Policy implications also extend to the regulatory environment surrounding digital innovations. Governments should enact policies that promote experimentation with emerging technologies while balancing these advancements with safeguards for public welfare. Policies encouraging collaboration between public institutions and private technology partners can further accelerate innovation, fostering an ecosystem where digital tools can be developed and refined directly relevant to public needs.

As new digital tools and challenges emerge, policies must be grounded in the latest insights regarding the interplay between technology, governance, and citizen welfare. Research exploring dynamic capability development, ethical AI applications, and citizen engagement in digital governance will provide valuable insights for shaping responsive and effective policy. Future policies should be designed as living documents, open to iteration and improvement based on evolving technological landscapes and societal expectations.

In conclusion, the long-term success of digital transformation in the public sector depends on policies that balance technological advancement with human-centred values, ethical considerations, and strategic resilience. By fostering a policy-making culture that prioritises adaptability, inclusivity, and good governance, public institutions can build a digital governance model that is efficient, resilient, and equitable. This approach will create a public sector prepared to meet the complex demands of future generations, serving as a model for digitally responsive governance that emphasises both innovation and public trust.

Acknowledgements "This work was supported by a grant from the Romanian Ministry of Research, Innovation and Digitalization, the project with the title "Economics and Policy Options for Climate Change Risk and Global Environmental Governance" (CF 193/28.11.2022, Funding Contract no. 760078/23.05.2023), within Romania's National Recovery and Resilience Plan (PNRR) - Pillar III, Component C9, Investment I8 (PNRR/2022/C9/MCID/I8) - Development of a program to attract highly specialised human resources from abroad in research, development and innovation activities."

Bibliography

Addis Tax Initiative (2023). The Digital Transformation of Tax Administrations. Retrieved from Addis Tax Initiative: https://www.addistaxinitiative.net/news/digital-transformation-tax-administrations-0

Aghakhani, G., Wautelet, Y., Dijkmans, D., Heng, S., Poelmans, S., Kolp, M. (2024). Supporting digital transformation strategy formulation through a customisable set of objectives: conceptual model and expert opinions. Enterp. Inf. Syst. 18(3), 363–396. https://doi.org/10.1080/17517575.2023.2300089

AlNuaimi, B.K., Singh, S.K., Ren, S., Budhwar, P., Vorobyev, D. (2022). Mastering digital transformation: The nexus between leadership, agility, and digital strategy. J. Bus. Res. 145, 636–648. https://doi.org/10.1016/j.jbusres.2022.03.03.038

Almusaed, A., Yitmen, I., Almssad, A. (2023). Reviewing and integrating AEC practices into Industry 6.0: Strategies for smart and sustainable future-built environments. Sustainability 15(18). https://doi.org/10.3390/su15181813464

Bousdekis, A., Kardaras, D. (2020). Digital Transformation of Local Government: A Case Study from Greece. 2020 IEEE 22nd Conf. Bus. Inform. (CBI). IEEE. https://doi.org/10.1109/CBI49978.2020.10070

Del Rio Castro, G., Gonzalez Fernandez, M.C., Uruburu Cosla, A. (2021). Unleashing the convergence amid digitalisation and sustainability towards pursuing the Sustainable Development Goals (SDGs): A holistic review. J. Clean. Prod. 280. https://doi.org/10.1016/j.jclepro.2020.122204

Dibeh, G., Fakih, A., Marrouch, W., Matar, G. (2021). Who cares about environmental quality in the MENA region? Soc. Indic. Res. 157, 603–629. https://doi.org/10.1007/s11205-021-02667-x

Estrada, R., Arturo, M. (2024). The Seventh Industrial Revolution (IR 7.0). https://doi.org/10.2139/ssrn.4720983

European Commission (2019). European environmental pact. Brussels. Retrieved from https://eur-lex.europa.eu/resource.html?uri=cellar.0020.02/DOC_1&format=PDF

European Commission (2022). Digital Economy and Society Index (DESI) 2022 - Methodological Note. Retrieved from https://ec.europa.eu/newsroom/dae/redirection/document/88557

European Commission (2023a). Digital Economy and Society Index (DESI) 2022 - Thematic chapters. European Commission. Retrieved from https://ec.europa.eu/newsroom/dae/redirection/document/88764

European Commission (2023b). Impact of digital transformation on public governance - New forms of policy-making and the provision of innovative, people-centric and inclusive public services. Luxembourg: Publ. Off. Eur. Union. https://doi.org/10.2760/204686

European Commission (2024). IST 2024 Flagship - Supporting the Digital Transformation of Tax and Customs Administrations. Retrieved from European Commission: https://reform-support.ec.europa.eu/tsi-2024-flagship-supporting-digital-transformation-tax-and-customs-administrations_en

European Commission (n.d.). Environmental Transition. Retrieved from https://research-and-innovation.ec.europa.eu/document/download/f9d78996-ddb6-496d-8aa0-58e863c584ee_en?filename=ec_rtd_tpi-2021-vi-environmental-transition.pdf

European Commission. Governance Transition. Retrieved from https://research-and-innovation.ec.europa.eu/document/download/f8f6dee9-df0e-4745-90f6-9eac2ec59089_en?filename=ec_rtd_tpi-2021-vii-governance-transition.pdf

European Commission. Europe's Digital Decade: Digital goals for 2030. Retrieved from https://commission.europa.eu/strategy-and-policy/priorities-2019-2024/europe-fit-digital-age/europes-digital-decade-digital-targets-2030_ro

European Council (2024). REPowerEU plan explained. Retrieved from https://www.consilium.europa.eu/ro/infographics/repowereu/

European Union (2020). NextGenerationEU. Retrieved from https://next-generation-eu.europa.eu/index_ro

Godse, V., Garg, A. (2007). From E-government to E-governance. Proc. 5th Int. Conf. e-Governance, 50–73. Mumbai. Retrieved from https://csi-sigegov.org.in/1/2_313.pdf

Gradillas, M., Thomas, L.D. (2022). Distinguishing digitisation and digitalisation: A systematic review and conceptual framework. J. Prod. Innov. Manag. 1–32. https://doi.org/10.1111/jpim.12690

Hartley, J. (2005). Innovation in governance and public services: Past and present. Public Money Manag. 25(1), 27–34. https://doi.org/10.1111/j.1467-9302.2005.00447.x

Hevner, A.R. (2007). A three cycle view of design science research. Scand. J. Inf. Syst. 19(2), 4.

Kirilor, R., Kazakova, M. (2022). Human capital as a factor for successful digitalisation of local administrative services. Bus. Manag., 48–58.

Konopik, J., Jahn, C., Schuster, T., Hossbach, N., Pflaum, A. (2022). Mastering the digital transformation through organisational capabilities: A conceptual framework. Digit. Bus. 2. https://doi.org/10.1016/j.digbus.2021.100019

Lanzolla, G., Pesce, D., Tucci, C.L. (2020). The digital transformation of search and recombination in the innovation function: Tensions and an integrative framework. J. Prod. Innov. Manag. 38(1), 90–113. https://doi.org/10.1111/jpim.12546

Levin, S.A., Anderies, J.M., Adger, N., Barrett, S., Bennett, E. Governance in the face of extreme events: Lessons from evolutionary processes for structuring interventions, and the need to go beyond. Ecosystems 25, 697–711. https://doi.org/10.1007/s10021-021-00680-2

Li, L., Su, F., Zhang, W., Mao, J.Y. (2017). Digital transformation by SME entrepreneurs: A capability perspective. Inf. Syst. J. 1–29. https://doi.org/10.1111/isj.12153

Linggren, I., Jansson, G. (2013). Electronic services in the public sector: A conceptual framework. Gov. Inf. Q. 30, 163–172. https://doi.org/10.1016/j.giq.2012.10.005

Mergel, I., Efdelmann, N., Haug, N. (2019). Defining digital transformation: Results from expert interviews. Gov. Inf. Q. 36. https://doi.org/10.1016/j.giq.2019.06.002

Noble, S.M., Mende, M., Grewal, D., Parasuraman, A. (2022). The Fifth Industrial Revolution: How harmonious human-machine collaboration is triggering a retail and service [r]evolution. J. Retail. 98, 199–208. https://doi.org/10.1016/j.jretai.2022.04.04.003

OECD (2022). Digital Transformation Maturity Model. Retrieved from https://www.oecd.org/tax/forum-on-tax-administration/publications-and-products/digital-transformation-maturity-model.htm

Ringson, J., Matshabaphala, M.J. (2023). Leadership, service delivery and managing human capital in the digital age in the public sector. Afr. J. Gov. Dev. 12(1). https://doi.org/10.36369/ajgd.v12i1.17

Sanina, A., Balashov, A., Rubtcova, M. (2021). The socio-economic efficiency of digital government transformation. Int. J. Public Adm. https://doi.org/10.1080/01900692.2021.1988637

Tangi, L., Janssen, M., Benedetti, M., Noci, G. (2021). Digital government transformation: A structural equation modeling analysis of driving and impeding factors. Int. J. Inf. Manag. 60. https://doi.org/10.1016/j.ijinfomgt.2021.102356

Tax Foundation Europe (2024). Retrieved from https://taxfoundation.org/data/all/eu/digital-tax-europe-2024/

Teece, D.J. (2018). Business models and dynamic capabilities. Long Range Plan. 51, 40–49. https://doi.org/10.1016/j.lrp.2017.06.007

Tullu, M.S. (2019). Writing the title and abstract for a research paper: Being concise, precise, and meticulous is the key. Saudi J. Anaesth. 13(Suppl 1), S12–S17. https://doi.org/10.4103/sja.SJA_685_18

US Congress (2002). H.R.2458 - E-Government Act of 2002. Retrieved from https://www.congress.gov/bill/107th-congress/house-bill/2458

Warner, K.S., Wäger, M. (2019). Building dynamic capabilities for digital transformation: An ongoing process of strategic renewal. Long Range Plan. 52(3), 326–349. https://doi.org/10.1016/j.lrp.2018.12.001

Williams, K., Chatterjee, S., Rossi, M. (2008). Design of emerging digital services: A taxonomy. Eur. J. Inf. Syst. 17, 505–517. https://doi.org/10.1057/ejis.2008.38

Yoo, Y., Henfridsson, O., Lyytinen, K. (2010). Research commentary: The new organising logic of digital innovation: An agenda for information systems research. Inf. Syst. Res. 21(4), 724–735. https://doi.org/10.1287/isre.1100.0322

Climbing the Digital Performance Ladder: Mapping the Peaks and Valleys Across EU Regions

Cristina Criste, Chi Wei Su, Sorana Vatavu, Oana Ramona Lobont, and Valeri Viorel Sitnikov

Abstract Given the disparities between the European Union member states in terms of the quality of governance, the management of financial resources and the efforts to improve economic performance and the well-being of society, digital innovation appears as an essential solution in stimulating digital governance. This research aims to rank the regions of the European Union from the perspective of digital performance and offers a new perspective on the digitalisation process and its effects on the European public system. The evolution of the intensity and impact of digitalisation will be examined through the e-government framework, specifically from the perspective of the 27 member states of the European Union (EU). This study employs a multifaceted methodological approach to analyse longitudinal data within the EU from 2017 to 2022: data mapping, robust regression, Gaussian and mixed-Markov graphical (GGMs), and analysis hierarchical clustering. First, we conducted data mapping to overview the variables under consideration comprehensively. Subsequently, we employed robust regression analysis to examine the direct impacts of key digitalisation, innovation, world governance, and economic indicators on economic development. To further explore the relationships between these variables, we utilised

C. Criste
Faculty of Economics and Business Administration, Doctoral School of Economics and Business Administration, West University of Timisoara, Timisoara, Romania
e-mail: cristina.criste@e-uvt.ro

C. W. Su
School of Economics, Qingdao University, Qingdao, China

S. Vatavu (✉) · O. R. Lobont
Faculty of Economics and Business Administration, Finance, Business Information Systems and Modelling Department, West University of Timisoara, Timisoara, Romania
e-mail: sorana.vatavu@e-uvt.ro

O. R. Lobont
e-mail: oana.lobont@e-uvt.ro

V. V. Sitnikov
Faculty of Economics and Business Administration, Eugeniu Carada Doctoral School of Economics, University of Craiova, Craiova, Romania

S. O. Idowu et al. (eds.), *Competitiveness and Sustainability in the Digitization Era*, Springer Proceedings in Business and Economics,
https://doi.org/10.1007/978-3-031-91778-3_2

Gaussian and mixed-Markov graphical modelling. Finally, we performed hierarchical clustering with Euclidean distance on the panel dataset, clustering EU countries based on their performance across the variables for 2017 and 2022. This clustering facilitated a more nuanced and comparative assessment of digital performance across different groups of EU member states. Our results highlight the significant disparities among the diverse nations and the multifaceted contemporary challenges EU member states encounter in implementing and adopting specific e-governance initiatives alongside the hierarchical performance patterns observed in digitalisation and innovation. The main findings imply that nations with substantial investment in research and development and digitalisation tend to exhibit robust economic progress. Denmark, Finland, and Sweden have shown the most adaptability and innovation in enhancing administrative efficiency. Notably, some nations with substantial economic potential, such as Bulgaria, Poland, and Romania, do not dedicate adequate resources to innovation. The results suggest that nations should adapt their digital transformation strategies to integrate digital technologies and continuous innovation to improve the effectiveness of e-government. Establishing effective e-government relies on more than just technology. It also requires carefully devised strategies, appropriate resource allocation, ongoing innovation, and dedication from the government to deliver accessible, secure, and user-friendly e-services.

Keywords European Union · Cluster analysis · Graphical models · e-government · Digitalisation · Innovation

1 Introduction

The primary objective of this research is to evaluate and rank the regions of the European Union based on their digital performance. Furthermore, this study offers a novel perspective on digitisation and its implications for the European public system. In addition, the research investigates and contextualises the intensity of the relationship between e-government and digital innovation, specifically examining this dynamic through the lens of e-government practices among the Member States of the European Union.

This chapter analyses the interaction between the public sector and digital technology within a multifaceted framework, examining these two domains' dynamic interplay and reciprocal influence. The analysis is based on advanced methodological approaches, including data mapping techniques, robust regression, hierarchical clustering using the k-means algorithm, and the Gaussian graphical Model (GGM) and Mixed-Markov Graphic Model (MGM). The findings underscore the close relationship between the public sector and digital technology, indicating that digitalisation plays a significant role in assessing the performance of the public sector.

Adopting digital technology has widespread implications for various facets of the national economy, particularly in enhancing problem-solving capabilities and facilitating the incorporation of new technologies and operational processes (Chiriac et al. 2021; Bolbotenko 2021; Stanimirović et al. 2012). The increasing interest in digitalisation can be attributed to its potential to optimise operational efficiency, minimise required working hours, and elevate the quality of e-government services and the public sector. Governments must prioritise data-driven digital governance to fully capitalise on digital technology's opportunities and ensure effective implementation (Arner et al. 2022). Integrating digital technologies enables data-driven decision-making, allowing public sector organisations to leverage data analytics for better policy formulation and resource allocation, enhancing operational efficiency and accountability.

Many Member States of the European Union highlight the importance of cultivating digital processes for economic progress, which implement comprehensive and multifaceted programs designed to promote the digital sectors within their national economies (Criste et al. 2024a). Despite the variations observed among European Union member states regarding governmental quality, sound public governance, appropriate allocation of public financial resources, rational public expenditures, and specific measures to foster economic performance and well-being (Houngbo et al. 2017), across both less developed and developed nations, the implementation of digitalisation emerges as a crucial driver in promoting economic prosperity (Myovella et al. 2020). One of the key technological challenges many countries worldwide face is the need for digital transformation against the backdrop of an increased adoption rate and a declining growth rate. Countries relying on solid political commitment supported by adequate funding continue to grapple with these difficulties due to the significant gaps in digital connectivity and access across their territories (Dhaoui 2022). Therefore, digitalisation affects multiple economic and social life dimensions, transforming how individuals, businesses, and governments interact and function. This digital transformation touches various aspects of society, including commerce, governance, healthcare, education, and more, reshaping how we live, work, and access services. Implementing innovative technological solutions to enhance e-government across various institutions faces numerous challenges. These challenges often vary depending on national contexts and specific e-government models. Beniwal (2013) identified several obstacles that may arise in the e-government implementation process, including constraints related to technical infrastructure and financial limitations.

Digital technologies are a domain with immense growth potential for Europe. Therefore, the European Commission is currently engaged in developing a Europe prepared for the digital age, where citizens, businesses, and administrations have access to new, efficient technologies. Thus, a transformational digital landscape is being established that will lead to future social benefits. At the same time, the European Commission is launching digital solutions specially designed for citizens (Martin and Grudziecki 2006), creating new opportunities for the entrepreneurial environment, encouraging the development of reliable and innovative technologies, and promoting a transparent and democratic society, as well as facilitating the transition to a sustainable economy. Furthermore, the following concepts associated with the digital transition are noted: the digital economy, research and innovation, digital public administration, digitalisation of healthcare, digitalisation of fiscal authorities, and the development of digital skills. Figure 1 describes these components. This establishes a transformative digital landscape that will lead to future social benefits. Therefore, the European Commission is currently engaged in developing a Europe prepared for the digital age, in which citizens, businesses, and administrations have access to new, efficient technologies.

This research offers several significant contributions to the field, primarily distinguished by its methodological innovations and the design of its empirical framework. The study distinguishes itself from previous research by applying advanced empirical techniques, employing methods such as data mapping, robust regression, hierarchical clustering, Gaussian graphical modelling, and Mixed-Markov graphic modelling to provide a nuanced analysis of the complex interactions between the public sector and digital technology. This diverse methodological approach enables a comprehensive examination of the data, capturing intricate patterns and relationships that may have been overlooked in earlier studies. Second, by focusing on the connections between

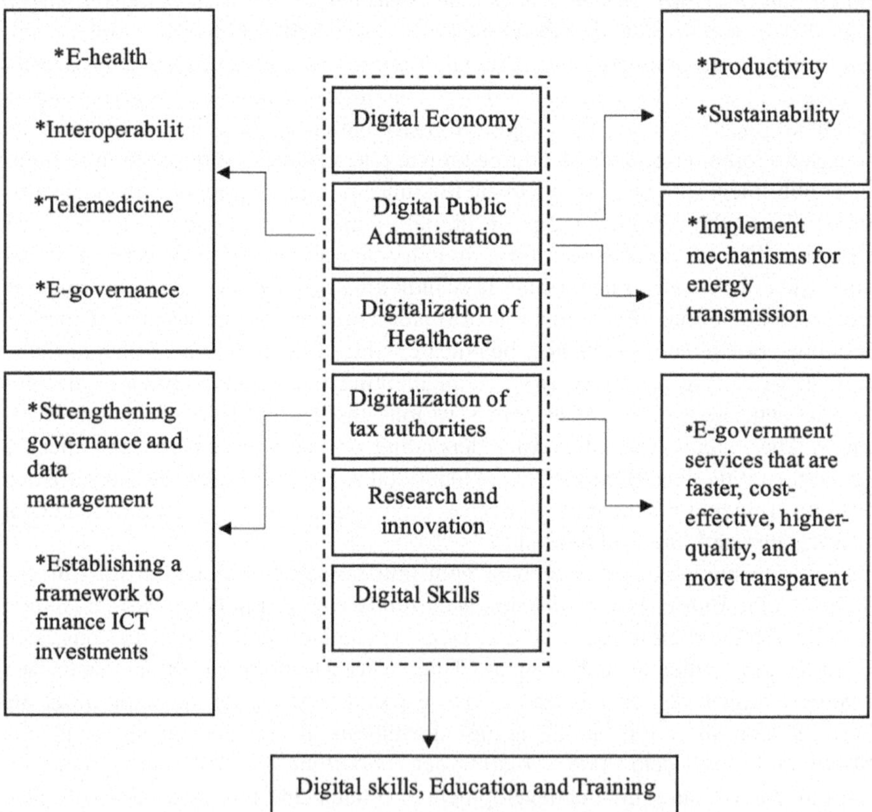

Fig. 1 Visions and concepts of the digital transition. *Source* Authors' own processing of information provided by the European Commission through digital transformation: EU strategy

the public sector and digital technology, this research sheds light on an area that has not been extensively explored in prior studies. This contribution is particularly relevant to ongoing digital transformation initiatives within the EU. Third, hierarchical clustering facilitates the identification of patterns among different member states, and Gaussian graphical modelling aids in understanding the conditional dependencies between variables. Meanwhile, Mixed-Markov graphic modelling allows for examining dynamic changes over time. Together, these techniques provide a sophisticated analytical toolkit that enriches the study's insights. Finally, by elucidating the intricate relationships between digital technology and public governance, the study provides valuable insights that can inform strategic decision-making, enhance policy formulation, and guide the implementation of effective digital initiatives.

The empirical findings of this research reveal ongoing challenges in achieving equitable and efficient digital transformation across the European Union. This analysis reveals a dynamic interplay between digital technology and public sector operations, with technological advancements increasingly shaping public service delivery. As expected, developed countries have exhibited higher digital performance than their less developed counterparts. Moreover, countries can formulate relevant policies and enhance the allocation of funds in the public sector, prioritising digital transformation. This strategic approach can ensure efficiency in the application of digital technology and can reduce the uncertainty associated with national policies. Furthermore, digitalisation has a significant impact on contemporary society and the economy.

Our empirical findings align with the model developed by Pandey (2023) and Cherdantseva and Hilton (2013), highlighting significant variations among EU member states regarding the digitalisation of public services through the interaction between digital technology and the uncertainty of government policies. Therefore, this research provides an overview of ways to determine digital performance while identifying the issues that may arise in implementing these digital technologies in the public sector. Accordingly, the main research questions are: (i) How do digital transformation policies and strategies within the public sector vary across the EU-27 member states?; (ii) What is the impact of these digital transformation policies and strategies on the digital performance of the public sector within every EU member state?; (iii) How can EU member states be ranked based on their digital performance in the public sector?

The paper is structured into distinct sections. After an introduction that sets the stage for research, outlining the significance of digital transformation in contemporary governance, Sect. 2 establishes the context for the study by discussing the growing importance of digital technologies in enhancing public efficiency, transparency, and service delivery. This review synthesises key theoretical frameworks and empirical studies relevant to the topic, highlighting the progress in understanding the interplay between digital technology and public governance. Section 3 outlines the data sources, including relevant datasets overviewed within the analysis. It details the econometric methods employed to analyse the data, i.e. regression analysis, clustering techniques, or other statistical tools that facilitate a robust examination of the relationships between digital transformation variables and public sector outcomes.

Section 4 systematically reports on the results, often using tables and figures to illustrate key trends and relationships. The findings provide empirical evidence regarding the impact of digital technologies on public sector performance, revealing insights into how various factors interact within the context of digital transformation. This data-driven approach allows for a nuanced understanding of regional dynamics among EU member states. The final section synthesises the study's conclusions, drawing the main insights derived from the analysis. This synthesis not only reiterates the significance of the findings but also discusses their broader implications for policymakers.

2 Literature Review

The digital transformation process brings various economic and social challenges requiring careful management and adaptation. These include the connections between digital technologies and economic conditions, such as employment, productivity, and competitiveness, as well as providing digital services to citizens and businesses. Additionally, the digital transformation has implications for areas such as digital infrastructure, digital skills, digital inclusion, and the adoption of new technologies across society and the economy (Laitsou et al. 2020; Đorić 2022; Martín et al. 2023). These interconnected facets showcase the multifaceted nature of the digital transition, underscoring the need for a comprehensive policy approach to address its challenges and harness its opportunities. Numerous studies have highlighted the significance of integrating digital technologies within the public sector for developed and developing economies, examining their wide-ranging implications and specific measurement indicators.

The digital transformation process can involve two key approaches: leveraging complexity to create value and harnessing digital innovation to enhance value. In this context, the government can influence citizens' participation and engagement with public service delivery (Lopes et al. 2019). Doran et al. (2023) suggest that e-government represents a reliable solution for modernising and improving the efficiency of public administration. Likewise, Nam (2014) investigated the relationship between e-government and the efficiency of government administration, demonstrating a significant influence between the two. Similarly, Archmann and Iglesias (2011) present the advantages of utilising digitalisation in the public sector, including enhanced efficiency and innovation. Digital public services constitute a novel form of interaction with citizens and enterprises. Digitalised public services constitute a novel modality of interaction with citizens and enterprises. Pathak et al. (2007) argue that e-government initiatives—by digitising governmental processes and services—can help reduce corruption by increasing transparency and accountability. Digital platforms make governmental actions more visible to the public, which limits opportunities for corrupt practices by reducing face-to-face interactions, where bribery and favouritism often occur. Bhatnagar and Singh (2010) classified the impact of digital public services on the interaction with citizens; three aspects were considered: financial implications, governance, and service quality. The financial implications involve the time and expenses associated with e-government services. Governance refers to eradicating corruption, transparency and government accountability, while service quality encompasses fairness and convenience. It is essential to note that digitalisation transcends the mere adoption of digital technologies. Furthermore, through digital media, platforms, and technology, digitalisation has reconfigured the economy, the public sector, and society (Karimi and Walter 2021).

The recent global COVID-19 pandemic has accelerated the technological development of public services worldwide, prompting governments to reconsider how they serve all segments of society (Mergel et al. 2019). As the intensity of digitalisation has increased, public institutions and administrations have changed, both at the structural level and in terms of the relationship between governments and citizens. The COVID-19 pandemic has directly impacted the implementation of digital services in the European Union and the significance of digital resources for a country's economy. Internet access, connectivity, artificial intelligence, and digital skills support the economy and facilitate the proper functioning of society. Public institutions and administrations have undergone several irreversible changes as digital governance has structurally increased how governments and citizens interact. Integrating digital work tools into the economy can generate future benefits for the entrepreneurial environment and the EU member states (Magomedov et al. 2020). The pandemic has revealed substantial gaps in digital capabilities across EU member states, requiring increased investment in digital infrastructure and competencies (Chan et al. 2020). Asogwa (2012), the widespread adoption of digital public services presents several advantages, including enhanced efficiency in public administration, increased transparency in decision-making, reduced corruption, and lower administrative costs. Sá et al. (2016) emphasise the importance and necessity of implementing a model to measure the quality of online public services compared to traditional services. Kovacikova and Stofkova (2020) noted a strong connection between a government information system and its components, identifying three categories of IT system integration: data-driven integration, process-based integration, and service-oriented integration. Deploying innovative digital technologies to bolster e-government across diverse institutions confronts numerous obstacles; these challenges often differ among nations and distinct e-governance frameworks, while some countries may face resource constraints or infrastructure deficits, others grapple with issues like digital divides or cybersecurity risks (Acheampong et al. 2024). Santiso (2022) has identified several challenges that can arise during the digitalisation of public services, including inadequate technical infrastructure, such as substandard telecommunications infrastructure and outdated equipment, a lack of digital literacy among citizens, as well as financial constraints that limit the resources available for digital transformation initiatives. These factors collectively constrain citizens' access to quality public services.

Based on the evolution of e-government and digital transformation within the public sector, we realised a mind map of the most important events and stages of

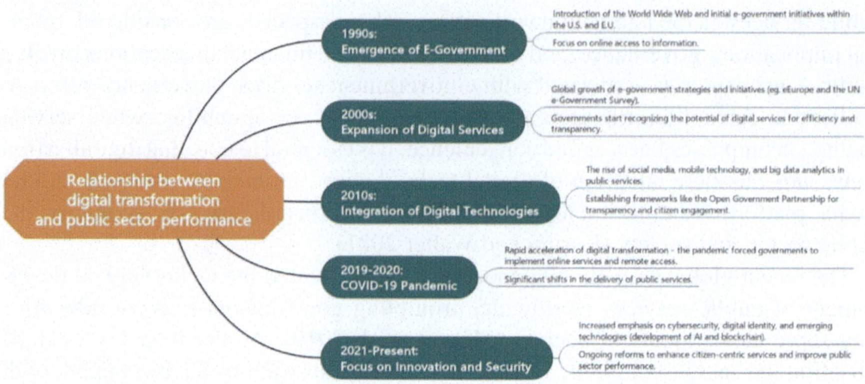

Fig. 2 The main stages for the development of digital transformation and public sector performance. *Source* Authors' own processing

developing the relationship between digital transformation and performance in the public sector; this is presented in Fig. 2.

However, the digitalisation process is not without its challenges. Febiri and Hub (2021) imply that Issues related to cybersecurity, personal data protection, digital exclusion, and adapting technological infrastructure are just some of the obstacles that need to be overcome to ensure an efficient and equitable transition to a digital society. Medaglia et al. (2021) evidence that maintaining citizens' trust in digital government services requires robust privacy safeguards and transparent data management practices. Eom and Lee (2022) argue that maintaining citizen trust in digital government services requires robust measures to safeguard privacy and security. Policymakers must carefully navigate these complex challenges to fully realise the benefits of digital government transformation. Moreover, Zhang et al. (2014) find that there is an imperative need to rethink the skills of public officials to ensure they are prepared to manage the new digital tools and technologies introduced as part of the transformation.

Implementing new digital technologies has also presented numerous challenges, with most of these challenges varying across countries and governance models. Nevertheless, the literature underscores the significant benefits that e-government initiatives can provide, including enhanced efficiency, transparency, and accountability, as well as the reduction of administrative costs and corruption (Ndou 2004; Uyar et al. 2021; Shareef et al. 2013).

In summary, the digital transformation of the public sector faces a range of obstacles that require careful consideration and strategic planning to overcome. These include technical, financial, and societal challenges, as well as the need to maintain citizen trust and ensure the security and privacy of digital services.

3 Data and Methodology

The main objective of this chapter was to rank the regions of the European Union based on digital performance and offer a new perspective on the digitalisation process and its effects on the European public system. The research process began with a data mapping technique, followed by an empirical analysis. The empirical analysis was divided into several complementary research stages: first, an analytical approach employing Robust Regression, followed by the Gaussian Graphical Model and Mixed-Markov Graphic Model. The final stage involved representing the digital performance of the public sector by applying vector quantisation through the K-means algorithm to determine the performance of digital public services. This approach allowed for ranking the European Union member states into efficient regions. Therefore, three different research methods were applied to achieve a ranking of EU Member States in terms of digital performance, as follows:

a. Robust Regression (RREG) to evidence the direct impacts of the significant variables. The Gross Domestic Product per capita served as the dependent variable in the macro-econometric models.
b. The Gaussian Graphical Model (GGM) and Mixed-Markov Graphic Model (MGM) evaluate the overall interlinkages between various factors influencing digital performance in the EU. To capture the complex interplay between economic, social, and technological factors influencing digital performance, we employ two complementary graphical modelling approaches: GGMs and MGMs. GGMs excel at revealing conditional dependencies between continuous variables, while MGMs are adept at handling datasets with both continuous and categorical variables, reflecting the diverse nature of our data.
c. Cluster analysis focused on disparities. Using the R software, the cluster technique and the K-means clustering algorithm will be applied, together with the hierarchical grouping technique, to partition the EU-27 countries into homogeneous groups; this analysis was conducted to assess the homogeneous groups of EU countries in depth to set tailored strategies.

Consistent with the methodologies utilised in prior studies by Noja et al. (2019), Dima et al. (2013, 2016), the present investigation incorporated comparable metrics and associated methodological specifications. Our study configured on the cross-sectional dataset of EU-27 MS for two specific years, 2017 and 2022; his approach allows for a comparative analysis of digital performance across EU countries at two distinct points in time. This analysis was grounded in macro-econometric models to evaluate the direct impacts of digital technology and other selected economic and social variables on economic development. To ensure stationarity, the variables were transformed using logarithms. The analysis was conducted using data available for these periods of 2017 and 2022, with data available from the European Commission, Eurostat, and Word Bank. The overall structure of the implemented model is outlined in Eq. (1), represented as a multiple regression model analysed using RREG.

$$LOG_{GDP_{Cit}} = \alpha_0 + \alpha_1 GII_{it} + \alpha_2 GERD_{it} + \alpha_3 IDT_{it} + \alpha_4 IUI_{it} + \alpha_5 IUS_{it}$$

$$+\alpha_6 LIAC_{it} + \alpha_7 OD_{it} + \alpha_8 R\&D_{it} + \alpha_9 THE_{it} + \alpha_{10} DPS_{it}$$
$$+\alpha_{11} Egov_{it} + \alpha_{12} FBS_{it} + \alpha_{13} Connect_{it}\alpha_{14} + ASD_{it} \quad (1)$$

To achieve our overarching objective and in alignment with the established methodological procedures, we have formulated the following two hypotheses (H) for testing:

H1: The digital transformation policies and strategies exhibit significant direct impacts on economic development, which are more pronounced in specific contexts.
H2: There are strong linkages between the dimensions of digital technology, digitalisation of the public sector, innovation, and economic performance.
H3: There are significant disparities among the EU-27 member states regarding their digital transformation policies and strategies for the public sector, which have resulted in outcomes that have fallen short of government expectations.

Digital transformation is a multifaceted phenomenon encompassing various interconnected dimensions influencing the overall process. This analysis explores these complex relationships and how they collectively contribute to successfully implementing digital transformation initiatives within the European Union. Therefore, rather than attributing digital transformation to a single dimension, viewing it as a multifaceted process where these dimensions are interconnected and influence each other is more accurate.

To accomplish the overall aim of this study, we have assembled a comprehensive dataset based on relevant literature; for methodological operationalisation, research variables were decomposed into dimensions. The data were extracted for the years 2017 and 2022 for all European Union member states (EU-27). The data were extracted from Eurostat, the European Commission and the World Bank. Eurostat for economic performance indicators and the digitalisation and e-governance dimension, we used the European Commission database; finally, data were collected from both the World Bank and Eurostat for the innovation indicators. At the same time, the data sample was divided into four dimensions: innovation, digitalisation, e-government and economic performance. Therefore, the variables are grouped into the following dimensions:

- Digitalisation: World Bank—People using the Internet (% of population); Fixed broadband subscriptions; High-tech exports (% of manufactured exports); Digital economy and society index—(i) Integration of digital technology (weighted score (0–100); (ii) Human capital—according to the skills of Internet users (weighted score (0–100); (iii) Connectivity—via mobile broadband (weighted score (0–100); (iv) Digital skills and competences, by ICT specialists (weighted score (0–100); (v) Eurostat- Internet access level—households (% of households);
- e-Government: Digital Economy and Society Index—(i) e-Government Users-Open Data (Percentage of people who have used the Internet in the last 12 months), (ii) Digital Public Services- e-Government (weighted score (0–100), (iii) Index of the digital economy and society e-government users (weighted score (0–100);

- Innovation: Global Innovation Index; Eurostat—(i) Gross domestic expenditure on research and development, (ii) GERD by performance sector and research and development fields.
- Economic performance: World Bank—GDP growth; Eurostat—GDP per capita (%) (annual%).

Graphical representation of the main dimensions consists of mapping the data through the STATA software, thus creating a hierarchy of countries. At the same time, the most representative indicators for each member country of the EU-27 will be graphically represented. The main dimensions of digitalisation are graphically represented in Fig. 3 at the European Union level for the year 2022.

To highlight the differences between EU member states regarding specific digitalisation indicators, we applied the data mapping technique for 2022 (Fig. 3). All indicators show significant levels, especially in the Nordic countries (Sweden, Denmark, Finland, Estonia, and Ireland), Germany, and Austria. At the opposite pole, with the lowest values for connectivity (Fig. 3a), human capital (Fig. 3c), integration of digital technology (Fig. 3g) and High-tech exports (Fig. 3e), there are countries such as Romania and Hungary, Bulgaria, Poland, Lithuania, Greece, Croatia and Slovakia. On the other hand, the lowest values for People using the Internet (Fig. 3f) and Fixed Broadband Subscriptions (Fig. 3d) were noticed in the countries of Bulgaria and Greece, Romania, and Malta, while Luxembourg, Denmark, Belgium, Sweden, Ireland, present the most significant values. Germany and France have the best internet access (Fig. 3h).

The results demonstrate the following aspects: e-Government users (% of people who have used the Internet) (Fig. 4a). The highest level is in Sweden, Denmark, Ireland and the Netherlands, while the lowest level is recorded in Romania, Bulgaria and Italy. Moreover, the EU member states with the lowest level of e-government (Fig. 4c) are represented by: Slovakia, Malta, Hungary and Belgium. While the most digital public services offered to citizens (Fig. 4b) were found in countries such as Malta and Luxembourg and, at the opposite pole, countries such as Romania, Greece, Cyprus and Bulgaria.

Regarding the indicators representative of the dimension of innovation at the level of the EU member states for the year 2022 (Fig. 5), we can attest to the fact that there are significant discrepancies between the states. The Global Innovation Index (Fig. 5a) shows the highest score in Sweden (61) but also Germany (57), Finland (56.9) and Denmark (55.9); on the other hand, countries such as Romania (34.1), Slovakia (34.3), Greece (34.5) and Croatia (35.6) are the states with the lowest level of innovation. In terms of gross domestic expenditures for research and development (Fig. 5c), the following countries attribute the highest share as a percentage of GDP: Belgium (3.43%), Sweden (3.4%), Austria (3.2%) and Germany (3.13%), while countries such as Romania (0.46%), Malta (0.65%), Latvia (0.75%), Cyprus (0.77%) and Bulgaria (0, 77) assign the lowest weight to expenses for research and development.

At the same time, results were also issued for the specific indicators of economic performance (Fig. 6). We note that in 2022, a higher level of GDP per capita was

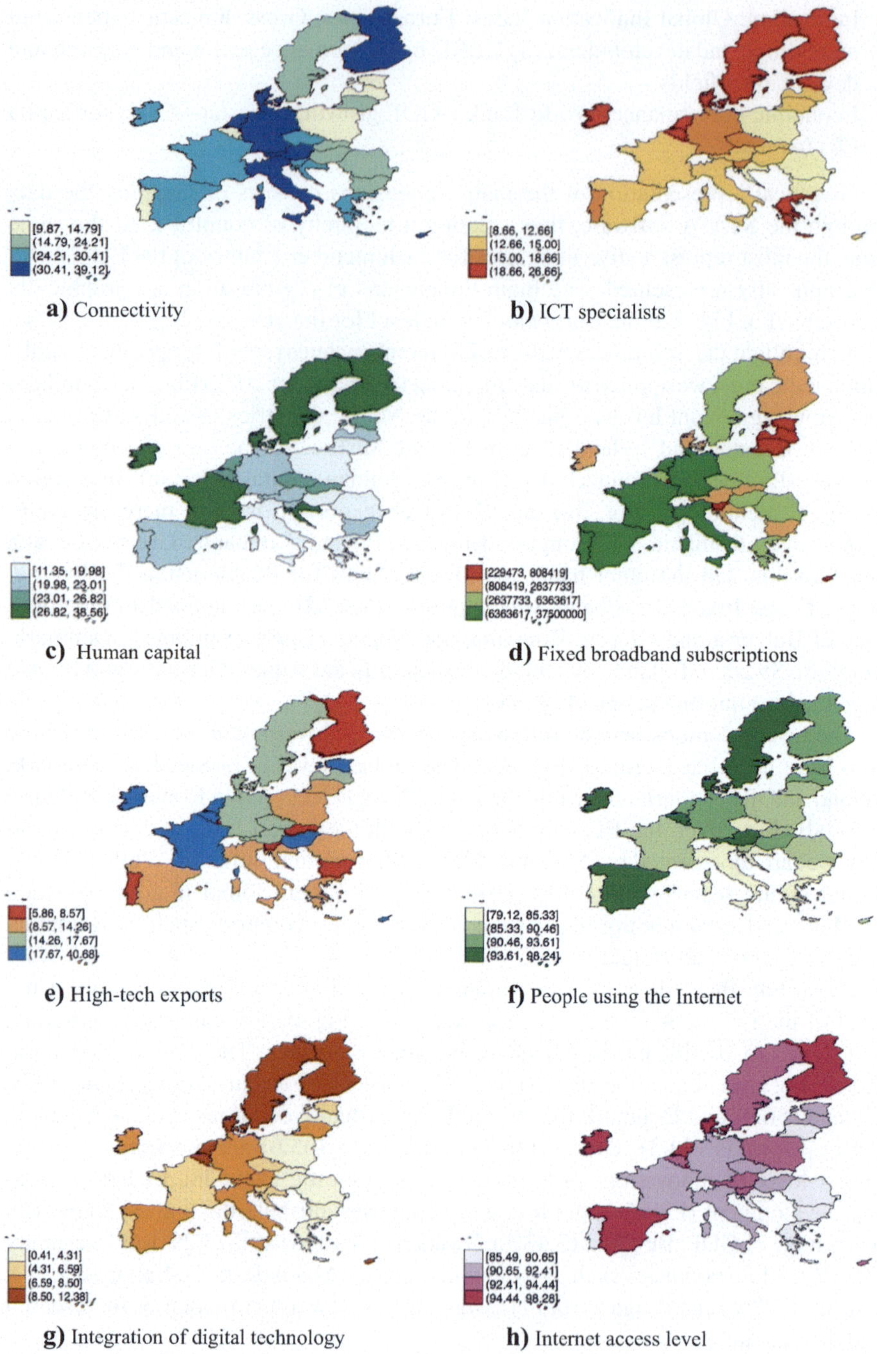

Fig. 3 Dimensions of digitalisation, year 2022 (EU-27). *Source* Authors' own processing in Stata 18 software

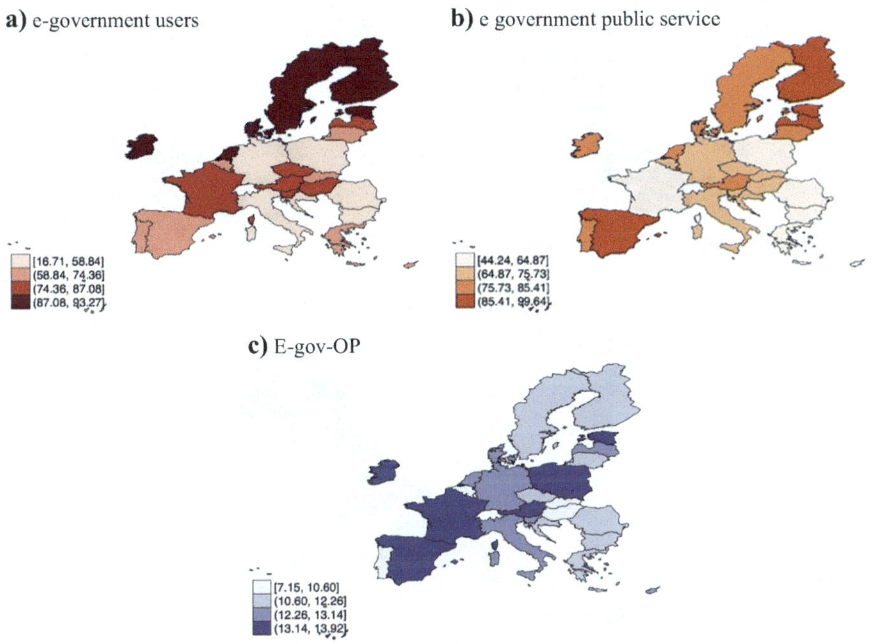

Fig. 4. Representative indicators, E-governance dimension. *Source* Authors' own processing in Stata 18 software

recorded (Fig. 6a) and also of the GDP rate per capita inhabitant. Bulgaria, Poland, Ireland, and Croatia recorded the highest GDP per capita compared to the EU-27 average, and Ireland, Malta, Portugal, and Croatia had the highest annual GDP growth (Fig. 6b).

4 Results

To test and validate the first hypothesis, which posits a direct impact of digital transformation policies on economic development, we began by constructing robust regression models (RREG). These models are presented in Table 1, showcasing the results for both Model 1 and Model 2.

The main results reveal a perfect association among variables and a notable impact on economic development (GDP per capita). The unfavourable direct implications of the Global Innovation Index and GERD on GDP per capita are in line with the results obtained for each advanced hypothesis in both models, the coefficient is negative and statistically significant, suggesting that an increase in the global innovation score is associated with a decrease in GDP per capita. This finding contradicts previous results reported in studies by Kotenok et al. (2020) and Maradana et al. (2017), who found

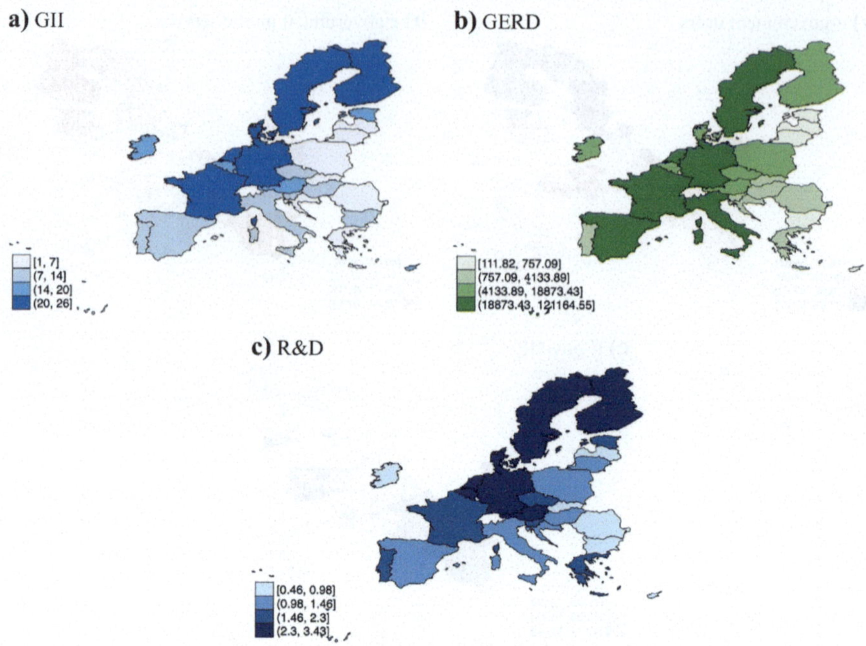

Fig. 5 Indicators of the innovation dimension. *Source* Author's own processing in Stata 18 software

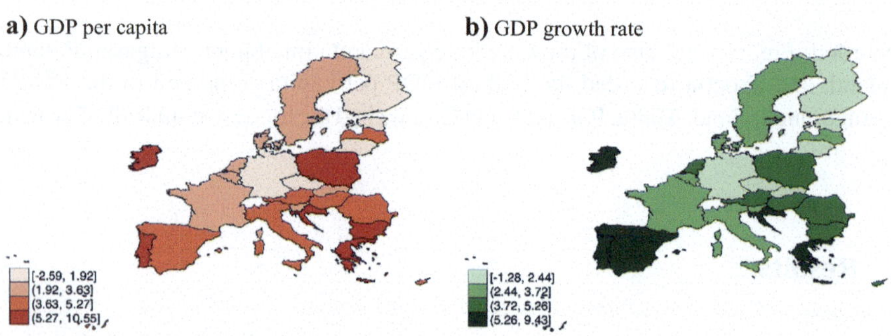

Fig. 6 Indicators specific to technology. *Source* Authors' own processing in Stata18 software

a positive and significant impact of innovation and R&D on economic growth indicators. For GERD, in Model 1, the coefficient is negative and significant, indicating a negative impact of research and development expenditures on GDP per capita; in Model 2, the effect becomes non-significant, suggesting a possible attenuation of the influence of R&D on GDP per capita. R&D, in Model 1, the coefficient is positive, implying that R&D contributes positively to GDP per capita, but in Model 2, the effect becomes non-significant, possibly indicating a reduction in the importance of R&D. Furthermore, the literature underpinnings have also revealed that the

Table 1 Results of robust regression models (RREG)

Dependent variable: GDP per capital		
Variables	Model 1 (2017)	Model 2 (2022)
GII	−1.684240***	−1.340911***
GERD	−1.328032*	−0.079617
IDT	−0.112475*	0.000780
IUI	1.075211*	−5.299013***
IUS	−0.117347	−1.432875***
LIAC	6.908200***	−2.336298**
OD	1.199256***	2.095301***
R&D	1.286695***	−0.148830
THE	0.167503***	0.356583***
DPS	1.045022***	2.266716***
E_Gov	−2.305637**	0.476415***
FBS	0.780087***	−0.089981
CONNECT	2.953342***	−0.717807***
ASD	−1.147367***	0.123573

Source Authors' own processing in EViews12 software. (*Note* statistically significant at '***': 1%; '**': 5%; '*': 10% level respectively)

effective impacts of digitalisation depend critically on the institutional frameworks and governments' ability to promote new technologies and address associated social challenges (Cristea et al. 2023).

The e-governance dimensions have registered favourable direct impacts on the GDP per capita. In Model 1, the coefficient for E_Govern is negative and significant, but it becomes positive and statistically significant in Model 2, indicating a change from a negative to a positive impact. The results regarding the direct impact of e-governance dimensions on GDP per capita are more encouraging; these results are reversed to those obtained by Laitsou et al. (2020) and Kusairi et al. (2023).

The results are mixed regarding the direct impacts of digital technology on the GDP per capita of the EU countries. While the results indicate favourable influences, the impacts of t Integration of Digital Technology, IUS, and Advanced Skills and Development by ICT Specialists were unfavourable (Ali et al. 2021; Cevik 2024). This highlights the complex and potentially context-dependent nature of the relationship between digital technology and economic development, which may depend on factors such as institutional frameworks, digital skills, and broader socio-economic conditions. Therefore, hypothesis H1, that the digital transformation policies and strategies exhibit significant direct impacts on economic development, with these effects being more pronounced in specific contexts, is partially fulfilled.

To explore the interconnections among digitalisation, innovation, the digitalisation of the public sector, and the economic performance of EU countries, referred to as hypothesis H2, we utilised both Gaussian Graphical Models (GGM) and a Mixed-Markov Graphic Model (MGM) as illustrated in Figs. 6 and 7. These models facilitate a comprehensive analysis of the complex relationships among these variables over the period from 2017 to 2022. In this context, the Gaussian Graphical Model allows us to understand how each variable functions as a node within a network. Each node is interconnected through significant pathways representing their interdependencies, thereby providing insights into how changes in one variable might influence others. Similarly, the Mixed-Markov Graphic Model enables us to account for the dynamics of these relationships over time, capturing the potential for shifts in these interlinkages. The analysis employed specific statistical techniques, including partial correlation, the extended Bayesian Information Criterion (EBIC), and absolute minimum selection. Partial correlation helps determine the strength and direction of the relationships between pairs of variables while controlling for the influence of other variables in the model. The EBIC is a sophisticated criterion used for model selection that balances the goodness of fit with model complexity, ensuring that the selected model is both parsimonious and representative of the underlying data. Estimates for the models were generated using two distinct methodologies: one based on partial correlation and the other utilising the Bayesian EBIC criterion. This dual approach enhances the robustness of our findings by allowing for cross-validation of results and providing a more nuanced understanding of the intricate web of relationships among the variables studied.

The integration of digital technologies (IDT) is intrinsically connected to various factors, including digital public services (DPS), economic growth as measured by gross domestic product (GDP), connectivity (CMB), and research and development activities (R&D). Moreover, domestic expenditures on research and development (R&D) exhibit a partially positive correlation with the integration of advanced skills (ADVS) and broader economic development, as well as with the utilisation of e-government services (EGOV) and GDP per capita (GDP per Cap). Digital public services (DPS) further demonstrate positive relationships with individual internet

a) Graphical Outcomes of the Mixed-Markov (MGM) Model, 2017

b) Ourcomes of the Mixed-Markov graphic model, 2022

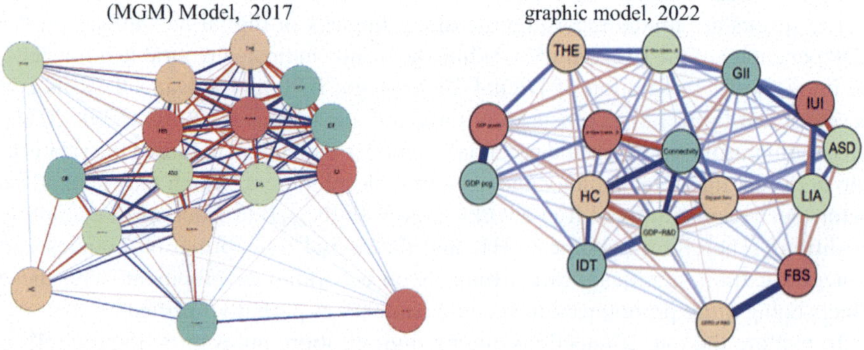

Fig. 7 Analytical Outcomes of the Mixed-Markov Model (MGM). *Source* Authors' own processing in RStudio software

usage (IUI), the development of advanced skills, the cultivation of information and communication technology (ICT) specialists, and open data initiatives (OP). These findings highlight the significant implications of the diverse aspects of digitalisation and innovation within the e-government landscape across the EU-27 member states. Such insights suggest that enhancing digital capabilities and fostering innovative practices can improve public service delivery and economic performance.

In the Mixed-Markov Graphic Model (MGM) depicted in Fig. 7, stronger connections illustrate various relationships between digital innovation and the dimensions of e-government. Specifically, positive associations are identified between the integration of digital technology (IDT) and factors such as gross domestic expenditure on research and development (R&D), gross domestic product (GDP), digital public services (DPS), connectivity (CMB), human capital (HC), and open data initiatives (OP). Conversely, the model reveals negative correlations with individual internet usage (IUI). Additionally, a positive impact on gross domestic expenditure on research and development (R&D) is noted in relation to GDP per capita growth (GDP per Cap), integration of digital technology (IDT), and internet usage for information-seeking about goods and services, as well as e-government utilisation (EGOV). However, adverse influences are observed among internet users engaged in fewer digital devices, including limited participation in online activities related to human capital (HC) and accessing public services that have integrated digital technologies (DPS). These findings highlight the complex interplay between digital innovation and e-government dimensions, suggesting that while certain elements of digital integration foster economic growth and enhance public service delivery, challenges may hinder broader engagement with digital technologies among the population. The model underscores the importance of promoting comprehensive digital literacy and encouraging active participation in e-government initiatives to maximise the benefits of digital transformation.

The Gaussian Graphical Model (GGM) presented in Fig. 8 reveals strong interconnections among various aspects of digital innovation and e-government dimensions. Positive associations are observed between the integration of digital technology (IDT) and factors such as gross domestic expenditure on research and development (R&D), GDP, Digital Public Services (DPS), connectivity (Connect), human capital (HC), and Open Data (OP). Conversely, negative synergies are found with individuals' Internet usage (IUI). Favourable influences on gross domestic expenditure on research and development (R&D) are seen in GDP per capita growth (GDP per_Cap), Integration of Digital Technology (IDT), Internet use, and e-government users (E-GOV). However, negative influences are observed among internet users (IUI) who participate in a limited range of activities involving digital devices, including various online engagements and the use of digitally integrated public services (DPS). These findings corroborate the results reported by Crăciun et al. (2023) and Criste et al. (2024a, b), reinforcing our research hypothesis (H2), which posits that there are strong linkages between the dimensions of digital technology, the digitalisation of the public sector, innovation, and economic performance. This underscores

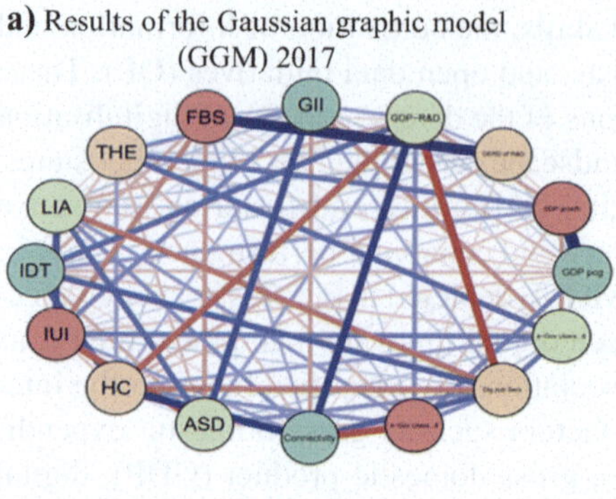

Fig. 8 Results of the Gaussian graphic model (GGM). *Source* Authors' own processing in RStudio software

the importance of fostering a comprehensive digital ecosystem that integrates technology within public services and encourages broader participation among citizens to maximise the potential benefits for economic growth and social engagement.

Moreover, cluster analysis was used to verify the third hypothesis, through which it was possible to group and visualise the relative distances of the already formed groups. So, K-means is a clustering algorithm that sets the cluster centres for some predefined number of clusters and assigns each data vector to a single cluster based on the Euclidean distance. Thus, the K-means algorithm allowed the data set to partition into k distinct, predefined subgroups (clusters). The K-means algorithm groups similar data points within a similar intra-group but, at the same time, keeps subgroups as distinct and distant from each other as possible. For the methodological operationalisation, we used the R software. According to Ţăran et al. (2022), the data grouping process based on the K-means algorithm involves establishing the number of "k" clusters and determining the centroid value based on the chosen number of clusters.

Thus, a preliminary stage of our study consisted of testing the optimal number of clusters Gap Statistic (GS) (Fig. 9) and Silhouette method (SSW) (Fig. 10), both for the first and for the last year retained in the analysis, respectively the year 2017 and 2022, an optimal number of 2 clusters resulted in the end. So, after determining the optimal number of clusters, a second stage consisted of applying the cluster analysis (Fig. 11) and the Hierarchical K-means dendrogram (Fig. 12).

We used the dendrogram to document the hierarchical relationships between countries and clusters. The dendrogram shows the intuitive distance of the formed groups/ clusters using a scale from 0 to 15. The height indicates the order in which the clusters were merged, and the lowest height indicates the connection, that is, similarities between countries. At the same time, the highest height indicates the distinctive characteristics between the countries. Figure 11. shows the dendrogram, the intuitive distance between the clusters becomes more extensive as we move towards the maximum point of the dendrogram 15. So, the dendrogram allows the grouping of countries in an innovative way based on the specifics of the group.

a) The number of clusters in 2017

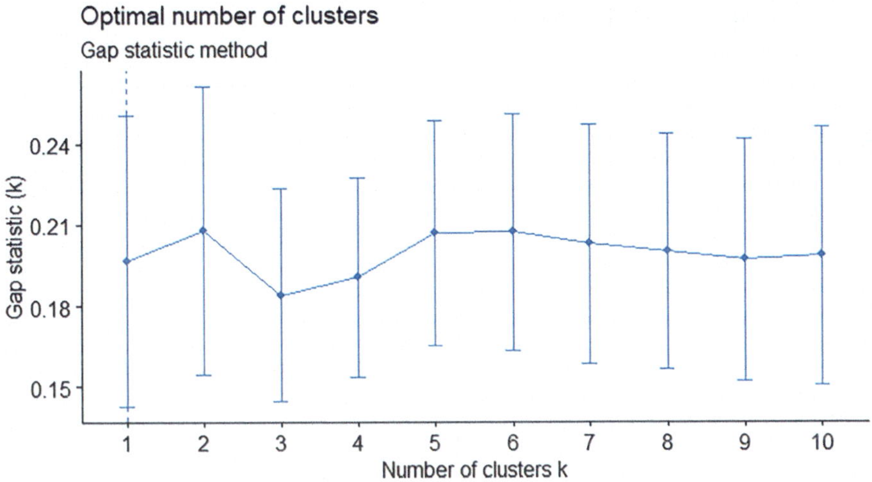

b) The optimal number of clusters in 2022

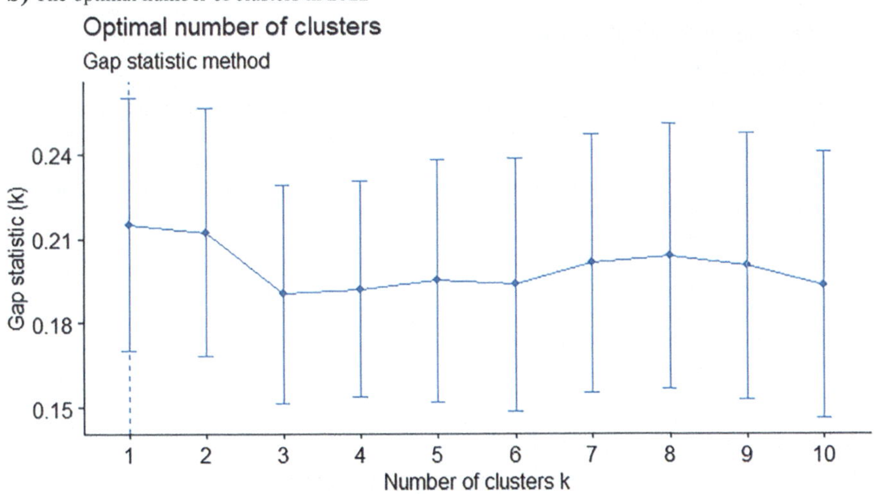

Fig. 9 The optimal number of GS clusters. *Source* Authors' own processing in R software

Figure 11 illustrates the clustering of EU countries based on digital performance for 2017 and 2022. In 2017, the yellow cluster predominantly consisted of Western and Northern European countries known for their advanced digital economies, while the blue cluster comprised mainly Southern and Eastern European nations. For the year 2017, the most similar countries in terms of the level associated with digital performance, for the year 2017, are the yellow cluster—Austria and Belgium; Spain, Luxembourg, Sweden and Denmark; Finland, the Netherlands; Germany, France, Ireland, Estonia and Malta. While in the blue cluster, we have identified countries

a) Cluster Determination 2017

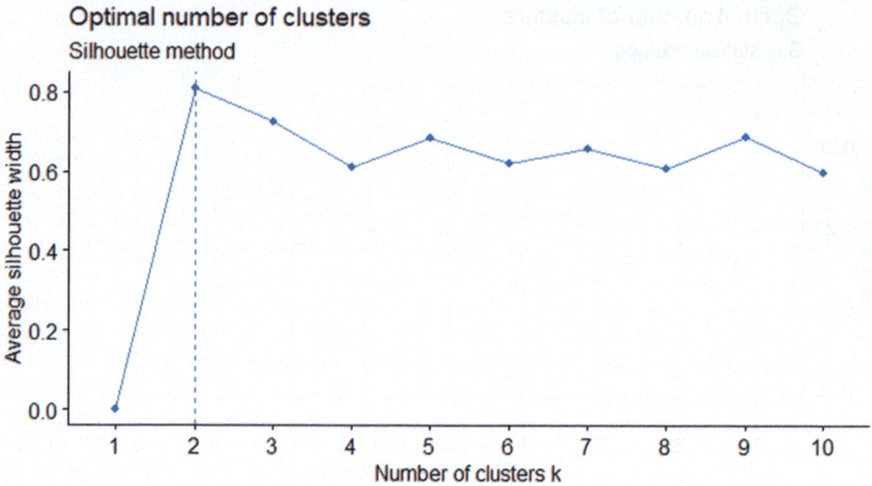

b) Cluster Determination 2022

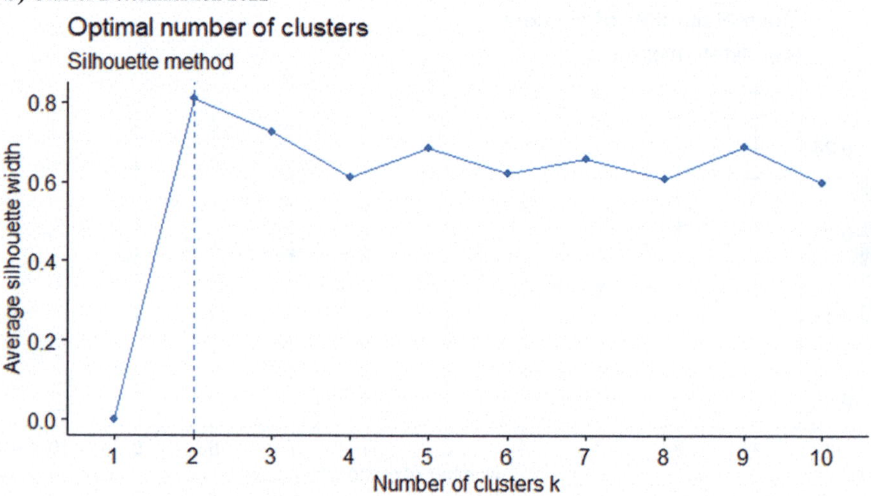

Fig. 10 Determination of the optimal number of SM clusters. *Source* Authors' own processing in R software

such as—Portugal and Lithuania, Croatia, Slovenia, Czech Republic, Poland, Cyprus, Latvia, Slovakia, Hungary, Greece, Bulgaria, Italy, and Romania.

As for the analysis for the year 2022, based on it, we identify the yellow cluster—Cyprus and Austria, Italy, Ireland, Latvia and Lithuania, Slovenia and the Czech Republic, Slovakia and Hungary, Malta, Luxembourg and Estonia, and Belgium. The yellow cluster includes Greece, Croatia, Portugal, Poland, Bulgaria, Romania, Germany, and France. At the same time, the blue cluster is Sweden, the Netherlands,

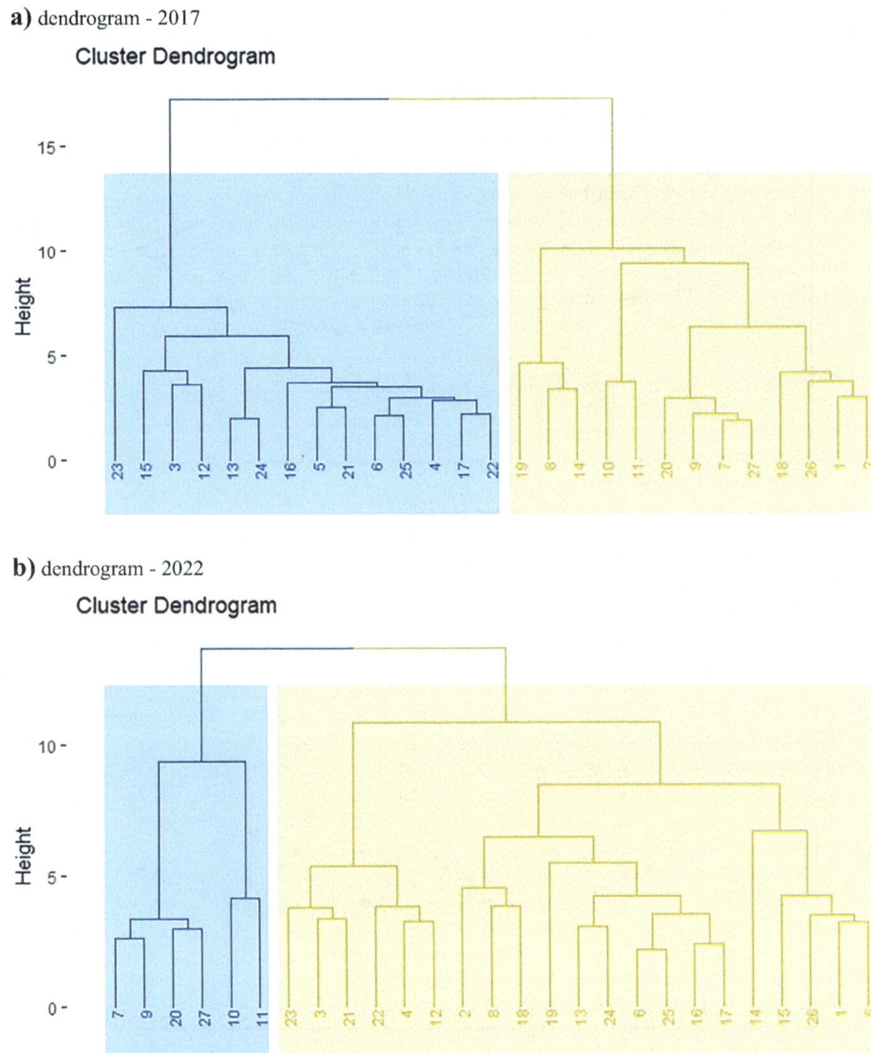

Fig. 11 Dendrogram results. *Source* Authors' own processing R software

Finland, and Denmark. It can also be observed that a noticeable shift occurs in several countries from the blue cluster, including Slovenia, Slovakia, Latvia, Lithuania, and the Czech Republic, transitioning to the yellow cluster. This shift suggests a convergence in digital performance among these nations, aligning more closely with the digital frontrunners. Conversely, the blue cluster in 2022 exhibits greater homogeneity. This observation highlights a potential widening digital performance gap between these top performers and the rest of the EU.

a) Cluster - 2017

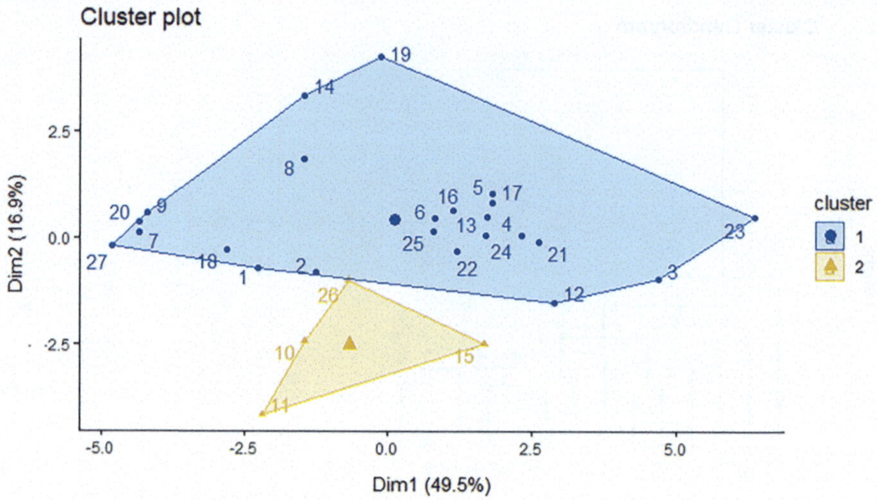

b) Cluster - 2022

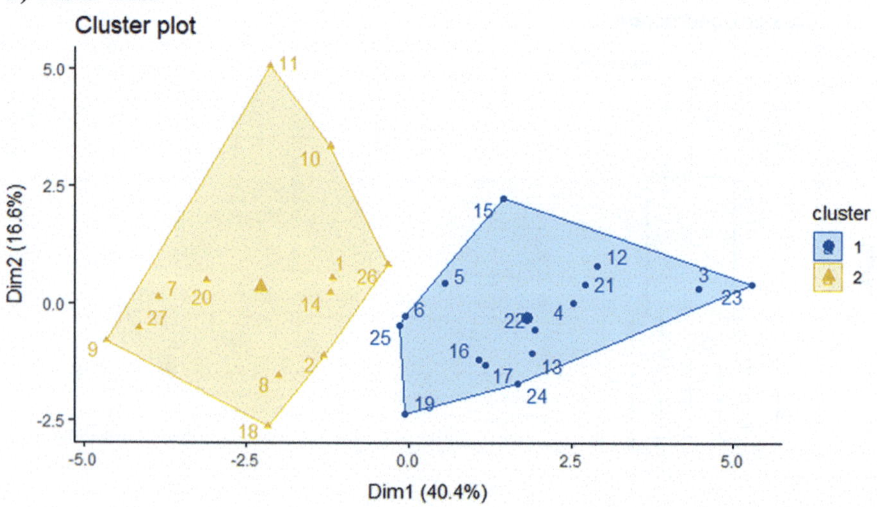

Fig. 12 Representation of clusters associated with digital performance. *Source* Authors' own processing in R software

The dendrogram analysis reveals that countries which joined the European Union more recently (Romania, Bulgaria, Croatia, and Slovakia), particularly former communist states, tend to demonstrate lower digital performance levels. These nations face challenges in the efficient use of public funds due to high levels of corruption and low transparency in decision-making compared to developed EU countries such as Finland, Sweden and Denmark. While perceptions of corruption and transparency play a significant role (Cruz-Jesus et al. 2012; Androniceanu et al. 2022), it's important to consider broader systemic factors, such as investment gaps, contributing to the disparity in digital performance. This country's relatively low public spending on research and development in digital technologies compared to high-performing countries like Denmark is a significant factor behind its lagging performance. Additionally, the emigration of highly skilled information technology professionals to higher-paying job markets within the European Union can further compound the challenges these countries face in developing a thriving digital economy (Pashkevich et al. 2020; Andrey et al. 2020). Furthermore, countries that transitioned from centrally planned economic systems frequently inherited obsolete technological infrastructure and rigid bureaucratic frameworks, which can impede swift digital transformation (Soja and Cunha 2015; Rubino-Hallman and Hanna 2007; Roztocki and Weistroffer 2014). In these contexts, addressing corruption is essential, but sustained investment in digital infrastructure, skills development, and institutional reforms is equally critical to enable more agile, responsive, and citizen-centric public services.

By utilising the clustering technique, a ranking was obtained at the level of the European Union's member states. This dendrogram-based ranking identified similarities that group countries into the same cluster. At the same time, employing the cluster analysis, the differences in digital performance among the EU countries were grouped and visualised (innovation, economic performance, digitalisation of the public sector). Therefore, the countries were divided into two groups based on their overall performance.

At the same time, Fig. 12. provides an overall picture of the 2 clusters for the year 2017: the first cluster (blue) consists of Germany, France, Italy and Spain. At the same time, the yellow cluster includes most countries: Austria and Belgium, Lithuania, Slovenia, Czech Republic, Poland, Slovakia, Latvia, Croatia, Bulgaria and Romania, Estonia, Luxembourg, Ireland, Netherlands, Denmark, Sweden and Finland, Portugal, Greece, Hungary and Cyprus and Malta.

The analysis at the level of 2022 reveals the composition of the 2 clusters: the first cluster (blue) is made up of the countries Malta, Slovenia, Slovakia, Latvia, Lithuania, Czech Republic, Hungary, Portugal, Italy, Croatia, Poland, Bulgaria, Romania, Greece, and Italy. The second cluster (yellow) includes Luxembourg, Finland, Estonia, Sweden, Bulgaria, Denmark, Holland, Ireland, Austria, Spain, France, and Germany.

Comparing the cluster analysis results, we observe a notable trend where several countries are transitioning from the relatively heterogeneous Yellow Cluster in 2017 to the more homogeneous Blue Cluster by 2022. This finding indicates a persistent digital divide between the more developed and less developed Member States of the European Union. The analysis suggests that Slovenia, Slovakia, Latvia, Lithuania, Czech Republic, Hungary, Portugal, and Croatia demonstrated notable advancements in their digital performance indicators during the period examined, resulting in these countries aligning more closely with the digital leaders within the European Union. In contrast, Spain transitioned from the Blue Cluster to the Yellow Cluster, suggesting a potential relative deterioration in its digital performance relative to the leading EU countries.

According to the cluster analysis foundation, countries with the same cluster show similar digital performance levels. EU countries on the same line are very close in terms of the value of the indicators. Based on these results, our 3rd hypothesis, H3, is partially validated, "there are significant disparities among the EU-27 member states in terms of their digital transformation policies and strategies for the public sector, which have resulted in diminished outcomes compared to government expectations". The present analysis shows significant differences in digital performance. The indicators' trends in recent years show a constant improvement, which can be attributed to the strategies and measures imposed by the European Union, such as the digital governance framework, structural reforms, and technical support. All these initiatives can contribute to the efficiency of the allocation of public funds and the improvement of services offered to citizens. The European Union persistently encourages and lends support to Member States in their efforts to enhance this critical sector, which is essential for the proper functioning of society.

This analysis indicates that a significant digital divide continues to exist between more developed and less developed countries within the European Union. Despite advancements in digital technologies and e-government initiatives, disparities in access, utilisation, and benefits from these technologies remain pronounced. This divide can affect economic growth, social equity, and overall development across the member states. To address these challenges, three strategic lines of action are proposed for the medium term: (i) evaluation of national and regional public policies to identify their effectiveness in promoting digitalisation and addressing inequalities; (ii) consideration of digital inclusion as a tool for reducing disparities to create a more equitable digital landscape where everyone can participate in the digital economy and benefit from e-government services and (iii) provision of training in advanced digital skills are essential for enhancing social communication processes and enabling individuals to navigate the digital environment effectively. Together, these actions aim to bridge the digital divide by promoting equitable access to technology, enhancing digital literacy, and fostering an inclusive digital economy that benefits all EU member states.

5 Conclusions

This study investigated the relationship between digital transformation and public sector performance within the European Union. A mixed-methods approach assessed the multifaceted connections between digital technology and e-government services. This approach incorporated data mapping, robust regression analysis, hierarchical clustering, and both Gaussian Graphical Models and Mixed-Markov Graphic Models. Our empirical findings highlight digital technology's complex and nuanced influences on e-government services across EU-27 member states, revealing both positive and negative impacts. These findings significantly impact understanding of the intricate nexus between digitalisation and Digital Public Services within the EU context.

Graphical representation of indicators has enabled evaluating public sector performance levels across the European Union member states. This encompasses assessing digital performance and innovation in the European public sector and their economic evolution. Subsequently, cluster analysis was conducted, revealing significant diversity in the digital performance of EU regions. Furthermore, recent trends in the indicators suggest a steady improvement in digital performance.

The main findings at the level of the EU member states indicate that several countries, including Portugal, Lithuania, Croatia, Slovenia, Czechia, Poland, Cyprus, Latvia, Slovakia, Hungary, Greece, Bulgaria, Italy, Hungary, and Romania, require substantial improvements across all four dimensions implemented in this study. Additionally, some of these nations have the lowest values in funding for research, development, and innovation. On the other hand, countries such as Austria, Belgium, Spain, Luxembourg, Germany, and France could follow the best practice models of the highly digitalised countries to achieve an optimal level of digitalisation. In contrast, Sweden, the Netherlands, Finland, and Denmark are the most representative of digitalisation. These findings directly address our research question regarding the variation in digital performance across EU regions.

At the same time, the relationship between the public sector and digital transformation, as illustrated by the Gaussian and Mixed Markov graphical models, underscores the dual nature of digital technology's impact on e-government services within the European Union. These models reveal that while digital technology has facilitated significant advancements and improvements in the delivery of public services, it has also introduced challenges and negative consequences that must be acknowledged. These findings are crucial for understanding how digitalisation influences public services in the EU-27. They demonstrate that digital technology is vital in enhancing the efficiency and effectiveness of e-government operations, contributing to better service delivery, increased transparency, and improved citizen engagement. However, the graphical analyses provided by the Gaussian and Mixed Markov models also allow for a nuanced visualisation of the relationships between various elements of digital technology and public sector operations, highlighting both positive outcomes and potential pitfalls. Moreover, the results indicate that enhancements in digital infrastructure over recent years have led to a broader integration of digital networks within the public sector. This improvement has created a more conducive environment for digital transformation, allowing for the effective deployment of e-government services. A comparison of the findings from the Gaussian Graphical Model (GGM) and the Mixed Markov Model (MGM) for EU member states during the period 2017–2022 reveals that innovation and the digitalisation of e-government have had a direct and substantial influence on economic performance.

The significant impact of digitalisation on e-government underscores the necessity for ongoing investments in digital infrastructure and technology. By leveraging these advancements, the public sector can further enhance service delivery, foster innovation, and ultimately drive economic growth across the EU. Our findings suggest that countries with advanced digital capabilities also possess a stable digital infrastructure, significantly influencing the provision of Digital Public Services and their associated implications for intensive innovation. Furthermore, data mapping indicates that countries with a substantial level of digitalisation also exhibit a significant degree of e-government. Finland, Denmark, and Sweden have recorded the highest levels of digital intensity. Additionally, the COVID-19 pandemic has been a potential factor in the intensified use of digital technology, as this unexpected event has driven the integration of digital technologies. However, Romania and Bulgaria continue to exhibit a low level of digitalisation, and this resistance to change may be attributed to the perception of digital infrastructure development as a cost rather than a long-term investment.

Based on the study's findings, several policy recommendations can be suggested: EU member states should incorporate digital technologies and continuous innovation into their digital transformation strategies to enhance e-government effectiveness. Also, ensuring adequate resource allocation, sustained creativity, and government commitment are essential for making electronic services accessible, secure, and user-friendly for all.

(i) Boosting Digital Performance in Lagging Regions: (a) Prioritize investments in digital infrastructure, particularly in countries with lower digital performance, such as those that recently joined the EU and former communist states. This includes expanding broadband access, improving network quality, and ensuring affordable internet connectivity; (b) Addressing the digital skills gap by developing education and training programs tailored to the needs of these countries' public sector and citizens. This should encompass promoting digital literacy, computational thinking, and specialised competencies in data analysis, cybersecurity, and emerging technologies.

(ii) Fostering Innovation and R&D: (While the study suggests a potential inverse correlation between the Global Innovation Index, GERD, and GDP per capita, further research is needed to understand this complex relationship fully) (a) Prioritize R&D investments in digital technologies that directly enhance the efficiency and service delivery of the public sector. This should include exploring innovative applications of emerging technologies such as artificial intelligence, blockchain, and big data analytics in domains like e-government, healthcare, and education; (b) encourage the establishment of collaborative public–private partnerships to leverage the expertise and resources of the private sector in driving digital innovation within the public sphere.

(iii) Systemic Challenges: (a) implementing institutional reforms that streamline bureaucratic processes, enhance transparency, and promote good governance in public administration. This should involve simplifying administrative procedures, digitising public services, and fostering a culture of accountability and citizen engagement.

(iv) Fostering Digital Equity and Inclusive Transformation: (a) Prioritize inclusivity and accessibility in digital transformation efforts to ensure no one is left behind. This entails addressing the unique needs of older adults and those in rural or disadvantaged areas; (b) Developing tailored digital literacy and skills training programs for diverse demographic groups to bridge the digital divide and fully empower all citizens to engage in the digital economy and society.

In conclusion, policymakers must take a holistic approach when evaluating the benefits of digital advancements in public service delivery. This evaluation should extend beyond merely assessing costs; it must also consider the overall value and effectiveness of such innovations to the services provided to citizens. Policymakers need to determine whether these digital innovations improve service quality, accessibility, and responsiveness while also contributing to broader socioeconomic benefits, such as enhanced economic growth, social equity, and increased citizen engagement. EU member states should incorporate digital technologies and continuous innovation into their digital transformation strategies to enhance e-government effectiveness. Ensuring adequate resource allocation, sustained creativity, and government commitment are all essential for making electronic services accessible, secure, and user-friendly. Policymakers must prioritise the user experience in designing and implementing digital services, making them intuitive and easy to navigate for all citizens, including those with varying levels of digital literacy. By focusing on these factors, EU member states can maximise the potential of digital technologies to enhance public service delivery, ultimately leading to a more efficient, effective, and equitable government that better serves its citizens.

References

Acheampong, D., Meso, P., Agyemang, I O., Cudjoe, J. (2024). Bridging the digital divide: Securing information and computer systems in an unequal world. In Chigona, W., Kabanda, S., Seymour, L.F. (eds) Implications of information and digital technologies for development. ICT4D 2024. IFIP Advances in information and communication technology (Vol. 709). Springer, Cham. https://doi.org/10.1007/978-3-031-66986-6_6

Ali, S A., Alharthi, M., Hussain, H I., Rasul, F., Hanif, I., Haider, J., Ullah, S., Rahman, S U., & Abbas, Q. (2021, February 4). A clean technological innovation and eco-efficiency enhancement: A multi-index assessment of sustainable economic and environmental management. Elsevier BV, 166, 120573–120573. https://doi.org/10.1016/j.techfore.2021.120573

Andrey, Z., Evgeniy, K., Yulia, B., & Zarema, D. (2020, January 1). Influence of the level of development of the digital environment on the trend of gross domestic product in the countries of the European Union. EDP Sciences, 211, 04006–04006. https://doi.org/10.1051/e3sconf/202021104006

Androniceanu, A., Georgescu, I., & Kinnunen, J. (2022, February 25). "Public Administration Digitalization and Corruption in the EU Member States. A Comparative and Correlative Research Analysis". Babeş-Bolyai University, 5–22. https://doi.org/10.24193/tras.65e.1

Archmann, S., & Iglesias, J. C. (2011). Perspectives on E-Government in Europe. In Information Communication Technologies and the Virtual Public Sphere: Impacts of Network Structures on Civil Society (pp. 195–206). IGI Global.

Arner, D. W., Castellano, G. G., &Selga, E. K. (2022). The transnational data governance problem. *Berkeley Tech. LJ*, *37*, 623.

Asogwa, B. E. (2012). The challenge of managing electronic records in developing countries: Implications for records managers in sub–Saharan Africa. Records Management Journal, 22(3), 198–211.

Beniwal, V. S. (2013). Instilling citizen-centric approach in civil service: Prospects and challenges. Journal of Politics and Governance, 2(1and2), 235–244.

Bhatnagar, S. C., & Singh, N. (2010). Assessing the Impact of E-government: A Study of Projects in India. Information Technologies & International Development, 6(2), pp. 109.

Bolbotenko, A. (2021, March 31). Analysis of the Practice of Providing Administrative Services by the Member States of the European Union. Wydawnictwo Adam Marszałek, 29(1), 28–40. https://doi.org/10.15804/ksm20210103

Cevik, S. (2024, February 1). Is Schumpeter Right? Fintech and Economic Growth. International Monetary Fund, 2024(020), 1–1. https://doi.org/10.5089/9798400266324.001

Chan, F K Y., Thong, J Y., Brown, S A., & Venkatesh, V. (2020, October 24). Service Design and Citizen Satisfaction with E-Government Services: A Multidimensional Perspective. Wiley, 81(5), 874–894. https://doi.org/10.1111/puar.13308

Cherdantseva, Y., & Hilton, J. (2013, September). A reference model of information assurance & security. In 2013 international conference on availability, reliability and security (pp. 546–555). IEEE.

Chiriac, A M., Mocanu, Ş., & Popa, C. (2021, March 25). Onto Digitalization of Public Services. https://doi.org/10.1109/atee52255.2021.9425172

Crăciun, A. F., Ţăran, A. M., Noja, G. G., Pirtea, M. G., & Răcătăian, R. I. (2023). Advanced modelling of public governance and digital transformation interplay: new empirical evidence from structural equation modelling and Gaussian and Mixed-Markov graphical models. Mathematics, 11(5), 1168. https://doi.org/10.3390/math11051168

Criste, C., Man, C. B., & Lobonţ, O. R. (2024a, July). Portraying the Level of Digital Performance and Innovation of the European Public Sector: Contextualising the Relationship Between E-government and Digital Innovation. In International Scientific Conference Strategic Management and Decision Support Systems in Strategic Management (pp. 363–372).

Criste, C., Man, C. B., Moldovan, N. C., Răcătăian, R., & Lobonţ, O. R. (2024b). EU Capacity to Bolster and Stimulate Research and Innovation: Who is the Leader in Development?. Studies in Business and Economics, 19(2), 60–77.

Cristea, M., Noja, G. G., Găinaru, T. A., & Tălăban, C. D. (2023). Digital transformation and its implications on educational quality: An empirical analysis within the European Union context. Oppor Chall. Sustain, 2(3), 130–140. https://doi.org/10.56578/ocs020302

Cruz-Jesus, F., Oliveira, T., & Bação, F. (2012, October 1). Digital divide across the European Union. Elsevier BV, 49(6), 278–291. https://doi.org/10.1016/j.im.2012.09.003

Dhaoui, I. (2022). E-government for sustainable development: Evidence from MENA countries. *Journal of the Knowledge Economy*, *13*(3), 2070–2099.

Dima, B., Dima, S.M., & Lobont, O. (2013). New empirical evidence of the linkages between governance and economic output in the European Union. Journal of Economic Policy Reform, 16:1, 68–89, https://doi.org/10.1080/17487870.2012.759427

Dima, B., Lobonţ, O., & Nicoleta-Claudia, N. (2016). Does the quality of public policies and institutions matter for entrepreneurial activity? Evidences from the European Union's member states. Panoeconomicus, 63(4), 425–439. https://doi.org/10.2298/pan1604425d

Doran, N. M., Puiu, S., Bădîrcea, R. M., Pirtea, M. G., Doran, M. D., Ciobanu, G., & Mihit, L. D. (2023). E-government development—A key factor in government administration effectiveness in the European Union. Electronics, 12(3), 641.

Đorić, Ž. (2022, January 1). Digitalisation of the economy and the issues of inequality in the global society. , 19(2), 123–155. https://doi.org/10.5937/skolbiz2-41090

Eom, S., & Lee, J. (2022, March 11). Digital government transformation in turbulent times: Responses, challenges, and future direction. Elsevier BV, 39(2), 101690–101690. https://doi.org/10.1016/j.giq.2022.101690

Febiri, F., & Hub, M. (2021, January 1). Digitalization of Global Economy: A Qualitative Study Exploring Key Indicators use to Measure Digital Progress in the Public Sector. EDP Sciences, 92, 05006–05006. https://doi.org/10.1051/shsconf/20219205006

Houngbo, P. T., Coleman, H. L. S., Zweekhorst, M., De Cock Buning, T., Medenou, D., & Bunders, J. F. G. (2017). A model for good governance of healthcare technology management in the public sector: learning from evidence-informed policy development and implementation in Benin. PloS one, 12(1), e0168842.

Karimi, J., & Walter, Z. (2021). The role of entrepreneurial agility in digital entrepreneurship and creating value in response to digital disruption in the newspaper industry. Sustainability, 13(5), 2741.

Kotenok, A., Kulaga, I., Klivak, V., & Ткаченко, O. (2020, January 1). The E-Government's Influence on the Country's Economy (At the Example of Ukraine and Estonia). https://doi.org/10.2991/aebmr.k.200318.022

Kovacikova, M., & Stofkova, K. (2020). SELECTED ASPECTS OF THE INTERNET OF THINGS DURING GLOBALIZATION. Proceedings of CBU in Economics and Business, 1, 112–119.

Kusairi, S., Wong, Z Y., Wahyuningtyas, R., & Sukemi, M N. (2023, January 1). Impact of digitalisation and foreign direct investment on economic growth: Learning from developed countries. Centre of Sociological Research, Ternopil, Ukraine, 16(1), 98–111. https://doi.org/10.14254/2071-8330.2023/16-1/7

Laitsou, E., Κάργας, A., & Varoutas, D. (2020, October 15). Digital Competitiveness in the European Union Era: The Greek Case. Multidisciplinary Digital Publishing Institute, 8(4), 85–85. https://doi.org/10.3390/economies8040085

Lopes, K. M. G., Macadar, M. A., &Luciano, E. M. (2019). Key drivers for public value creation enhancing the adoption of electronic public services by citizens. International Journal of Public Sector Management, 32(5), 546–561.

Magomedov, I. A., Murzaev, H. A., & Bagov, A. M. (2020, May). The role of digital technologies in economic development. In *IOP Conference Series: Materials Science and Engineering* (Vol. 862, No. 5, p. 052071). IOP Publishing.

Maradana, R P., Pradhan, R P., Dash, S., Gaurav, K., Jayakumar, M., & Chatterjee, D. (2017, January 10). Does innovation promote economic growth? Evidence from European countries. Springer Nature, 6(1). https://doi.org/10.1186/s13731-016-0061-9

Martin, A., & Grudziecki, J. (2006). DigEuLit: Concepts and tools for digital literacy development. Innovation in Teaching and Learning in Information and Computer Sciences, 5 (4), 249–267. Режим доступа: https://doi.org/10.11120/ital.

Martín, M Á G., Martínez, M S C., & Picazo, M T M. (2023, March 16). Digitalization, entrepreneurship and competitiveness: an analysis from 19 European countries. Springer Science+Business Media, 17(5), 1809–1826. https://doi.org/10.1007/s11846-023-00640-1

Medaglia, R., Misuraca, G., & Aquaro, V. (2021, June 9). Digital Government and the United Nations' Sustainable Development Goals: Towards an analytical framework. https://doi.org/10.1145/3463677.3463736

Mergel, I., Edelmann, N., &Haug, N. (2019). Defining digital transformation: Results from expert interviews. Government Information Quarterly, 36 (2).

Myovella, G., Karacuka, M., & Haucap, J. (2020). Digitalization and economic growth: A comparative analysis of Sub-Saharan Africa and OECD economies. Telecommunications Policy, 44(2), 101856.

Nam, T. (2014). Determining the type of e-government use. Government information quarterly, 31(2), 211-220.

Ndou, V. (2004, June 1). E – Government for Developing Countries: Opportunities and Challenges. Wiley, 18(1), 1–24. https://doi.org/10.1002/j.1681-4835.2004.tb00117.x

Noja, G. G., Cristea, M., Sîrghi, N., Hategan, C., & D'Anselmi, P. (2019). Promoting good public governance and environmental support for sustainable economic development. International Journal of Environmental Research and Public Health, 16(24), 4940. https://doi.org/ https://doi.org/10.3390/ijerph16244940

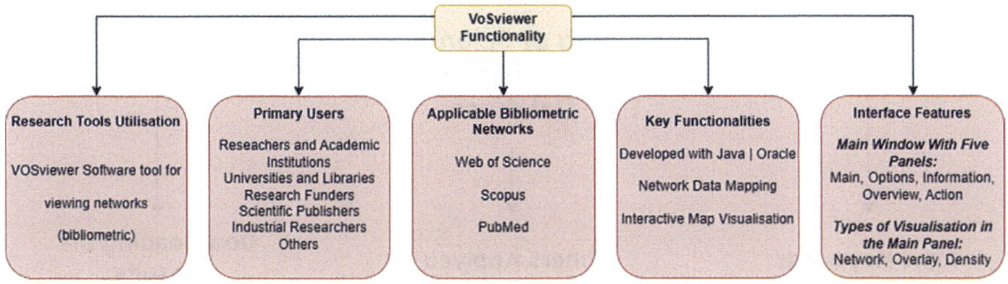

Fig. 1 The functionality of the VOSviewer bibliometric software. *Source* Data processed by the authors from the VOSviewer manual (Eck and Waltman 2023)

insights into thematic developments, academic impact, and the interconnected areas shaping the fields of digital transformation and sustainability research, as illustrated in Fig. 1.

In bibliometric networks, pivotal nodes are established through essential publications, influential researchers, and key terminologies. Connections between these nodes represent different relational structures: bibliographic coupling between publications, co-authorship links among researchers, and keyword co-occurrence within the literature. The strength of these connections is quantified, with higher values representing more robust ties, such as a large number of shared citations or frequent collaborations. These metrics illustrate the relational depth and highlight prominent themes and contributors within the research landscape.

In VOSviewer's network visualization, clusters emerge as groups of interconnected articles, each exclusively assigned to a single cluster, signifying distinct research communities. Although the majority of articles fall into clusters, some remain as relevant outliers. Each cluster is labeled numerically, and articles within these clusters carry attributes such as "weight" and "score," indicating their prominence and influence. Key metrics, "Links" and "Total Link Strength," quantify an article's integration within the scholarly network, reflecting its level of connectivity and influence.

Our study utilized data from the WoS Core Collection by Clarivate Analytics, a database known for its comprehensive high-impact journals. To refine the dataset to digital transformation and public sector performance, we applied targeted keyword filters using the expressions "digital transformation" AND "public sector" across Web of Science's domains. This dataset, consisting of English-language articles through 2024, was saved as a Tab-Delimited file,.txt format, containing "Full Record and Cited References" for a comprehensive analysis (Fig. 2).

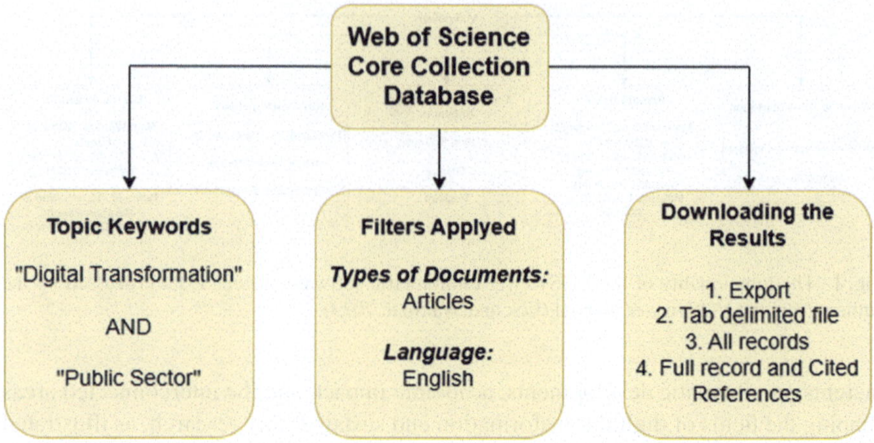

Fig. 2 Extraction of data from WoS C.C. Database. *Source* Data processed by the authors

3 Results

Our study initiates a bibliometric analysis to explore the relationships among digital transformation, public sector performance, and sustainability. Drawing on a carefully selected dataset of 225 documents from the WoS Core Collection by Clarivate Analytics, the study utilizes advanced bibliometric tools to systematically investigate these interconnected themes.

The co-authorship analysis begins by designating authors as the central unit of analysis. With an initial threshold of three publications, we identify 13 authors out of a total of 635 who meet this criterion (see Fig. 3). Adjusting the threshold to two publications broadens the set to 42 authors. Finally, including authors with at least one publication captures all 635 authors in the dataset, resulting in a network composed of 189 clusters, with 957 links and an aggregate link strength of 996.

Table 1 lists the 13 authors who meet the minimum threshold of 3 publications in the field of digital transformation research. Citation counts for these authors vary widely, with some, like Fredrik Carlsson and Marcus Matteby, receiving no citations, while Ines Mergel leads with a notable 496 citations, marking her as the most cited author in this cohort. Noella Edelmann also demonstrates significant influence, with 475 citations, emphasizing the impactful contributions of these key researchers to the digital transformation discourse. Johan Magnusson emerges as the most prolific author, with 8 publications, emphasizing his consistent scholarly output. In terms of Total Link Strength—an indicator of the author's collaborative connections within the field—Johan Magnusson, Fredrik Carlsson, and Marcus Matteby each achieve a top score of 6, highlighting their strong integration within the research network. The publication frequency and citation impact reveal a diverse landscape in digital transformation studies, with some authors excelling in output and others in citation

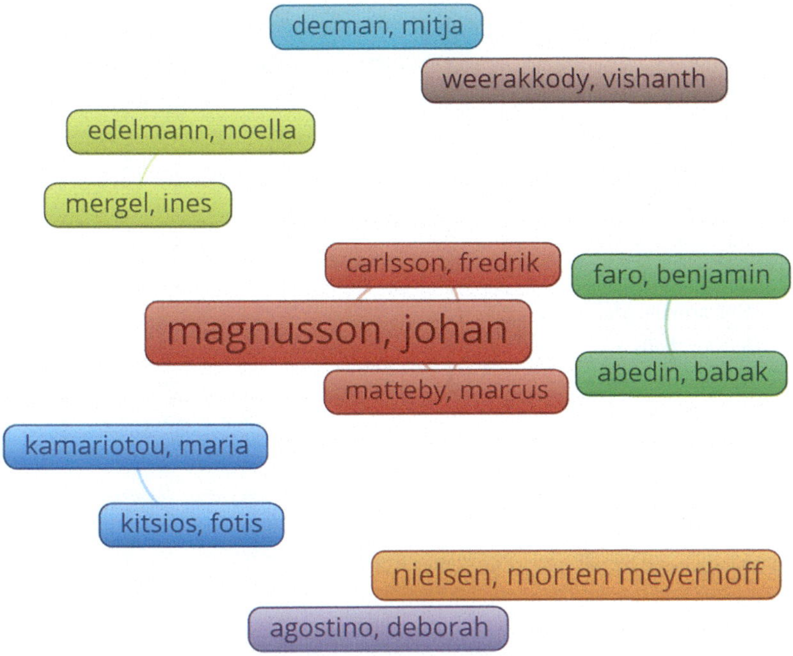

Fig. 3 Mapping of the authors that meet the threshold. *Source* Data processed by the authors in VOSviewer software

influence. Notably, authors from the bibliometric analysis align with those in the literature review, collectively enriching the field.

Continuing with the co-authorship analysis, Fig. 4 displays the organizational affiliations actively contributing to digital transformation research, specifically highlighting those that meet a threshold of three or more documents. Starting with a minimum of one document per organization, the analysis identifies 348 organizations engaged in the field. The resulting network comprises 155 clusters, 346 links and a cumulative link strength of 359, underscoring the collaborative network and institutional ties that are instrumental in advancing digital transformation research in the public sector. Raising the threshold to two documents reduces the pool to 46, while a further increase to three documents narrows it to 15 organizations.

Table 2 presents an overview of the 15 organizations that meet a threshold of at least 3 publications in the realm of digital transformation research. Leading in citation impact, University of Konstanz stands out with 496 citations, demonstrating notable influence and visibility within the field. Danube University Krems follows closely with 475 citations, emphasizing its significant contributions to advancing research focused on public sector performance, digital transformation, and sustainability. When examining Total Link Strength, which indicates the degree of scholarly collaboration, University of Gothenburg and Kristiania University College both

Table 1 13 authors that meet the thresholds of 3 documents/author

ID	Author	Documents	Citations	Total link strength
4	Abedin, Babak	3	22	3
12	Agostino, Deborah	3	175	0
99	Carlsson, Fredrik	3	0	6
153	Decman, Mitja	3	8	0
177	Edelmann, Noella	3	475	2
190	Faro, Benjamin	3	22	3
280	Kamariotou, Maria	3	2	3
294	Kitsios, Fotis	3	2	3
348	Magnusson, Johan	8	7	6
371	Matteby, Marcus	3	0	6
379	Mergel, Ines	3	496	2
408	Nielsen, Morten Meyerhoff	4	30	0
599	Weerakkody, Vishanth	3	17	0

Source Data processed by the authors in VOSviewer software

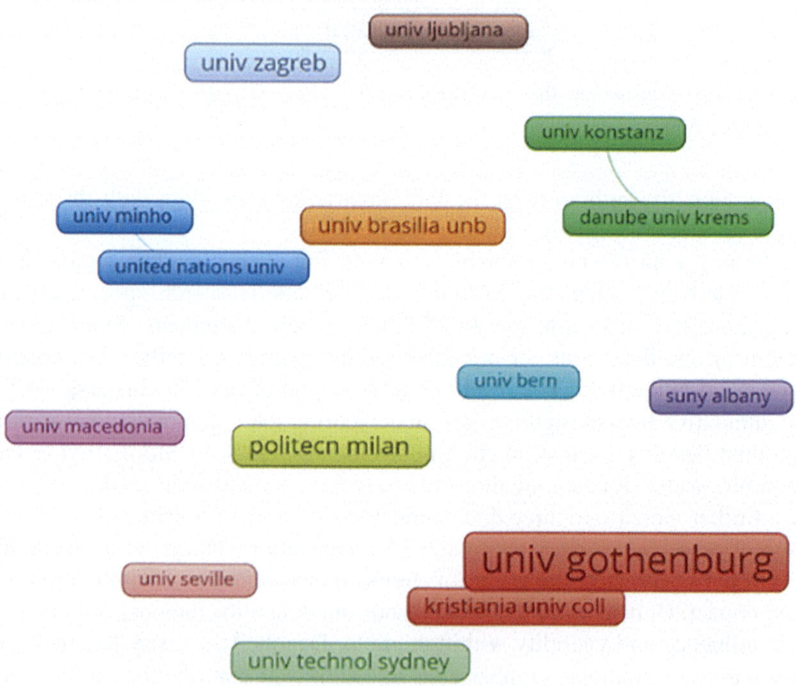

Fig. 4 Mapping of the organisations which meet the thresholds. *Source* Data processed by the authors in VOSviewer software

attain the highest score of 4, reflecting their active engagement and strong connections within the academic network. Other institutions, like Politecnico di Milano with 6 publications and University of Zagreb with 5 publications, also contribute meaningfully, showcasing their dedication to this field. This table underscores a broad geographic and institutional representation, with European organizations playing a particularly prominent role in driving advancements in digital governance and innovation.

Table 2 illustrates the distribution of institutions contributing to digital transformation research, with a concentration in regions known for strong research infrastructures, particularly Europe and Asia. Countries such as Germany, Austria, and Italy are prominent, reflecting a global emphasis on exploring how digital transformation shapes public sector efficiency and supports sustainability goals. The high volume of publications from these regions highlights the role of well-funded programs and collaborative networks that facilitate in-depth investigations and high-impact research within this field.

Figure 5 illustrates the final component of the co-authorship analysis, focusing on the countries of origin for authors engaged in digital transformation research. Setting a baseline of one document per country includes contributions from all 64 countries, emphasizing the widespread international interest in this field. Increasing the threshold to two documents refines the dataset to 47 countries, and applying a higher standard of three documents further narrows the analysis to 34 countries with notable research activity.

Table 2 15 organizations that meet the thresholds of a minimum of 3 documents

ID	Organisation	Documents	Citations	Total link strength
49	Danube Univ Krems	3	475	2
108	Kristiania Univ Coll	4	7	4
161	Politecn Milan	6	253	0
195	SUNY Albany	3	2	0
216	United Nations Univ	3	19	1
230	Univ Bern	3	23	0
233	Univ Brasilia UNB	4	3	0
265	Univ Gothenburg	15	22	4
274	Univ Konstanz	3	496	2
282	Univ Ljubljana	3	8	0
285	Univ Macedonia	3	2	0
288	Univ Minho	3	13	1
315	Univ Seville	3	28	0
324	Univ Technol Sydney	4	23	0
335	Univ Zagreb	5	47	0

Source Data processed by the authors in VOSviewer software

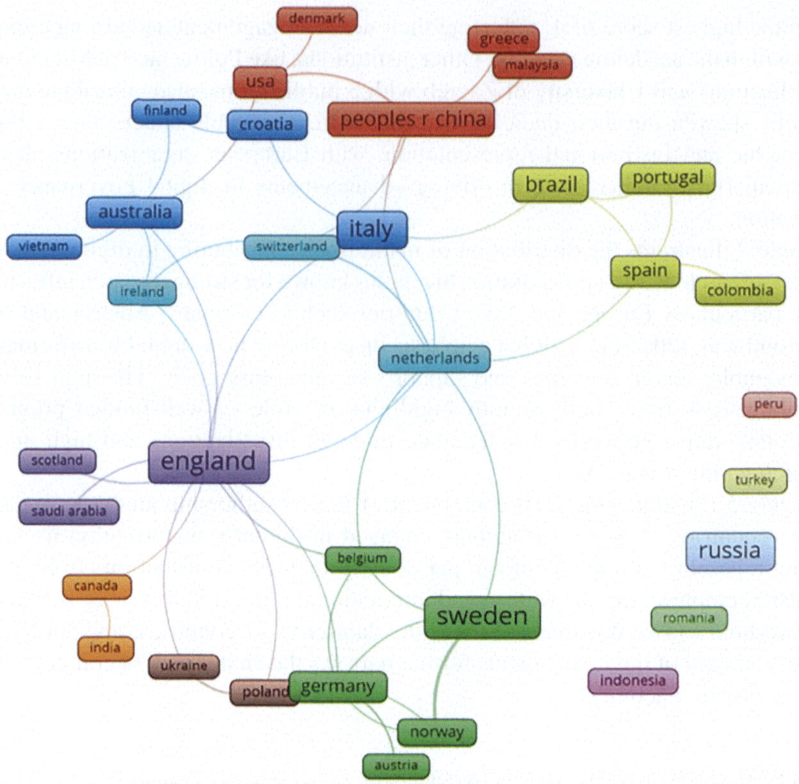

Fig. 5 Mapping of the countries which meet the thresholds. *Source* Data processed by the authors in VOSviewer software

The resulting network structure comprises 26 clusters, representing regional and thematic research alliances, connected by 77 links, with a cumulative link strength of 92. These figures highlight a dynamic international research landscape, with certain regions showing stronger collaborative networks, reflecting both strategic focus and substantial institutional support for advancing digital transformation globally.

Table 3 provides an overview of the 34 countries surpassing the 3-document threshold in digital transformation research. England and Sweden lead in document count, each with 20 publications, followed by Italy and Russia with 18 documents each. In terms of citation impact, People's Republic of China is prominent with 609 citations, while England, Germany, and the USA follow closely with 560, 526, and 521 citations, respectively. Additionally, England shows the highest total link strength among these countries, reflecting its strong collaborative presence within the field.

In conclusion, Table 3 highlights the prominent role of countries like England, China, and Germany in digital transformation research. High citation counts and

Table 3 34 countries that meet the thresholds of a minimum of 3 documents

ID	Country	Documents	Citations	Total link strength
2	Australia	11	266	5
3	Austria	3	475	2
6	Belgium	4	47	5
7	Brazil	14	190	3
9	Canada	3	100	2
11	Colombia	7	10	2
12	Croatia	8	57	2
16	Denmark	3	73	1
18	England	20	560	14
20	Finland	3	30	2
21	Germany	10	526	6
23	Greece	7	135	2
25	India	3	17	1
26	Indonesia	5	9	0
28	Ireland	3	194	3
30	Italy	18	471	4
33	Malaysia	4	109	3
35	Netherlands	7	210	8
38	Norway	6	8	7
40	Peoples R China	14	609	7
41	Peru	3	0	0
42	Poland	5	27	5
43	Portugal	11	450	2
45	Romania	3	1	0
46	Russia	18	99	0
47	Saudi Arabia	3	13	2
48	Scotland	3	18	2
54	Spain	11	74	5
55	Sweden	20	61	8
56	Switzerland	4	23	4
59	Turkey	3	8	0
62	Ukraine	3	23	4

Source Data processed by the authors in VOSviewer software

collaboration strengths underscore these countries' influence and connectivity, reflecting a robust global network advancing the field.

The study advances by shifting to a co-occurrence analysis with a focus on keywords as the primary unit of investigation. This analysis encompasses a dataset of 1,036 keywords. By setting an initial occurrence threshold of one, all 1,036 keywords are included, offering a broad view of the terminology within the digital transformation research domain. As the threshold increases, the dataset becomes progressively refined: a threshold of two occurrences narrows it to 232 keywords, capturing widely referenced themes. Raising the threshold to three occurrences further focuses the analysis on 123 keywords, while a threshold of four occurrences includes 72 keywords. At the highest threshold, set at five occurrences, the core dataset is distilled to 58 central keywords, reflecting the most frequently discussed terms in the field (Fig. 6).

In addition, Table 4 displays the 58 keywords that meet the threshold of five or more occurrences. Leading the list is "Digital Transformation," with 138 occurrences, totaling a link strength of 409. The term "Innovation" is coming next, appearing 39 times and holding a link strength of 163, while "E-Government" is mentioned 32

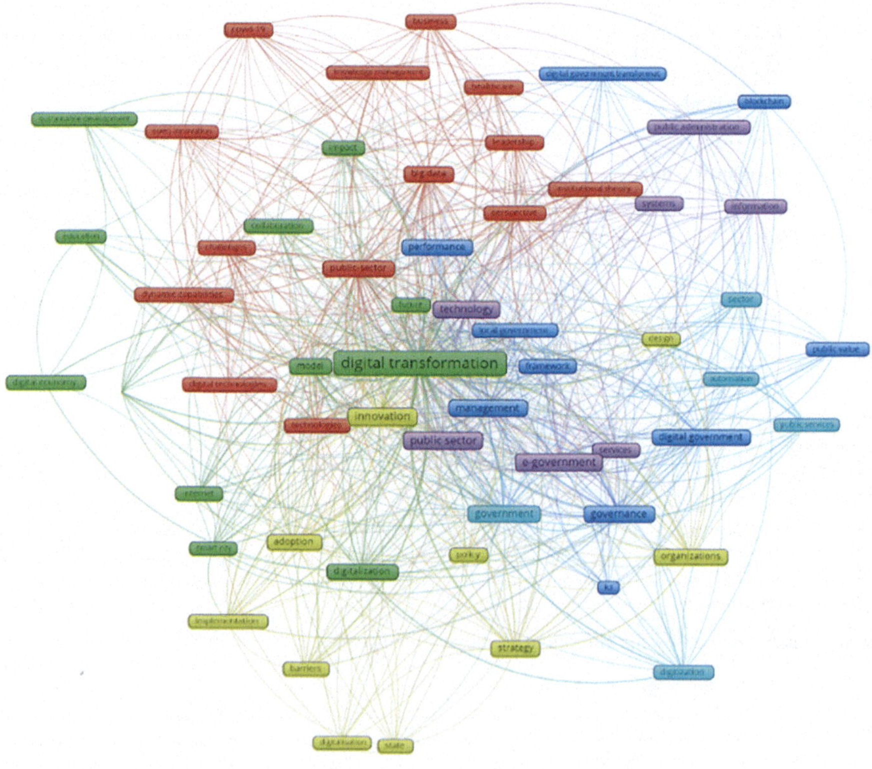

Fig. 6 Mapping of the 58 keywords that meet the thresholds. *Source* Data processed by the authors in VOSviewer software

times with a link strength of 125. "Public Sector," encompassing both hyphenated and non-hyphenated forms, has 52 occurrences and a combined link strength of 212. "Governance" shows up 28 times with a link strength of 124, indicating its substantial presence in the research field. Lastly, "Technology" and "Management" occur 24 and 31 times, with link strengths of 103 and 124, respectively, underscoring their importance within the digital transformation discourse.

The recurring presence of these keywords underscores the influential function of digital transformation in advancing public sector performance, governance, and sustainability. The frequent pairing of terms like "Innovation," "E-Government," "Public Sector," and "Technology" highlights a multidisciplinary perspective focused on enhancing public service capabilities in the digital era. This trend suggests that researchers are examining both the immediate impacts of digital transformation and its broader implications for policy-making, citizen engagement, and resource efficiency. Additionally, the focus on "Governance" and "Management" signals the importance of adaptive strategies that enable public institutions to remain responsive amid ongoing technological and societal shifts. The integration of sustainability into these themes reflects a rising recognition of the need to aling technological progress with enduring environmental and social objectives, ensuring that digital transformation supports sustainable development.

Examining the interconnections between these keywords is crucial for understanding the core drivers of public sector performance, governance, and sustainability within the digital transformation framework. Key terms from the bibliometric analysis, such as "Innovation," "Management," "Public Sector," and "Governance," serve as focal points in disentangling complex relationships in the field. These terms offer valuable insights into how various elements collectively foster

Table 4 58 keywords that meet the thresholds of 5 occurrences of a keyword

Keyword	Occurrences	Total link strength
Digital Transformation, Innovation, E-Government, Public Sector	100–138	106–409
Governance, Management, Technology, Digitalization, Big Data, Digital Government	20–50	42–163
Performance, Policy, Information, Adoption, Barriers, Collaboration, COVID-19, Framework, Dynamic Capabilities, Impact	10–20	30–69
Challenges, Future, Implementation, Strategy, Education, Model, Internet, Organizations, Sustainable Development, ICT, Public Services, Public Value, Automation, Blockchain, Digital Economy, Design, Digitization, Local Government, Knowledge Management, Leadership, Open Innovation, Public Administration, Smart City, Healthcare, Services, State, Systems, Institutions, Resources, Conservation, Carbon, Security, Development	5–10	10–56

Source Data processed by the authors in VOSviewer software

progress in digital public services and inform policy-making that is both responsive and forward-looking.

- Interplay between Digital Transformation and Public Sector Efficiency: The analysis underscores the significant nexus between "Digital Transformation" and key public sector performance indicators, including "Efficiency" and "Transparency." This relationship highlights a growing recognition that digital technologies are pivotal in streamlining government operations, reducing administrative burdens, and enhancing the transparency of public processes. As digital tools enable faster, more accurate data handling and service delivery, they serve as essential drivers of a more efficient and transparent public sector.
- Governance and Adaptability in a Digital Era: Keywords such as "Governance," "Management," and "Policy" point to the necessity for governance structures that can evolve with the demands of rapid digital transformation. This emphasizes the importance of flexible policies and management frameworks that enable public institutions to respond effectively to technological advancements. Such adaptive governance is vital to balance accountability, responsiveness, and innovation in an increasingly digital public administration landscape.
- Sustainability and Resource Management in Digital Initiatives: The frequent occurrence of terms like "Sustainable Development," "Resource Efficiency," and "Innovation" highlights the significance of embedding sustainability within digital transformation strategies. This indicates a commitment to ensuring that technological progress aligns with environmental goals and sustainable resource use. Digital transformation, when strategically aligned with sustainability objectives, holds the potential to make public sector operations not only more efficient but also more ecologically responsible, supporting long-term societal well-being.
- Citizen Engagement and Social Impact through Digital Platforms: Keywords like "E-Government," "Public Sector," and "Citizen Engagement" point to an emphasis on strengthening the relationship between governments and citizens through digital platforms. This focus on digital channels for public engagement underscores efforts to create more accessible, responsive, and participatory governance structures. By leveraging technology, public institutions aim to increase citizen participation, enhance service accessibility, and foster trust in government through transparent and user-friendly interfaces.
- Sector-Specific Digital Advancements: The analysis of terms like "Healthcare," "Public Services," and "Education" reveals a targeted approach to digital transformation within specific sectors of the public domain. This focus underscores the need for specialized digital strategies to address unique challenges, improve service delivery, and meet sector-specific requirements. Sector-tailored digital advancements enable public institutions to respond more effectively to the diverse needs of citizens and stakeholders across various fields.
- Global and Regional Emphasis on Digital Public Services: The presence of region-specific keywords, such as "Europe," "USA," and "China," along with terms related to "Digital Transformation" and "Public Sector," illustrates a shared international commitment to advancing digital government services. This global

interest highlights both the common and unique challenges faced by different regions, suggesting a need for context-specific approaches that consider regional priorities, technological readiness, and socio-political factors.
- Technological Innovation as the Cornerstone of Transformation: Keywords like "Technology," "Innovation," and "Big Data" suggest that advancements in technology are at the heart of the digital transformation movement. These innovations enable public institutions to modernize service delivery, optimize resource use, and create data-driven policy frameworks that are agile and responsive to citizens' needs. The role of technology as a core enabler of digital transformation underscores the potential for continued advancements that further enhance the efficiency, transparency, and sustainability of public sector operations.

In conclusion, the keyword analysis offers an in-depth perspective on the primary themes and interconnections shaping research in digital transformation within the public sector. The frequent recurrence and co-occurrence of terms like "Digital Transformation," "Innovation," "Public Sector," "Governance," and "Sustainability" reflect a comprehensive approach to tackling the complexities of contemporary public administration. This analysis underscores the essential role of technology in improving efficiency, transparency, and citizen engagement, while also highlighting the importance of flexible governance frameworks that promote sustainable and adaptive progress.

4 Conclusion

This study offers an in-depth bibliometric analysis to illuminate the current research landscape at the intersection of digital transformation, sustainability, and public sector performance. By examining 225 articles from the WoS Core Collection Database and utilizing VOSviewer for science mapping and performance analysis, we identified key themes, influential contributors, and significant geographic distributions across the research domain. The findings indicate a global interest, with notable contributions from China, England, Germany, Sweden, the USA, and Italy, highlighting the widespread commitment to advancing digital public sector innovation.

Our analysis underscores the core themes of innovation, governance, technology, management, and sustainability, revealing a multidisciplinary approach that reflects diverse yet interconnected public sector applications. This study also highlights key gaps in the literature, emphasizing the need for more comprehensive explorations of sustainability's role within digital transformation initiatives and their long-term impacts on public sector efficiency and resilience.

The results of our bibliometric analysis reveal a highly interconnected research landscape at the intersection of digital transformation, public sector performance, and sustainability. The keyword co-occurrence analysis shows that core terms such as "Digital Transformation," "Innovation," "Public Sector," "Governance," and

"Technology" are central to the field, reflecting a multidimensional approach to exploring digital advancements in public administration. The frequent co-occurrence of terms like "E-Government" and "Management" further underscores a focus on improving governance and operational efficiency through digital means, with an emerging emphasis on sustainable development as a guiding principle for technology integration within public institutions.

The co-authorship analysis highlights the global nature of this research field, with significant contributions from scholars based in China, England, Germany, Sweden, the USA, and Italy. This geographical distribution indicates strong collaborative networks, particularly among European and Asian institutions, where research infrastructure and funding support digital innovation initiatives. Authors such as Ines Mergel and Noella Edelmann emerge as influential contributors, with high citation counts that reflect their impact on shaping digital transformation discourse in the public sector. The results demonstrate both the depth and reach of research in this field, offering a foundation for future explorations that balance technological progress with sustainable, resilient governance frameworks.

An additional insight from our study is the alignment between our literature review findings and the bibliometric analysis, reinforcing the relevance of key contributors in digital transformation research. Several authors who emerged as influential figures during the literature review also stood out prominently in the bibliometric analysis, such as Ines Mergel and Noella Edelmann, both recognized for their significant contributions and high citation counts. This overlap suggests a robust consensus within the field regarding foundational research and thought leadership. The recurring presence of these authors across both qualitative and quantitative analyses underlines their work's impact on shaping the discourse on digital transformation, governance, and sustainability in the public sector. This consistency validates our study's approach, confirming that our findings reflect not only the current research landscape but also the field's most influential voices.

The use of bibliometric analysis and VOSviewer in this study offers valuable insights but also has certain limitations. One primary limitation is the dependence on database coverage, as only articles indexed in the Web of Science Core Collection Database were analyzed. Additionally, bibliometric methods primarily measure quantitative aspects, such as citation links, keyword co-occurrence and co-authorship, which may not entirely reflect the nuanced, qualitative dimensions of the study, like in-depth theoretical contributions or contextual factors within individual studies. Lastly, temporal limitations are also present, as this analysis provides a snapshot of research at a specific point in time. Rapid developments in digital transformation and public sector practices mean that the research landscape could evolve, necessitating continual updates to reflect emerging trends and new contributors.

Sustainability emerges as a crucial dimension in the discourse on digital transformation within the public sector, as indicated by the recurring keywords and themes in our analysis. The frequent mention of "Sustainable Development," "Resource Efficiency," and "Innovation" underscores a growing recognition of the need to align technological advancements with long-term environmental and social goals. By incorporating sustainability, digital transformation strategies can support public sector institutions in achieving efficient resource management and resilient infrastructure, ensuring that technological progress contributes to sustainable governance. This emphasis on sustainability reflects a shift in public sector priorities towards creating systems that not only enhance operational efficiency and citizen engagement but also address broader social and environmental responsibilities.

In closing, this study advocates for expanding research in the overlap between digital transformation and sustainability, calling for frameworks that integrate technological advancements with resilient and sustainable governance practices. As public institutions increasingly adopt digital tools, there is a pressing need to develop approaches that go beyond efficiency, addressing environmental impacts, social equity, and long-term sustainability. By aligning digital transformation initiatives with sustainable goals, public sector entities can enhance their adaptability, ensuring that new technologies support immediate operational improvements and future resilience.

The insights presented here are intended to guide policymakers, researchers, and public administrators in harnessing digital transformation to achieve higher performance standards, stronger citizen engagement, and responsible resource management. Embracing a balanced approach to digitalization can create public services that are not only efficient and transparent but also equipped to respond to evolving societal and environmental challenges. As digital transformation continues to shape the public sector landscape, this study underscores the necessity of integrating sustainability into governance frameworks, fostering a public sector that is both innovative and sustainably oriented for the future.

Acknowledgements This work was supported by a grant from the Romanian Ministry of Research, Innovation and Digitalization, the project with the title „Economics and Policy Options for Climate Change Risk and Global Environmental Governance" (CF 193/28.11.2022, Funding Contract no. 760078/23.05.2023), within Romania's National Recovery and Resilience Plan (PNRR)—Pillar III, Component C9, Investment I8 (PNRR/2022/C9/MCID/I8)—Development of a program to attract highly specialised human resources from abroad in research, development and innovation activities.

References

Alathamneh, F.; Al-Hawary, S.: Impact of digital transformation on sustainable performance. International Journal of Data and Network Science (2023).

Agostino, D.; Saliterer, I.; Steccolini, I.: Digitalization, Accounting and Accountability: A Literature Review and Reflections on Future Research in Public Services. Financial Accountability & Management, 38, 152–176 (2021).

Camodeca, R.; Almici, A.: Digital Transformation and Convergence toward the 2030 Agenda's Sustainability Development Goals: Evidence from Italian Listed Firms. Sustainability, 13, 11831 (2021).

Crusoe, J.; Magnusson, J.; Eklund, J.: Digital Transformation Decoupling: The Impact of Willful Ignorance on Public Sector Digital Transformation. Government Information Quarterly, 41, 101958 (2024).

Edelmann, N.; Mergel, I.; Lampoltshammer, T.: Competences That Foster Digital Transformation of Public Administrations: An Austrian Case Study. Administrative Sciences, 13, 44 (2023).
Feroz, A.K.; Zo, H.; Chiravuri, A.: Digital Transformation and Environmental Sustainability: A Review and Research Agenda. Sustainability, 13, 1530 (2021).
Gils, B.; Weigand, H.: Towards Sustainable Digital Transformation. 2020 IEEE 22nd Conference on Business Informatics (CBI), 1, 104–113 (2020).
Gomez-Trujillo, A.; Gonzalez-Perez, M.: Digital transformation as a strategy to reach sustainability. Smart and Sustainable Built Environment (2021).
Kwilinski, A.; Lyulyov, O.; Pimonenko, T.: Unlocking Sustainable Value through Digital Transformation: An Examination of ESG Performance. Information, 14, 444 (2023).
Lobonţ, O.R.; Vătavu, S.; Jicărean, L.; Moldovan, N.C.: A Cross-cultural Study on the Digitalisation of Public Services. Contemporary Studies in Economic and Financial Analysis, 109A, 69–88 (2022).
Mergel, I.; Edelmann, N.; Haug, N.: Defining Digital Transformation: Results from Expert Interviews. Government Information Quarterly, 36, 101385 (2019).
Milukutu, A.; Siachisa, M.: Assessing the Impact of Digital Transformation on Employee Performance in the Public Sector: A Case Study of Zambia's Ministry of Health Headquarters (2017–2022). International Journal of Humanities, Social Sciences and Education (2023).
Nicolescu, A.C.; Lobonţ, O.R.; Vătavu, S.; Bozga, E.: Entrepreneurship and digitalisation in the EU: Twinning insights through a panel threshold regression. Journal of Business Economics and Management, 25(2), 315–336 (2024).
Su, C.W.; Yuan, X.; Umar, M.; Lobonţ, O.R.: Does technological innovation bring destruction or creation to the labor market? Technology in Society, 68, 101905 (2022).
Van Eck, N.; Waltman, L.: Manual for VOSviewer version 1.6.20. Weblink: https://www.vosviewer.com/documentation/Manual_VOSviewer_1.6.20.pdf (2023).

Domains and Lexical Fields of Digital and Digitization

Floriana Anca Păunescu, Mihaela Ileana Chirițescu, Svetlana Caterenciuc, and Anyila Poor

Abstract It is well known, accepted and studied that the evolution of digital technologies and practices and the emergence and development of the Internet have had a significant impact on several types of languages and on languages in general: (1) on online communication, that is, on the languages used on *websites* and on those used on social media platforms or chat; so on Computer-Mediated Communication (and similar devices: tablets, phones, *smartwatches/*intelligent watches, etc.) and the Internet; (2) On specialized terminologies and languages, related to domains with activity and practices in the online environment; (3) On scientific languages, from fields such as philology (with its multitude of linguistic disciplines), philosophy, anthropology, sociology, education sciences, respectively on interdisciplinary discourses, through which digital technologies are studied, analyzed and integrated into educational processes.

Keywords Digital (r)evolution · Social networks · Socializing · Migratory lexicon · E-Learning

F. A. Păunescu (✉) · M. I. Chirițescu
Faculty of Letters, Department of Modern Applied Languages, University of Craiova, Craiova, Romania
e-mail: anca.paunescu18@gmail.com

S. Caterenciuc
Department of Modern Languages Applied, University State Technical University of Moldova, Chisinau, Republic of Moldova
e-mail: svetlana.caterenciuc@lm.utm.md

A. Poor
Faculty of Education and Philology, Foreign Language Department, Fan S. Noli University, Korçë, Albania

S. O. Idowu et al. (eds.), *Competitiveness and Sustainability in the Digitization Era*, Springer Proceedings in Business and Economics,
https://doi.org/10.1007/978-3-031-91778-3_4

1 Digital Age

The polysemy of the term *digital* requires from the beginning a series of delimitations and clarifications regarding the meanings in which it will be used throughout this paper. We note the presence of *digital* into a series of phrases that describe realities and extremely vast and complex areas: *the digital age* (which is found and in the title of our thesis), *digital civilization*, *digital society*, *digital education*, etc. It presupposes, above all, an accumulation of technologies and related practices that have transformed all fields of activity, which is also reflected in general and specialized dictionaries.

It was used and is being used. and the expression "*digital revolution*", analogous to a *mental mutation*, according to anthropologists, who have also signaled the tendency of some of us to invert the ratio between the two dimensions: "If the digital revolution scares you, ask yourself why we were running away when we set out on the path of such a revolution. Look for the intelligence that generated the digital revolution; it is much more important than studying the one that was generated by it, because the generating intelligence is the matrix of the generated intelligence".[1] The quote is from the book *The Game. The Game of Digital Civilization* by the internationally renowned philosopher and novelist, Alessandro Baricco. We will not insist on his arguments and analytical descriptions, but we will take some general information in this introductory subchapter and we will also extract from the book a series of terms for the corpus of texts that we propose, respectively for the compilation of the field and the lexical subsets that we will compile and analyze. (We note, in this sense, that the translator opted, in agreement with the editor, to preserve the English form *The Game* in the title, for its meanings in the context of digitalization.)

Baricco believes that "The digital revolution is born from three broad gestures that mark a new playing field." These are, in fact, a series of solutions and innovative technological achievements:

> A. The digitization of texts, sounds and images, the liquefaction of the world's tissues. It is an endeavor that goes from CD to DVD, passing through MP3, between 1982 and 1995. Around the same time as the development of the PC.// B. The inventory of the PC. It is an endeavor with distant roots, which becomes truly remarkable in the mid-1980s – with the three PCs that I mentioned [MAC, COMANDORE 64, IBM] and becomes irreversible in the mid-1990s – with the appearance of Windows 95.// C. The interconnection between all computers, through a network. It is an endeavor that begins in 1969 with ARPANET and. passing through the invention of the Web, reaches the finish line in 1998, with the launch of the Google search engine.[2]

There are several intermediate stages to these episodes, but they really represent the domain *of the digital* in a broad sense. The three aspects involve, on the one hand, new methods (generically called *digital*) of storing and reproducing text, image, and sound (music), and on the other, the construction of *the machine* that would make these things possible and mediate them. And thirdly, the connection of data, the

---

[1] Baricco (2023, p. 32).

[2] Ibid., p. 64.

circulation of and mediating their access, based on the theories of computation, programming, and computational linguistics.

To these we would add a fourth opening and manifestation of *the digital*: the generation through the technologies attributed to it of what we call *virtual reality/ augmented reality.* It began to be used in video games in the early 2000s.

In recent years, the third component of those listed above has had the most social, linguistic and psychological implications: "The Internet as a network of networks of planetary dimensions, which integrates technologies and the most diverse and complex applications, represent the foundation of the *Digital Society*."[3]

The way we think about the relationship between humans and *the digital world is* also reflected in language, in the lexico-semantic fields that this macro-domain contains. When we use terms from its lexical family, we refer to different aspects and areas of action that it has created or whose functioning has been decisively changed. Moreover, there are expressions that also include references that refer to the identity of individuals. The phrase *digital native*, originating from English, *Digital Natives, is* used in public speeches, official documents and specialized articles, especially in the field of pedagogy and didactics, being first used in an article by Marc Prensky. In this context, the issue of *digital skills* began to be systematically raised, which, however, are not learned automatically, only from the presence in an environment where new technologies are omnipresent. What is needed, first of all, is the ability to adapt them to specific requirements, to specific actions and educational or professional practices with goals and clear purposes. And this fact also presupposes the individual's ability to relate critically to *new technologies*, to know their constraints, limits and the effects they can have on behavior in general. Along with the expression *digital natives*, the expression *digital immigrants* was also used, initially in opposition—through it, individuals from societies that have not (r)known digital evolution are named. The two expressions have already been used for more than a decade, being put in relation to *digital education.*

2 The Influence of Digital on the Use and Development of the English Language

The English language has functioned and functions in *the digital age* as *a lingua franca.* But the impact of the neologisms imposed by the *digital revolution has* also been felt at its level. There is a rich specialized bibliography that reveals the enrichment of the English vocabulary and the formation of new words, expressions, metaphorical constructions and lexical fields in this context. The process is relevant because it reflects the relationship between language and a new type of referent, of reality—augmented, virtual. Over time, exclusively digital domains and subdomains have emerged, such as gaming, which has had an important contribution to the formation of digital language. Although researchers have been drawn to the new

[3] Târziman (2023, p. 10).

type of communication, we must also take into account the actual activities to which users relate in this communication.

One of the most important English authors who has drawn attention to the linguistic mutations that have occurred through the Internet is David Crystal. His work *Language and the Internet*, with a first edition in 2001, represents the main landmark for discussions initial issues of transformations and linguistic variations in specialized bibliographies. It theorized, for example, the concept of *Netspeak*, which we will also use throughout this thesis. The author starts from the concern publicly expressed in the early 2000s by specialists and politicians, regarding the future of languages in the Internet age. Thus, he raises a question that is still valid among many commentators and specialists today: "Will the English- dominated Internet spell the end of the other tongues?"[4] Such fears have caused all the great revolutions throughout time, especially the technological and scientific. A second question raised by the author was, in the early 2000s, "*What is it like to be a regular citizen of the Internet, a netizen?*", which would translate: "How is it to be a regular citizen of the Internet, a *netizen*?"[5] I mentioned the years to highlight the age of these problems that still concern us, but also the emergence of specific terms, such as the one I have highlighted, which reveal a new condition socio-cultural and professional of the individual. He extracts these questions from the press and bibliography of the time. There have been several sites since then that drew attention, more or less with scientific arguments, to the symptoms that individuals should pay attention to if they wanted to know to what extent they are predisposed and exposed to internet addiction. The author drew attention to the fact that the use of the Internet was the prerogative of certain classes, being at the beginning, but he anticipated the extent that it would take, which is why he set out to research the linguistic trends of communication on the Internet, which he called *Netspeak*. He also drew attention to many shortcomings, which were generally related to the non-verbal aspects of communication, because, however, telephone services (with camera), augmented reality and the new graphics that we use today are still very poorly developed.

David Crystal formulated a series of questions, contextualizing them through the lens of debates related, in general, to the idea of globalization and local community:

> What happens, linguistically, when members of the human race use a technology that allows any one of them to be in routine contact with anyone else? There has been much talk about the notion of a *global village,* which is at first glance a persuasive metaphor. However, such a concept raises all sorts of linguistic questions. A village is a close-knit community, traditionally identified by a local dialect or language that distinguishes its members from those elsewhere: *That's not how we say things around here.* Then we must ask ourselves *What is its dialect?* What *are the common features of the language that give the global community of users their sense of identity?* And, if we cannot discern any unifying dialect or language, or a tendency toward such unity, we must ask ourselves whether this *global village* is anything more than a media fiction. Similar questions could be asked of related notions such as *digital citizens, virtual community,* and the network[6] *generation.*

[4] Crystal (2006, p. 1).

[5] Ibid., p. 4.

[6] Ibid., pp. 5–6.

The increase in access to the Internet has further accelerated and amplified some of these questions. The task set by the British researcher was to investigate whether the Internet is developing as a homogeneous linguistic environment or whether it will contain a collection of distinct dialects, reflecting the different environments, needs, purposes and attitudes of its users, or whether it is an aggregation of trends and uses specific to each spontaneous community, which still defies any form of classification. The intuitive answers, given the scale that the Internet has taken, would be the latter, but we note, however, the existence of many words and expressions with circulation international, amid increasing interaction through highly organized environments, such as experience exchanges international—at the level of the European Union and beyond. Specifically, we refer to programs such as *Work and Travel* or *Erasmus*, carried out initially in the university environment, for students and teacher, and later the second one in pre-university education.

Another phenomenon was represented by online *gaming*, with competitions international gaming, and with the specific language of this exclusively digital field. The means and strategies *of gaming have* also begun to be used in education, to make teaching—learning—evaluation modules more attractive. And the practice *of gaming* has an international dimension. And the large online social media platforms have imposed specific language elements, shared globally, namely a linguistic behavior summarized by the concept of *Netspeak* and its equivalents.

Therefore, notes David Crystal, "in a setting where linguistic differences are likely to become large, the concept of *linguistic variation* will be helpful.[7]" This is also our main working hypothesis, but we will try to explain what the characteristics and the ramifications of this variation. The English researcher greatly simplified the language specific to the study of language in the pioneering book I cited. He admitted that as *Internet linguistics* develops, more sophisticated models will be needed to capture all the elements of variation. And indeed, in the specialized literature, the terminology varies greatly when discussing the different types of situations on the Internet, such as the environment, the setting and interactive activity, the virtual space, the languages of domains that have developed a digital dimension.

Grammatical, lexical, and discursive features play, of course, a distinctive role in all spoken variations of a language, just as they do in writing. A television commentary, for example, is characterized not only by pronunciation, but also by the use of grammar, vocabulary, and discourse in general. There are a number of changes analogous to those produced by the Internet in the history of the audio–video press and the evolution of the written press. Moreover, the press has adapted quickly to the Internet.

New questions regarding the research of linguistic variation produced on the Internet concern, therefore, the aspects that give homogeneity to the language used *online*. Can we speak of the generation of a single variety of language, defined using canonical theories of linguistic variation? Are there recurrences? and graphic, orographic, grammatical, lexical and discursive characteristics common to the languages used on the internet? Such a question implies the identification of

[7] Ibid., p. 6.

several types of communication situations, several types of content—depending on the fields of activity to which we refer. The nature of these fields is different: in a certain way we must relate to everyday communication on social media platforms, in another to *digital education* programs, for example, initiated by states or various NGOs. If the first aims to maintain and the development of personal relationships and relates to what we call, generically, *loisir*, with an anglicism that has long entered the Romanian language, and to online social life, the second relates to systematized *training,* based on the principles of contemporary psychopedagogy and didactics. Therefore, the important linguistic features of each situation must be described and to identify and extract the common features that give homogeneity to the variations.

In this way we can realize and analyze the strategies that people use and the linguistic attitudes they have in this environment, through its digital channels, and, thus, will allow us to develop theories regarding the language and languages used on the Internet. A good part of these situations have stabilized, have been systematized by specialized studies. Other types of activities continue to experience a dynamic induced by emerging technologies and are changing rapidly, with consequences at the lexico-semantic level.

Moreover, as far as we are concerned, we must relate to these *varieties* linguistic features in Romanian, a Romance language, therefore significantly different structurally from English. The lexico-semantic borrowings and linguistic behaviors of *netspeak users* have a different impact on the system. The changes and the mutations are much greater for the native speaker of Romanian, but they are, however, prepared, also in our case, by the penetration of new terminologies through the press, fiction, scientific literature and bureaucracy. This is why we find a series of studies on the circulation of and borrowings of Anglicisms even before the internet became an everyday reality that took over all forms of activity.

There is already a generation of digital natives who have completed high school and, in part, university studies and entered the workforce. The previous generation also adapted quickly, because technological changes were not so sudden as to create a real generational divide. Romanian technical education has always been remarkable, with fields such as electrical engineering, cybernetics and computer science being quite popular in the academic environment. For this reason, sociolinguistic perspectives are indispensable in approaches to the development of languages in digital environments. The adherence of the languages of new technologies and new media has been quite high in the Romanian language.

In 2014, the same David Crystal, that it is too early to say what permanent effect the internet will have on languages:

> Electronically mediated communication (EMC) has been in routine use for only twenty years, and that is a blink in the history of a language. It takes time – a long time – for a change to occur, for individuals to get used to its novelty, for them to start using it in everyday speech and writing, and eventually for it to become so widely used that it becomes a permanent feature of a language, recorded in dictionaries, grammars, and style guides. There are already some telltale signs of what may be happening, but everything must be provisional.[8]

[8] Crystal (2014).

From our point of view, the changes have happened much faster. The extent and pace have depended and depend, of course, on the characteristics of each language. Although generated from within and from the English language, its structures are much too strong to undergo rapid changes in a short time. They are standardized in the spirit of already existing languages. One thing seems certain to us, however: technologies and virtual spaces will not destroy languages. We believe that the problem should not even be posed in these terms.

A descriptive-objective look reveals that technology enriches language with new components, and language as a means of communication ultimately behaves naturally. The Romanian language assimilates the new necessary lexico-semantic constructs, but also allows for a series of *luxury Anglicism borrowings.*

3 Anglicisms in the Digital Domain in European Languages

Specialists from all over the world have raised, on the one hand, the issue of the changes that have occurred in the English language, as *a lingua franca*, under the impact of *(r) digital evolution*, and on the other hand, the effects and the consequences of these changes on other languages, which have massively borrowed Anglicisms. At the level of the European Union and its linguistic spaces and in proximity, there has been much discussion about these phenomena. Romanian linguists have also been and are very receptive to the objects and research themes in this new area, which offers huge virtual corpora through search engines, databases and online dictionaries. A coherent and standardized use of Anglicisms and neologisms is attempted and recommended, in general, for several reasons, the most important being the security of the Romanian language and for reasons of cultural identity.

The reality is that a very large amount of new words that entered the Romanian language were created in English under the influence of digital technologies. The same thing happened in all European languages. Many terms come from the field of computer science, but from the moment they enter the language used on the Internet, they acquire a new series of connotative meanings, new derivations and inflections. They entered the common lexicon through *gaming* and the *Internet*, respectively, social networks. Can we talk, however, about a terminology of the digital and/or the Internet? We can certainly talk about complex lexico-semantic fields of the digital and the Internet. In this sense, from a methodological point of view, we consider that lexico-semantic analysis must be doubled by contextual analysis.[9]

In the specialized literature of Romanian linguistics, the term *neologism* was avoided for a long time, according to *the Dictionary of Language Sciences* (2001), being equated with phrases such as *recent word* or *loanwords*. However, Anglicisms in the digital field fall under the scope of this term. It has, in the meantime, acquired greater conceptual consistency, being used with the meaning in European linguistics (see DTG).

[9] See in this regard the work: Bidu-Vrănceanu (2008).

The phenomenon is extremely complex and extensive, difficult to summarize in a subchapter, especially when we bring into discussion the presence of Anglicisms in the languages of circulation As we also note in Argument, many of the terms introduced into the category of Anglicisms have, in fact, multiple etymologies and equivalences, of similar meaning and spelling, in the languages of the countries that participated in the digitalization revolution. We will give a few examples that we consider representative, then we will attempt a taxonomy of Anglicisms, depending on how they have been used and treated by users from various fields, as well as by linguists.

In a paper analyzing the impact of new digital technologies on the English language, Juraj Miština believes that the rise of the Internet has produced a lot of neologisms that have made their way into both common languages: "Official linguistics has not yet accepted the terms' tech 'neologism' (*technological neologism*) or 'modern- day neologism' (*modern neologism*), but defines in this context those newly emerged words and often frequently used by cybernetic communities and Internet subcultures, which, in addition to the fact that many have enriched the formal and informal English vocabulary, have become common terms used in everyday conversation and writing". The author[10] also gives a relevant example through the neologism that appeared in the context of the Internet: the verb *to Google.* The immense popularity of *the Google search engine* has led *the American Dialect Society* to consider it "*most useful word of the year*" *in 2002. The example* also reveals the fact that it was and is typical for technological neologisms, intensively used in today's digital environments, to quickly enter dictionaries, with numerous forms and meanings. *To Google* was introduced, according to this source, into *the Oxford English Dictionary* and the Merriam-Webster Collegiate Dictionary in 2006. *To google* soon entered other languages, among which the author renders: *googlit'/vygooglit'* (Slovak), *googeln* (German), *загуглить* (Russian) etc. In Romanian it did not establish itself, although it is sporadically used with the form *a da un google* (pronounced like in English). It did not become, therefore, a verb, nor was it recorded in dictionaries. Romanian Academy. However, we find in DOOM3 the word *search*, which is in a relationship of partial synonymy with *google*, but as a neuter noun, with pl. *search*—uri, in *a da search.* Both have the meaning of searching. *To When the company* was founded, *Google* was a new word for the English language, but in a very short time it became established through the expression *Google it*!—which means *searching for something on the Internet using the Google search engine.*

Influences between European languages have always existed, mainly due to trade, but also to other types of interactions, such as those in the sphere of religion and the languages of the colonizing empires had a very large impact on languages from different corners of the world: English, French, Spanish, Portuguese, etc. In this subchapter, however, we will focus on the terminologies related to digitalization.

English is used intensively as an international language, offering a rich vocabulary that we find in most other languages international. There are *measurements* of speech and the influence of language in relationships international. Anda-Ileana Duţă

[10] Miština (2018, p. 101).

synthesized some data in the work *Anglicisms in Romanian Online Communication Between Theory and Practice.* The author informs us, based on an extensive bibliography, that English is dominant from this point of view, and French would be the third most powerful language due to its high position in diplomatic circles. Despite the small number of native speakers (80 million), it has a large number of speakers as a second language, being considered a complex and useful language. According to this ranking, Spanish is in fourth place on the global diplomatic scene and in third place in facilitating global communication, after English and French. In terms of the number of native speakers, it is in second place, after Mandarin (limited, however, to the Chinese diaspora and expatriate communities). German ranks seventh in *the Power Language Index*. The influence of the German language is limited by its rather small geographical coverage, but it is spoken by citizens with the highest standard of living, with the highest incomes.[11] Such criteria matter in terms of population mobility and on free commercial markets. Language is closely related to realities, of which commerce, which has been in the digital era for decades, is a very important component.

Moreover, specialized literature produced in academic environments is another *vehicle* of the English language, imposing technical terminologies and cross-cutting terms (*digital* and *digitization*, being, in fact, such terms), which relate to the protocols of research and the distribution of its results.

The previously cited study also presents some data on the presence of Anglicisms in French, Spanish and German. Numerous *open access* articles (a common expression in academic language in Romania, meaning that they are freely accessible) and on the influence on languages such as Italian, Norwegian, Chinese, etc. are available in current online databases. A relevant case is the borrowing and adaptation of Anglicisms in Italian, showing numerous similarities with French and Romanian.

Anda-Ileana Duţă informs that in the comparative study of English borrowings into French from France and Quebec, six types of Anglicisms are mentioned in French: semantic, lexical, syntactic, morphological, phonetic and graphic Anglicisms. Curiously, in the list of the most frequent words, those from the sphere of digitalization and online communication are not found. The bibliography she consulted, however, mentions evidence of cultural and basic borrowings from English in the lexicon of many languages, especially in mass media, promoted products, technology, sports and everyday communications and the lack of lexical elements to designate new concepts in communication technology. And this fact led to borrowings from English into French: *tweeter*—"to Sendai tweets", *likers*—"to like a link on Facebook", poker—"to send a poke on Facebook, texter to send an SMS", *blogger*—"to use blog", *faire le buzz*—"to engage in what is talked about at the moment", *Instagramer*—"to take a picture via Instagram", *webmaster*—"someone in charge of a web site", *chatter*—"to chat".[12] Obviously, we encounter Anglicisms from other fields as well.

---

[11] Duţă (2021, p. 36).

[12] Ibid., pp. 38–39.

Specialized studies show that there is also a large flow of Anglicisms in the Spanish language, most of which come from digitalized environments. Anda-Ileana Duţă I have also compiled a list in this regard, a list that respects the frequency criterion: *blog, playoff (play-off), retail, mall, commodity, notebook, challenger, online, peak, mail, top ten, coach, on line, tag, pen drive, link, resort, think, tank, cover, game, laptop, berry, team, e-mail, major, retailer, cluster, e- learning, partner, court, cooler, switch, timing, indoor, joint venture, lodge, lounge, paper, voucher, know how, power, nerd, factoring, freak, trailer, trainer, upgrade, head hunter (head hunter), outdoor, outsourcing, backstage, part time, blockbuster, gamer, express, focus group, top one, club house, ringtone, shopping, sitcom, stopper, talk show, wild card.*[13]

Things are roughly similar in terms of the flow of Anglicisms in German. Here too, we encounter words used to name new technological objects, in a broad sense, that appeared after the year 2000, their shape being square like in English: *computer, mouse, internet, screen, download* etc., but also Germanized words such as *chatten, downloaden, texten,* etc. In the research of words borrowed from English in the German media, the presence of hybrid Anglicisms is also noted: a combination of German and English words, created according to internal forms of vocabulary enrichment.

In this brief illustration, we only consider the morpho-syntactic adaptations of Anglicisms. We have not discussed the phonetic aspect.

To support the internationalization hypothesis and globalization of Anglicisms, we also provide some data about their presence in the Italian language, taken from a work often cited in specialized articles, *The Influence of English on Italian* by Virginia Pulcini. Linguistics reveals the behavior of borrowed verbs, verbs that enter into different processes of adaptation and enrichment of the Italian vocabulary. He notes, in this sense, that "verbs must be adapted to the internal grammatical system", and this happens, to a large extent. "The most common category of inflection of the verb ending in *-are* is applied to borrowed words", the verbs recorded being related to the following areas:

- web communication: e.g. banning (*block access to an internet page*—"block access to an internet page"), chattare (*chat*), clicare (*click*), craccare (in Romanian, *to crack*—unregistered, but used in the *gaming field*, both with the meaning of "breaking the security barriers of a computer system" and of "*pirating*"), downloading ("downloading"—*download*), formatting ("a format"—*format a hard disk, a computer disk* or *a memory stick*), google ('search on *google*'), hacking ('break into *a* computer system to steal confidential information'), linkare (link), loggare ('log into a computer program'), postare ('post something on the internet'), resettare ('reset a machine or device'), retweet (retweet), scannerizzare (scan), scrollare ('scroll on a computer screen'), spammare ('to Sendai unwanted emails'), surfing ('surf the internet'), tagging ('assign an electronic code'), trolling ('upset an online discussion by sending offensive or irrelevant messages'), twittare ('send a message on Twitter'), zippare ('compress a computer file')

[13] Ibid., p. 38.

- young people's discourse: pogare (*pogo*), friendzonare ('regard someone only as a friend, despite their unreciprocated romantic or sexual interest'), flirtation (flirt)
- other technical words from digitalized domains: mixing (*mix*), performing (*perform*), remixing (remix); bluffing (bluff), flopping (flop), geotagging (geotag), microchipping ('implant a microchip'), monitoring (monitor), processing (process), setting (set), spoilering ('anticipate the plot of a TV series, film, or book that could spoil the someone's enjoyment who shoo note yet seen or read it'), storage (stock), and zoom in.

Many of these verbs are also found in Romanian, being generally adapted with the lexico-grammatical suffix *–a* (*a scana, a downloada, a login* etc.).[14]

We can talk about a *neological lexicon* (an expression also used in *DGT*) present in all European languages, formed by the Anglicisms of new technologies. There is a great interest from linguists for this phenomenon, which has been materialized in an international project. A research platform called *the Global Anglicism Database has been created. Network* (GLAD) on which academic contributions from all over the world are centralized. The acronym GLAD appears recurrently in specialized studies, the platform providing both corpora and statistics, as well as theoretical and methodological frameworks. The motivation of the creators is:

> The GLAD network aims to share and compare strategies and resources to stimulate cooperation among scholars interested in linguistic and cultural *Anglicization, involving* the widest possible range of speech communities in Europe and beyond. The Global Anglicism Database (GLAD) network *is* motivated by the current and growing interest of linguists and laypeople alike in the influence of English on other languages. Both through face-to-face interaction and through remote (online) contact situations, English influences languages globally at the lexical, morphological, syntactic, phraseological and pragmatic levels, thus transforming English, a traditionally receiving language, into the donor language par excellence.[15]

The resources offered by this database are updated, being an ongoing project. There is also an exhaustive bibliography, with over 4500 titles on Anglicisms and their influence on language dynamics. The list is open, being periodically completed, the most recent edition being from 2023.[16]

The most recent *newsletter* announces that the platform can be accessed directly, without a password, and that the database was edited by a team from the Dutch Language Institute, led by Nicoline van der Sijs, having been removed, since the last update, four languages with incomplete data (Bulgarian, Catalan, Finnish and Welsh). Instead, Ukrainian has been added and, "very soon, Romanian records will also be included". As of May 2023, the GLAD database contains a total of 81,000 anglicisms in 17 languages, of which ten record more than 3,000 anglicisms, as follows (Fig. 4.1).

---

[14] Pulcini (2023, pp. 108–109).

[15] https://www.nhh.no/en/research-centres/global-anglicism-database-network/background/—last accessed on 1 June 2024.

[16] https://www.nhh.no/globalassets/centres/glad/glad_bibliography_fall_2023.pdf—last accessed on 1 May 2024.

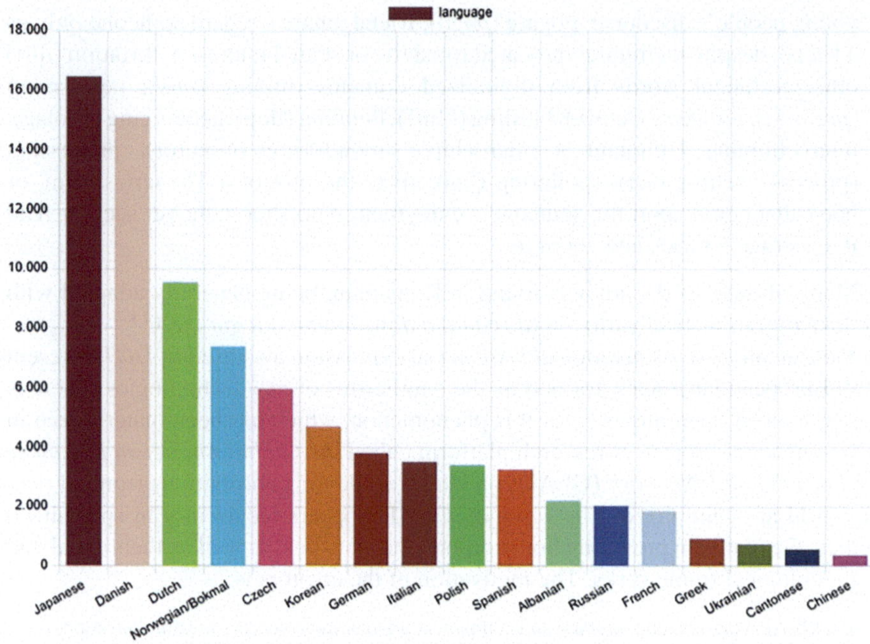

Fig. 4.1 The amount of Anglicisms in 17 languages[17]

Although the number varies at small intervals of time, we note that there is an inventory of these terms, a neological lexicon of Anglicisms, which in some languages have already exceeded 15,000 words: Japanese—16,470, Danish—15,100, while in German it is approaching 10,000.[18] The fewest Anglicisms are reported in the Ukrainian language, but we believe that also because it is recent, the articles we identified online reveal that in this country too the phenomenon is more extensive with the opening of free markets and technology transfer. Specialists have initiated a common reporting methodology, respecting, however, the specifics of each language, offering ample contextual analyses. These are necessary especially in terms of *adaptation* of terms. Of course, not all Anglicisms are recent and only a percentage have appeared under the influence of digitalization, but the share is very high, especially if we take into account those that have entered through *computer-mediated communication* and the *internet*, and *new mass media.*

[17] GLAD NEWSLETTER # 11—MAY 2023—https://www.nhh.no/globalassets/centres/glad/glad_newsletter_11_may_2023.pdf—last accessed on 1 May 2024.
[18] Ibid.

4 International Theoretical Framework

Specialists participating in GLAD have proposed various theories regarding the circulation and the adaptation of Anglicisms, regarding their influence on the dynamics of the languages in which they have imposed themselves, diachronic and synchronic, lexicological, sociolinguistic perspectives.

For the definition and general theoretical framework, the platform refers to the article "Introducing and developing GLAD—The Global Anglicism Database Network", published in the publication scientifically *The ESSE Messenger* (Vol. 27-2 Winter 2018), a publication published under the aegis of The European Society for the Study of English. The article is signed by university specialists from Denmark, Norway, Germany, Poland, Finland and Italy. After a brief presentation of the project, hosted by Norwegian School of Economics (NHH), in Bergen, the authors also propose a theoretical synthesis.

There is no single definition of the term, therefore, such a synthesis is all the more important. According to the aforementioned study, a first explanation that should be mentioned is that of Manfred Görlach (A Dictionary of European Anglicisms. A Usage, 2001). Therefore, Görlach suggests the following meaning of the term: "A word or idiom that is recognizably English in its form (spelling, pronunciation, morphology, or to th century one of the three (three), but is accepted to to it is me the vocabulary oh yeah the receptor language". In translation, Anglicism is: "A word or idiomatic expression recognized in its forms (spelling, pronunciation, morphology, or at least one of the three) in English that is accepted as an element in the vocabulary of the recipient language" (tn[19]).

Affiliated researchers consider the definition insufficiently comprehensive, as it includes other less identifiable types of lexical influence, although, in fact, such types were partly present in Görlach's Dictionary of English Anglicisms (2001), in the form of loan translations, borrowings, neologisms, hybrids (calculi) and pseudo-Anglicisms. For this reason, Henrik Gottlieb's definition (Anglicisms and translation, 2005): "any individual or systemic language feature adapted or adopted from English, or inspired (...) by English models, used intralingually communication in a language other than English is an Anglicism", in translation: "any individual or systemic feature of the language adapted or adopted from English, or inspired (...) by English models, used in intralinguistic communication in a language other than English is an Anglicism".[20] GLAD specialists have imposed as a rule and the presence of these words in at least one of the 17 languages in which research is currently being conducted.

Anticipating a little the theoretical synthesis of Romanian linguistics works that we will do in a future subchapter, we highlight and one of the conditions proposed, since 1972, by Theodor Hristea regarding the adoption of neologisms: the presence of new words in languages other than the one of origin, which denotes the tendency and

---

[19] Henrik Gottlieb et al. (2018, pp. 5–6).

[20] Ibid.

their international character, a condition fully fulfilled by contemporary technological Anglicisms.[21]

Adopting a very general definition, GLAD proposes several types of Anglicisms, which, however, better delimits this category of neologisms.

(1) *Non-adapted loans* (of which the newest are called in Romanian terminology and *xenisms*—DGT), which can be simple words (e.g., *browse*), phrases (*bed and breakfast*), acronyms (*OMG*), terms from non-English speaking communities ("terms originating in non-English speaking communities in the Anglosphere")*, for example *tomahawk* and *jungle*, and with a circulation international language for which an origin language cannot be established ("and internationalisms", e.g. *hologram*, present in English.

(2) *Adapted loans* (e.g. Norwegian *blogg* < English "blog")*, representing the same categories as those mentioned above, but showing signs of orthographic/ morphological adaptation in the recipient language.

(3) Proper names became generic nouns, for example in Danish *plimsoller* < English (British MP) Samuel Plimsoll (1824–1898).

(4) Semantic borrowings, which refer to domestic words or assimilated borrowings ("referring to domestic words or assimilated borrowings taking on English sense /s") which have meaning/senses as in English, for example: italianescu *realize*—"to become aware of"—from the English "realize".

(5) Derived from unit-for-unit translations of English compounds, multi-word units, or phraseological units. These include idioms, similes, various types of discourse markers, speech act formulas, attitude formulas, commonplaces, proverbs, and slogans; for example, Norwegian *gratis monsj*—"free lunch"—from "free lunch".

(6) *Hybrids,* including adapted compounds with at least one English component or an English productive affix, e.g. *blogginnlegg* in Norwegian, from "blog post".

(7) *Pseudo-anglicisms*, which have different forms: (a) cuts, i.e. shortened English words as in *parking* < English "parking lot", present in large numbers in many European languages; (b) resemantizations ("domestic sense for English words")—as in German *handy* from "mobile phone" or in Polish *handicap*—"an advantage imposed on a competitor" or c) internal compositions of elements originating from English.

Phono-semantic adaptations ("Phono-semantic matchings"), in which new Anglicisms (words or expressions) match already adapted, pre-existing elements, similar phonetically and semantically, e.g. German Was gibt's? < from the English "What" gives?[22]

Researchers admit that even this taxonomy does not exhaust the phenomenon, but it is the theoretical model on which the project was built. In the meantime, other theoretical articles have appeared based on the GLAD database. We consider this project relevant for several reasons. First, the theoretical framework is indicative for

---

[21] Theodor Hristea (1972, pp. 185–186).

[22] Henrik Gottlieb et al. (2018, p. 7).

our own research. Second, it can help us to more easily identify relevant *neologisms* that transit Romanian languages, anticipating which will be adapted and will enter the local lexicons. It helps us, ultimately, to understand and to describe the influence of Anglicisms on the dynamics of the current Romanian language in an international context. The GLAD project also reveals the scientific attitude that we can adopt towards this phenomenon, an attitude of balance. We cannot reject Anglicisms—which spread spontaneously through computer-mediated means of communication and the Internet and through the evolution of technology, respectively through digitization projects, which have taken an institutional form. But we must contribute, scientifically, to their adaptation and explanation.

In the process of adapting Anglicisms into Romanian, what matters, on the one hand, are the pre-existing linguistic mechanisms and intervention specialists (press articles, TV shows, *podcasts*, etc.), both through popularization materials and through specialized works and dictionaries. On the other hand, spontaneous cultural mechanisms also matter, the level of critical assimilation by the population of new technical and cultural elements. It is a combination of educational, institutional factors or through the prism of non-institutionalized cultural settings.

There are a number of categories of words that have their origin in English that do not fall into the internal classification. Among these are many specialized terms, technological terms, which, as we will see, tend to eventually enter the common lexicon with approximate meanings.

The concern for a comparative perspective on the presence of Anglicisms in other languages is not new. In 2001, *A Dictionary of European Anglicisms (known in bibliographies with the acronym DEA, ed. Manfred Görlach, Oxford University Press)* was published. However, it has not seen any revised editions. However, the pace of spread of Anglicisms intensified greatly, especially in the 2000s, with the development and increased access to the Internet. If at first communication mediated by computers and the Internet was the prerogative of the wealthy or middle classes, now access to the Internet has become free in the spaces and public institutions and a growing part of the population allows you to purchase an access device.

We have previously presented only the starting point of what we could call an international theory of Anglicisms. The *international attribute* is necessary here for *the theory* because we are working with the mechanisms of national languages, languages that have many specific elements at the phonetic and morpho-syntactic level. Moreover, any language involves characteristic relations with reality, culturally constructed. Analogies and similarities are, obviously, present, especially since intercultural dialogue has always been a reality.

Affiliated researchers have begun to discuss various methodological and taxonomic aspects after consulting data from and recorded in 17 languages, with the possibility of comparative approaches, which could lead to new theoretical descriptions. However, we do not find many studies that address the issue of an overall perspective. Such an approach would require a very high level of knowledge of at least three foreign languages, in order to understand the linguistic behaviors of some communities, their relationship with the common lexical fund, with different professional terminologies.

Chosen Klégr, a lecturer at Charles University in Prague, proposes such an article, entitled *Anglicisms: Towards defining their concept and typology.* He notes the lack and difficulty of establishing and theorizing common criteria, based on which descriptions and typologies of Anglicisms are made. Analyzing the definitions and the categories that I presented above, note the existence of recurring arguments of a logical nature, which cannot be applied systematically. The proteism of languages very often confronts the researcher with novel cases, difficult to capture in an argumentative pattern or which respond, simultaneously, to criteria from different categories.

However, to highlight the very effective, functional features, the Czech linguist recommends starting the research from the most obvious forms of borrowing, the direct ones, often called *quoted*, being transferred without changes directly from the English language, according to some needs or for stylistic reasons. Most examples come to us, in this case, from the field of digital and digitization, including among the acronyms or words formed specifically for the instruments, spaces and the languages of the Internet, in general: *Internet*—with the abbreviation *net, site, chatbot, web*, but also from related domains, which have experienced rapid digitalization. These provide a solid starting point, because they are the most obvious in form, etymology and, when applicable, in formation (abbreviations—as I said, compounds, changes in grammatical value, etc.).

By adopting words like *chatbot* or *influencer*, "(a) a concept (a certain meaning) that occurs in English, (b) a certain word that conveys the concept/meaning (and can serve as a model or template for word formation in the recipient language), and (c) a graphic/phonetic form specific to English are adopted.[23]" That is, all the important dimensions of a lexical unit. Moreover, contextual elements specific to technological development are also imported.

A decisive point, which the linguist emphasizes, is that of the three determining aspects, a borrowed word must meet at least two of them. So it is not mandatory to have all three, at least this is considered in the current methodology for registering Anglicisms. In some cases, they have been accepted even if they meet a single criterion. Combinations of the three characteristics form several definition models, which are theoretically proven. Therefore, from these, the following possible formal definitions of Anglicisms could be obtained: "an Anglicism is a lexical item in the RL's vocabulary that (a) realizes a borrowed concept from English, (b) exhibits an English form (graphical, phonological), or (c) is an actual English word or its RL copy (for which it provides a model), or (d) is any combination of (a) to (c), while it is enough for the word's status of Anglicism to exhibit at least one of these constitutive features"//"an Anglicism is a lexical item from the RL vocabulary [*Recipient Language=host language, target language*] that (a) reproduces a concept borrowed from English, (b) presents an English form (graphic, phonological) or (c) is an English word proper, which provides a model for the RL; (d) is any combination of (a), (b) and (c), it being sufficient for the status of the word as an Anglicism to present at least one of these constitutive features".[24] Combinations based on the three features

[23] Klégr (2023, p. 105).

[24] Ibid., pp. 105–106.

	types of loan (Anglicism)	features borrowed from English		
		concept/sense	model/word	form
1.	concept-model-form loan	+	+	+
2.	concept-model loan	+	+	–
3.	model-form loan	–	+	+
4.	concept-form loan	+	–	+
5.	concept loan	+	–	–
6.	model loan	–	+	–
7.	form loan	–	–	+

TABLE 1: Hypothesized types of loan (Anglicism) based on feature patterns

Fig. 4.2 Table with the categories of Anglicisms proposed by Aleš Klégr[25]

(i.e. concept/meaning, word/model and form) can actually impose seven categories of Anglicisms. The linguist also proposes a structuring of them in the form of a table (Fig. 4.2).

Also indicate the levels of analysis that Anglicisms require, in fact, to create more complex lexical fields. For this reason, we also find the clarifications that the Czech researcher continues to provide relevant. These categories, be they formal or not, influence the dynamics of the current Romanian language in different ways.

Chosen Klégr analyzes these characteristics as follows[26]:

- Concept/meaning—a concept can be expressed by different word classes, usually nouns, but also adjectives, verbs, adverbs, etc. By borrowing a concept is meant its transfer into the recipient language in the word class it has in the source language (the particular word, as a signifier or as a model that stands at the beginning of the transfer). In contrast, the transposition of a concept into another word class in the recipient language, i.e. the conversion (of a noun into a verb, for example), must be considered a process of a different nature, which takes place in the host language. It is so different from the borrowing itself that, according to the Czech linguist, it should not even be considered a direct borrowing of a concept. Indeed, the process takes place according to internal rules, and the change in grammatical value also comes with changes in meaning, even if sometimes hardly perceptible.

It should also be mentioned and that in the case of polysemantic words, a single specific meaning is usually transferred, whether dominant in the source language or necessary in the host language. Usually both of these conditions are met. The deviations that occur in the host language from the meaning that the word has in English are an eminently internal change, the result of a process of word formation in the host language and not an act of borrowing. The terminology may vary in this case. Because these changes lead rather to the category of neologisms that appear within the RL than concept/meaning borrowings.

[25] Ibid., p. 106.

[26] Ibid., pp. 106–107.

Given that language always implies meaning, is about meaning, we might think that this criterion is an indisputable, fixed constant, the most solid of the three presented. But the borrowing of words from English is not always motivated by the taking over of new concepts for the meanings they entail. We often find the entry into circulation of words that have one or more synonyms in the host language. They are even more useful, due to their usage and their knowledge in various contexts.

The phenomenon led specialists to distinguish between *necessary* and *luxury loans/luxury anglicisms* ("on necessary and luxury, or catachrestic and non-catachrestic, loans"). Their appearance has different motivations. In the conceptual register, it is considered that they bring additional clarification and/or the assumption of a clearly delimited theoretical position, of a trend, a theory or a school. But, very often, they have a stylistic motivation and, moreover, they come from the playful predisposition of users of anglicisms, on different platforms. It has been noted, in the specialized bibliography, that there is a tendency to create word games in *Internet-mediated communication*, both in discussions on forum-type sites and in chat. This tendency has also been cultivated in advertising, as well as in other forms of manifestations on the Internet, *blogging* and *vlogging*, for example, are terms that have entered DOOM3. Such cases do not fall into the category of "concept/meaning borrowings". The reason for their borrowing is their English form; they are often pragmatically motivated and used not only to introduce variety, but also because they are associated with prestige and novelty and considered to be stylistically or otherwise appropriate to certain types of discourse.

- Model/word. The feature denotes either a particular English word directly adopted by speakers of the host language, or an English word or phrase that serves as a model to be copied into the host language by matching it (its components) with internal elements (words or morphemes considered standard, or present in dictionaries, equivalent). Aleš Klégr gives us an example from the Czech language: citizen ("citizen") and scientist ("scientist") are translated as "občan" and "vědec", respectively, and thus the new concept of "citizen scientist" borrowed from English is expressed in Czech by translating the model text through its component equivalents as *občanský vědec.* With single-word patterns (and occasionally multi-word patterns) used with a specific meaning in English, the standard equivalents in the host language that translate them take over and assume the new meaning. Sometimes, English patterns are difficult to match with the standard equivalents and the resulting rendering can deviate from them to varying degrees. In a more abstract sense, English words and their combinations can provide "structural plans", i.e. word formation and syntactic patterns borrowed from English and copied by speakers of the host language to produce words internally by analogy. It is a phenomenon that is very little analyzed in specialized Romanian bibliographies, although it exists as such in Romanian as well, and can be considered a new method of *composition*, for example, *hybridization* or *linguistic calculus,* be it *lexical calculus* or *grammatical calculus.* The DGT mentions: "Grammatical calculus has a lower frequency than lexical calculus, since grammatical structure is characterized by greater stability and resistance to foreign influences than vocabulary".

- Form. The distinction is subtle compared to the previous category. "To borrow an English form means to use an English spelling (orthography) and/or an English phonetic form (pronunciation) in RL"—states the Czech linguist. This is the case of direct loanwords in which the characteristics of "model/word (English)" and "form (English)" overlap. However, there are RL words that are deliberately written using English spelling, or pronounced with English pronunciation (usually to attract attention). That is why it is useful to separate "form (English)" from "model word (English)", even if in direct loans they coincide. If the written (or spoken) form of the loanword is consistent with English, it is said to be unadapted. If the form is modified (intentionally or unintentionally) in accordance with the norm of the orthography and pronunciation, is said to be adapted. This adapted/unadapted distinction, however, is not without its problems. The written form of English words is difficult to maintain across different writing systems and also across different types of alphabets. When it comes to the spoken form, it can be difficult to draw the line between the unadapted and adapted form of a loanword because of interference between the phonological systems of the host language and English (especially with less proficient non-native speakers of English).[27]

The GLAD platform also provides us with a series of statistics that we consider relevant to understanding the impact of Anglicisms on the dynamics of the language. One of them concerns the percentages of Anglicism categories (Fig. 4.3).

We note that the number of adapted Anglicisms is approximately equal to that of unadapted Anglicisms. Going through several articles in this database, but also according to the general impression, the amount of unadapted Anglicisms is justified and digital evolution, namely the lexical fields related to digitalization. Many of them are in the process of adaptation, acquiring inflections depending on the characteristics and the frequency with which they are used in each language. In Romanian, in this sense, the tendency of changing grammatical values and verbalization is noticeable, which denotes that not only the objects that Anglicisms name are new, but also many of the actions related to digitalization (Fig. 4.4).

Another interesting statistic is that of the morphological categories of Anglicisms.

As we have previously noted, most Anglicisms are nouns, sensitively maladapted and adapted, for various reasons related to the characteristics of the host languages and to certain cultural aspects. We consider that the number of verbs or adjectives is also impressive, although much smaller. The appearance of new objects, in a broad sense, is much more frequent in everyday life. Everyday, rather than new types of action, in the broad sense, or states. These statistics give us an overview of the influence that Anglicisms have on European languages. The category of phraseological units, which are included in the statistics under "other", includes expressions like *no comment* or *game over. They are* also very common in Romanian, because they

27 Ibid., p. 107.

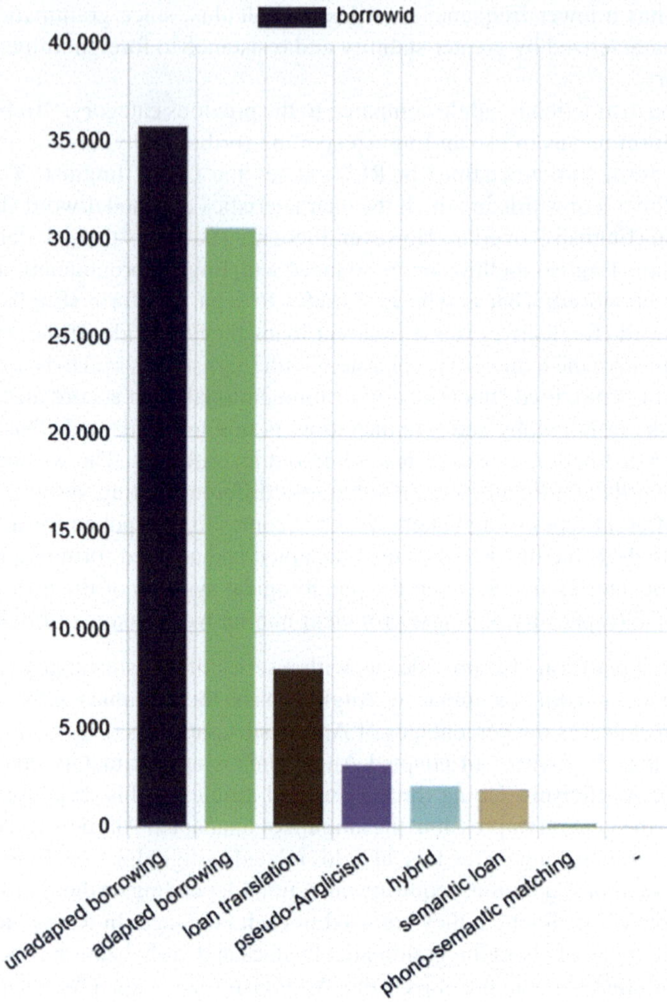

Fig. 4.3 Distribution of Anglicisms according to adaptation, according to GLAD, from the studied European languages[28]

express, in the context of digitalization, actions and recurring activities. The distribution by lexico-grammatical classes from the initial list drawn up by GLAD members, in 2022, reveals the following percentages: nouns 81%, adjectives 8.1%, verb 6.7%, others 1.9%, adverb 0.9%, interjection 0.9%.

International studies are descriptive, not regulatory, in nature. The objective has generally been to observe and analytically describe the spontaneous, social, and

[28] GLAD NEWSLETTER #11—MAY 2023—https://www.nhh.no/globalassets/centres/glad/glad_newsletter_11_may_2023.pdf—last accessed on 1 June 2024.

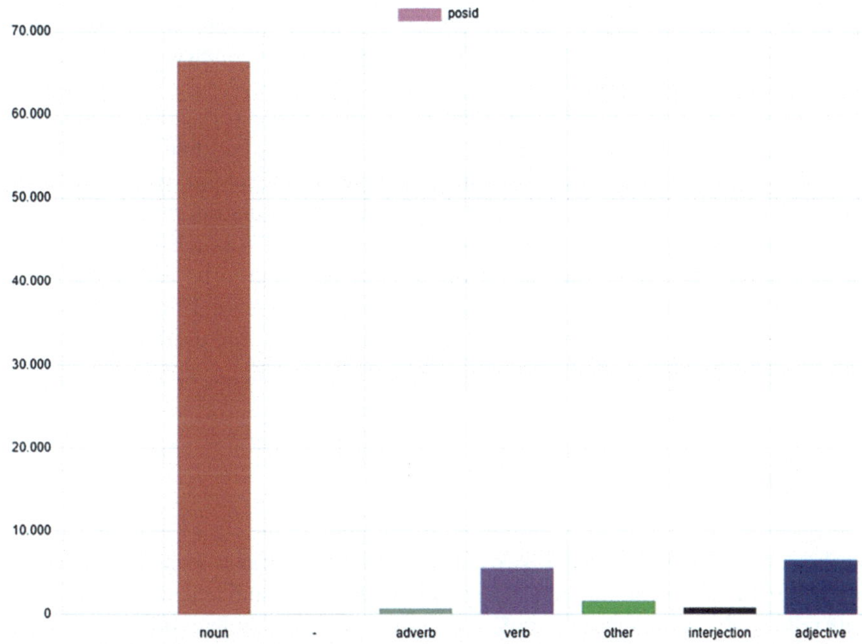

Fig. 4.4 Distribution by morphological categories of Anglicisms, according to GLAD, from the studied European languages[29]

contextual behavior of Anglicisms. Adaptability and adaptation are topics of great interest, as has become the internationality of Anglicisms.

Also took over these data because I had not encountered them until the time of writing the paper present, in the specialized bibliographies in Romanian. In the most recent GLAD *newsletter*, from 2023, we saw that they are announced and future contributions and Romanian statistics.

Therefore, from our point of view, two conclusions can be drawn. First, *digital skills*, whether we are talking about didactics, psychopedagogues and teachers, or whether we are talking about students and students, require specific linguistic skills. Secondly, the language used in the macro-context of digitalization has become so widely known that this problem is not yet being raised. It has become more of a problem for linguists, who have the duty to analyze how the notions and the constructions used are or can be standardized. And in support of this latter idea, the fact that the first classes of *digital natives* have already entered the workforce, including education, can also be invoked. This language was formed during their schooling and, according to the specialized bibliography, in the very first decade of this century. These realities were clear from the beginning, so that the observations. The linguists of that time are still valid today, anticipating the evolution of this

[29] GLAD NEWSLETTER #11—MAY 2023—https://www.nhh.no/globalassets/centres/glad/glad_newsletter_11_may_2023.pdf—last accessed on 1 June 2024.

language that has decisively changed the way we think. Its influence on the dynamics of today's language is very great, and through this thesis we wanted to highlight as many facets of it as possible.

We also observe that there is no longer any unfounded resistance against the flow of Anglicisms. The reality has been accepted as such, but there are measures that seek a balance in their case. Romanian equivalents are sought, which circulate in parallel, and sometimes it seems that they win. Self-regulation mechanisms are therefore increasingly effective, decreasing the number of Anglicisms. Luxury, at least in written texts. In online conversations they continue to be very numerous, because they keep and the expressive side of this style. General dictionaries still integrate them inconsistently and at a low rate, although they are used in contexts as relevant as possible to be given attention, respectively, in several registers.

5 Conclusions

Therefore, from our point of view, two conclusions can be drawn. First, *digital skills*, whether we are talking about didactics, psychopedagogues and teachers, or whether we are talking about students and students, require specific linguistic skills. Secondly, the language used in the macro-context of digitalization has become so widely known that this problem is not yet being raised. It has become more of a problem for linguists, who have the duty to analyze how the notions and the constructions used are or can be standardized. And in support of this latter idea, the fact that the first classes of *digital natives* have already entered the workforce, including education, can also be invoked. This language was formed during their schooling and, according to the specialized bibliography, in the very first decade of this century. These realities were clear from the beginning, so that the observations The linguists of that time are still valid today, anticipating the evolution of this language that has decisively changed the way we think. Its influence on the dynamics of today's language is very great, and through this thesis we wanted to highlight as many facets of it as possible.

We also observe that there is no longer any unfounded resistance against the flow of Anglicisms. The reality has been accepted as such, but there are measures that seek a balance in their case. Romanian equivalents are sought, which circulate in parallel, and sometimes it seems that they win. Self-regulation mechanisms are therefore increasingly effective, decreasing the number of Anglicisms. luxury, at least in written texts. In online conversations they continue to be very numerous, because they keep and the expressive side of this style. General dictionaries still integrate them inconsistently and at a low rate, although they are used in contexts as relevant as possible to be given attention, respectively, in several registers.

References

Alessandro Baricco, *The Game. The Game of Digital Civilization,* Translation from Italian and notes by Anamaria Gebăilă, Bucharest, Humanitas Publishing House, 2023.

Anda-Ileana Duţă, Anglicisms in Romanian Online Communication Between Theory and Practice, Bucharest, Pro Universitaria Publishing House, 2021.

Angela Bidu-Vrănceanu, *Lexical fields in the Romanian language. Theoretical and practical applications,* University of Bucharest Publishing House, 2008.

Chosen Klégr, "*Anglicisms : Towards defining their concept and typology* ", in *Linguistica Pragensia,* November 2023 – available at https://www.researchgate.net/publication/375120996_Anglicisms_Towards_defining_their_concept_and_typology?enrichId=rgreq-80a4de6b182b199d37931bd44f13059e-XXX&enrichSource=Y292ZXJQYWdlOzM3NTEyMDk5NjtBUzoxMTQzMTI4MTIwMjM5Mjg4NkAxNjk4ODMxNjMxODU5&el=1_x_3&_esc=publicationCoverPdf - last accessed on 01.06.2024.

David Crystal, "The Internet: Changing the Language ", in AS STELLS, Manu, it is a *l* ., *Change: 19 Key Essays on How Internet Yes Changing Egg Lives,* Turner House Publications, 2014.

David Crystal, *Language and the Internet,* Second Edition, Cambridge University Press, 2006.

Elena Târziman, *Digital Society,* Bucharest, Pro Universitaria Publishing House, 2023.

Henrik Gottlieb et al., "Introducing and developing GLAD – The Global Anglicism Database Network ", in *The ESSE Messenger,* Vol. 27–2, Winter 2018 – available at: https://essenglish.org/messenger/vol-27-2-winter-2018/ - last accessed on 01.06.2024.

Juraj Miština, „Impact of Digital Technologies on the English Language", in *Online Journal for Research and Education,* Special Issue 13, 2018, available at https://www.researchgate.net/publication/349118564_Impact_of_Digital_Technologies_on_the_English_Language_2018_In_RE-SOURCE_httpsjournalph-noeacat - last accessed on 15.05.2024.

Theodor Hristea, "Neological loanwords and lexical creations in contemporary Romanian". In the journal *Limba română,* Editura Academiei, Bucharest, 1972, no. 3.

Virginia Pulcini, *The Influence of English on Italian: Lexical and Cultural Features,* De Gruyter Mouton, Berlin, Boston, 2023 – available at https://doi.org/10.1515/9783110755114-004/html - last accessed on 01.06.2024.

Books and Papers

Academia Română. Institutul de Lingvistică „Iorgu Iordan", *Enciclopedia limbii române,* Bucureşti, Editura Univers Enciclopedic, 2001.

Anghelina, Alexandru Dan, „Observaţii asupra vulgarizării ştiinţifice în terminologia IT" – disponibil pe http://anale.litere.ro/doc/anale/2015/anghelina.pdf.

Athu, Cristina, *Influenţa limbii engleze asupra limbii române actuale (în limbajul conomic şi de afaceri),* Editura Universitară, Bucureşti, 2011.

Avram, Mioara, *Anglicismele în limba română,* Bucureşti, Editura Academiei, 1997.

Badea, Georgiana I., *Mic dicţionar de termeni utilizaţi în teoria, practica şi didactica traducerii,* Timişoara, Editura Universităţii de Vest, 2012.

Badea, Oana, *Privire bibliografică asupra anglicismelor în limba română,* în.

Baltă, Alexandru, *Gamingul, un nou „Gesamtkunstwerk" - opera de artă a secolului XXI,* Teză de doctorat susţinut la Universitatea Naţională de Artă Teatrală şi Cinematografică „I.L.Caragiale" Bucureşti, 2019.

Baricco, Alessandro, *The Game. Jocul civilizaţiei digitale,* Traducere din italiană şi note de Anamaria Gebăilă, Bucureşti, Editura Humanitas, 2023.

Baron, Naomi S., *Always On: Language in an Online and Mobile World,* Oxford, Oxford University Press, 2008.

Baudrillard, Jean, *Simulacre şi simulare*, Traducere de Sebastian Big, Cluj-Napoca, Editura Idea Design & Print, 2008.
Bidu-Vrănceanu, Angela, *Câmpuri lexicale din limba română. Probleme teoretice şi aplicaţii practice*, Editura Universităţii din Bucureşti, 2008.
Bidu-Vrănceanu, Angela, *Lexicul specializat în mişcare. De la dicţionare la texte*, Editura Universităţii din Bucureşti, 2007.
Bidu-Vrănceanu, Angela; Călăraşu, Cristina; Ionescu-Ruxăndoiu, Liliana; Mancaş, Mihaela; Pană Dindelegan, Gabriela, *Dicţionar de ştiinţe ale limbii*, Bucureşti, Editura Nemira, 2001.

Dictionaires

DEX-2019: Dicţionarul explicativ al limbii române. [Coordonator: Monica Busuioc. Colaboratori: Alexandru Anghelina, Mihaela Marin, Nicoleta Mihai, Carolina Popuşoi, † Radu Trif, Florin Vasilescu] [versiune electronică, de uz intern al Academiei Române, nepublicată]. www.dexonline.ro.
DEX-2016: *Dicţionarul explicativ al limbii române*, Institutul de Lingvistică „Iorgu Iordan – Al. Rosetti", Bucureşti, Editura Univers Enciclopedic, 2016.
DEX-2009: *Dicţionarul explicativ al limbii române*, Institutul de Lingvistică „Iorgu Iordan – Al. Rosetti", Bucureşti, Editura Univers Enciclopedic Gold, 2009.
DOOM3: *Dicţionarul ortografic, ortoepic şi morfologic al limbii române*, Institutul de Lingvistică „Iorgu Iordan – Al. Rosetti", Bucureşti, Editura Univers Enciclopedic, 2022. https://doom.lingv.ro/.

Webografie

https://www.researchgate.net/publication/349118564_Impact_of_Digital_Technologies_on_the_English_Language_2018_In_RE-SOURCE_httpsjournalph-noeacat.
https://doi.org/10.1515/9783110755114-004/html.
https://www.nhh.no/en/research-centres/global-anglicism-database-network/background/.
https://www.nhh.no/globalassets/centres/glad/glad_bibliography_fall_2023.pdf.
https://essenglish.org/messenger/vol-27-2-winter-2018/.
https://www.researchgate.net/publication/375120996_Anglicisms_Towards_defining_their_concept_and_typology?enrichId=rgreq-80a4de6b182b199d37931bd44f13059e-XXX&enrichSource=Y292ZXJQYWdlOzM3NTEyMDk5NjtBUzoxMTQzMTI4MTIwMjM5Mjg4NkAxNjk4ODMxNjMxODU5&el=1_x_3&_esc=publicationCoverPdf.
https://www.nhh.no/globalassets/centres/glad/glad_newsletter_11_may_2023.pdf.
https://epale.ec.europa.eu/ro/blog/nivelul-de-competente-digitale.
https://www.researchgate.net/publication/281647681_Terminologia_informatica.
http://anale.litere.ro/doc/anale/2015/anghelina.pdf.
https://www.umpcultura.ro/Files/Ghid%20de%20digitalizare.pdf.
https://brio.ro/rapoarte/State-of-the-Nation-2-Alfabetizarea_Digitala_in_Romania-RO.pdf.
https://www.researchgate.net/publication/281647217_De_la_monosemie_la_polisemie_in_terminologia_stiintifica_actuala_Teza_de_doctorat.

Where is the Land in the New Digital Economy?

Paula Cobzaru and Alexandru Tugui

Abstract Although land may no longer be considered a traditional production factor in the new digital economy, it remains essential to our existence and the infrastructure that supports digital products and services. As the world increasingly relies on the internet and data-driven technologies, the role of land, while less visible, continues to underpin the digital ecosystem. This research aims to explore the evolving role of land in the digital economy and smart agriculture through a systematic literature review and qualitative thematic analysis. Our findings reveal that land serves as a foundational element for digital infrastructure, such as cloud computing centers, which support data production and drive the new economy. These infrastructures represent the modern equivalent of land in a digital context, enabling the emergence of data as a key resource. On the other hand, land remains the main production factor in the digital (smart) agriculture, meaning an agriculture that is more productive by automation tools (GPS and IoT sensors), reduced waste and optimized resource use (remote sensing, satellite and automated machinery), digital cadastral technologies, weather forecasting done with machine learning algorithms to increase accuracy and more sustainable by green and lower carbon print (smart tractors and drones). In the same time, population is increasing over the world, and the smart digital agriculture becomes a high demand for the survival of our global economy. So, land in the digital economy has evolved from a static physical resource to a dynamic infrastructure supported by digital technologies, critical for both urban and rural development. Our study traces the transformation of land from its traditional role to its contemporary form in the digital ecosystem, emphasizing the need to integrate digital economics into broader discussions of global economic dynamics. We also recommend further research into the role of technological innovation in a resource-constrained world, particularly in terms of sustainability and land use, with a focus on localized and bottom-up approaches to sustainable development.

P. Cobzaru · A. Tugui (✉)
Faculty of Economics and Business Administration, Alexandru Ioan Cuza University of Iași, Iași, Romania
e-mail: alexandru.tugui@uaic.ro

P. Cobzaru
e-mail: paula.cobzaru@staff.uaic.ro

S. O. Idowu et al. (eds.), *Competitiveness and Sustainability in the Digitization Era*, Springer Proceedings in Business and Economics,
https://doi.org/10.1007/978-3-031-91778-3_5

Keywords Land · Digital economy · Smart agriculture · IoT · AI

1 Introduction

The rise of the digital economy (Tugui and Gheorghe 2016) is the promise for an upcoming shift not only in the digital realm of industry—such as online connectivity, automation of processes, transportation, and virtual products or services—but also in ubiquitous agriculture and land optimization and use in the global economy (Bukht and Heeks 2018).

According to UNCTAD (2019), the land has become a means for efficiently and sustainably developing the global ecosystem for a daily growing population.

Classic economists such as Schultz (1964) predict that the agricultural sector, which remains the primary production factor among capital and labor, must prioritize efficiency and efficacy in order to accommodate growing needs and population. On the other hand, in the digital era, Brynjolfsson and McAfee (2014) distinguish that the industry and infrastructure that are also based on technical innovation are transforming these production factors into new levels and forms that we want to analyze in this paper.

As Diamond (1997, pp. 85–92) explains, early human societies began mastering land and domesticating animals using primitive techniques, laying the foundation for agriculture and settled civilizations. Through historical analysis, Polanyi (1944) considers that the evolution over time was slow, but over thousands of years, it transitioned from a barter economy to one based on currency and circulation to small craft workshops, as ancestors of the factories from the post-industrial revolution period.

The emergence and concentration of capital as a factor of production, on one hand, as well as increasingly frequent technological innovations, such as the telegraph, telephone, electric current, and later complex computing systems and the internet, have represented major development factors. By their widespread application in industry, they made the emergence of new economic sectors, new needs, products, and services possible over hundreds of generations (Rifkin 2000).

Over time, innovation and development have concentrated in certain countries and territories, some of which have grown into empires or global leaders (Landes 1998). In this continuous race to find new markets and customers, as well as more or less skilled labor, global trade is increasing simultaneously. Regional and global policies, such as those of the World Economic Forum (2020), have played a role in the more equitable distribution of these resources and the broader development of the world's regions. If wars have halted or introduced new elements of innovation to the military, these developments have gradually benefited the civilian world during peacetime. The world has managed to adapt to the new conditions and recover from the massive destruction, turning it into competitive advantages.

For example, World War II significantly accelerated technological innovation, many of which transitioned to civilian use, reshaping modern life. Mowery and

Rosenberg (1998) discussed how wartime innovations—such as radar, jet engines, and early computers—shaped civilian life post-war, driving advancements in transportation, communication, and healthcare. Advances in aviation, such as jet engines and pressurized cabins, revolutionized air travel. Radar, initially developed for military purposes, became essential in civil aviation and meteorology. Computers, designed for wartime calculations, laid the foundation for the information age, transforming industries worldwide.

Medical breakthroughs, including the mass production of penicillin and improved surgical techniques, revolutionized healthcare. Despite its origins in warfare, nuclear technology found its way to energy production. Materials like nylon moved from military to consumer applications, while logistics innovations improved global trade. These wartime developments not only addressed immediate needs but also spurred long-term progress, defining the postwar modern world.

In order to improve the standard of living, the world has entered a period of disruptive technological transformation. This transformation aims to eliminate the paradigm of resource scarcity and opportunity costs by increasing the abundance of products and lowering their prices, thereby increasing the global population's access to them (Kelly 2016).

However, despite its transformation in the digital era, land remains a limited resource, with the price of land typically only decreasing in economically underdeveloped areas. According to the United Nations (2021), this connection increasingly highlights the dependence between digitalization, infrastructure, urban planning, and agricultural areas.

Another type of land, seen as a digital asset, has appeared in the virtual space as a mirror of the real world and represents a paradigm of changes not so much due to the scarcity of resources, but especially due to the abundance of their forms of manifestation (Tapscott 1996).

Our study aims to identify and analyze multiple aspects of land in the context of digitalization in the new millennium. We discovered a deficiency in the available research on this topic. To build new bridges for sustainable progress and social welfare, we must more deeply understand the gap between the role of land in the context of the digital economy and the ongoing digital transformation in all aspects of the economy (OECD 2020).

Thus, our research questions are accordingly to our objective:

RQ1 **How has the role of land as a production factor transformed with the rise of the digital economy, particularly in its integration into digital infrastructure and smart agriculture?**

RQ2 **What strategies can optimize the dual role of land in supporting digital economic systems and sustainable development amidst global challenges like climate change and population growth?**

To answer this questions we use a systematic literature review, with some elements of bibliometric analysis, followed by a qualitative analysis as methodologies that will help us to understand the role of land in the research literature up to date and find solutions for the future.

The remaining sections of the paper are classically structured as follows: Sect. 2—Methodology, Sect. 3—Results, Sect. 4—Discussion, Sect. 5—Conclusion and follow-up.

2 Methodology

As previously mentioned in the introduction, we will initially employ a systematic approach based on the Scopus scientific database, which is widely regarded as the most comprehensive among other databases such as WOS, ProQuest, Google Scholar, or ResearchGate. Therefore, we began our systematic review by searching for the keywords "digital economy" and "land" in the titles, abstracts, and keywords of the papers indexed by Scopus. Our initial search yielded 121 papers, as of November 23rd, 2024.

To reach our results, we systematically applied the filters of the PRISMA flow, as suggested by the authors of this scientific tool, Page et al. (2021). We meticulously proceeded with the subsequent steps for removal and result analysis. We analyzed the initial pool of 121 papers, finding only 103 articles and conference papers, as document types (17 papers removed from the pool), 100 final papers (3 press articles removed), 96 only journals and conference proceedings (4 other formats removed from the 100), 84 only English (12 papers written in different languages from the total 96 removed), and 43 only open access (41 non-open access papers removed from the 84), as detailed in Table 1 of this paper.

As a quantitative method to establish the conjecture of features that took this area of interdisciplinary interest to the interest of researchers all over the world, we will bring in front some bibliometric analysis (BA) elements. Firstly, we utilize the analysis maps from Scopus, which are shown in the following figures.

Figure 1 illustrates the novelty of the subject, with the resulting papers covering the short period from 2016 to 2024. However, the initial 121 results, which span a larger period from 2001 to 2024, are not substantially included in all the intermediate results.

Figure 2 will also showcase the interdisciplinary journals or conference proceedings that published articles based on our search, with an emphasis on environmental (26.70%), earth and planet (13.30%), and social sciences (11.1%), making up 51.10% of the total, while economics (7.8%), computer science (5.60%), or business and management (2.20%) areas support such publications, but not in high percentages.

We also consider it important to present the main countries that contribute to the research in the field, as in Fig. 3 from below.

Maybe it is not a rule for all the other countries that contributed to the field, but China (24 papers) and Russia (12 papers), meaning 36 of the prefinal step of 43 papers, are among the largest countries in the world (Russia) or the most populated ones (China). Australia (a country as well as a continent), Estonia (a tiny country compared with the previous ones), Finland, Germany, Hong Kong, Kyrgyzstan, Ukraine, and Romania have one publication each.

Table 1 Summary of the Results from the Scopus Database

No	Name of the paper	Methodology	Results
1	Digital Economy and Green and Low-Carbon Transformation of Land Use: Spatial Effects and Moderating Mechanisms (Ai et al. 2024)	Spatial Durbin Model (SDM) and panel threshold model applied to panel data from 283 Chinese cities (2011–2019) to analyze spatial and moderating effects	The digital economy promotes green and low-carbon transformation of land use both locally and regionally, with effects peaking at 450 km. Moderators like financial agglomeration and intellectual property protection amplify this impact, but regional disparities exist
2	Assessing the potential of the digital economy in agriculture (Akmarov et al. 2021)	Statistical and comparative analysis, forecasting and modeling	Digitalization ehances productivity, cost efficiency, and innovation in agriculture
3	City as a Growth Platform: Responses of the Cities of Helsinki Metropolitan Area to Global Digital Economy (Anttiroiko et al. 2020)	Theoretically oriented case study with interviews and analysis of city strategies	Cities adopt platform and ecosystem thinking but struggle with the complexity of platform economy integration
4	How digital skills affect farmers' agricultural entrepreneurship? An explanation from factor availability (Cheng et al. 2024)	Panel Logit fixed-effects model using data from China Land Economic Survey (2020–2022)	Digital skills significantly farmers' agriculture entrpreneurship by improving access to credit, modern technology, and social capital
5	The economic impact of digitalization and the creation of digital products on the development of the state (Dziatkovskii et al. 2021)	Analysis of investment strategies, global trends, and government programs for digitalization	Digitalization fosters economic efficiency and competitiveness through technology integration and investment
6	Innovative Research on Industrial Upgrading and Transformation Path of Regional Economy in the Perspective of Digital Economy (Ge 2024)	Spatial data mining, self-organizing neural networks, and empirical analysis	Digital economy drives industrial upgrading and enhances significantly regional economic growth

(continued)

Table 1 (continued)

No	Name of the paper	Methodology	Results
7	Treating the Symptoms as Well as the Root Causes: How the Digital Economy Can Mitigate the Negative Impacts of Land Resource Mismatches on Urban Ecological Resilience (Gu et al. 2024)	Empirical analysis using data from 280 cities (2007–2021), with fixed-effects regression and heterogenity tests	The digital economy mitigates the negative effects of land resource mismatches on urban ecological resilience through optimization and digital infrastructure
8	Digital Economy as a Buffer: Alleviating the Adverse Effects of Land Resource Mismatch on Food Security (Li et al. 2024)	Panel data analysis using a baseline regression model, robustness tests, and heterogeneity analysis, complemented by mechanism and moderating effect models, to examine the impact of land resource mismatch (LRM) on food security (FS) across 30 Chinese provinces (2011–2022)	LRM negatively affects FS by reducing land, labor, and capital resources for food production. The digital economy mitigates these effects through digital technologies and open government data, enhancing FS and resource allocation efficiency
9	The Design of a Remediation Device for Heavy Metal Contaminated Soil Under Digital Economy (Li et al. 2022)	Experimental design using electrodynamic remediation to test the removal of heavy metals in soil	The remediation device effectively removes heavy metals and supports resource recycling within the digital economy framework
10	Does Land Urbanization Affect the Catch-Up Effect of Carbon Emissions Reduction in China's Logistics? (Liu et al. 2022)	Logarithmic Mean Divisia Index (LDMI) decomposition method and comparative analysis at national and regional levels	Land urbanization factors significantly impact carbon emissions reduction in logistics, with heavy varying effects across regions
11	Evaluation of coupling coordination development between digital economy and green finance: Evidence from 30 provinces in China (Liu et al. 2023)	Modified Coupling Coordination Degree (CCD) model and clustering algorithms for data from 30 provinces in China (2015–2021)	Coupling coordination between digital economy and green finance is increasing but uneve, with the eastern region outperforming others

(continued)

Table 1 (continued)

No	Name of the paper	Methodology	Results
12	Australian farmers left behind in the digital economy: Insights from the Australian Digital Inclusion Index (Marshall et al. 2020)	The study combines quantitative analysis using data from the Australian Digital Inclusion Index (ADII) and qualitative interviews with farmers. The digital inclusion is based on access, affordability, and digital skills in rural and urban areas	Australian farmers are significantly disadvantaged in digital inclusion due to poor connectivity, high costs, and limited digital literacy. These barriers restrict their participation in the digital economy, affecting productivity and market access. Targeted policies are needed to address these challenges
13	Sustainable Development of Organic Agriculture: Strategies of Russia and Its Regions in Context of the Application of Digital Economy Technologies (Nesterenko et al. 2020)	Analysis of environmental, social, and economic indicators across Russian regions, integrating digital technologies with organic agriculture strategies	Identifies regional strategies and niches for organic agriculture development, emphasizing the role of digital technologies in achieving sustainability
14	On Creating Digital Land Management in the Framework of the Program on Digital Economy of the Russian Federation (Papaskiri et al. 2019)	Proposal for a digital land management system using GIS (Geographic Information System), CAD (Computer Aided Design), ICT (Information and Communication Technology), and automated models for land use and planning	Developed an integrative system design (ICAS-AGRO) for optimizing land use, reducing economic losses, and supporting sustainable agriculture
15	Information and technological support of digital land management (Papaskiri et al. 2021a)	A conceptual and technical analysis of existing systems, identifying gaps and proposing solutions for digital land management. It also integrates Geographic Information Systems (GIS) and Building Information Modeling (BIM) technologies to enhance data storage, analysis, and decision-making processes	The study proposes a framework for digital land management, emphasizing automation and informatization as essential for improving land use and management efficiency. It highlights the role of advanced technologies like GIS and BIM in modernizing land management systems to align with global trends

(continued)

Table 1 (continued)

No	Name of the paper	Methodology	Results
16	Digital land management technologies (Papaskiri et al. 2021b)	Technical and conceptual analysis focusing on integrating advanced technologies like GIS, CAD, BIM, and Big Data into digital land management systems	Proposes a framework for modernizing land management through digital tools, emphasizing automation, improved efficiency, and comprehensive spatial data integration for land use optimization
17	Principles and Regularities of Functioning of the Organizational and Economic Mechanism of Land Tenure and Land Use in the Digital Economy (Pototskaya et al. 2022)	Dialect and system-functioning approaches using economic-statistical, computational-constructive, and monographic methods	Proposed an organizational-economic mechanism integrating digital tools to optimize land tenure and land use, addressing market and regulatory challenges
18	Optimizing the Use of Intangible Assets in Industry to Overcome Poverty: A Cross-Country Analysis (Rysalieva et al. 2024)	Historical and logical analysis, system analysis, expert opinions, and forecasting applied to cross-country data	Intangible assets (intellectual property, technological know-how, human capital) contribute to poverty alleviation through industrial optimization, in post-Soviet countries
19	Relationship between the Categories of Digital and Commodity Rents (Shcherbakova et al. 2023)	System approach using analysis, synthesis, deduction, and induction to compare raw material and digital rents in the mining industry	Digital rent, driven by the digital revolution, coexists with raw material rent in mining but is more transient and rooted in technological and creative resources
20	The Telework Paradigm in the IoE Ecosystem: A Model for the Teleworker Residence Choice in the Context of Digital Economy and Society (Stoica and Ghilic-Micu 2021)	Development of a mathematical model based on von Thunen's land use theory to study teleworker residence choices influenced by digital economies factors	Teleworking shifts residential preferences toward suburban areas, impacting urban land use and commuting patterns, with implications for metropolitan infrastructure and development policies
21	Who isn't online? Mapping the 'Archipelago of Disconnection' (Straumann and Graham 2016)	Spatial mapping and analysis of internet penetration rates using global datasets to identify disconnected regions	The"Archipelego of Disconnection" highlights areas with low internet penetration, mainly in Sub-Saharan Africa, emphasizing their exclusion from digital economic, cultural, and social participation

(continued)

Table 1 (continued)

No	Name of the paper	Methodology	Results
22	The Impact Mechanism and Spillover Effect of Digital Rural Construction on the Efficiency of Green Transformation for Cultivated Land Use in China (Tang and Chen 2022)	Panel data analysis of 30 Chinese provinces (2011–2020) using two-way fixed effect and spatial Durbin model to assess regional and spatial spillover impacts	Digital rural construction enhances the efficiency of green transformation in cultivated land use and generates positive spillover effects across neighboring regions
23	Three-dimensional Cadastre in Creating an Information Base for a Spatial Model of a Real Estate Object (Shevchenko et al. 2020)	Case study involving ground-based laser scanning and 3D modelling of real estate objects using Cyclone software to create semantic databases	Demonstrated the potential of a 3D cadastre system to improve land and property registration accuracy, though implementation in Russia faces legal and technical challenges
24	Does the digital economy exhibit multiplier effects? A case study on the optimization of agricultural production structure in the rural digital economy (Wang et al. 2024a,)	Panel data analysis (2011–2020) with econometric models and threshold tests to study the rural digital economy's impact on agricultural production structure upgrading (APSU)	The rural digital economy significantly drives APSU through technological innovation, industrial integration, and consumption upgrading, demonstrating a multiplier effect consistent with Metcalfe's Law
25	Research on the Integrated Development of China's Marine Industry Empowered by the Digital Economy: Architecture Design and Implementation Pathways (Wang et al. 2024b,)	Grounded theory coding and text analysis of 67 case studies using Nvivo software to design an integration framework	Developed a digital architecture and four pathways for integrating the marine industry with the digital economy, focusing on resource optimization, industrial chain integration, ecosystem-based clusters, and land-sea linkage
26	Impact of the digital economy on urban land green use efficiency: Evidence from Chinese cities (Wen and Li 2024)	Empirical analysis using the super-efficiency SBM model and econometric techniques on data from 286 Chinese cities (2011–2019)	The digital economy significantly enhances urban land green use efficiency through industrial optimization, green technology innovation, and digital talent agglomeration, with land finance dependence moderating these effects negatively

(continued)

Table 1 (continued)

No	Name of the paper	Methodology	Results
27	Digital economy, binary factor mismatch and sustainable economic development of coastal areas in China (Wu et al. 2024)	Empirical analysis using intermediary and regulating effect models applied to panel data from 11 Chinese coastal provinces (2009–2018)	The digital economy enhances sustainable development in coastal areas by reducing land and marine factor mismatches and improving green total factor productivity, moderated by market integration
28	Resilient cities governance when encountering external turbulence in the Greater Bay Area of China: An ESG perspective (Xu and Zhao 2024)	Conceptual analysis of urban resilience using the ESG framework (Environment, Social, Governance) and case study insights from the Greater Bay Area of China	The study highlights the integration of ESG principles in urban governance to enhance resilience, focusing on sustainable energy, digital economy, public health, and collaborative policies to address environmental and social vulnerabilities
29	Exploring the influence of the digital economy on marine pollution mitigation: A spatial econometric study of coastal China (Xu et al. 2024)	Spatial Durbin Model (SDM) analysis of panel data from 42 Chines coastal cities (2006–2015) to asses direct, indirect, and non-linear impacts of the digital economy on marine potion	The digital economy reduces marine pollution through technological innovations and exhibits significant spatial spillover effects, following an inverted U-shaped relationship
30	Can e-commerce adoption improve agricultural productivity? Evidence from apple growers in China (Yan and Liu 2023)	Propensity Score Matching (PSM) and Stochastic Frontier Analysis (SFA) based on survey data from 827 apple farmers in China	E-commerce adoption improves agricultural production efficiency by optimizing resource allocation, including land transfer, labor structure, and agriculture investments
31	Digital economy development, rural land certification, and rural industrial integration (Yan and Cao 2024)	Spatial econometric models, including a double fixed-effects model and mediation effect model, using panel data from 108 cities in China'Yangtze River Economic Belt (2011–2021)	The digital economy drives rural integration through land certification, exhibits an inverted U-shaped effect, and has significant spatial spillover effects across regions
32	The Concept of the New Information System of Electronic Services in the Field of Land and Property Relations (Zakharov and Kryakhtunov 2019)	Comparative analysis of existing geographic information systems to develop a new concept for electronic land and property service integration	Proposed a unified GIS-based system enabling interactive land and property management, addressing limitations of existing platforms and facilitating economic land use

(continued)

Table 1 (continued)

No	Name of the paper	Methodology	Results
33	The Impact of Digital Finance on the Green Utilization Efficiency of Urban Land: Evidence from 281 Cities in China (Zhang and Sun 2024)	Super-SBM model, fixed-effect regression, and mediation effect models using panel data from 281 Chinese cities (2010–2020)	Digital finance significantly enhances urban land green utilization efficiency through green technology innovation, with stronger effects in eastern and southern cities. Environmental regulation amplifies the impact, but industrial structure optimization shows no regulatory effect
34	Digital Transformation and Corporate Tax Avoidance: An Analysis Based on Multiple Perspectives and Mechanisms (Zhang and She 2024)	Theoretical and empirical analysis using signal theory, information asymmetry theory, and the T-O-E framework, applied to A-share listed companies in China from 2007 to 2022	Digital transformation reduces corporate tax avoidance by improving transparency, resource allocation, and internal controls, with stronger effects in growing firms and regions with lower financing constraints
35	A new method of crop yield prediction based on artificial intelligence (Zhang et al. 2023)	A novel AI-based yield prediction model combining environmental data, crop growth states, and big data analytics, with weights adjusted based on growth speed	The method significantly improves the accuracy of crop yield predictions by integrating real-time growth conditions with environmental variables through advanced AI algorithms
36	The Impact of the Digital Economy on Land Transfer-Out Decisions Among Chinese Farmers: Evidence from CHFS Micro-Data (Zheng et al. 2024)	Linear Probability Model (LPM) using data from the China Household Finance Survey (CHFS) spanning 2013–2019, supported by robustness and heterogeneity analyses	The digital economy promotes rural land transfer-out by enhancing non-agricultural employment, entrepreneurship and information acquisition, with a 3,39% increase in transfer likelihood per unit increase in the digital economy index
37	Transformations in Agricultural Land Use: Through Changes in Land Functions to Changes in Information Support for Land Management (Zhigulina et al. 2021a)	Analysis and synthesis, supported by a transdisciplinary approach, to examine the transformation of land functions during the transition to a digital economy,	Proposed a digital cadastral information resource to enhance the management of agricultural land use by assessing its ecological and economic states, bridging the gap between digital economy requirements and land administration systems

(continued)

Table 1 (continued)

No	Name of the paper	Methodology	Results
38	Digital transformation in land use and cadastre: Towards adaptive cadastral systems (Zhigulina et al. 2021b)	Systems approach grounded in systems theory, focusing on the structural and functional transformation of cadastral systems in response to digital transformation	Highlights adaptability as a critical property of modern cadastral systems, driven by the digitalization of land use processes and integration of unified cadastral information systems to address global land-use challenges
39	E-Commerce and Land Use Optimization in Agriculture: Case Studies from Southeast Asia (Zhou and Tang 2023)	Propensity Score Matching (PSM) and Stochastic Frontier Analysis (SFA) applied to survey data from 827 apple farmers in Shaanxi Province, China, to examine the impact of e-commerce adoption on agricultural productivity	E-commerce adoption significantly enhances agricultural production efficiency by optimizing labor, land, and capital allocation. It helps farmers access better market opportunities, increase investments in sustainable farming practices, and modernize agricultural operations
40	Has the Digital Economy Improved the Urban Land Green Use Efficiency? Evidence from the National Big Data Comprehensive Pilot Zone Policy (Zhou et al. 2024)	Utilized a super-efficiency slack-based measure (SBM) model incorporating undesirable outputs and applied a difference-in-differences (DID) approach to analyze panel data from 281 Chinese cities (2006–2021)	The establishment of National Big Data Comprehensive Pilot Zones (NBDCPZs) significantly improved Urban Land Green Use Efficiency (ULGUE) through mechanisms such as technological innovation, resource allocation, and industrial agglomeration. Positive spillover effects were observed in neighboring cities
41	Spatial and Temporal Interaction Coupling of Digital Economy, New-Type Urbanization, and Land Ecology and Spatial Effects Identification: A Study of the Yangtze River Delta (Zhu et al. 2023)	Modified Coupled Coordination Model and Spatial Panel Model applied to data from 41 cities in the Yangtze River Delta from 2011 to 2020, analyzing temporal evolution and spatial interactions	The digital economy enhances coordination among urbanization and land ecology but exhibits spatial disparities, with a "high in the east, low in the west" pattern, promoting sustainable regional development

(continued)

Table 1 (continued)

No	Name of the paper	Methodology	Results
42	The Role of Digital Platforms in Urban Land Transformation: Evidence from Case Studies in Coastal Regions (Zhu et al. 2024)	Modified coupling coordination model and spatial panel vector autoregression (PVAR) model applied to city-level data from the Yangtze River Delta (2011–2020)	The digital economy promotes coupling between new urbanization and land ecology, enhancing coordinated development, with spatial spillovers showing stronger effects in eastern cities
43	The Synergistic Role of Smart Agriculture in Optimizing Land Use and Enhancing Sustainability (Zhuo and Chen 2023)	Spatial Durbin Model (SDM) analysis using panel data from 42 coastal cities in China (2006–2015) to assess direct and spillover effects of the digital economy on marine pollution	The digital economy mitigates marine pollution through technological advancements and spatial spillovers, exhibiting an inverted U-shaped relationship with pollution levels

Source Adapted from Scoupus (as of November 23rd, 2024)

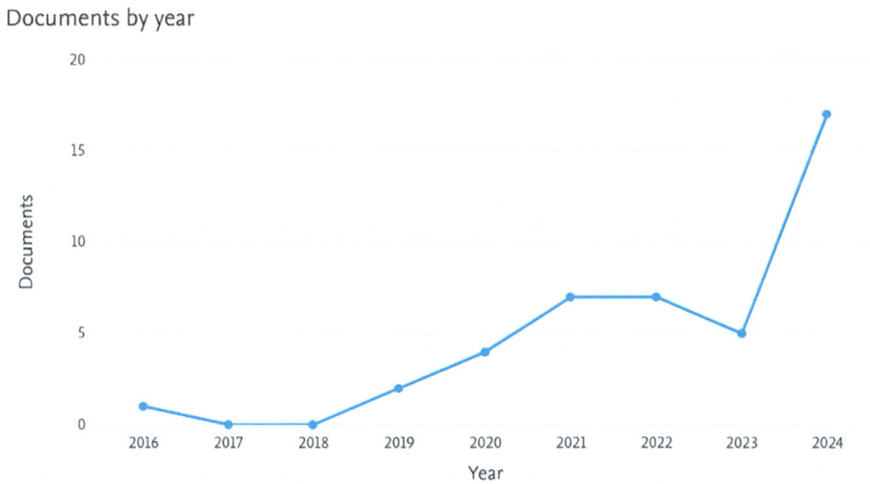

Fig. 1 Documents by year (*Source* Scopus analysis for the research)

Observing the papers by source for each year, from 2019 to 2024, is intriguing. The majority of the papers are published in journals such as Land, Sustainability Switzerland, and PLOS ONE, accounting for 9 out of the top 10 presented in Fig. 4, while the remaining two are conference proceedings, specifically the E3S Web of Conferences and the IOP Conference Series Earth and Environmental Science, each with 10 papers. Usually, the scientific conferences are the research communities that bring new and revolutionary ideas and proposals to a field.

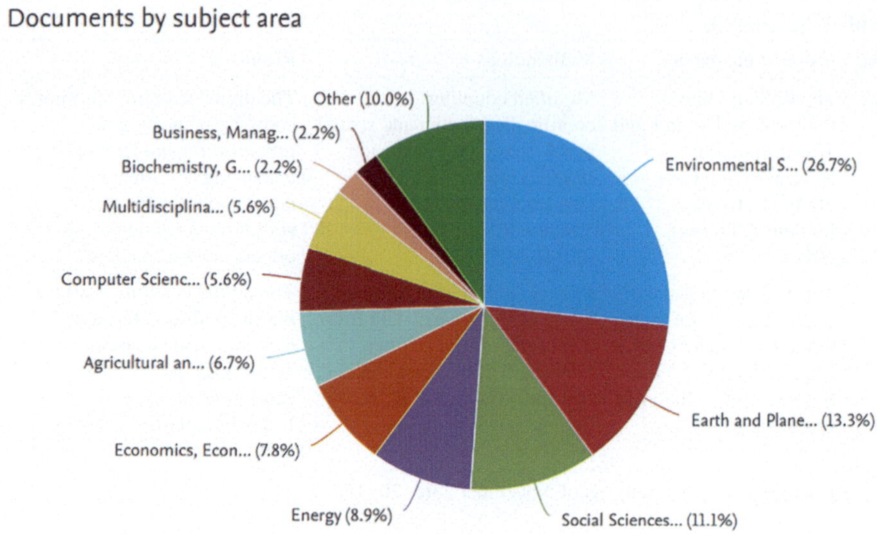

Fig. 2 Documents by subject area (*Source* Scopus analysis for the research)

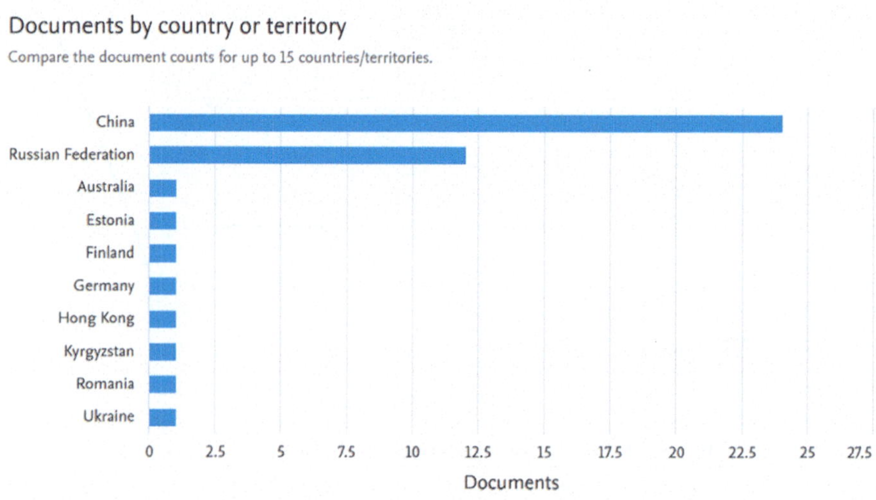

Fig. 3 Documents by country or territory (*Source* Scopus analysis for the research)

We mention that of the 43 papers, 30 are articles (69.80%), and 13 conference papers (30.20%).

We use the VOS Viewer software tool (van Eck and Waltman 2010) as a bibliometric analysis tool for networked data to identify the network correlations between

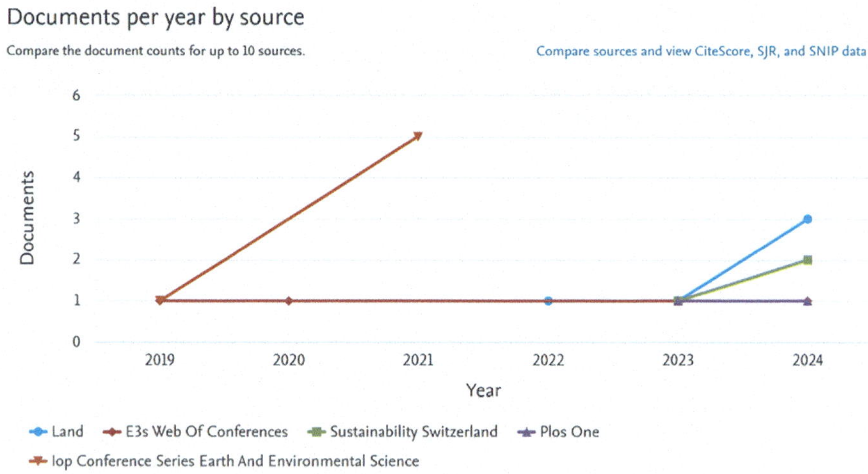

Fig. 4 Documents per year by source (*Source* Scopus analysis for the research)

the most important terms or items of the articles, which are found in the titles, articles, and keywords fields. Using the full counting method, we showcased 1576 items and retained those with at least 2 occurrences, resulting in 147 relevant items out of 228. We have grouped them into 13 clusters, which you can view in Fig. 5 or the link below.

Fig. 5 VOS Viewer co-occurrence map (See link: https://app.vosviewer.com/?json=https%3A%2F%2Fdrive.google.com%2Fuc%3Fid%3D1-wzjZmNrsYtMd08r4Ak1yPP8Q8frAiAG) (*Source* VOS Viewer network map of co-occurences)

These 43 papers are the outcome of the systematic literature review methodology, which is illustrated in this section. We applied some bibliometric analysis to understand the time, territory, or source context, as well as the correlation between the terms and the fields involved in this type of research, which is interdisciplinary in nature.

3 Results

This section will provide the findings of our research inquiries through a qualitative and thematic analysis of the 43 articles identified in the systematic literature review.

First we will synthesize the papers in the Table 1, below.

The above systematic results will be subsequently given as a topic and content analysis, addressing the research questions of the study.

RQ1 **"How has the role of land as a production factor transformed with the rise of the digital economy, particularly in its integration into digital infrastructure and smart agriculture?".**

The evolution of land as a production factor in the digital economy signifies a substantial paradigm change, particularly evident in its incorporation into digital infrastructure and smart agriculture. Liu et al. (2023) examined the adaptation of land use to facilitate digital infrastructure, including data centers and broadband networks, highlighting its significance in underpinning the spatial and technological framework of the digital economy. They contend that the advancement of digital infrastructure necessitates smart urban planning, as land allocation for such purposes increasingly competes with conventional uses.

Papaskiri et al. (2019) analyzed digital land management systems, emphasizing how the emergence of cadastral digitalization has transformed land governance and ownership frameworks. These tools facilitate improved transparency and efficiency, integrating land management with the requirements of digital infrastructure development.

Moreover, Zakharov and Kryakhtunov (2019) observed that the digital transformation of land records amalgamates physical and digital economies, facilitating more efficient decision-making processes for urban and rural development. According to Yan and Liu (2023), the e-commerce adoption enhances land productivity through better market access, labor allocation, and agricultural investments, while Papaskiri et al. (2021a) go further with the integration of GIS and BIM technologies into land management systems has modernized land governance, making it adaptive to the requirements of the digital economy.

In smart agriculture, Akmarov et al. (2021) highlighted the significance of digital technologies in optimizing land productivity. They investigated how Internet of Things (IoT) devices and artificial intelligence systems facilitate precision agriculture, thereby optimizing land utilization. Yan and Cao (2024) illustrated how rural land certification and smart agricultural technologies promote land optimization, facilitating rural industrial integration and economic sustainability.

Tang and Chen (2022) examined the facilitation of the green transformation in cultivated land usage through digital rural development efforts. Their research shows that digital technologies improve agricultural productivity while also reducing environmental harm, hence rethinking the ecological and economic roles of land. Ai et al. (2024) consider too that the digital economy transforms land use by promoting green and low-carbon practices, optimizing land productivity, and integrating technology for sustainable development.

Zhu et al. (2023) underscored the synergistic impacts of digital economy policies and land ecology, proposing that the incorporation of digital infrastructure into land use planning maintains a balance between development and sustainability.

The digital economy has transformed land into both a tangible and virtual asset. Zhigulina et al. (2021b) state that digital transformation has shifted land functions toward supporting both physical and virtual assets in urban planning and agricultural optimization.

The findings of Liu et al. (2023), Papaskiri et al. (2019), and Tang and Chen (2022) jointly demonstrate that land, in this contemporary setting, fulfills two functions: underpinning physical infrastructure for digital ecosystems and facilitating revolutionary agricultural practices through technology. This dual functioning highlights the increasing economic importance of land in the digital era.

An other important shift of the land in the era of digital transformation is the electronic land. It appears not so evident, but the papers that treat this idea are very complex. According to Zhigulina et al. (2021a) and Papaskiri et al. (2021b), the digitization of records and processes leads to unified platforms for managing land transactions, cadastral data, and usage planning. The same electronic land comes from the integration with smart technologies: IoT, GIS, and Big Data for real-time monitoring, precision planning, and optimization (Ai et al. 2024; Tang & Chen, 2022) or from promoting green and efficient land use through digital platforms for sustainability and efficiency (Ai et al. 2024; Zhou et al. 2024). These papers collectively emphasize that land, as a resource, is increasingly managed as a digital asset, aligning with the broader vision of electronic land.

Given that land has evolved into a complex and dynamic resource in the digital era, independent of its static functionality, we can delve deeper into its dual roles in supporting the digital ecosystem, sustaining sustainable development, and reducing poverty.

This is particularly relevant as the climate confronts global challenges due to the uncertainty of sustainability in the twentieth century, as well as population growth in certain areas where economic development and people's well-being are not the primary focus. This is the aim of the second research question, which is presented below.

RQ2 **"What strategies can optimize the dual role of land in supporting digital economic systems and sustainable development amidst global challenges like climate change and population growth?".**

The dual role of land in supporting digital economic systems and sustainable development necessitates innovative strategies to balance economic growth with environmental stewardship.

Tang and Chen (2022) highlighted that integrating digital technologies into land use planning can promote sustainable practices, particularly in rural areas. They proposed that digital rural development programs, which include precision agriculture and IoT-enabled monitoring, optimize land productivity while reducing environmental degradation.

In their paper related to the Australian farmers, Marshall et al. (2020) address that the digital inclusion gaps in rural areas is critical for leveraging land-based digital economic opportunities and achieving equitable development.

Liu et al. (2023) emphasized the need for policy frameworks that prioritize land allocation for digital infrastructure without compromising environmental goals. They argued that urban planning policies should incorporate land use efficiency models that accommodate the spatial needs of data centers and broadband networks while maintaining green spaces. This approach aligns with the findings of Nesterenko et al. (2020), who advocated for the integration of digital tools into organic agriculture strategies to enhance land's ecological function while supporting rural economies.

Gu et al. (2024) proposed that addressing land resource mismatches through digital technologies can enhance urban ecological resilience. Their study emphasized strategies such as using AI to optimize urban land use and leveraging digital platforms to mitigate land-use conflicts. Similarly, Zhu et al. (2023) underscored the importance of coupling digital economy policies with green land use initiatives, suggesting that spatial and temporal interaction models can guide sustainable urbanization.

In the context of climate change, Zakharov and Kryakhtunov (2019) identified the potential of digital land management systems to support adaptive strategies for land use. These systems, which integrate geospatial technologies and real-time data, allow for more responsive land planning that accommodates shifting climatic patterns and population pressures.

Additionally, Yan and Cao (2024) suggested that rural land certification programs, supported by digital frameworks, enable better resource management and scalability, especially in regions facing demographic and environmental challenges.

The findings from these studies underscore that effective strategies must combine technological innovation with regulatory oversight. As Liu et al. (2023), Gu et al. (2024), and Tang and Chen (2022) collectively demonstrated, optimizing the dual role of land requires a holistic approach that integrates digital technologies, sustainable practices, and forward-looking policies. This approach not only supports the growth of digital economic systems but also ensures land's viability as a resource for future generations amidst global challenges.

4 Discussion

The role of land as a fundamental factor of production has undergone a profound transformation from its classical conceptualization to its multifaceted functions in the digital economy. Traditionally viewed as a static and finite resource underpinning agriculture and industrial growth, land has evolved into a dynamic asset shaped by technological, economic, and social forces. This discussion explores the trajectory of land's transformation, highlighting its integration into digital infrastructure, its efficiency-driven application in smart agriculture, and its virtualization within emerging digital ecosystems like the metaverse.

The subsequent analysis addresses how land's historical role has adapted to meet the demands of a rapidly changing economy (Genete and Tugui 2008). It examines the transition from land as a foundational element of early economies to its modern dual role as a physical and digital resource. Central to this transformation are the strategies employed to balance land use for digital economic systems and sustainable development amidst global challenges (Georgescu et al. 2015), such as climate change and population growth. Evidence from the reviewed literature contextualizes these shifts, providing insights into the evolving economic and social significance of land.

4.1 The Classical Role of Land in Economics

In classical economics, land has traditionally been one of the three fundamental factors of production, alongside labor and capital. Liu et al. (2023) discussed the historical view of land as a fixed and limited resource, fundamental for agricultural and industrial productivity.

Zakharov and Kryakhtunov (2019) highlighted the unique characteristic of land as a non-reproducible factor, forming the basis for economic value creation through agriculture and real estate.

This classical perspective underpinned centuries of economic theory, focusing on land as a primary and essential input in production processes.

4.2 Evolution of Land's Role: From Primary Resource to Digital Asset

Historically, land has evolved from a primary resource integral to agriculture to a versatile industrial and real estate asset. Nesterenko et al. (2020) explored land's transformation into a market product during industrialization, where it became commodified and traded for urban development and industrial expansion. In recent decades, however, land's role has diversified significantly with the rise of the digital economy. Tang and Chen (2022) discussed how smart agriculture technologies have redefined land use, making it more efficient in meeting the food demands of an increasing global population.

Simultaneously, Gu et al. (2024) analyzed the urbanization-driven shift where land supports digital infrastructure such as data centers and cloud computing facilities. These facilities underpin the operational backbone of the digital economy, highlighting land's critical role in enabling technological advancements. Moreover, Zhu et al. (2023) demonstrated how digital tools replicate and virtualize land as assets in smart city planning, creating more efficient urban spaces.

At its most sophisticated level, land has become a virtual asset within the metaverse economy, as described by Zhang et al. (2023). Gaming, augmented reality, and other applications replicate these virtual land assets, showcasing their versatility and economic value for users. This evolution illustrates land's transition from a physical to a hybrid digital-virtual resource, addressing multiple economic and social needs simultaneously.

4.3 *Research Methods and Interdisciplinary Frameworks*

The research methods employed in these studies emphasize the interdisciplinary nature of analyzing land's role in the digital economy. Papaskiri et al. (2019) employed digital land management models to explore how cadastral systems integrate geospatial technologies. Liu et al. (2023) used spatial econometric analysis to evaluate urban land efficiency, while Zhu et al. (2023) applied coupling coordination models to assess the synergy between digital economy policies and land use sustainability.

These methods reflect a growing need for interdisciplinary research frameworks, where economics converges with technology, environmental science, and urban planning. Such an approach is essential for understanding the scalability of land's roles and its regulatory implications. Tang and Chen (2022) advocated for stronger regulatory frameworks to guide the sustainable development of digital and physical land resources, ensuring equitable access and balanced development.

4.4 *The Future of Land in a Sustainable Digital Economy*

Looking ahead, research on land in the digital economy must address critical objectives. Zakharov and Kryakhtunov (2019) argued for integrating regulatory frameworks that promote fair resource distribution and equitable technological access. Furthermore, Gu et al. (2024) emphasized using digital platforms to mitigate resource misallocation and poverty, aligning with the broader goal of creating an economy of abundance, as opposed to the classical economy's focus on resource scarcity.

To support sustainable growth, Zhuo and Chen (2023) highlighted the importance of reducing resource consumption in affluent economies while promoting sustainable practices globally. This transition from a consumerist to a sustainable consumption economy must incorporate digital innovations to ensure equitable development. The studies collectively illustrate that land, in its digital and physical forms, can drive social connectivity and reduce poverty by enabling scalable and fair economic systems.

The role of land in the digital economy represents a paradigm shift from classical economic views, with its evolution now reflecting technological advancements and interdisciplinary applications. As land continues to serve as a production factor, it must also support sustainable and equitable development goals.

Land has the ability to revolutionize the digital economy, according to Liu et al. (2023), Tang and Chen (2022), and Zakharov and Kryakhtunov (2019). These studies call for sustainable, technological, and regulatory measures to make the most of this potential.

It seems that the role of land in the global economy is also a subject of the spatial economy, while the population is experiencing an unprecedented growth in the digital economy upgrade of the classical paradigm. The next research efforts should focus more on eliminating disparities between poor populations and highly developed countries, where technology represents the cutting edge of the economic system but also amplifies the interconnectedness between global markets and the social economy.

5 Conclusion

This paper has explored the evolving role of land in the digital economy, highlighting its transformation from a foundational production factor in classical economics to a dynamic and versatile resource in the digital age.

Traditionally, people valued land for its fixed and finite nature, using it as a foundation for agricultural and industrial development. This perspective, as demonstrated in the reviewed literature, underscored the importance of land as a primary economic driver in pre-digital economies.

As economies transitioned toward industrialization and urbanization, land became a commodified market product, utilized for real estate and urban development.

However, the digital economy has redefined this relationship, as land now serves as a critical resource for digital infrastructure, such as data centers and cloud computing hubs. These facilities represent the backbone of digital services, integrating physical land use with technological advancements.

In smart agriculture, the integration of IoT, AI, and other digital technologies has revolutionized land use, enabling higher productivity and resource optimization. This evolution aligns with global challenges such as population growth and climate change, which demand more efficient and sustainable approaches to land use. Furthermore, the virtualization of land in applications such as metaverse economies highlights its versatility, with virtual land assets creating new dimensions of value and economic activity.

The discussion emphasized the dual role of land as both a physical and digital resource, advocating for interdisciplinary frameworks and regulatory strategies to maximize its potential. The research that was looked at used a variety of approaches, such as spatial econometric models, digital cadastral systems, and coupling coordination analyses, to show the pros and cons of land use in the digital economy.

Looking ahead, further research should focus on empirical case studies to better understand localized strategies for optimizing land use in resource-constrained environments. Such studies should also explore the social and economic benefits of digital land management systems, particularly in addressing poverty and inequality. Moreover, future work should emphasize the role of sustainable growth in reducing resource overuse in consumerist economies while promoting equitable access to digital technologies globally.

In conclusion, land's role in the digital economy is a testament to its adaptability and enduring significance. As we integrate technological innovations into economic systems, there is an urgent need for collaborative research and policymaking to ensure that land continues to serve both economic and societal needs in a sustainable and inclusive manner.

References

Ai, K., Li, H., Zhang,W., Yan, X.-W. 2024. Digital Economy and Green and Low-Carbon Transformation of Land Use: Spatial Effects and ModeratingMechanisms. *Land*, 13, 1172.

Akmarov, P.B., Knyazeva, O.P., & Tretyakova, E.S., 2021. Assessing the potential of the digital economy in agriculture. IOP Conference Series: Earth and Environmental Science, 666, p. 042036.

Anttiroiko, A.V., Laine, M., & Lönnqvist, H., 2020. City as a Growth Platform: Responses of the Cities of Helsinki Metropolitan Area to Global Digital Economy. Urban Science, 4(67), pp. 1–20.

Brynjolfsson, E. & McAfee, A., 2014. *The Second Machine Age: Work, Progress, and Prosperity in a Time of Brilliant Technologies*. New York: W.W. Norton & Company.

Bukht, R. & Heeks, R., 2018. Defining, Conceptualising and Measuring the Digital Economy. *Development Informatics Working Paper*, no. 68.

Cheng, C., Gao, Q., Ju, K., & Ma, Y., 2024. How digital skills affect farmers' agricultural entrepreneurship? An explanation from factor availability. Journal of Innovation and Knowledge, 9, p. 100477.

Diamond, J., 1997. *Guns, Germs, and Steel: The Fates of Human Societies*, pp. 85–92. New York, NY: W.W. Norton & Company.

Dziatkovskii, A., Hryneuski, U., Dudov, A., & Krylova, A., 2021. The economic impact of digitalization and the creation of digital products on the development of the state. Economic Annals-XXI, 193(9-10), pp. 4–14.

Ge, X., 2024. Innovative Research on Industrial Upgrading and Transformation Path of Regional Economy in the Perspective of Digital Economy. Applied Mathematics and Nonlinear Sciences, 9(1), pp. 1–17.

Genete, L. D., & Tugui, A., 2008. From ERP systems to digital accounting in relations with customers and suppliers. In Selected Papers from the WSEAS Conferences in Spain September 2008, pp. 57–63.

Georgescu, M., Păvăloaia, V.D., Popescul, D. and Țugui, A., 2015. The race for making up the list of emergent smart cities. An Eastern European country's approach. Transformations in Business & Economics, 14(2A), pp. 529–549.

Gu, H., Guo, G., & Li, C., 2024. Treating the Symptoms as Well as the Root Causes: How the Digital Economy Can Mitigate the Negative Impacts of Land Resource Mismatches on Urban Ecological Resilience. Land, 13, p. 1463.

Kelly, K., 2016. *The Inevitable: Understanding the 12 Technological Forces That Will Shape Our Future.* New York: Viking.

Landes, D.S., 1998. *The Wealth and Poverty of Nations: Why Some Are So Rich and Some So Poor.* New York: W.W. Norton & Company.

Li, W.; Guo, G.; Gu, H.; Lai, S.; Duan, Y.; Li, C. 2024. Digital Economy as a Buffer: Alleviating the Adverse Effects of Land Resource Mismatch on Food Security. *Land*, 13, 1742.

Li, Y., Liu, J., & Jia, S., 2022. The Design of a Remediation Device for Heavy Metal Contaminated Soil Under Digital Economy. Frontiers in Energy Research, 10, p. 893335.

Liu, B., Wang, Y., Chang, X., Nie, B., Meng, L., & Li, Y., 2022. Does Land Urbanization Affect the Catch-Up Effect of Carbon Emissions Reduction in China's Logistics? Land, 11, p. 1503.

Liu, Z., Zhang, X., Wang, J., Shen, L., & Tang, E., 2023. Evaluation of coupling coordination development between digital economy and green finance: Evidence from 30 provinces in China. PLoS ONE, 18(10), p. e0291936.

Marshall, A., Dezuanni, M., Burgess, J., Thomas, J., & Wilson, C. K. 2020. Australian farmers left behind in the digital economy: Insights from the Australian Digital Inclusion Index. *Journal of Rural Studies, 80*, 195–210.

Mowery, D.C. & Rosenberg, N., 1998. *Paths of Innovation: Technological Change in 20th-Century America.* Cambridge: Cambridge University Press.

Nesterenko, N.Y., Pakhomova, N.V., & Richter, K.K., 2020. Sustainable Development of Organic Agriculture: Strategies of Russia and Its Regions in Context of the Application of Digital Economy Technologies. St. Petersburg University Journal of Economic Studies, 36(2), pp. 217–242.

OECD, 2020. *Digital Economy Outlook 2020.* Paris: OECD Publishing.

Page, M.J., McKenzie, J.E., Bossuyt, P.M., Boutron, I., Hoffmann, T.C., Mulrow, C.D., Tetzlaff, J.M., Akl, E.A., Brennan, S.E., Chou, R., and Glanville, J. (2021). The PRISMA 2020 statement: An updated guideline for reporting systematic reviews. *BMJ*, 372, n71.

Papaskiri, T., Kasyanov, A., & Ananicheva, E., 2019. On Creating Digital Land Management in the Framework of the Program on Digital Economy of the Russian Federation. IOP Conference Series: Earth and Environmental Science, 274, p. 012092.

Papaskiri, T.V., Burov, M.P., Ananicheva, E.P., Shevchuk, A.A., & Popova, E.S. (2021). Information and technological support of digital land management. *IOP Conference Series: Earth and Environmental Science, 867*(1), 012174.

Papaskiri, T.V., Semochkin, V.N., Alekseenko, N.N., Krasnyanskaya, E.V., & Zatsepina, E.A. 2021. Digital land management technologies. *IOP Conference Series: Earth and Environmental Science, 867*(1), 012159.

Polanyi, K., 1944. *The Great Transformation: The Political and Economic Origins of Our Time.* Boston: Beacon Press.

Pototskaya, L., Ukolova, N., & Novikova, N., 2022. Principles and Regularities of Functioning of the Organizational and Economic Mechanism of Land Tenure and Land Use in the Digital Economy. BIO Web of Conferences, 43, p. 3041.

Rifkin, J., 2000. *The Age of Access: The New Culture of Hypercapitalism Where All of Life is a Paid-For Experience.* New York: Tarcher/Putnam.

Rysalieva, G., Razhapbaeva, M., Kolosha, V., Muzychenko, M., Butenko, D., & Zhang, L., 2024. Optimizing the Use of Intangible Assets in Industry to Overcome Poverty: A Cross-Country Analysis. Multidisciplinary Science Journal, 6, p. e2024ss0730.

Schultz, T.W., 1964. Transforming Traditional Agriculture. *The Journal of Farm Economics*, 46(1), pp. 200–204.

Shcherbakova, L.N., Evdokimova, E.K., Fedulova, E.A., & Rada, A.O., 2023. Relationship Between the Categories of Digital and Commodity Rents. E3S Web of Conferences, 458, p. 05019.

Shevchenko, G., Gura, D., Moskvina, P., Popova, I. & Akopyan, G., 2020. Three-dimensional Cadastre in Creating an Information Base for a Spatial Model of a Real Estate Object, 2020. E3S Web of Conferences, 164, p. 07012.

Stoica, M., & Ghilic-Micu, B., 2021. The Telework Paradigm in the IoE Ecosystem: A Model for the Teleworker Residence Choice in the Context of Digital Economy and Society. Economic Computation and Economic Cybernetics Studies and Research, 55(3), pp. 263–271.

Straumann, R.K. & Graham, M., 2016. Who isn't online? Mapping the 'Archipelago of Disconnection'. Regional Studies, Regional Science, 3(1), pp. 96–98.

Tang, Y., & Chen, M., 2022. The Impact Mechanism and Spillover Effect of Digital Rural Construction on the Efficiency of Green Transformation for Cultivated Land Use in China. International Journal of Environmental Research and Public Health, 19, p. 16159.

Tapscott, D., 1996. *The Digital Economy: Promise and Peril in the Age of Networked Intelligence.* New York: McGraw-Hill.

Tugui, A., & Gheorghe, A.M., 2016. Identifying difficulties encountered by the accounting profession in accessing documents, in the digital economy context of Romania. Audit Financiar, 3, pp.291–301.

UNCTAD, 2019. *Digital Economy Report 2019: Value Creation and Capture—Implications for Developing Countries.* Geneva: United Nations.

United Nations, 2021. Our common agenda: Report of the Secretary-General. United Nations. Available at: https://www.un.org/en/common-agenda

van Eck, N.J. and Waltman, L., 2010. Software survey: VOSviewer, a computer program for bibliometric mapping. *Scientometrics*, 84, pp. 523–538.

Wang, F., Wang, H., & Xiong, L., 2024. Does the digital economy exhibit multiplier effects? A case study on the optimization of agricultural production structure in the rural digital economy. International Journal of Agricultural Sustainability, 22(1), p. 2386821.

Wang, J., Lu, Y., & Li, Z., 2024. Research on the Integrated Development of China's Marine Industry Empowered by the Digital Economy: Architecture Design and Implementation Pathways. Water, 16, p. 2381.

Wen, R., & Li, H., 2024. Impact of the digital economy on urban land green use efficiency: Evidence from Chinese cities. Environmental Research Communications, 6(5), p. 055008.

World Economic Forum, 2020. *The Future of Jobs Report 2020.* Geneva: WEF.

Wu, S., Tang, J., Li, M., & Xiao, J., 2024. Digital economy, binary factor mismatch and sustainable economic development of coastal areas in China. Heliyon, 10, p. e26453.

Xu, W., Wang, Q., & Wei, L., 2024. Exploring the influence of the digital economy on marine pollution mitigation: A spatial econometric study of coastal China. Water, 16, p. 1990.

Xu, Y. & Zhao, Z. 2024. Resilient cities governance when encountering external turbulence in the Greater Bay Area of China: An ESG perspective. *E3S Web of Conferences, 512*, 01021.

Yan, B., & Liu, T., 2023. Can e-commerce adoption improve agricultural productivity? Evidence from apple growers in China. Sustainability, 15(150), pp. 1–16.

Yan, M., & Cao, X., 2024. Digital economy development, rural land certification, and rural industrial integration. Sustainability, 16, p. 4640.

Zakharov, Z., & Kryakhtunov, A., 2019. The Concept of the New Information System of Electronic Services in the Field of Land and Property Relations. E3S Web of Conferences, 110, p. 12222.

Zhang, J., & Sun, T., 2024. The Impact of Digital Finance on the Green Utilization Efficiency of Urban Land: Evidence from 281 Cities in China. Sustainability, 16, p. 2003.

Zhang, Q., & She, J., 2024. Digital Transformation and Corporate Tax Avoidance: An Analysis Based on Multiple Perspectives and Mechanisms. PLoS ONE, 19(9), p. e0310241.

Zhang, Y., Liao, Y., & Li, Y., 2023. A new method of crop yield prediction based on artificial intelligence. Journal of Physics: Conference Series, 2665, p. 012019.

Zheng, P., Li, Y., & Li, X., 2024. The Impact of the Digital Economy on Land Transfer-Out Decisions Among Chinese Farmers: Evidence from CHFS Micro-Data. Scientific Reports, 14, p. 19684.

Zhigulina, T.N., Luchnikova, N.M., & Lebedeva, L.V., 2021. Transformations in Agricultural Land Use: Through Changes in Land Functions to Changes in Information Support for Land Management. IOP Conference Series: Earth and Environmental Science, 677, p. 042097.

Zhigulina, T.N., Kostritsina, M.N., Luchnikova, N.M., & Lebedeva, L.V., 2021. Digital transformation in land use and cadastre: Towards adaptive cadastral systems. *IOP Conference Series: Earth and Environmental Science, 839*, 022071.

Zhou, H., & Tang, Z., 2023. E-Commerce and Land Use Optimization in Agriculture: Case Studies from Southeast Asia. Agricultural Economics Journal, 15(6), pp. 112–127.

Zhou, G., Xu, H., Jiang, C., Deng, S., Chen, L., & Zhang, Z. (2024). Has the Digital Economy Improved the Urban Land Green Use Efficiency? Evidence from the National Big Data Comprehensive Pilot Zone Policy. *Land, 13*(7), 960.

Zhu, Y., Shen, S., Du, L., Fu, J., Zou, J., Peng, L., & Ding, R., 2023. Spatial and Temporal Interaction Coupling of Digital Economy, New-Type Urbanization, and Land Ecology and Spatial Effects Identification: A Study of the Yangtze River Delta. Land, 12(3), p. 677.

Zhu, Z., Zhao, L., & Zhang, X., 2024. The Role of Digital Platforms in Urban Land Transformation: Evidence from Case Studies in Coastal Regions. Land Use Policy, 142, p. 104239.

Zhuo, L., & Chen, Y., 2023. The Synergistic Role of Smart Agriculture in Optimizing Land Use and Enhancing Sustainability. Environmental Research Letters, 18, p. 105012.

Need to Lead: Romania's Leadership Traits on the Global Stage

Sander Schroevers, Laurentiu Mihai, and Aynur Dogan

Abstract In an era defined by swift digital transformation, this study examines the evolving leadership traits of Romanian professionals, focusing on decision-making adaptability, hierarchical dynamics, and cross-cultural positioning. Drawing on survey data, qualitative interviews, heatmaps, and a forest plot analysis, the research identifies a duality in Romanian leadership: a commitment to conventional hierarchical principles coexists with emerging participative practices, particularly among emerging leaders within private-sector firms. The study contextualises Romania within a global leadership framework, highlighting its alignment with structured, task-oriented cultures like Germany and Spain, while contrasting with participative environments such as the Netherlands. Additionally, digital transformation emerges as a critical driver reshaping leadership adaptability and communication preferences in Romania. This paper contributes to leadership literature by integrating quantitative and qualitative data with comparative visualisations, offering actionable insights for practitioners and researchers. Limitations include reliance on self-reported data and the need for expanded sectoral representation. Future research could explore the interplay of digitalisation, generational shifts, and cross-sector dynamics in Romanian leadership. These findings provide practical guidance for Romanian (expatriate) leaders as they navigate the complexities of digital transformation and the intricacies of global professional landscapes.

Keywords Leadership · Leadership style · Romania · Culture · Digital transformation

S. Schroevers · A. Dogan
Amsterdam University of Applied Sciences, Amsterdam, Netherlands
e-mail: s.schroevers@hva.nl

L. Mihai (✉)
University of Craiova, Craiova, Romania
e-mail: laurentiu.mihai@edu.ucv.ro

S. O. Idowu et al. (eds.), *Competitiveness and Sustainability in the Digitization Era*, Springer Proceedings in Business and Economics,
https://doi.org/10.1007/978-3-031-91778-3_6

1 Introduction

Each year, a demographic equivalent to the population of Braşov leaves Romania. Among EU member states, Romania has the largest proportion of citizens residing in other EU countries, with 24% of working-age adults living abroad. Remarkably, nearly two out of five Romanian expatriates (44%) occupy senior roles, significantly surpassing the global average (IOM 2023). This trend reflects not only patterns of migration but also the transferability of Romanian expatriates across cultural and organisational contexts (Den Hartog and De Hoogh 2024). To achieve professional success abroad, leaders must possess a nuanced understanding of their own leadership styles while adapting to the cultural and professional norms of host countries (Urbach et al. 2021). This study explores Romania's leadership traits within a global framework, particularly in areas such as decision-making, power distance, and perceptions of status.

Leadership practices in Romania are equally relevant to those who remain within its borders. Since Romania's integration into the European Union and NATO, its management systems have become increasingly globalized. In parallel, the influence of digital transformation has emerged as a critical factor shaping leadership dynamics and organisational competitiveness. As businesses worldwide embrace the digital era, effective leadership must foster collaboration across diverse teams, a capacity that cross-cultural leadership uniquely provides (Alvarez and Sahija 2022).

Romanian cities such as Cluj-Napoca, now a prominent hub for Europe's digital sector, illustrate the role of leadership in leveraging digital platforms to enhance organisational performance. Digitalisation challenges traditional top-down management styles, encouraging Romanian leaders to adopt participative approaches that enhance decision-making and leadership efficacy (Krishna Murthy et al. 2024). As Romanian leaders navigate this dual challenge of preserving cultural authenticity while adapting to global digital capabilities, they must integrate traditional and modern methodologies to remain competitive in an interconnected marketplace (Lifintsev and Wellbrock 2019).

Hierarchical organisational structures, which have long characterised Romanian leadership, are being reshaped by the participative styles enabled by digital technologies. This evolution reflects a broader trend in human resource management, where leadership methodologies are influenced by historical, societal, and economic factors specific to a region (Schühly 2022). In this context, Romanian leaders face the task of reconciling deeply rooted hierarchical traditions with the adaptive demands of the digital age, fostering innovation while retaining their cultural identity.

Romania's unique geographic and historical context adds further complexity to its leadership landscape. Situated at the crossroads of Central and Eastern Europe, Romania has been shaped by diverse influences, from Latin-Byzantine legacies to the Ottoman administrative practices of Wallachia, the Slavic influences of Moldova, and the Austro-Hungarian traditions of Transylvania (Gâf-Deac 2019; Zait and Zait 2016). These cultural and historical layers have created distinct leadership paradigms across Romania's regions, resulting in a non-linear progression of managerial practices. Over time, leadership in Romania has evolved in response to socio-political shifts. From the autocratic rule of the Ceaușescu era to the demands of European integration, Romanian leadership has undergone significant transformations (Aioanei 2006). This evolution has fostered a distinctive environment where hierarchical structures coexist with participative and transformational leadership paradigms, particularly within the private sector (Littrell and Valentin 2005; Mihai 2016). In the public sector, the transition has been slower, reflecting the inertia of historical systems that prioritize stability and control.

This study aims to analyse how Romanian leadership practices respond to both local and global demands, with particular emphasis on how these practices align with emerging trends in digitalisation and cross-cultural management. By situating Romanian leadership within a global framework, this research seeks to provide actionable insights for expatriates and organisations navigating Romania's dynamic cultural and professional landscape. The paper is structured as follows: after this introduction, the second section discusses relevant works from the leadership literature, followed by the methodology section which presents the research and survey designs, as well as the data collection and processing methods. Moreover, our paper continues with the results section, which presents our general findings, followed by a section which thoroughly discusses these findings, as well as aligning them with other similar studies. Lastly, our paper concludes with a final section, which presents our general conclusions, as well as the limitations of our study and future recommendations for other researchers who want to tackle this topic.

2 Literature Review

2.1 Romanian Leadership: Cultural and Organisational Characteristics

Romanian leadership practices have been significantly shaped by cultural dimensions such as collectivism, high uncertainty avoidance, and a complex blend of hierarchical traditions and modern influences. Historically, leadership styles in Romania reflected task-oriented and autocratic tendencies, particularly in state-owned enterprises, as noted by Hurduzeu (2015). This approach emphasized bureaucratic consistency and managerial authority but limited employee autonomy. Similarly, Aioanei (2006) observed persistent hierarchical tendencies, wherein managers were perceived as authoritative figures providing clear direction.

In recent decades, however, Romania has seen gradual shifts toward participative and transformational leadership, particularly in private sector firms and SMEs.

Mihai (2016) attributes this shift to Romania's European Union integration, exposure to global business practices, and the growing emphasis on employee engagement. Moldovan and Macarie (2016) identify merit-based leadership and participative decision-making as emerging values in public organisations. Private enterprises, by contrast, continue to prioritize adaptability, reflecting Romania's transition to a market economy.

Crăciun et al. (2015) further elaborate on leadership attributes in SMEs, identifying cooperation, charisma, and motivational skills as crucial for effective management. Despite these shifts, challenges remain, with many organisations struggling to balance traditional hierarchical norms and evolving participative models.

2.2 Perceptions of Status and Power Distance

Romanian leadership styles reflect a historical interplay of hierarchical dominance, collectivist values, traditionally shaped by authoritarian governance and entrenched power distance, leadership practices in Romania have transitioned significantly post-Ceaușescu, driven by economic liberalisation and integration into the European Union (Aioanei 2006). Power distance remains a defining feature of Romanian organisational culture, albeit with sectoral variations. Littrell and Valentin (2005) highlight hierarchical relationships and status consciousness as dominant in private enterprises. Employees in these settings often expect leaders to maintain authority and provide clear guidance. However, Moldovan and Macarie (2016) report lower power distance in public organisations, where employees value open communication and merit-based recognition.

Guluță and Rusu (2016) describe the prevalence of autocratic leadership styles in some Romanian companies, reflecting high power distance norms. These styles are often characterised by clear directives and limited employee input. Nonetheless, there is growing evidence of a preference for transformational leadership, which fosters inspiration, motivation, and collective goal achievement (Hintea 2015).

Regional differences further complicate the leadership landscape in Romania. Neculăesei and Tătărușanu (2008) highlight cultural contrasts between regions such as Transylvania, with its lower power distance and more participative tendencies, and Wallachia, where traditional hierarchical norms prevail. These findings underscore the dynamic nature of Romanian leadership, shaped by historical legacies, regional influences, and sectoral demands.

2.3 Comparative analysis of leadership styles worldwide

Romanian leadership styles occupy a distinctive place in the global leadership landscape, balancing hierarchical traditions with emerging participative approaches.

Littrell and Valentin (2005) compared Romanian, German, and UK managers, identifying Romania's collectivist and high power distance culture as key differentiators. The GLOBE study (Javidan et al. 2023, House et al. 2004) reinforces these findings, highlighting self-protective and humane-oriented leadership as prevalent traits in Romania. These traits contrast with the more autonomous and participative styles observed in Western Europe. In the public sector, Romanian leadership increasingly aligns with global transformational trends, emphasizing employee satisfaction, motivation, and merit-based practices (Ţiclău & Hintea 2016). However, resource constraints and cultural inertia continue to limit the widespread adoption of participative models. In SMEs, Crăciun et al. (2015) identify a hybrid approach that combines transformational and transactional techniques, distinguishing Romanian leadership from Western counterparts. Emerging research highlights the adaptability of Romanian leaders in cross-border contexts. As Romanian professionals increasingly migrate to countries like Germany and the UK, they face challenges navigating cultural differences in leadership practices. For instance, the UK's emphasis on interpersonal qualities such as charisma contrasts with Romania's preference for technical expertise, while Germany's flatter hierarchies challenge traditional Romanian expectations of authority and status (Budrina 2019).

2.4 *Decision-Making, Hierarchy and Authority*

Romanian leadership is characterised by centralized decision-making and adherence to hierarchical structures, particularly in larger organisations. Nicolescu and Nicolescu (2020) describe a model where decision-making authority is concentrated at the top management, streamlining processes but often preventing innovation. This methodology embodies cultural inclinations towards robust leadership and explicit chains of command, as observed by Budrina (2019).

In practice, Romanian managers often blend traditional hierarchical control with relational leadership traits. Văduva (2016) notes the enduring influence of paternalistic leadership, where leaders act as benevolent patriarchs, balancing authority with responsibility. This duality enables Romanian leaders to navigate complex organisational challenges while maintaining stability and order. However, it may also pose challenges in multicultural work environments, where more collaborative and egalitarian approaches are preferred.

Recent studies emphasize the evolving role of decision-making in Romanian leadership. Forest plots and heatmaps from the Global Leadership Survey provide empirical evidence of Romania's unique positioning on dimensions such as decision-making adaptability and hierarchical respect. These visualisations underscore the contrasts between Romania and key expat destinations, such as Germany and the Netherlands, offering actionable insights for Romanian expatriates.

2.5 Research gaps and future directions

Despite substantial progress in understanding Romanian leadership, research gaps remain. Much of the literature focuses on public sector practices, with limited exploration of leadership in multinational private enterprises operating in Romania, or digital transborder leadership practices. Additionally, the interaction between traditional cultural traits and modern leadership demands warrants deeper investigation. Addressing these gaps could enhance the understanding of how Romanian leadership adapts to global trends, such as an increasing emphasis on transformational leadership, digital transformation, and employee engagement.

Emerging areas of research include the role of digital leadership in Romania's evolving economy and the impact of generational shifts on leadership practices. For instance, younger Romanian leaders, often educated abroad, are increasingly adopting participative and inclusive styles, signalling a potential departure from hierarchical norms (Alexandru and Catana, 2010; Crăciun et al. 2015). This development reflects broader efforts to align leadership practices with the international market. Consequently, our review of existing literature establishes the foundation for an in-depth examination of the associated practices and their ramifications for both domestic and international contexts.

This being said, our paper aims to bridge these gaps and contribute to the leadership literature by assessing how leadership manifests in Romanian companies. In this context, our analysis is based on four main research questions:

RQ1 Which are the dominant traits of Romanian leaders?
RQ2 How are Romanian leaders perceived by their followers, in terms of status and power distance?
RQ3 How do Romanian leadership practices align with or diverge from global norms.

2.6 Implications for Research Questions

This review highlights several key themes relevant to the research questions guiding this study. For RQ1, exploring cultural and organisational characteristics of Romanian leadership, the literature underscores the tension between traditional hierarchical structures and emerging participative models. For RQ2, examining power distance and status perceptions, insights from GLOBE and Hofstede frameworks provide a robust comparative basis. Finally, for RQ3, analysing comparative insights across nations, the integration of Romania's leadership profile with global trends offers a nuanced understanding of its unique positioning within cross-cultural contexts.

3 Methodology

3.1 Research Design and Approach

This study employs a mixed-methods approach, integrating both quantitative and qualitative data sources to provide a comprehensive analysis of leadership practices in Romania. The methodological design is formulated to include survey-driven quantitative data gathering, thematic evaluation of qualitative interviews, and psychometric and statistical assessments to guarantee reliable and applicable conclusions. This approach aligns with the recommendations of Bryman (2012) for combining numerical and thematic data to address intricate research questions within the realm of leadership studies.

3.2 Survey Design and Translations

The primary dataset comprises responses from 152 qualified Romanian participants, extracted from a broader survey conducted across 158 countries with over 10,000 global respondents. Data collection spanned October 2022 to May 2024 and utilised both Qualtrics and SurveyMonkey platforms, supplemented by paper surveys during in-person academic visits to Romania. The survey consisted of 27 items, combining multiple-choice, Likert-scale, and open-ended formats to attain a comprehensive understanding of leadership practices and viewpoints. The topics included hierarchical respect, decision-making styles, interpersonal traits, and formal communication norms. To ensure cultural and linguistic accessibility, the survey was translated into 52 languages globally. For the Romanian sample, translations were available in Romanian, English, Hungarian, and German. These translations were carefully vetted by native speakers and back-translated where feasible to ensure accuracy and cultural relevance.

3.3 Quantitative Data Processing and Analysis

Survey responses were subjected to systematic analysis. Quantitative analysis began with normalising responses to account for varying sample sizes across countries, enabling cross-national comparisons. Likert-scale responses have been coded numerically, assigning values from 1 ("strongly disagree") to 6 ("strongly agree"), to facilitate the calculation of the mean scores. These mean scores were ranked to identify significant differences between Romania and other nations, highlighting leadership trends. Data visualisation techniques, including forest plots and heatmaps, were employed to contextualise Romania's leadership landscape within global trends.

3.4 Qualitative Data Collection and Analysis

Qualitative insights were gathered through nine in-depth interviews with Romanian leadership experts, including academics, executives, and organisational consultants. Conducted in-person and by using video conferencing, these interviews lasted between 15 and 60 min and were recorded for transcription and analysis. Braun and Clarke's (2006) guidelines were used to code and triangulate these qualitative findings, ensuring they complemented the quantitative data. Open-ended survey responses were also translated and thematically categorized, focusing on recurring patterns such as hierarchical norms, generational divides, and leadership authenticity. Select illustrative quotes from paper surveys and digital datasets were integrated into the analysis to enrich the study's findings.

3.5 Visual Representation and Analytical Tools

Forest plots, developed using an R-based Shiny dashboard, visualized inter-country differences for key survey questions, such as hierarchical respect and decision-making adaptability. Heatmaps depicted leadership trait preferences across six selected countries, showcasing Romania's alignment or divergence with regional and global trends. Mean score comparisons using Excel-based frequency tables facilitated the ranking of countries based on survey responses, offering actionable insights for both academic and professional audiences.

3.6 Respondent Demographics and Context

The Romanian subset of survey respondents included participants from diverse professional backgrounds, predominantly C-suite executives (44%), with the remainder representing mid-level managers and industry experts. The sample spanned various sectors, with a slight overrepresentation from technology, manufacturing, and public administration. The inclusion of multiple languages and in-person paper surveys further enhanced the study's representativeness, reflecting the multilingual and multicultural dimensions of Romanian leadership.

4 Results

RQ1 Which Are the Dominant Traits of Romanian Leaders?

This study investigates cross-cultural leadership preferences by analysing the frequency of traits or prevalence of attributes, deemed important for leaders across various nations. The traits, which are sourced from established leadership theories and practices, encompass: technical competence, organisational experience, market expertise, charismatic personality, and interpersonal abilities. Romania's leadership profile is characterised by a strong emphasis on practical competencies.

The findings highlight (i) technical competence (61 mentions), (ii) organisational experience (41 mentions), and (iii) market expertise (48 mentions) as the dominant traits identified in the Romanian dataset. This emphasis aligns with the nation's historical focus on task-oriented leadership and structured decision-making processes. Visionary thinking and charismatic personality were less frequently mentioned, underscoring a preference for practical, measurable leadership over interpersonal influence.

Figure 1 presents a heatmap illustrating the comparative frequencies of leadership traits across six selected countries, including Romania, reflecting aggregated frequencies from survey responses as well as highlighting variations in the importance placed on competencies, interpersonal skills, and influential resources. The visualisation emphasizes Romania's task-oriented preferences for technical competence (61 mentions) and organisational experience (41 mentions), while highlighting divergences in interpersonal and hierarchical leadership traits with countries like Turkey and Algeria.

The heatmap emphasizes Romania's leadership traits within a global context, showcasing the task-oriented focus while highlighting critical contrasts with hierarchical and relational leadership paradigms in other nations. Romania's alignment with structured, competency-driven traits mirrors German and Spanish preferences,

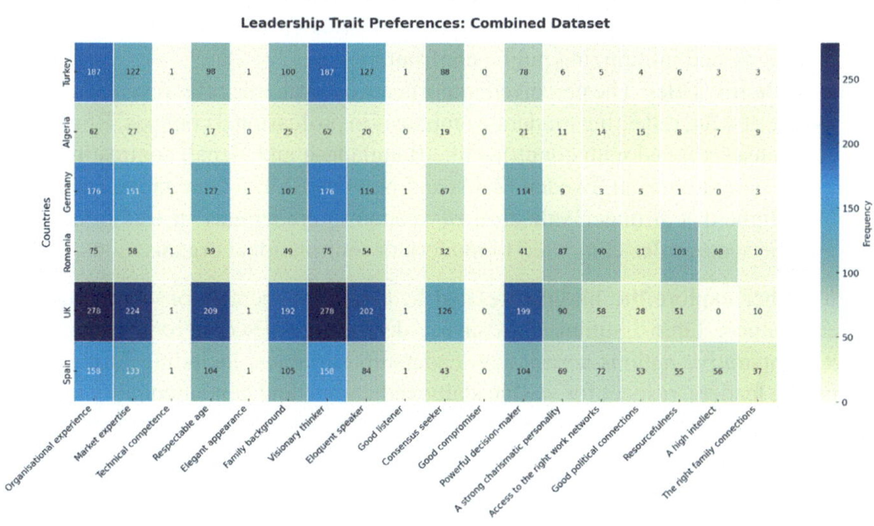

Fig. 1 Heatmap of leadership trait preferences across six countries (*Source* The authors' own analysis)

while the divergence with the UK, Algeria, and Turkey underscores distinct cultural dynamics.

By visually comparing Romania's leadership profile to key expat destinations, the heatmap provides actionable insights for Romanian professionals navigating international roles. This comparative approach underscores the importance of adaptability in cross-cultural environments, where interpersonal and task-oriented expectations may differ significantly.

RQ2 How Are Romanian Leaders Perceived by Their Followers, in Terms of Status and Power Distance?

The analysis of hierarchical norms and power dynamics offers nuanced insights into the cultural dimensions of Romanian leadership.

(i) **Visible Status Markers**: Respondents expressed mixed attitudes toward the significance of visible status markers, such as office space and transportation perks. Approximately 36% agreed or strongly agreed that these symbols reflect leadership respect, while 28% disagreed. This suggests a divide between traditional hierarchical practices and modern multinational trends that prioritize meritocracy and skills over material markers.
(ii) **Formal Address**: The use of formal titles when addressing leaders remains prominent, with 59% of respondents frequently adhering to this norm. However, 31% stated that they rarely or never use formal titles, reflecting an emerging shift toward informality in global organisations and among younger professionals.
(iii) **Communication Preferences**: Indirect communication styles dominate Romanian leadership, with a mean score of 3.16 for delivering criticism subtly rather than directly. This preference aligns with broader cultural norms favouring harmony and minimizing public confrontation.
(iv) **Academic Titles**: The perceived importance of academic titles revealed a mean score of 4.34, reflecting moderate emphasis in professional contexts. Romanian responses aligned with countries like Bangladesh and Nepal, contrasting with flatter hierarchies in Sweden (2.44) and Norway (2.87). Qualitative responses highlighted a stronger valuation of academic credentials in traditional and public sector roles compared to modern or multinational organisations.

To further explore the findings related to followers' perceptions of status and power distance, Table 1 summarizes survey-derived mean scores for Romania and select comparative nations across key leadership variables, including formality in addressing leaders, respect for visible status indicators, and gender equality in leadership. Moreover, the table highlights areas of alignment and divergence in practices such as the use of formal titles, the importance of visible status indicators, and gender equality in leadership. These insights underscore Romania's nuanced position within global leadership paradigms, balancing traditional hierarchical norms with evolving preferences influenced by cross-cultural exposure.

RQ3 How Do Romanian Leadership Practices Align with or Diverge from Global Norms?

Table 1 Comparative analysis of leadership practices based on followers' perceptions

Survey question	Mean score for Romania	Top 3 Highest scores *(countries)*	Top 3 Lower scores *(countries)*	Sample scores for countries with High Romanian Expat Representation
Use of First Names	1,68	South Korea (1.09), Iran (1.21), Bangladesh (1.25)	Tunisia (1.68), Moldova (1.67), Sri Lanka (1.67)	Germany: 1.09, Netherlands: 1.21, Belgium: 1.63
Addressing Leaders by Titles	4,39	Norway (2.01), South Korea (4.66), Wales (2.19)	Georgia (4.40), Kazakhstan (4.37), Austria (4.42)	Italy: 2.05, Canada: 4.42, Austria: 4.13
Importance of Academic Titles	4,34	Sweden (2.44), Ethiopia (5.94), Faroe Islands (2.80)	Bangladesh (4.34), Nepal (4.32), Uruguay (4.36)	France: 3.48, USA: 3.97, Spain: 3.21
Respect via Visible Status Indicators	3,35	Afghanistan (4.56), North Cyprus (4.44), UAE (4.34)	Spain (3.33), Bolivia (3.38), Serbia (3.38)	Germany: 3.75, Netherlands: 3.42, Canada: 3.69
Indirect Criticism	3,16	Basque Country (1.93), UAE (4.38), South Korea (4.25)	Finland (3.16), North Cyprus (3.16), Trinidad & Tobago (3.17)	UK: 3.4, Belgium: 3.12, Austria: 3.69
Personal Distance	3,03	Afghanistan (4.56), North Cyprus (4.44), UAE (4.34)	Switzerland (3.05), Oman (3.01), Canada (3.05)	France: 3.07, Spain: 2.82, USA: 2.96
Gender Equality	4,53	South Korea (3.02), Italy (3.05), Philippines (5.91)	Malawi (4.53), Pakistan (4.54), Bahamas (4.54)	Italy: 3.05, Austria: 3.95, Canada: 4.63

Source The authors' own analysis

The cross-national survey data provided rich insights into how Romanian leadership practices align with or diverge from global norms. Six specific dimensions derived from the survey questions form the basis for this analysis, with Romania's scores serving as a baseline.

(i) *Use of First Names:* Romania's preference for formal communication is reflected in a mean score of 1.68 for comfort in addressing leaders by their first name. Comparatively, South Korea (1.09) and Iran (1.21) demonstrated even stronger adherence to formality. In contrast, the USA's score of 1.90 and Germany's 1.50 reflect more relaxed communication norms, while Tunisia (1.68) and Moldova (1.67) closely align with Romanian practices.

(ii) *Importance of Titles:* Romania's mean score of 4.39 for the importance of formal titles positions it closer to hierarchical societies like South Korea (4.66) and Afghanistan (4.51). Meanwhile, Germany (3.22) and the USA (3.47) reflect lower scores, signalling more egalitarian approaches.
(iii) *Status Symbols in Leadership:* Visible status indicators, such as office space and transportation perks, scored a mean of 3.35 in Romania. This places Romania between hierarchical contexts like Afghanistan (4.51) and egalitarian cultures like Norway (2.01). Countries like Spain (3.33) and Bolivia (3.38) displayed alignment with Romanian preferences, reflecting regional similarities.
(iv) *Indirect Communication:* Romania's score of 3.16 for indirect criticism illustrates a cultural balance between directness and subtlety. Higher scores in South Korea (4.25) and Afghanistan (4.20) emphasize indirectness, while the USA (3.03) and Italy (3.38) align moderately with Romanian practices.
(v) *Personal Distance:* Romanian leaders' preference for maintaining personal distance scored 3.03, reflecting a cautious approach to balancing respect and approachability. Similar scores were observed in Switzerland (3.05) and Oman (3.01), whereas Afghanistan (4.56) and North Cyprus (4.44) demonstrated stronger hierarchical preferences.
(vi) *Gender Equality*: The mean score of 4.53 for gender equality in leadership highlights Romania's transitional position, closely aligning with Pakistan (4.54) and Australia (4.54). By comparison, Germany (3.91) and Italy (3.05) reported lower scores, indicating ongoing challenges in achieving parity.

5 Discussion

This study provides an analysis of Romanian leadership traits, focusing on decision-making styles, hierarchical dynamics, and international positioning within leadership standards. By integrating survey data, qualitative insights, and comparative forest plot analyses, we explore Romania's unique leadership profile while addressing the research questions (RQs).

RQ1 Which Are the Dominant Traits of Romanian Leaders?

The findings highlight technical competence, organisational experience, and market expertise as the dominant leadership traits in Romania. The emphasis on practical, task-oriented leadership reflects a historical alignment with structured decision-making processes, particularly within traditional sectors such as state-owned enterprises. From a cultural perspective, Romania's task-oriented leadership mirrors German and Spanish approaches, as depicted in the heatmap. For example, the frequency of technical competence (61 mentions) and organisational experience (41 mentions) underscores Romanian leaders' preference for measurable results and structured authority. However, visionary and charismatic traits received fewer mentions, suggesting a focus on stability over innovation. These trends resonate with post-communist legacies that prioritize hierarchy, consistency, and clear chains of command (Nicolescu and Nicolescu 2020).

The generational divide further nuances the analysis. Younger Romanian leaders in multinational companies are increasingly adopting participative leadership styles influenced by globalisation and digital transformation. A shift that reflects an emerging duality in Romanian leadership—one rooted in traditional hierarchical norms but evolving in the direction of relational and participative approaches, particularly in the private-sector.

RQ2 How Are Romanian Leaders Perceived by Their Followers, in Terms of Status and Power Distance?

The forest plot analysis provides critical insights into hierarchical respect, decision-making preferences, and status perceptions. Romania's baseline score of 3.96 reflects moderate adaptability in decision-making, positioning it between highly rigid contexts like South Korea and participative systems like Sweden.

(i) *Hierarchical Respect:* Romania's mean score (4.39) for addressing leaders by formal titles aligns closely with other hierarchical societies such as Kazakhstan and Poland. The continued importance of titles and academic credentials (mean score: 4.34) reinforces Romanian organisational norms, particularly in public institutions and traditional sectors. These findings are consistent with Aioanei's (2006) description of Romania's enduring power distance.
(ii) *Status Markers and Communication:* The preference for indirect communication (mean score: 3.16) highlights Romanian leaders' emphasis on maintaining harmony within hierarchical structures. Visible markers of leadership status, such as office spaces and transportation perks, remain relevant but show variability across sectors. For instance, younger professionals in multinational companies prioritise merit-based recognition over material status indicators. These findings underscore a transitional phase in Romanian leadership, where traditional hierarchies coexist with evolving meritocratic and participative practices. This duality reflects Romania's broader socio-economic transformation and growing exposure to global leadership norms.

RQ3 How Do Romanian Leadership Practices Align with or Diverge from Global Norms?

The forest plot in Fig. 2 situates Romania's leadership practices within a global framework, providing actionable insights for Romanian professionals operating in cross-cultural environments. Key observations include:

Alignment with Germany and Spain: Romania's task-oriented leadership traits align with German and Spanish preferences, suggesting smoother cultural transitions for Romanian expatriates in these contexts. The structured, competency-driven focus shared by these countries highlights an emphasis on measurable performance and clear decision-making processes.

Contrasts with Sweden and South Korea: The stark divergence between Sweden's participative leadership (low decision-making rigidity) and South Korea's hierarchical approach underscores the challenges Romanian leaders may face in adapting to culturally distinct environments. For example, South Korea's higher rigidity reflects

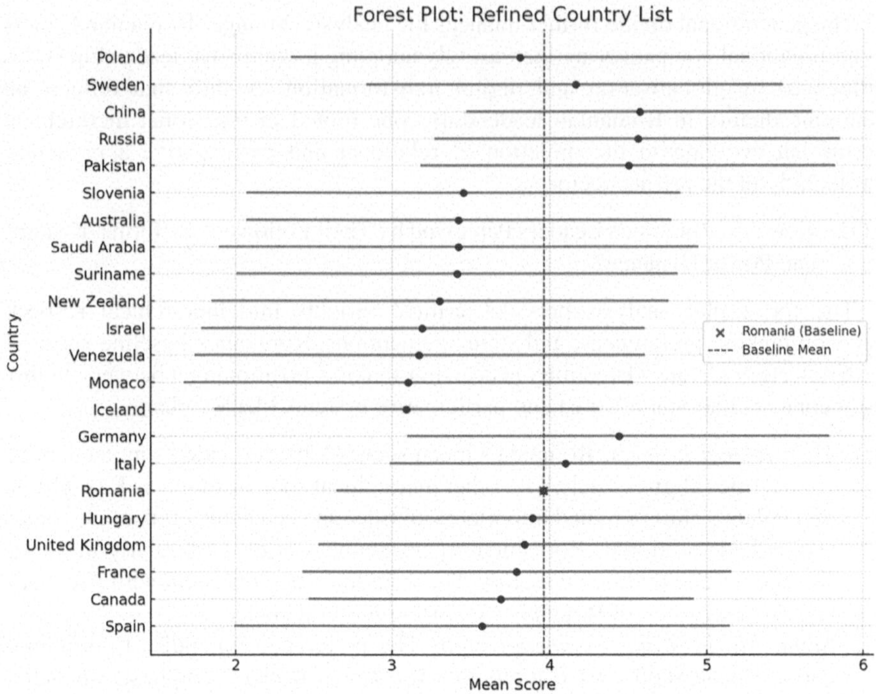

Fig. 2 Comparative analysis of decision-making adaptability across selected countries (*Source* the authors' contribution)

Confucian traditions that emphasise top-down decision-making, while Sweden prioritises egalitarian collaboration (Vrânceanu & Iorgulescu, 2016).

Regional Similarities: Countries like Poland and Hungary display leadership styles similar to Romania's, reflecting shared historical legacies and post-communist transitions. This regional alignment provides opportunities for cross-border collaboration and knowledge exchange among Eastern European leaders.

These insights highlight Romania's adaptive potential in global leadership contexts. The balance between hierarchical respect and emerging participative trends positions Romanian leaders uniquely, enabling them to navigate both traditional and modern professional environments effectively.

5.1 Visual Context: Forest Plot Integration

Figure 2 highlights Romania's baseline position relative to key expat destinations and cultural outliers, providing critical context for the discussion on Romanian leadership adaptability.

The forest plot visually reinforces the nuanced positioning of Romanian leadership, providing empirical support for the discussion. By comparing Romania's decision-making adaptability to other nations, the plot contextualises its standing within global leadership paradigms. The observed regional similarities and global divergences offer practical insights for Romanian professionals and organisations seeking to enhance cross-cultural leadership effectiveness.

5.2 Implications for practitioners and researchers

For practitioners, this study offers implementable frameworks for understanding Romanian leadership traits in domestic and international settings. The forest plot analysis provides comparative benchmarks that can guide Romanian expatriates in navigating cultural differences. For example, leaders transitioning to participative environments like Sweden or the Netherlands may benefit from fostering relational skills and decentralised decision-making.

For researchers, the findings underscore the need for further exploration of generational and sectoral differences in Romanian leadership. The duality between conventional standards and contemporary methodologies offers fertile ground for future studies on digital leadership, intersectoral comparisons, and the impact of globalisation on leadership transformations.

6 Conclusion

This research provides perspectives on Romanian leadership traits, focusing on decision-making adaptability, hierarchical dynamics, and their positioning within a global framework. The findings address the research questions and highlight Romania's distinctive leadership profile:

RQ1 Romanian leaders demonstrate a strong emphasis on technical competence, organisational experience, and market expertise, reflecting their task-oriented and structured decision-making preferences.

RQ2 Followers' perceptions of leadership reveal the enduring importance of hierarchical respect, formal titles, and indirect communication. These traditional norms coexist with emerging participative trends, particularly among younger professionals in the private sector.

RQ3 Comparative analysis shows Romania's alignment with Germany and Spain, while contrasting sharply with participative cultures like Sweden and rigid hierarchical contexts like South Korea. This highlights Romania's adaptive potential within diverse cultural environments.

The study makes several contributions to leadership research. By combining quantitative and qualitative data with forest plot visualisations, it provides an empirical basis for understanding Romania's evolving leadership landscape. The integration of cross-national comparisons offers actionable insights for practitioners, particularly Romanian expatriates navigating international leadership contexts. However, the study has certain limitations. The reliance on self-reported survey data may introduce response bias, and the sample size, though robust, may not fully capture sectoral or regional nuances. Future research could address these limitations by incorporating longitudinal data and expanding the sample to include underrepresented sectors, such as SMEs and digital startups.

Further directions include exploring the impact of digitalisation and generational shifts on Romanian leadership, as well as cross-sectoral analyses in multinational organisations. Investigating leadership dynamics in rapidly changing industries will provide deeper insights into how Romanian leaders adapt to global trends while preserving their cultural identity.

In conclusion, this study underscores Romania's leadership duality—balancing traditional hierarchical norms with modern participative practices. These findings contribute to the broader leadership literature and offer practical frameworks for enhancing leadership effectiveness in both digital domestic and global contexts.

References

Aioanei, I. (2006). Leadership in Romania. *Journal of Organizational Change Management, 19*(6), 705–712. https://doi.org/10.1108/09534810610708350

Alexandru, C. G., & Catana, D. (2010). Prospective Romanian Leaders' view on leadership dimensions. *Annals of Faculty of Economics, 1*(1), 645–650. https://ideas.repec.org/a/ora/journl/v1y2010i1p645-650.html

Alvarez, S. C., & Sahija, D. (2022). *A review of cross-cultural leadership and management in international projects.* Technoarete Transactions on Economics and Business Systems, 1(2), 23–28.

Braun, V., & Clarke, V. (2006). Using thematic analysis in psychology. *Qualitative Research in Psychology, 3*(2), 77–101.

Bryman, A. (2012). *Social research methods* (4th ed.). Oxford University Press.

Budrina, I. (2019). *Multiculturalism: United in diversity—A Romanian perspective.* Coresi Publishing House.

Catana, D., & Pucko, D. (2012). Prospective managers about cultural dimensions and Leadership Styles: A Comparison Between Romania and Slovenia. *Studia Universitatis Babes-Bolyai, 57*(3), 27–44.

Catana, D., Catana, A. G., Neal, M., & Finley, J. L. (2006). *Leadership authority and CEO motivations in Romania: Max Weber revisited.*

Crăciun, L., Năstase, M., Stamule, T., & Vizitiu, C. (2015). Leadership in Romanian small to medium enterprises. *Sustainability, 7*(4), 4183–4198. https://doi.org/10.3390/su7044183

Den Hartog, D. N., & De Hoogh, A. H. (2024). Cross-Cultural Leadership: What We Know, What We Need to Know, and Where We Need to Go. *Annual Review of Organizational Psychology and Organizational Behavior, 11*(1), 535–566.

Fein, E. C., Vasiliu, C., & Tziner, A. (2011). Individual values and preferred leadership behaviors: A study of Romanian managers. *Journal of Applied Social Psychology, 41*(3), 515–535. https://doi.org/10.1111/j.1559-1816.2010.00724.x

Gâf-Deac, I. (2019). The concept of Romanian management culture in the United European management model. *Contemporary Social Science: Journal of the Academy of Social Sciences, 4*, 1334–1340.

Guluță, M. C., & Rusu, C. (2016). Leadership styles and managerial behavior in Romanian companies. *Polish Journal of Management Studies, 13*(2), 69–80. https://doi.org/10.17512/pjms.2016.13.2.07

Hintea, C. (2015). Transformational leadership and performance in the Romanian public administration. *Revista de Cercetare si Interventie Sociala, 51*, 103–121. https://doi.org/10.1007/s11280-019-00738-2

House, R. J., Hanges, P. J., Javidan, M., Dorfman, P. W., & Gupta, V. (Eds.). (2004). *Culture, leadership, and organizations: The GLOBE study of 62 societies*. Sage.

Hurduzeu, R.-E. (2015). Culture and leadership: The case of Romania. *The Romanian Economic Journal, 18*(56), 119–134.

Ignat, S. (2024). Microsoft Teams Interview. 9 May.

International Organization for Migration (IOM). (2023). Migration and leadership dynamics: An analysis of expat trends. International Organization for Migration. https://romania.iom.int/

Javidan. M, Carolyn, P., Egri., Peter, W., Dorfman., Richard, G.H., Cotton., Medha, Satish, Kumar., Anirban, Kar., Amanda, Bullough. (2023). *The New GLOBE Leadership Model and Measures: Cross-Culturally Validated in 134 Countries/Societies*. Proceedings—Academy of Management, https://doi.org/10.5465/amproc.2023.15777symposium

Krishna Murthy, K. K., Khan, S., & Goel, O. (2024). *Leadership in technology: Strategies for effective global IT operations management*. Journal of Quantum Science and Technology, 1(3), 1–9. https://doi.org/10.36676/jqst.v1.i3.23

Landscape Report (2023). *Romania's Leadership Landscape*. KPMG Romania.

Lifintsev, D., & Wellbrock, W. (2019). *Cross-cultural communication in the digital age*. Estudos em Comunicação, 28(1), 93–104. https://doi.org/10.25768/fal.ec.n28.a05

Littrell, R. F., & Valentin, L. N. (2005). Preferred leadership behaviours: Exploratory results from Romania, Germany, and the UK. *Journal of Management Development, 24*(5), 421–442. https://doi.org/10.1108/02621710510598445

Lupu, Dr. Prof. C. (2022, November 2). *Interview Prof. Dr. Lupu on How Romanians characterize leaders* (J. Imansoeradi & E. Beukers, Interviewers) [Personal communication].

Marius, Constantin, Guluta., Costache, Rusu. (2016). *Leadership styles and managerial behavior in Romanian companies. Polish journal of management studies*, https://doi.org/10.17512/PJMS.2016.13.2.07

Mihai, L. (2016). The particularities of the leadership styles in Romanian organisations. *Annals of the University of Craiova, Economic Sciences Series, 14*(2), 579–587.

Mihai, L. (2024). Microsoft Teams interview. 9 May.

Moldovan, O., & Macarie, F. C. (2016). Organizational culture in public administration: A comparative analysis. *Revista Transilvană de Ştiinţe Administrative, 2*(39), 123–139.

Neculăesei, A., & Tătăruşanu, M. (2008). Romania–cultural and regional Differences. *Scientific Annals of the Alexandru Ioan Cuza University of Iasi LV*, 198–204.

Nicolescu, O., & Nicolescu, C. (2020). The dynamics of the Romanian national management strengths and weakness between 2009 and 2018. *The Best Romanian Management Studies, 2017–2018*, 1.

O. Nicolescu et al. (eds.), *Romanian Management Theory and Practice*, Contributions to Management Science. https://doi.org/10.1007/978-3-031-60343-3_13

Ogarcă, R. F., Crăciun, L., & Mihai, L. (2016). Leadership styles in smes: an exploratory study in Romania. *Directory of Open Access Journals*. https://doaj.org/article/7e9ea4d1cbf14d788bf57de83c5acff1

Onea Angelica-Nicoleta (2011), *Diversitatea culturală în management. O abordare regională*, Iaşi, Editura Universităţii „Alexandru Ioan Cuza".

Peter, T., van, den, Berg. (2020). *Comparing the cultures of Romania and the Netherlands: When East meets West*. https://doi.org/10.24837/PRU.2010.2.302

Schühly, A. M. (2022). The influence of culture on strategic management and its processes. In: A. M. Schühly (Ed.), *Cultural influences on the process of strategic management: Using scenario planning for decision making in multinational corporations, MIR series in international business* (pp. 137–237). Springer. https://doi.org/10.1007/978-3-030-86660-0_3
Ţiclău, T., & Hinţea, C. (2016). Public sector leadership: A review of Romanian research done in the field between 2007–2016. *Transylvanian Review of Administrative Sciences, Special Issue*, 91–101. https://doi.org/10.1007/s11280-019-00738-2
Ulrich, K., Rodríguez-García, M., Gallego-Nicholls, J. F., & Pagán-Castaño, E. (2021). Family Council From A Cultural Approach: the case of eastern european countries. *KnE Social Sciences.*, pp.116–125. https://doi.org/10.18502/kss.v5i9.9889
Urbach T, Den Hartog DN, Fay D, Parker SK, Strauss K. 2021. Cultural variations in whether, why, how, and at what cost people are proactive: a followership perspective. *Organ. Psychol. Rev.* 11(1):3–34
Văduva, S. (2016). *Between globalization and integration: The Europeanization of Romania.* Springer International Publishing. https://doi.org/10.1007/978-3-319-27009-8
Vaduva, S. (2016). *From corruption to modernity—The evolution of Romania's entrepreneurship.* https://doi.org/10.1007/978-3-319-26997-9
Văduva, S., Prisac, I., & Lîsîi, A. (2025). The particularities of Romanian management. In O. Nicolescu et al. (Eds.), *Romanian Management Theory and Practice* (pp. 211–219). Springer. https://doi.org/10.1007/978-3-031-60343-3_13
Vrânceanu, C. A., & Iorgulescu, M.-C. (2016). A look at Hofstede's cultural dimensions in two service sectors from Romania. *Amfiteatru Economic Journal, 18*, 875–884.
Zaiţ D., (coord.) (2002), *Management intercultural. Valorizarea diferenţelor culturale*, Bucureşti, Editura Economică.
Zait, D., & Zait, A. (2016). Issues of organizational culture in Romania—A case study. *Review of Economic and Business Studies, 9*, 253. https://doi.org/10.1515/rebs-2016-0043

Leveraging Digital Tools and Artificial Intelligence for Optimizing Organizational Processes and Decision-Making: A Bibliometric Analysis

Laurențiu Mihai, Cătălina Sitnikov, Mirela Sichigea, Laura Vasilescu, Anca Băndoi, and Leonardo-Geo Mănescu

Abstract The integration of digital tools, including Artificial Intelligence (AI), is reshaping organizational processes and decision-making within businesses. This bibliometric study investigates the scientific literature related to the use of digital tools, AI, and software solutions in optimizing organizational processes and decision-making, analyzing a dataset of 1,204 peer-reviewed articles from the Web of Science database, published between 2020 and 2024. The study focuses on publications that explore how businesses utilize digital innovations to streamline operations, enhance decision-making processes, and improve overall management efficiency. The research query was designed to capture articles addressing the application of AI, software tools, and digital technologies in business contexts, particularly in process optimization and decision-making frameworks. The analysis employs tools like VOSviewer, Bibliometrix in RStudio, and Microsoft Excel to map the key trends, authors, influential publications, collaborative networks, and thematic clusters within this domain. Initial findings reveal a strong concentration of research interest in AI

L. Mihai (✉) · C. Sitnikov · M. Sichigea · L. Vasilescu · A. Băndoi
Faculty of Economics and Business Administration, University of Craiova, Craiova, Romania
e-mail: laurentiu.mihai@edu.ucv.ro

C. Sitnikov
e-mail: catalina.sitnikov@edu.ucv.ro

M. Sichigea
e-mail: mirela.sichigea@edu.ucv.ro

L. Vasilescu
e-mail: laura.vasilescu@edu.ucv.ro

A. Băndoi
e-mail: anca.bandoi@edu.ucv.ro

L.-G. Mănescu
Faculty of Electrical Engineering, University of Craiova, Craiova, Romania
e-mail: leonardo.manescu@incesa.ro

S. O. Idowu et al. (eds.), *Competitiveness and Sustainability in the Digitization Era*, Springer Proceedings in Business and Economics,
https://doi.org/10.1007/978-3-031-91778-3_7

applications in decision-making, with emerging trends indicating a growing focus on digital tools for process optimization across various industries. The study highlights key areas of advancement, as well as gaps in the literature, offering insights for future research directions. Furthermore, the research identifies the most prolific authors, influential journals, and notable international collaborations, providing a comprehensive overview of the academic landscape in this field. This study offers a valuable reference for both academics and practitioners, emphasizing the critical role that AI and digital technologies play in enhancing organizational effectiveness and guiding managerial decisions in a data-driven era.

Keywords Digital tools · Artificial Intelligence (AI) · Organizational processes · Decision-making · Bibliometric analysis

1 Introduction

The rapid transformation of the digital environment presents both opportunities and challenges for businesses. Emerging digital technologies, such as social media, IoT, cloud computing, and big data, are revolutionizing traditional business models, enabling companies to innovate and optimize processes at an unprecedented pace. Leading companies actively respond to customer and market changes by adopting digital technology capabilities, maintaining corporate earnings increase and competitive edge, and creating sustainable business competitiveness through persistent efficiency improvement. Companies nowadays are developing business models in which producers and consumers are connected with networks and the platform ecosystem based on data-centered technological capabilities in the conventional business model through technology-based digital transformation (Kim and Kim 2022).

Artificial Intelligence (AI) is at the forefront of this transformation, offering capabilities that extend beyond traditional computing. AI systems can perform tasks requiring human intelligence, such as decision-making and predictive analytics, empowering businesses to harness massive volumes of data. The integration of AI into decision-making processes allows organizations to evaluate complex scenarios, improve operational efficiency, and maintain a competitive edge in dynamic markets. AI has evolved from theoretical constructs to practical applications, playing a significant role in enabling organizations to achieve operational excellence and strategic agility.

AI technologies, including machine learning, neural networks, deep learning, and swarm intelligence, have demonstrated their versatility across different business processes. For example, AI-powered natural language processing and computer vision are transforming customer service and quality control, respectively. In healthcare, predictive models assist in diagnosing diseases, while in manufacturing, AI-driven automation improves production efficiency. In supply chain management, AI helps optimize logistics networks and forecast demand with unprecedented accuracy. These advancements not only enhance business agility but also foster innovation by uncovering novel approaches to problem-solving. Such applications underscore the potential of AI to act as a transformative agent across industries, from logistics and finance to marketing and beyond.

The current paper consists of a bibliometric analysis of the scientific literature regarding the use of AI in improving business processes and decisions, aiming to map the evolution of AI use in business over to time in order to identify major breakthroughs, emerging trends and gaps in the literature. Moreover, in this paper, we will identify they key research themes on this topic, categorizing and clustering topics where AI is most effectively used in business, such as supply chain management, customer relationship management (CRM), decision support systems, and process automation. Last but not least, the paper seeks to study the scholarly impact of the research papers published on this topic after 2020, in order to identify to most influential studies, authors, institutions and journals, as well as the regional and institutional collaborations networks.

After this introduction, the paper is structured as follows: the second section is a critical literature review of the most relevant studies on the use of AI in business process and decision optimization, followed by a third section which details the methodological approach of this paper, highlighting the search query, the refining process using exclusion and inclusion criteria as well as the analysis techniques. In the second part of the paper, we will present and discuss the results of our analysis, the paper ending with a section that presents our concluding remarks, the theoretical and practical implications as well as the study's limitations and suggestions for future research directions.

2 Literature Review

In the digital era, in order to gain a competitive edge, many firms are leveraging new digital technologies, with Artificial Intelligence (AI) emerging as a pivotal innovation (Akhtar et al. 2019). AI refers to a machine's ability to learn from experience, adapt to new inputs, and perform tasks traditionally requiring human intelligence. Several authors highlight AI's technology as a disruptive force capable of, fostering human creativity by enabling the exploration of new approaches to developing products, services, processes, and business models (Duan et al. 2019; Haan and Watts 2023; Lichtenhaler 2020). It enhances innovation, operational agility, and strategic decision-making, equipping firms with a competitive advantage in an ever-evolving global market (OECD 2022).

Moreover, other authors argue that AI can support businesses in developing strategies for entering international markets, providing critical insights into political, economic, legal, and regulatory environments, as well as market, industry, and competitor data (Menzies et al. 2024; Hughes 2023). Similarly, Neubert and Van Der Krogt (2018) highlighted how AI algorithms can forecast the future appeal of foreign markets, helping lean global companies make more accurate market selection decisions and identify opportunities for long-term growth. Beyond strategy development, AI is expected to drive productivity gains, foster economic growth, and create new opportunities in international trade. It encourages businesses to engage with an expansive global network of loosely connected external communities through digital platforms, partnerships, crowdsourcing, international freelancers, and open-source ecosystems (Nambisan and Luo 2022).

Moreover, according to Visinescu et al. (2017), AI can enhance efficiency across various manufacturing processes, including production, quality control, packaging, warehousing, and transportation, by providing valuable analytical insights. For instance, Lee et al. (2014) used machine learning to predict parameters of the Bass model before introducing a new product, demonstrating its superiority over traditional methods. Similarly, Li et al. (2015) employed data mining and machine learning to analyze limited experimental data for new products prior to mass manufacturing, highlighting AI's analytical precision.

AI's role extends beyond manufacturing to broader organizational processes. Borges et al. (2009) emphasized the importance of novel internet-based technologies in optimizing production and distribution processes. Spanaki et al. (2022) explored the transformative impact of disruptive AI technologies on agricultural operations, while Grover et al. (2022) found that AI and data analytics are driving new requirements for oil and electricity in sectors such as manufacturing, product development, and supply chain management.

Furthermore, AI technology has become deeply integrated into corporate networks, transforming data processing methodologies across devices and applications. This integration often necessitates modifications to business models, as well as changes in automation and operating systems (Kim and Kim 2022). Companies are leveraging AI not only to digitize analog information or digitalize existing processes but to drive digital transformation by reimagining organizational management and operations (Reis et al. 2018). These efforts aim to deliver corporate value, generate profits, and enhance efficiency through innovative strategies. Moreover, Li et al. (2015) identified several applications for AI in an organizational setting, including customer behavioral scoring for financial institutions, predictive process control to enhance product quality for manufacturers, security management in airlines, risk-controlled investment management, and stock price forecasting.

In their literature review, Kitsios and Kamariotou (2021) identified several applications for AI in business: enhancing corporate strategy through predictive analytics; employing image recognition to discern consumer behavior; selecting optimal IT infrastructure design plans effectively developing decision support systems; enhancing innovation capacity; mitigating specific challenges related to product attributes and machine functionalities and improving product quality while augmenting business performance.

Moving on, Toorajipour et al. (2021) highlighted the use of various AI technologies in supply chain management, including artificial neural networks, fuzzy logic, genetic algorithms, and data mining. Among these, artificial neural networks are the most widely utilized method for information processing and pattern recognition.

They have diverse applications across different business processes, such as sales forecasting, decision support systems, and customer segmentation. Similarly, Al-Surmi et al. (2022) examined the strategic alignment between marketing and digital initiatives, proposing a decision-making framework to enhance operational performance based on a unique model integrating artificial neural network) into a decision-making framework.

Machine learning (ML), a subset of AI, is widely applied in manufacturing optimization, according to Buchmeister et al. (2019) and Zhou et al. (2018) who emphasize its applications in smart manufacturing. ML techniques enable the comparison of actual and projected data, helping decision-makers uncover hidden relationships among processes, products, workflow patterns, and deviations from desired outcomes. Kang et al. (2020) note that ML methods are commonly employed in production optimization to enhance output quality, while reinforcement learning and deep learning are increasingly used in scheduling. Moreover, according to Messner (2022) beyond manufacturing, ML applications can support market and cultural segmentation, offering insights that go beyond simply selecting suitable countries for business operations (Messner 2022).

3 Methodology

This paper aims to realize a bibliometric mapping of the scientific production that has been published since 2020, regarding the use of artificial intelligence for improving business processes and decisions. In order to fulfil this aim, the paper is structured on two main research questions:

RQ1 To what degree is the use of AI for optimizing business processes and decisions represented in the scientific literature published since 2020?

RQ2 How is the research on the use of AI for optimizing business processes and decisions structured from a conceptual point of view?

In order to achieve the proposed objectives and to formulate relevant answers to the research questions, we have decided to use bibliometric analysis as the research method, as it as it facilitates the analysis of extensive scientific data and yields significant research effects (Donthu et al. 2021; Brabete et al. 2024). Moreover, the literature has shown that a bibliometric analysis, as opposed to conventional qualitative reviews, are able to reduce the subjectivity and bias of reviewers (Vogel and Güttel, 2012), hence lowering human error and bias in the literature review process (van Oorschot et al. 2018). In this regard, our methodology adhered to the two primary aspects characteristic of bibliometric analyses, namely performance analysis (RQ1) and scientific mapping (RQ2) (Donthu et al. 2021).

After choosing the research method, we proceeded to the data collection phase. In this phase, we decided to use Web of Science as the main academic database, since, in our opinion, it is the most comprehensive scientific database, and it is frequently used in literature reviews and bibliometric analyses (Liu 2019). Moreover, Brabete et al. (2024) as well as Puenete et al. (2024) have shown that Web of Science provides pertinent statistics on various types of papers, journals, scientific categories, authors, affiliations, and lists references, thus enabling researchers to efficiently search, filter, and download relevant scientific articles' records.

The quality of the results of a literature review or bibliometric analysis is largely depended on the quality of the records used in the analysis and thus, we tried to come up with a comprehensive query syntax that would cover all the relevant topics related to the use of AI for business process optimization. In order to select the relevant keywords that would make up the query, we did a preliminary analysis of the scientific literature in this field, which was followed up by an internal debate.

Following these steps, we used the following query to search the Web of Science Database: ((TS = "business" AND TS = "decision") OR (TS = "management" AND TS = "Decision") OR TS = "Decision making process" OR (TS = "business" AND TS = "process") OR (TS = "organizational" AND TS = "process") OR (TS = "business process" OR TS = "organizational process") AND (TS = "digital tool" OR TS = "AI" OR TS = "Artificial Intelligence" OR "Software" OR "Computer program"). Based on this query, on 25.09.2024, Web of Science returned 22.180 results. In order to further refine the query, we have employed several inclusion or exclusion criteria:

- Document types: Open Access Articles, Review Article (N = 8.704);
- Publication Year: 2020, 2021, 2022, 2023, 2024 (N = 5.713);
- Web of Science Categories: Computer Science Information Systems, Management, Business, Operations Research Management Science, Economics, Business Finance (N = 1.296)
- Language: English (N = 1.275)
- Automatic exclusion criteria: early access, retracted publications (N = 1.269)
- Manual Exclusion criteria: we have excluded all the papers that have been published in medical, computer programming, machine learning, agriculture or engineering related journals (N = 1.204).

After we have reached the final sample of 1.204 papers, we proceeded to download, process and analyze the data and visualize and discuss the results. Thus, we have downloaded the full Web of Science records (title, authors, affiliation, source, publication year, keywords, abstract, times cited and Web of Science category) including the cited references, in Excel, BibText and Tab Delimited File formats. In order to process, analyze and visualize the data we have employed Microsoft Excel, Bibliometrix R-Package and VOSViewer, which are the industry standard software for bibliometric and scientometric analysis (Aria and Cuccurullo 2017; Brabete et al. 2024; Puente et al. 2024). Several authors (Brabete et al. 2024; Van Eck and Waltman 2010) have shown that combining MS Excel with Bibliometrix and with VOSViewer yields a more comprehensive bibliometric analysis with more relevant results than using either software on its own.

The last phase of our study involved discussing the results obtained through our analysis and establishing a set of conclusions and recommendations for future research. The analysis of the data acquired in the previous phase facilitated discussions that enabled us to formulate significant responses to the study questions and important findings.

4 Results and Discussion

4.1 Descriptive Statistics

In order to examine to what degree is the use of AI for business process and decision optimization, represented in the scientific literature published since 2020, we began our research endeavor with a scientific literature performance analysis.

As it can be seen in Table 1, our research is focused on 1.204 eligble documents, published between 2020 and 2024 in 344 different journals, with an yearly average growth rate of 23,07%, which shows a constant increase in the scholar's interest regarding the use of AI for business process and decision optimization. Moreover, the papers included in our sample have an average of 14,34 citations per document, with almost 80.000 references, while using 4758 keywords (as defined by the authors), all of these showing that the use of AI for business process and decision optimization is a complex, but thoroughly researched issue. Furthermore, our research includes 4904 authors, out of which, 73 are authors of 74 single-authored documents, while, on average, each paper has 4,47 authors and a little less than half (42,52%) of the 1.204 documents have international co-authorships. These statistics also show the complexity of the subject and at the same time, the need for international collaboration in order to thoroughly research this topic. Last, but not least, our research has shown, that out of the 1.204 documents, 1.079 are research article, while 125 are literature reviews.

Looking at Fig. 1, we can see a clear positive trend regarding the number of papers published each on the use of AI for organizational process and decision optimization and at the same time, even if the search has been conducted at the end of September, 2024 is already the most prolific year from this point of view. In our opinion, the reason for this increased interest on the subject is the fact, that starting with 2020, more and more companies allowed their employees to work remotely and thus, the use of AI, including Artificial Intelligence, for the optimization of various business processes and decision has become imperative.

An additional analytical element, correlated with the yearly scientific production, is the average citation count, encompassing two dimensions: the average citations/paper and the average citations/year. As we can see in Table 2, 2021, the second to last from the scientific production point of view, was the most cited year with almost 6.915 citations, while averaging almost 8 citations/year, the most of the 5 years that were included in this analysis. At the same time, 2020, which has the lowest scientific production, has registered the highest average citations/paper count, with a value of 34,01. The fact that both the average citations/paper and the average citations/year

Table 1 Descriptive statistics

Description	Results	Description	Results
GENERAL INFORMATION		AUTHORS COLLABORATION	
Timespan	2020–2024	Single-authored docs	74
Sources (journals, books etc.)	344	Co-Authors per Doc	4,47
Documents	1204	International co-authorships %	42,52
Annual Growth Rate %	23,07	DOCUMENT TYPES	
Document Average Age	1,66	article	1079
Average citations per doc	14,34	review	125
References	78.976		
DOCUMENT CONTENTS			
Keywords Plus	2006		
Author's Keywords	4768		
AUTHORS			
Authors	4904		
Authors of single-authored docs	73		

Source The authors' own analysis, using bibliometrix

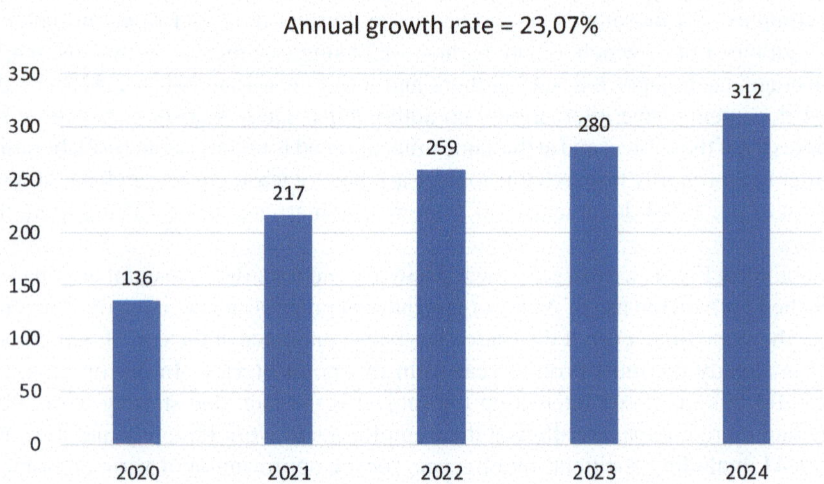

Fig. 1 Yearly scientific production (*Source* The authors' own analysis, using MS Excel)

are registering a downward trend doesn't mean that scholars are losing their interest towards this subject as time passes, but can be explained from a purely objective reason: both indicators are heavily influenced by the total number of citations, which accumulates and grows as the years are passing and thus is to be expected that more recent papers to have a lower citation count and, at the same time, by the number of

Table 2 Average number of citations

Publication year	No. of papers	Citations	Average citations/paper	Citable years	Average citations/year
2020	136	4626	34,01	5	6,80
2021	217	6915	31,87	4	7,97
2022	259	3504	13,53	3	4,51
2023	280	2227	7,95	2	3,98
2024	312	667	2,14	1	2,14

Source The authors' own analysis, using Bibliometrix

papers, which, due to the ever increasing scientific interest in this subject is growing steadily by the year.

4.2 *Authors' and Journals' Bibliographic Mapping*

In Table 3, we can see first ten journals that have published the most papers in the field of the use of AI for business process and decision optimization, 446 out of the total of 1.204 (37%). Thus, we can see that the most prolific journal, by far is IEEE Access with 219 papers, more than four times as many papers as the second journal, Electronics, accounting for almost half of the papers published in the first 10 journals. Analyzing the general topics of the top ten journals, we can see that there are only two who focus solely on business or management, while the rest have a much wider scope, covering both IT and business and in some cases, even sociology. This large array of subjects covered by the top ten journals highlights the complexity and the multidisciplinary nature of the topic at hand.

Moving on to Fig. 2, we can observe the scholars that have authored the most papers in the field of using AI for improving business or organizational processes and decisions. For the 5 years that were included in our study, we can see Kumar, A. as the most productive author, with 12 papers, closely followed by Liu, Y with 10 papers and Li, J with 8 published papers on this subject. Moreover, we can see, that in the second half of this ranking, the last six authors are sharing the last two places, with 5 or 6 published papers on this topic.

Figure 3 is showcasing how the top ten authors' production has evolved over time. Thus, we see that Kumar, A., the most prolific author on this topic, has published 3 papers in 2021, 4 papers in 2022 and 2023 and 1 paper in the first three quarters of 2024, while the second most productive author, Liu, Y. has started publishing on this subject only in 2022, when they published 4 papers, same as 2023, while in the first three quarters of 2024, they published only one paper. Furthermore, Li, Y, the third ranking author in terms of scientific production, has an interesting linear evolution, publishing at least one paper every year from 2020 to 2024, with 2022 being his most prolific year with 4 published papers. Along with Li, J., out of the first 10 authors,

Table 3 Top ten journals

Rank	Journal	No. of Papers
1	IEEE Access	219
2	Electronics	53
3	Information	35
4	CMC - Computers, Materials and Continua	32
5	Expert sytems with applications	22
6	Journal of Business Research	20
7	Technological forecasting and social change	18
8	International Journal of production research	17
9	Frontiers in artificial intelligence	17
10	Wireless communications and mobile computing	13

Source The authors' own analysis

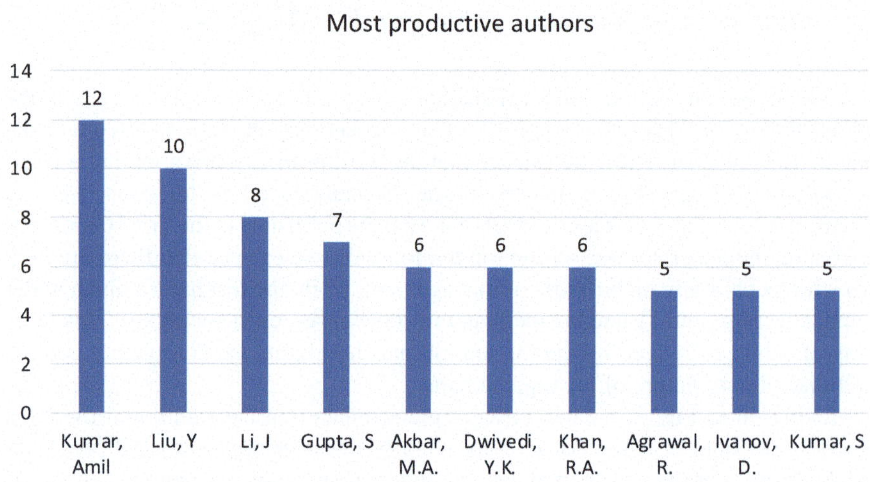

Fig. 2 Most productive authors (*Source* The authors' own analysis in MS Excel)

only one other, Ivanov, D. managed to publish at least one paper every year, on this subject. Overall, for the first 10 most productive authors, 2022 has been the most prolific year (as opposed to 2024, which is already the most productive year if we consider all the 1.204 papers included in our study) with 22 published papers, in which all but two authors from the top ten have published at least one paper.

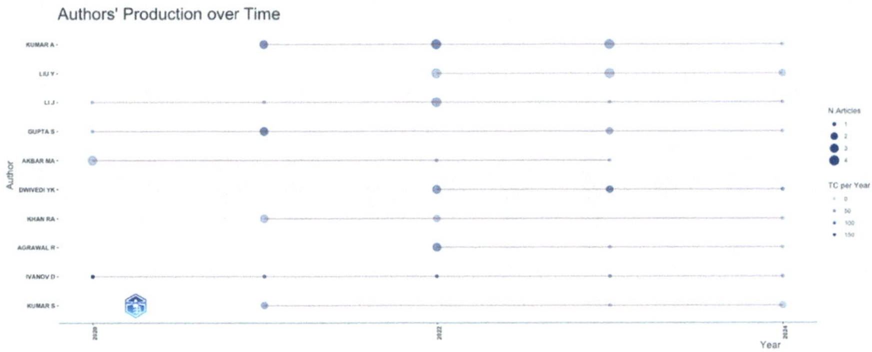

Fig. 3 Authors' production over time (*Source* The authors' own analysis, Bibliometrix)

4.3 Affiliation Bibliographic Mapping

The next part of our bibliographic analysis is focusing on the affiliation of the authors who have published papers on the topic of using AI for improving organizational processes and decisions. We have focused our bibliographic mapping of the authors' affiliation on two variables, the academic institution, and the country of origin, which allowed us to analyze the inter-institutional and/or multinational collaborations that were the basis of the scientific production this field.

Figure 4 is showing us the higher learning institutions, which, through affiliated authors, have published the most papers on topics related to the use of AI for improving organizational processes and decisions. We can see King Saud University from Saudi Arabia as the most productive institution in this field, with 31 papers published between 2020 and 2024, followed by Norwegian Science and Technology University—Norway and Prince Sattam bin Abdulaziz University—Saudi Arabia, both with 25 papers and Universitat Politecnica De Valencia—Spain with 18 papers. In the lower half of this ranking, we find 5 different universities, each with 16 papers: Aston University—England, Umm al-Qura University—Saudi Arabia, University of Craiova—Romania, Universiti Kebangsaan—Malaysia and University of Seville—Spain and one institution with 15 papers—Neoma Business School. Thus, we can see that Saudi Arabia has 3 universities in the top ten most productive institutions in this field of research, followed by Spain with two and Romania, England, Malaysia, Norway, and France with one higher learning institution each.

Moving on, Fig. 5 is highlighting the global distribution of the scientific production in the field of using AI for business process and decision optimization. Thus, we can see an almost global interest in this subject, with few exceptions: Greenland, Iceland, Belarus and Georgia in Europe, Kazakhstan, Mongolia, Myanmar, Laos, Cambodgia, North Korea, the Phillipines and Papua New Guinea in Asia, several countries in Easter, Central and South-Eastern Africa, Central America and the Caribbean island countries as well as Guyana, Surinam, French Guyana, Bolivia and Paraguay. Besides the global distribution of scientific production, Fig. 5 is also

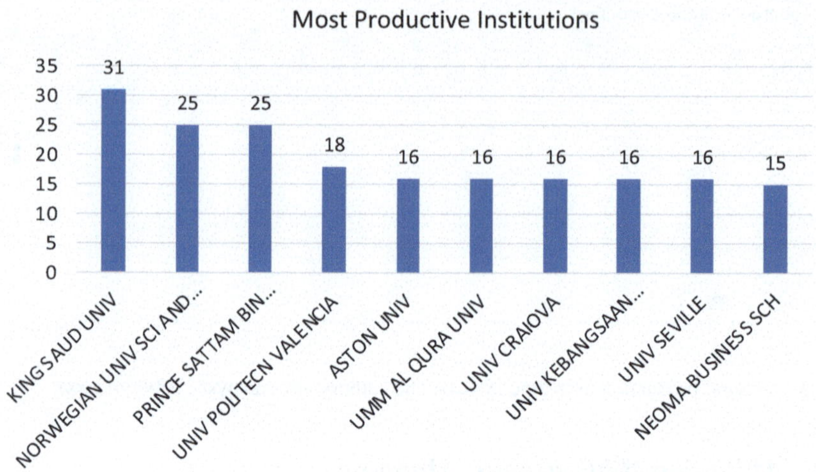

Fig. 4 Most productive institutions (*Source* The authors' own analysis in MS Excel)

highlighting each country's scientific output size, darker shades of blue meaning larger scientific productions.

Similar to Fig. 5, Table 4 is highlighting the top ten countries according to their scientific production on the subject of using AI for business processes or decision optimization. Thus, we can see that China is the most productive country, with 118 papers published on this subject (9,8% of the total published), out of each 84 were single country publications and 34 papers were published as a result of a international collaboration. Closely behind China, we can see the UK with 102 papers published (8,5% of the total papers included in our sample) on this topic, out of which 62 papers (60,8%) were published as a result of an international collaboration between multiple

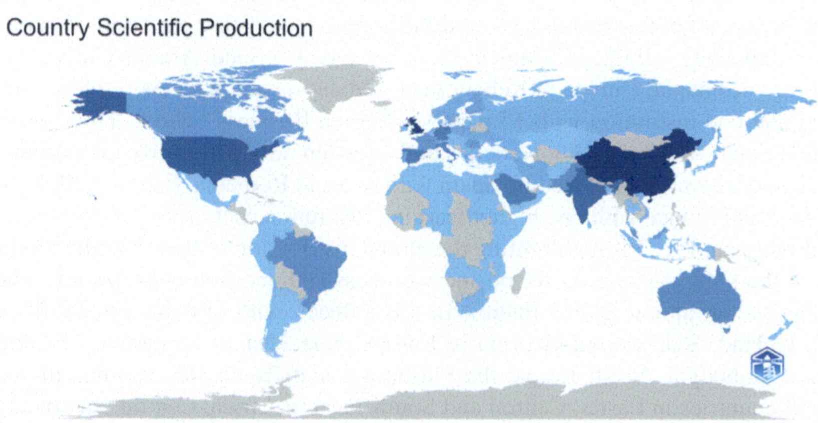

Fig. 5 Global distribution of scientific production (*Source* The authors' own analysis, Bibliometrix)

Table 4 Scientific production ranking, by country

Country	Articles, by corresponding author - value -	Articles, by corresponding author - % -	Single Country Publications	Multiple country publications - value -	Multiple country publications - % -
CHINA	118	9,8	84	34	28,8
UNITED KINGDOM	102	8,5	40	62	60,8
USA	62	5,1	48	14	22,6
GERMANY	54	4,5	37	17	31,5
INDIA	54	4,5	34	20	37
SPAIN	48	4	38	10	20,8
SOUTH KOREA	43	3,6	23	20	46,5
BRAZIL	40	3,3	29	11	27,5
ITALY	39	3,2	27	12	30,8
SAUDI ARABIA	35	2,9	14	21	60

Source The authors' own analysis with Bibliometrix

authors. From the point of view of the international collaborations, the UK is, by far, the leader with 60% of its papers being published as a result of an international collaboration, closely followed by Saudi Arabia with 60% and South Korea with 45,5%.

4.4 *Content Analysis of the Research Regarding the Use of AI for Business Process and Decision Optimization*

In order to answer the second research quest and identify the social, intellectual and conceptual structure of the research on the use of AI for business process and decision optimization, we continue our study with a content analysis of the scientific literature. This content analysis is primarily done by studying the co-occurrence of different author keywords, which allowed us to identify the main sub-topics of this field, how well were these sub-topics researched until the last quarter of 2024 and predict how will the research in this field evolve in the future (Donthu et al. 2021).

In this regard, we should observe Fig. 6 which shows which are the most used author keywords: "artificial intelligence" (19%), "machine learning" (10%), "decision making" (4%), "software" (3%), "management" (3%) and many others. This figure shows the complexity of the topic at hand, highlighting its multi-disciplinary nature, as most of the frequently used keywords are either related to business/ management or to computer science and technology.

Fig. 6 Keywords distribution (*Source* The authors' own analysis, Bibliometrix)

Moving on to Fig. 7, we can observe a word cloud highlighting the most used words in the abstracts of the 1.204 papers that have been included in this study. Thus, we can see that words like "management", "data", "research", "business", "decision", "study", or "process" frequently appear in the abstracts, highlighting the thematic focus of our dataset. Moreover, we can see words such as "ai", "artificial", "software", "system" or "technology" which signal the types of AI emphasized across studies. Another interesting conclusion that we can draw from Fig. 7 is the prevalence of terms as "research", "study" or "model", which means that most of the research on this topic is rather theoretical in nature, highlighting the need for more practical oriented future studies.

In a co-occurrence analysis, it is essential to identify the relationships among the analyzed elements, specifically the keywords, and to accurately interpret the significance of these connections. Therefore, the examination of the conceptual structure must be further enhanced through cluster analysis (Brabete et al. 2024). Bibliometrix is a powerful tool for this type of cluster analysis, being able to group the keywords into four categories: niche topics, motor themes, basic themes and emerging or declining topics (Puente et al. 2024; Brabete et al. 2024).

In this regard, we should observe Fig. 8 which represents the authors' keywords thematic map, which uses two dimensions, development degree (density) and relevance degree (centrality), grouping the keywords in the four above mentioned clusters. This map provides a structured view of the focus areas and emerging trends in the use of AI for business optimization, with motor and basic themes driving the

Fig. 7 Occurrence word cloud for abstracts (*Source* The authors' own analysis, Bibliometrix)

field, niche themes providing specialized insights, and emerging themes hinting at possible future directions.

From the thematic map, we can observe in the niche themes category we can find three groups of keywords "chat gpt, generative AI", "bibliometric analysis,

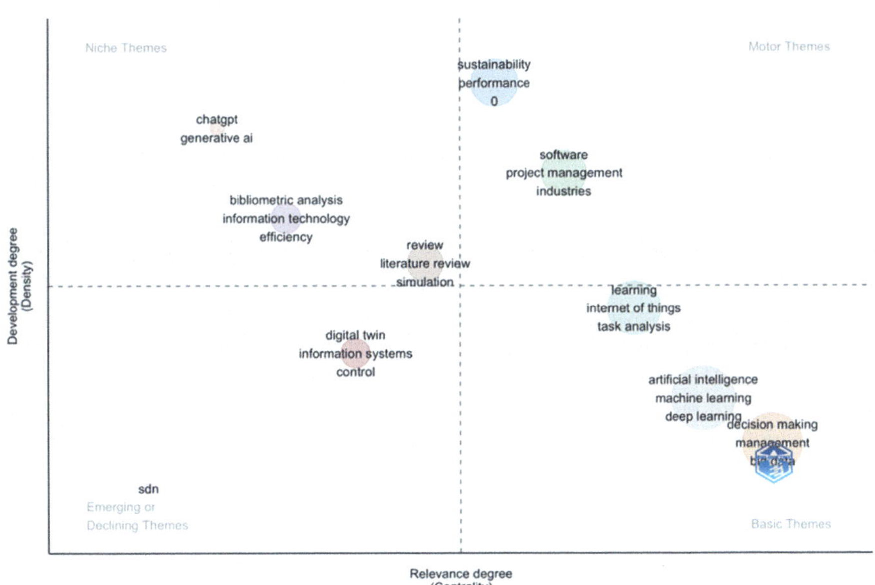

Fig. 8 Authors' keywords thematic map (*Source* The authors' own analysis, generated by Bibliometrix)

information technology", efficiency" and "review, literature review and simulation". According to Brabete et al. (2024), the niche theme cluster focuses on certain subjects, concentrate on a wider academic discipline, receive less attention or fewer citations compared to more contemporary themes, yet may be crucial for the advancement of knowledge in a given area of interest. For instance, the rise of generative AI and tools like ChatGPT highlights the increasing relevance of AI-driven conversational agents in business contexts, albeit as a focused area. Meanwhile, bibliometric analysis and literature reviews provide structured insights into the field, serving as meta-level research approaches for understanding developments in digital optimization. Though these topics receive less attention overall, their relevance to developing deeper, targeted insights may prove crucial as the field evolves, thus proving the novel aspect of our own research.

The second quadrant represents the motor themes and includes two groups of keywords "sustainability, performance" and "software, project management, industries". Brabete et al. (2024) states that motor themes refer to critical subjects or notions within a research domain, attract considerable attention, produce a substantial quantity of publications, and exert a profound influence on the field of study. "Sustainability" and "performance" suggest a strong focus on the strategic integration of AI to achieve long-term operational goals, addressing both ecological and efficiency concerns. Similarly, keywords like "software" and "project management" reflect practical applications of digital solutions in enhancing productivity across various industries, making these themes instrumental in shaping best practices and technological advancements in business process optimization. These topics are pivotal in the digital optimization of business processes, receiving significant attention due to their impact on improving business performance and sustainability goals.

Basic themes can be observed in the bottom left quadrant of Fig. 8, include keywords such as "learning, internet of things, task analysis," "artificial intelligence, deep learning, machine learning," and "decision making, management, big data," and represent fundamental pillars within the field. These terms capture foundational concepts that serve as the groundwork for both theoretical and applied research in the field digital optimization of business processes (Brabete et al. 2024). These topics are extensively studied and provide essential knowledge that supports more advanced or applied research. For instance, artificial intelligence (AI) and machine learning (ML) continue to be essential tools for data-driven decision-making, while the Internet of Things (IoT) and task analysis are integral to optimizing connected processes within businesses. As widely studied topics, these themes constitute the essential knowledge base, driving ongoing research and practical implementations in business process optimization.

The bottom-left quadrant, representing themes that are either emerging or on the decline, includes "digital twin," "information systems," and "control." These topics suggest areas that may be gaining traction or perhaps losing relevance in the current research landscape (Brabete et al. 2024). The digital twin, for example, is an innovative technology used for real-time simulation and optimization of business processes, through creating virtual replicas of physical systems, which might be in the early stages of adoption within some sectors. The position of this cluster suggests that it could be an area of future interest as the technology matures or may not be as widely adopted, depending on industry needs and research developments. The low density and centrality of these topics highlight their nascent stage, indicating a potential area for future research exploration or a possible trend that might phase out without substantial new interest.

We continue our content analysis with a keyword co-occurrence map (Fig. 9), generated with VOSViewer which provides a comprehensive visualization of the research landscape surrounding AI for optimizing business processes and decisions. This map displays keywords as nodes, with the size of each node indicating its frequency of occurrence across the 1.204 scientific papers. The links between nodes represent the strength of co-occurrence, suggesting how often keywords appear together within the same documents. Clusters of similarly colored nodes indicate groups of keywords that frequently co-occur, reflecting distinct thematic areas within the research field. Thus, as we can see from Fig. 9, the co-occurrence map reveals several prominent clusters, each representing a key area of research:

- **Artificial Intelligence and Machine Learning Cluster** consists of the following keywords Artificial Intelligence, Machine Learning, Deep Learning, Big Data, Decision Making, Management. This cluster highlights the foundational role of

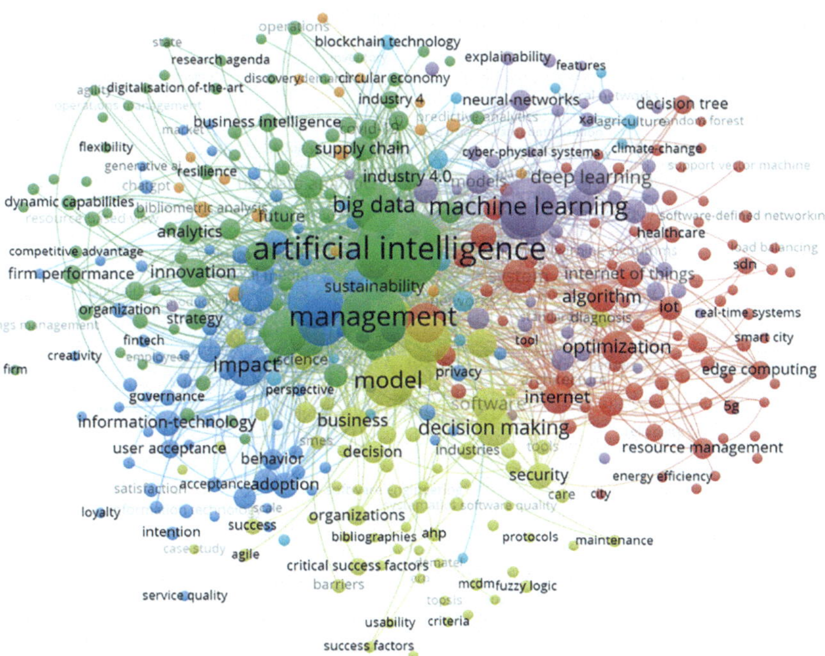

Fig. 9 Keywords co-occurrences map (*Source* The authors' own analysis with VOSViewer)

AI and machine learning in optimizing business processes. The frequent co-occurrence with terms like *big data* and *decision making* highlights how these technologies are leveraged to analyze large datasets for informed management decisions.

- **Internet of Things (IoT) and Task Analysis Cluster**, includes the following keywords Internet of Things, Task Analysis, Learning, Data Analytics. This group emphasizes the integration of IoT devices in business environments to streamline tasks and enhance operational efficiency. The association with *learning* and *data analytics* indicates a focus on continuous improvement and adaptive processes driven by real-time data.
- **Sustainability and Performance Cluster** includes key keywords such as Sustainability, Performance, Efficiency, Environmental Impact, Resource Management. Reflecting the growing importance of sustainable practices, this cluster connects digital optimization with environmental and performance metrics. It suggests that businesses are increasingly utilizing AI to achieve sustainable growth while maintaining or enhancing performance levels.
- **Software, Project Management, and Industry Applications Cluster** formed using keywords such as Software, Project Management, Industries, Implementation, Agile Methodologies. This cluster highlights the critical role of software solutions and project management methodologies in deploying AI across various industries. The co-occurrence with *Agile* and *implementation* signifies a focus on flexible and efficient project execution strategies.
- **Emerging Technologies Cluster** consisting of keywords such as *Digital Twin, Generative AI, ChatGPT, Simulation, Information System.* Representing the frontier of research, this cluster includes cutting-edge technologies like digital twins and generative AI. Their association with *simulation* and *information systems* points to innovative approaches being explored for advanced business process optimization.

Last but not least, based on the analysis of the keywords distribution tree map (Fig. 6), the abstract word cloud (Fig. 7), the keyword thematic map (Fig. 8) and co-occurrences map (Fig. 9), we try to suggest a few future directions of research in the field of using AI for optimizing business decisions and processes (Table 5).

5 Conclusion

This research provides a comprehensive bibliometric analysis of the academic contributions on the use of artificial intelligence (AI) for business process and decision optimization. Between 2020 and 2024, the topic experienced a substantial annual growth rate of 23.07%, with a total of 1,204 documents analyzed. The research demonstrates the multidisciplinary nature of the field, combining insights from business, management, and computer science domains. Key findings indicate that international collaborations, particularly involving the UK, Saudi Arabia, and China,

Table 5 Future research directions in the field of using AI for optimizing business decisions and processes

Research topic	Rationale	Research Direction
Integration of Artificial Intelligence (AI) with Internet of Things (IoT) for Real-Time Decision-Making	AI and IoT are among the most prominent keywords across the analyses, with both appearing frequently and forming central themes. Research on their integration could explore how real-time data from IoT sensors can be processed by AI algorithms to optimize decision-making in dynamic business environments	Topics could include AI-driven predictive maintenance, IoT-based real-time supply chain optimization, and adaptive AI algorithms that respond to IoT inputs for just-in-time decision-making. Additionally, issues like data privacy and security in real-time AI-IoT applications would be essential areas to address
Sustainability and Performance Optimization through Digital Twins and Simulation Technologies	Sustainability is a motor theme, indicating its increasing relevance, while "digital twin" appeared as an emerging theme and has significant potential in this context. Digital twins and simulation technologies can play a critical role in improving resource efficiency, reducing waste, and monitoring environmental impact in real time	Investigating the applications of digital twins for sustainability metrics, such as carbon footprint reduction, resource usage tracking, and waste minimization. This research could also explore creating hybrid digital twin models that integrate AI, IoT, and simulation to offer more accurate and dynamic predictions for sustainability performance
Explainable AI (XAI) for Enhanced Transparency and Trust in Business Decision-Making	The treemap highlights "explainable AI" as a growing area, reflecting a response to challenges in AI transparency, ethics, and trust. As AI becomes increasingly integral to business decision-making, it is crucial to make these processes interpretable and understandable for stakeholders	Studies could focus on developing frameworks for integrating explainability in decision-support tools, particularly in high-stakes areas like finance, healthcare, and human resources. Research can explore how XAI impacts user trust, compliance with regulatory standards, and overall business outcomes, as well as investigate trade-offs between model accuracy and interpretability

(continued)

Table 5 (continued)

Research topic	Rationale	Research Direction
Ethics and Governance in AI-Driven Business Optimization	"Ethics" and "governance" appear as keywords, suggesting a growing awareness of ethical issues associated with AI and data usage in business. As AI-driven tools make more autonomous decisions, understanding and managing the ethical implications becomes increasingly essential	Topics may include creating ethical guidelines for AI deployment in business, frameworks for accountability in automated decision-making, and strategies for mitigating algorithmic bias. Additionally, the role of governance frameworks in ensuring ethical use of AI and data within organizational structures could be explored, as well as developing tools that help monitor and enforce these standards
Application of Blockchain and Decentralized Technologies for Secure and Transparent Business Processes	Blockchain appears as a keyword, indicating its perceived potential for enhancing security, transparency, and traceability in business processes. This is particularly relevant as data integrity and security remain critical issues in digital optimization	Research could investigate blockchain applications in supply chain management, digital identity verification, and secure data sharing between business partners. Additionally, combining blockchain with AI and IoT can open new possibilities for securely managing data from connected devices. Future studies could focus on the scalability and efficiency of blockchain in business contexts, as well as on its integration with legacy systems and its compliance with privacy regulations

drive much of the scientific output, emphasizing the global interest and applicability of AI in this area.

Moreover, our findings illustrate the increasing complexity of AI-related research, characterized by significant international collaboration, high citation metrics, and diverse keyword clustering Our analysis reveals critical themes such as "Artificial intelligence" and "machine learning", which emerged as foundational concepts, frequently co-occurring with terms like "decision making" and "big data." Sustainability and performance, identified as motor themes, reflect the increasing emphasis on aligning AI-driven business optimization with ecological and efficiency goals. Emerging themes, such as digital twins and generative AI, highlight the potential for innovative applications, although their current impact remains limited. The study also shows a balanced distribution of foundational and exploratory themes, reflecting the dual focus on theoretical development and applied innovation.

From a theoretical perspective, this research contributes to the broader understanding of the role of AI in business by identifying key research clusters and trends. Thus, it offers a foundational framework for future studies to explore under-researched areas, such as ethical considerations and emerging technologies like generative AI and digital twins.

Practically, the findings highlight the growing relevance of AI in achieving business efficiency and sustainability goals. Organizations can leverage insights on clustering and thematic trends to align AI strategies with global best practices and emerging technologies, fostering innovation and competitive advantage. At the same time, the paper provides a roadmap for implementing AI-driven solutions in business operations, particularly in areas like sustainability, performance optimization, and real-time decision-making.

Limitations of the study include its reliance on Web of Science as the sole database, which, while comprehensive, may not capture all relevant publications. The exclusion of non-English and non-academic sources may also limit the scope of insights. Additionally, the focus on bibliometric techniques may overlook qualitative nuances in how AI technologies are implemented in practice.

Based on our research, we recommend that future researchers should focus on subjects such as the integration of AI and IoT for real-time organizational process optimization, explore the role of the digital twin technology in sustainability efforts, examine de application of explainable AI to enhance trust and transparency in decision-making, develop ethical and governance frameworks for deployment of AI in business or assess the potential of blockchain technology to enhance data security and transparency in AI-based business processes.

Acknowledgements The research within this paper was conducted within and with the support of the Interdisciplinary Research Center for Economics and Social Sciences, INCESA (Research Infrastructure in Applied Sciences), University of Craiova, a part of the project „HUB-UCv - Support Center for International CD Projects for the Oltenia region" project code POC/80/1/2/107885, cofinanced by the European Social Fund within the Sectorial Operational Program COMPETITIVENESS 2014–2020.

References

Akhtar, P., Frynas, J. G., Mellahi, K., & Ullah, S. (2019). Big Data-Savvy Teams' Skills, Big Data-Driven Actions and Business Performance. *British Journal of Management*, *30*(2), 252–271. https://doi.org/10.1111/1467-8551.12333

Al-Surmi, A., Bashiri, M., & Koliousis, I. (2022). AI based decision making: Combining strategies to improve operational performance. *International Journal of Production Research*, *60*(14), 4464–4486. https://doi.org/10.1080/00207543.2021.1966540

Aria, M. & Cuccurullo, C. (2017) Bibliometrix: An R-tool for comprehensive science mapping analysis. *Journal of Informetrics 11(4)*, 959–975. https://doi.org/10.1016/j.joi.2017.08.007

Borges, M., Hoppen, N., & Luce, F. B. (2009). Information technology impact on market orientation in e-business. *Journal of Business Research, 62*(9), 883–890. https://doi.org/10.1016/j.jbusres.2008.10.010

Brabete V., Sichigea M., Cîrciumaru D. & Goagără D. (2024) Bibliometric Mapping of the Relationships Between Accounting, Professional Accountants, and Sustainability Issues. *Sustainability.* 16(21):9508. https://doi.org/10.3390/su16219508

Buchmeister, B., Palcic, I., & Ojstersek, R. (2019). Artificial Intelligence in Manufacturing Companies and Broader: An Overview. In B. Katalinic (Ed.), *DAAAM International Scientific Book* (1st ed., Vol. 18, pp. 081–098). DAAAM International Vienna. https://doi.org/10.2507/daaam.scibook.2019.07

Donthu, N., Satish, K., Debmalya, M., Nitesh, P. & Weng, M.L. (2021) How to conduct a bibliometric analysis: An overview and guidelines. *Journal of Business Research,* 133, 285–296. https://doi.org/10.1016/j.jbusres.2021.04.070

Duan, Y., Edwards, J. S., & Dwivedi, Y. K. (2019). Artificial intelligence for decision making in the era of Big Data—evolution, challenges and research agenda. *International Journal of Information Management, 48*, 63–71. https://doi.org/10.1016/j.ijinfomgt.2019.01.021

Grover, P., Kar, A. K., & Dwivedi, Y. K. (2022). Understanding artificial intelligence adoption in operations management: Insights from the review of academic literature and social media discussions. *Annals of Operations Research, 308*(1–2), 177–213. https://doi.org/10.1007/s10479-020-03683-9

Haan, K., & Watts, R. (2023). How businesses are using artificial intelligence in 2023. Retrieved from https://www.forbes.com/advisor/ business/software/ai-in-business/, Accessed on 24th September 2024

Hughes, C. (2023). Maximizing business potential with AI-generated plans: Tools and tips for success. Forbes Business Council. Retrieved from https://www.forbes.com/sites/forbesbusinesscouncil/2023/05/03/m aximizing-business-potential-with-ai-generated-plans-tools-and-tips-for-success/?sh=75d025c06fd3

Kang, Z., Catal, C., & Tekinerdogan, B. (2020). Machine learning applications in production lines: A systematic literature review. *Computers & Industrial Engineering, 149*, 106773. https://doi.org/10.1016/j.cie.2020.106773

Kim, K., & Kim, B. (2022). Decision-Making Model for Reinforcing Digital Transformation Strategies Based on Artificial Intelligence Technology. *Information, 13*(5), Article 5. https://doi.org/10.3390/info13050253

Kitsios, F., & Kamariotou, M. (2021). Artificial Intelligence and Business Strategy towards Digital Transformation: A Research Agenda. *Sustainability, 13*(4), 2025. https://doi.org/10.3390/su13042025

Lee, H., Kim, S. G., Park, H., & Kang, P. (2014). Pre-launch new product demand forecasting using the Bass model: A statistical and machine learning-based approach. *Technological Forecasting and Social Change, 86*, 49–64. https://doi.org/10.1016/j.techfore.2013.08.020

Li, D.-C., Chen, W.-C., Chang, C.-J., Chen, C.-C., & Wen, I.-H. (2015). Practical information diffusion techniques to accelerate new product pilot runs. *International Journal of Production Research, 53*(17), 5310–5319. https://doi.org/10.1080/00207543.2015.1032437

Liu, W. (2019) The data source of this study is Web of Science Core Collection? Not enough. *Scientometrics 121*, 1815–1824. https://doi.org/10.1007/s11192-019-03238-1

Lichtenthaler, U. (2020). Building Blocks of Successful Digital Transformation: Complementing Technology and Market Issues. *International Journal of Innovation and Technology Management, 17*(01), 2050004. https://doi.org/10.1142/S0219877020500042

Menzies, J., Sabert, B., Hassan, R., & Mensah, P. K. (2024). Artificial intelligence for international business: Its use, challenges, and suggestions for future research and practice. *Thunderbird International Business Review, 66*(2), 185–200. https://doi.org/10.1002/tie.22370

Messner, W. (2022). Advancing our understanding of cultural heterogeneity with unsupervised machine learning. *Journal of International Management, 28*(2), 100885. https://doi.org/10.1016/j.intman.2021.100885

Nambisan, S., & Luo, Y. (2022). *The digital multinational: Navigating the new normal in global business*. MIT Press.

Neubert, M., & Van Der Krogt, A. (2018). Impact of Business Intelligence Solutions on Export Performance of Software Firms in Emerging Economies. *Technology Innovation Management Review*, *8*(9), 39–49. https://doi.org/10.22215/timreview/1185

OECD. (2022). Artifici*al intelligence and international trade.* Retrieved from https://www.oecd-ilibrary.org/deliver/13212d3e-en.pdf?item Id=/content/paper/13212d3e-en&mimeType=pdf. Acessed on 24th September 2024

Puente, L., Char, C., Patel, D., Thilakarathna, M.S. & Roopesh, M.S. (2024) Research Trends and Development Patterns in Microgreens Publications: A Bibliometric Study from 2004 to 2023. *Sustainability*, *16*, 6645. https://doi.org/10.3390/su16156645

Reis, J.; Amorim, M.; Melão, N. & Matos, P. (2018) Digital transformation: A literature review and guidelines for future research. In Trends and Advances in Information Systems and Technologies. WorldCIST'18 (2018). A*dvances in Intelligent Systems and Computing;* Springer: Cham, Switzerland, z; Volume 747, pp. 411–421

Spanaki, K., Sivarajah, U., Fakhimi, M., Despoudi, S., & Irani, Z. (2022). Disruptive technologies in agricultural operations: A systematic review of AI-driven AgriTech research. *Annals of Operations Research*, *308*(1–2), 491–524. https://doi.org/10.1007/s10479-020-03922-z

Toorajipour, R., Sohrabpour, V., Nazarpour, A., Oghazi, P., & Fischl, M. (2021). Artificial intelligence in supply chain management: A systematic literature review. *Journal of Business Research*, *122*, 502–517. https://doi.org/10.1016/j.jbusres.2020.09.009

van Eck, N.J. & Waltman, L. (2010) Software survey: VOSviewer, a computer program for bibliometric mapping. *Scientometrics*, *84*, 523–538. https://doi.org/10.1007/s11192-009-0146-3

van Oorschot, J.A.W.H.; Hofman, E.; Halman, J.I.M. (2018) A bibliometric review of the innovation adoption literature. *Technological Forecasting Social Change*, *134*, 1–21. https://doi.org/10.1016/j.techfore.2018.04.032

Visinescu, L. L., Jones, M. C., & Sidorova, A. (2017). Improving Decision Quality: The Role of Business Intelligence. *Journal of Computer Information Systems*, *57*(1), 58–66. https://doi.org/10.1080/08874417.2016.1181494

Vogel, R. & Güttel, W.H. (2012) The Dynamic Capability View in Strategic Management: A Bibliometric Review. *International Journal of Management Review, 15,* 426–446. https://doi.org/10.1111/ijmr.12000

Zhou, J., Li, P., Zhou, Y., Wang, B., Zang, J., & Meng, L. (2018). Toward New-Generation Intelligent Manufacturing. *Engineering*, *4*(1), 11–20. https://doi.org/10.1016/j.eng.2018.01.002

Like, *Comment*, *Share*, and *View*: Interpersonal Communication and Engagement in Social Media Environment Among Malaysians

Jamilah Ahmad

Abstract Social media has fundamentally reshaped interpersonal communication, transforming how individuals interact and seek information in an increasingly digital society. This study investigates the behavioural patterns of social media usage among Malaysians, emphasizing interpersonal communication through the lens of the Uses and Gratifications Theory. Using data from 406 respondents collected via an online national survey, the research identifies four key engagement behaviours—liking, commenting, sharing, and viewing—that define Malaysian social media culture. Notably, the study introduces the concept of "non-click" behaviour, where users engage passively with content without leaving explicit digital traces. This nuanced behaviour, often overlooked in social media research, has significant implications for understanding online engagement's social and psychological dimensions. The findings contribute to the growing discourse on digital communication by offering valuable insights into the motivations and hidden dynamics underlying Malaysian social media interactions.

Keywords Interpersonal communication · Social media · Uses and gratifications theory

1 Introduction

Social media has become an indispensable tool in contemporary society, offering unparalleled interactivity and connectivity that transcends geographical boundaries. Defined by Hudson (2020) as platforms enabling real-time content creation and sharing, social media encompasses a wide array of digital communication tools that facilitate seamless interaction among users and the public at large. Since the early 2000s, platforms like Myspace, Facebook, YouTube, Instagram, and TikTok have

J. Ahmad (✉)
Universiti Sains Malaysia, George Town, Malaysia
e-mail: jahmad@usm.my

S. O. Idowu et al. (eds.), *Competitiveness and Sustainability in the Digitization Era*, Springer Proceedings in Business and Economics,
https://doi.org/10.1007/978-3-031-91778-3_8

gained immense popularity, especially among teenagers and young adults, establishing themselves as integral components of everyday life (Teng and Joo 2021). As Abdallah et al., (2024) observes, the prevalence of internet-enabled devices ensures that social media continues to connect billions globally. This growing trend underscores the transformative power of social media in shaping how knowledge, communication, and relationships are navigated in the digital age.

Southeast Asia continues to experience exponential digital growth, with 1.42 billion internet users in the region as of 2024 (Petrosyan 2024). Malaysia stands out, with 83.1% of its population actively engaging in social media by January 2024, marking a 4.6% increase from the previous year (Siddharta 2024). This growth underscores the pivotal role of social media in the lives of young Malaysians, who leverage these platforms for connection, information sharing, entertainment, and communication. Such widespread adoption reflects Malaysia's commitment to technological advancement and the seamless integration of digital tools, illustrating how social media has become a cornerstone of modern living in a rapidly evolving digital landscape.

Powerful social media platforms such as Facebook, Twitter, and Instagram have evolved to change how humans communicate in today's society. However, as researchers battle to understand the current and future consequences of social media contact, social media interaction has positive and negative elements. For example, according to Paul (2014), youth can interpret online communication as accurately as in-person connection since the brain will process the information as if it were real, while others argue that it would not be. Meanwhile, another study found that society is regarded as developing disparities in digital contact, which improves the capacity to relate to others, accept differences, and communicate ideas and feelings healthily (Burleson 2003; Hinduja and Patchin 2008).

Indeed, the more significant the influence of technology, the more changes in communication styles and types of interpersonal communication. According to Booth (2013), there are three key issues regarding social media's role in communication styles. First, communication through social media tends to trust the people at the end of the communication. Therefore, the message tends to be more open. Second, social connections are not strengthened as much through social media as face-to-face. Hence don't tend to deepen the relationship. Third, tend to follow and interact with people who agree with our points of view, thus getting the same diversity of viewpoints. Although communication in the real world is exchanging with the contact in the virtual world, on social network sites, communication can be formed differently, not only to discuss personal subjects but also public issues.

While considering the function of social network sites, many positive contributions to interpersonal communication and adverse effects. Houghton (2012) has also mentioned that interpersonal communication, established online, has a certainty feature. It increases the frequency of both passive and interactive communication. In this sense, social media users use this platform for interpersonal communication for four (4) different purposes (Petrič & Pinter 2011);

- Informational-cooperative use: People get and give information, learn, dissemination information, join business projects
- Relational use: Developing social relations, executing social norms, sustaining relations, gaining social support, making friends, and maintaining the relationship
- Expressive use: People express themselves, their persona, experiences, wishes, beliefs, presenting internal communication, self-presentation, and obtaining identity.
- Strategic use: People have conscious or unconscious personal aims (controlling, organizing, entertaining, observing, and viewing) that can be realized by communication

Consequently, social network sites allow people to share information about themselves by creating accounts and expressing likes, comments, and sharing as a way to express their thoughts (Bateman et al., 2011). Thus, social networks make people interested in everyday things get together, help share information and get support. Obtaining mutual relations and sustaining these relations bring out emotional support. Consequently, the quality of life has been improved. The connections built via social networks help users know each other closely.

and get detailed information (Valenzuela et al., 2009). The profile information of the person is the most important source of information for others to make an impression. Social media users' profiles are compelling even when others have decided about others' personalities and personality traits are evaluated on their profiles (Bachrach et al., 2012). Therefore, it is interesting to explore how people use and engage in social media sites for intrapersonal communication.

1.1 Interpersonal Communication and Uses and Gratifications Theory on Social Networking Sites (SNS)

The uses and gratification theoretical approach were developed to evaluate users' motivations and gratifications for specific media (Katz et al., 1973). Uses and gratifications have four primary assumptions; (1) media use is goal-directed or motivated, (2) people use media to satisfy their needs and desires, (3) social and psychological factors mediate media use, and (4) media use and interpersonal communication are related (Rubin, 1993). In addition, some of the gratifications identified in the literature include social interaction, information seeking, entertainment, passing time, relaxation, communication, convenience, surveillance or knowledge about others, and self-status seeking (Alhabash and Ma 2017).

Previous studies have examined the effects of gratifications both sought and obtained in selecting different social media sites within uses and gratifications. For instance, one study found that Instagram use intensity was higher than Facebook and Twitter use passion among university students (Alhabash and Ma 2017). It was also found that self-documentation was related to Facebook and Instagram use intensity, and convenience was associated with a higher power of Twitter use. Other studies have found that individuals use Instagram to gratify surveillance, documentation, coolness, and creativity (Sheldon and Bryant 2016). Similarly, Facebook has also been found to keep up with close and distant friends for informational and educational gratifications, to pass the time, and for self-promotion (Manasijevic et al., 2016; Sendurur et al., 2015). Finally, activities such as reading comments, viewing, liking, disliking, and sharing videos on YouTube are associated with the gratification of relaxing entertainment (Khan 2017). As a result, this study implemented how people use and engage in social media sites for intrapersonal communication.

1.2 *Reflecting Social Media Behaviour:* Like, Comment, Share, *and* View

A previous study highlighted that social media behaviour is categorized into three levels: level of consumption, level of contributing, and level of creating (Muntinga et al., 2011). Consuming is the lowest, involving participation in behaviour without contributing to or creating content such as reading and viewing. At the middle level, donating is the interactions between users and contents and among users, including comments. Finally, creating task is the highest level, which involves producing and publishing content.

Clicking serves a variety of interpersonal and other goals. For example, Hayes et al., (2016) explored Sumner et al., (2018) showed that meta-communication using the Like button to acknowledge that users have seen a post was the most common interpersonal motivation behind its use. Sumner et al., (2018) also found that liking can be an act of self-presentation, publicly displaying one's desire to be associated with a particular piece of content. Employing a uses and gratifications approach, Lee et al., (2016) explored different motivations for one-click responses on social media, including interpersonal motivations, enjoyment, monetary incentives, pleasing others, and passing the time. Interpersonal and enjoyment motivations were the most predictive motivations of more Liking (Lee et al., 2016).

Similarly, social media behaviours also fall into discrete levels. First, like is the lowest. Like requires less commitment than others do. While a click is enough for like, comment, share, and view needs additional actions that ask for extra commitment or cognitive effort. Second, a share may be a higher level than a comment. When commenting on a post, the post appears on News Feed. On the other hand, when sharing a post, the post appears on News Feed and goes to the user's profile page, suggesting that the shared post constitutes a part of the user's self- presentation. Social media users are strategic in self-presentation (van Dijck 2013). In other words, when sharing a post, users are more committed to assessing its value regarding the self than when commenting on a post. In addition, technologically, social media platform allows users to add comments on the shared post.

Based on the discussion, the present research categorizes share as the highest, comment as the intermediate, and like as the lowest level. However, regardless of social media users' hierarchical levels, each behaviour must have a psychological (at least cognitive) implication different from the other. Additionally, social networking sites use several user interactions to enabling user responses, such as posts, likes, comments, and shares. Hence, this study looked into how people use and engage in social media sites for intrapersonal communication.

2 Methods

This study used original data from an online survey in Malaysia. Online survey research using Google Form helped recruit Malaysian youth respondents 30 years old and below. Because this study focused on social media use, only those who reported using social media were included. The sample was not probabilistic to ensure respondents reflected the Malaysian population's gender and geographical location. This study analysed the 406 respondents who completed the survey.

2.1 Social Networking Sites for Interpersonal Communication Purposes

The creation of social networking sites has a significant impact on communication and interaction with people. Therefore, to evaluate the behaviour of social media usage among Malaysian based on social interaction for interpersonal communication purposes, this study designed survey questionnaires with the guideline of previous literature (Petrič & Pinter 2011) and highlighted four (4) interpersonal communication purposes on social media in the questionnaire, including (1) information-cooperative use—seeking and share information, (2) relational use—developing social relations, gaining social supports, making friends and maintaining the relations, (3) expressive use—express themselves, self-presentation, obtaining identity and presenting internal communication, and (4) strategic use—conscious or unconscious personal aims (controlling, organizing, entertaining, observing, and viewing).

2.2 Identify Social Media Users' Behaviour as Social Interaction and Information Seeking

Through various means of communication and technologies, Morse (2003) says that human beings are love to socialize, develop and maintain a complex social network of friends, family, and acquaintances. Meanwhile, Zawawi (2008) noted that information and knowledge sharing were based on values that are crucial to knowledge development among Malaysian were honesty, knowledgeable and trustworthiness. Therefore, this study highlights the terms of Uses and Gratifications theory to indicate the behaviour of social media users as social interaction and information seeking. Thus, the indicators to identify the social media users' behavior are based on a previous study (Alhabsh and Ma 2017), include social interaction, information seeking, entertainment, passing time, relaxation, communication, convenience, surveillance, or knowledge about others, and self-status seeking.

2.3 People Use and Engage in Social Media Sites for Intrapersonal Communication

Social networking sites represent a cultural paradigm shift. In this study, culture is defined as the shared patterns of behaviours and interaction as an adequate understanding of learning through socialization. The facilities on social networking sites showed that it provides users an avenue to interact easily daily to connect with people at any time and anywhere. In addition, social networking sites use several user interactions to enable user responses, such as posts, likes, comments, and shares. In addition, a click is enough to like, comment, share. However, the view needs additional actions that ask for extra commitment or cognitive effort. Hence this study, used (1) like (2) share, (3) comment, and (4) view as indicators to identify the use of these actions as engagement in social media sites, particularly for intrapersonal communication.

3 Results and Discussion

The finding data on the evaluation of social media usage behaviours among Malaysian for interpersonal contact are shown in Table 1 below. According to the findings, respondents use social networking sites for (1) connecting friends and family, (2) keeping up with the latest news, (3) following community leaders and celebrities, (4) sharing pictures, articles, and status updates, and (5) stalking people you know or friends. Therefore, data findings may be classified into four (4) types of interpersonal communication on social media. As a result, the highest usage of interpersonal communication on social networking sites correlates with the most recent news, cooperative information use, which indicated that respondents actively seek and share information on social networking sites.

According to the data below, respondents often contact friends and family and usually follow the lifestyles of community leaders and celebrities as the second-highest use of interpersonal communication. Consequently, the findings demonstrate

Table 1 Interpersonal communication on social networking sites

Item	Very Often	Often	Sometimes	Seldom	Rarely	Never
Contacting friends/family	110 (27.1%)	105 (25.9%)	87 (21.4%)	43 (10.6%)	52 (12.8%)	9 (2.2%)
Follow the latest news	125 (30.8%)	148 (36.5%)	70 (17.2%)	38 (9.4%)	21 (5.2%)	4 (1.0%)
Following community leaders and celebrities	55 (13.5)	114 (28.1)	87 (21.4%)	63 (15.5%)	62 (15.3%)	25 (6.2%)
Share photos and status updates	53 (13.1%)	101 (24.9%)	80 (19.7%)	62 (15.3%)	90 (22.2%)	20 (4.9%)
Stalking people that you know or friends	36 (8.9%)	60 (14.8%)	68 (16.7%)	60 (14.8%)	125 (30.8%)	57 (14.0%

that interpersonal communication produced on social networking sites contributes to the development of social relationships, the acquisition of social support, the formation of friendships, and the maintenance of those relationships. Based on the data, the third category is expressive use. Respondents frequently share photos and status updates on social networking sites as one of the interpersonal communication purposes of expressing themselves, self-presentation, obtaining the identity, and presenting internal communication.

Based on the data findings, interpersonal communication on social networking sites is rarely utilized for strategic use. Respondents rarely stalk individuals or friends, implying that people use social networking sites not to learn more about other people in their lives. However, they may choose to do so non-public in some situations, as represented by the terms "stalking" (Lyndon et al., 2011). Even though the data indicates low percentages, the result revealed that in some cases, individuals are engaged in the information they are viewing but do not want their actions to be acknowledged, so they do not click (Thompson 2017).

Communication and interaction benefit the respondents in getting information while doing social networking. As a result, this benefit bridges the gap between them by allowing them to be updated from time to time readily. Thus, data results indicate that respondents actively seek social networking sites while building social interaction among users. Based on the findings in Table 2 below, the data shows that respondents neither agree nor disagree with the information on social media shared by social influencers. The uses and gratification theory explains that the respondents actively select media according to their specific needs. At this point, the user is always active in choosing the desired medium (Bryant and Oliver 2009). In other words, each user decides different mediums meet their diverse needs and acquires certain motives with this use.

Hence, the basic assumption of the uses and satisfaction approach is "medium as a source of influence within the context of other possible influence" (Bryant and Oliver 2009). Consequently, respondents strongly agree that reliable information influences followers, whereas fake news causes them to unfriend or block information sources.

Table 2 Social interaction and information seeking on social networking sites

	Strongly Agree	Agree	Neither Agree Nor Disagree	Disagree	Strongly Disagree
I trust the information	24	103	155	77	47
on social media shared	(5.9%)	(25.4%)	(38.2%)	(19.0%)	(11.6%)
by social influencer					
I am interested in	62	206	77	25	36
becoming a follower if	(15.3%)	(50.7%)	(19.0%)	(6.2%)	(8.9%)
the information is					
trustworthy					
Fake news makes me	141	128	87	32	18
(unfriend/block)	(34.7%)	(31.5%)	(21.4%)	(7.9%)	(4.4%)

Furthermore, as shown in Table 3, withholding clicks is sometimes a conscious decision that results in platform actions that are more beneficial relationship preservation. As a result, classifying non-clicks as "passive activity" might be concealing significant results for social media researchers. This pattern is consistent with research suggesting that people's attitudes toward clicks evolve (Hayes et al., 2016). Based on data findings below, non-clicking, in addition to social grooming, is a way for users to limit the exposure of their social media behaviours to their networks, notably by limiting their reactions to specific social media information. The non-click is a valuable concept for academics trying to understand how individuals regulate their online exposure since visibility is a primary "root" affordance in computer-mediated communication (Treem et al., 2020).

Overall, data findings in Table 4 below highlighted that the majority of respondents of this research are "indiscriminate clickers" who are individuals who frequently provide visual one-click feedback on Friends' content but do so without extended and attentive viewing. Clicks typically signal a post has been viewed but are ambiguous markers of engagement or time investment. The second type is the "engaged clicker" that individuals who pay close attention to social media content and engage in clicking feedback (share or repost) use social media is beneficial. Then the third type is "engaged lurker," who do not click but spend time viewing social media content. Looking but not clicking is a privacy-protecting act, especially in cases where users fear that third-party audiences will judge their responses or the opinions they hold (Wu et al., 2020).

Table 3 Engagement in social media sites for intrapersonal communication

	Strongly Agree	Agree	Neither Agree Nor Disagree	Disagree	Strongly Disagree
I often compare	37	141	91	83	54
how I socialize	(9.1%)	(34.7%)	(22.4%)	(20.4%)	(13.3%)
(social skills)					
(viewing)					
I like reading	103	228	48	15	12
opinions related to	(25.4%)	(56.2%)	(11.8%)	(3.7%)	(3.0%)
my problem					
(viewing)					
I like to see other people post on social media (viewing)	72 (17.7%)	194 (47.8%)	69 (17.0%)	47 (11.6%)	24 (5.9%)

Table 4 Engagement behaviours on social networking sites

		Responses	
		N	Percent
Engagement behaviors on social networking sites	Like" post entry	241	62%
	Share" or "Repost" post entry	183	47%
	Post comment	134	35%

4 Conclusion

The findings and discussion have shed some light on how interpersonal communication on social media activities creates behavioural culture on social media platforms among Malaysians through four behaviours—*like, comment, share,* and *view.* Additionally, indicating the benefits and effects of each behaviour towards Malaysian social media users. Therefore, the findings data highlighted two categories of Malaysian cultural behaviour on social media; *like* (click) and *view* (non-click). Furthermore, this study shows that the most common interpersonal behaviour motivation on social media is clicking the *like* button and viewing the social content. Thus, a Uses and Gratifications approach to different responses to social media interpersonal motivations reveals the concept of "non-click" and viewing social media content among Malaysians. In this case, users are highly engaged in the content they are viewing but want their activities to go unnoticed and thus refrain from clicking. However, the "non-click" is a vital component of today's online communication environments, as well as the indicator of social and psychological processes it facilitates.

Acknowledgements The author would like to extend appreciation to the Universiti Sains Malaysia with Project Code R501-LR-RND003-0000000559-0000. This article is one of the stated tangible outputs. The author also acknowledges the contributions of individuals who assisted directly or indirectly in completing the paper.

References

Abdallah, R. A. Q., Hatamleh, I. H. M., Nemer Abu Eid, Y. S., & Mahroum, M. (2024). Communication in the Digital Age: The Impact of Communication Skills and Cultural Restraint on the Use of Social Media Platforms in the Case of Jordan. *Journalism and Media, 5*(3), 1244–1258. https://doi.org/10.3390/journalmedia5030079

Alhabash, S., & Ma, M. (2017). A tale of four platforms: Motivations and uses of Facebook, Twitter, Instagram, and Snapchat among college students. *Social Media + Society, 3*(1), 2056305117691544. https://doi.org/10.1177/2056305117691544

Bachrach, Y., Kosinski, M., Graepel, T., Kohli, P., & Stillwell, D. (2012). Personality and patterns of Facebook usage. In *Proceedings of the 4th Annual ACM Web Science Conference* (pp. 24–32). https://doi.org/10.1145/2380718.2380722

Bateman, P. J., Gray, P. H., & Butler, B. S. (2011). The impact of community commitment on participation in online communities. *Information Systems Research, 22*(4), 841–854. https://doi.org/10.1287/isre.1090.0265

Bryant, J., & Oliver, M. B. (Eds.). (2009). Media effects: Advances in theory and research (3rd ed.). Routledge.

Burleson, B. R. (2003). The experience and effects of emotional support: What the study of cultural and gender differences can tell us about close relationships, emotion, and interpersonal communication. *Personal relationships, 10*(1), 1–23. https://doi.org/10.1111/1475-6811.00033

Hayes, R. A., Carr, C. T., & Wohn, D. Y. (2016). It's the audience: Differences in social support across social media. *Social Media + Society, 2*(4), 2056305116678894. https://doi.org/10.1177/2056305116678894

Hinduja, S., & Patchin, J. W. (2008). Personal information of adolescents on the Internet: A quantitative content analysis of MySpace. *Journal of adolescence, 31*(1), 125–146.

Houghton, D. (2012). Worst ideas of 2012: Celebrities oversharing. The Guardian. https://www.theguardian.com/lifeandstyle/2012/dec/28/worst-ideas-2012-celebrities-oversharing

Hudson, M. (2020). What is social media? Definition and examples of social media. Retrieved from, https://www.thebalancesmb.com/what-is-social-media-2890301

Katz, E., Blumler, J. G., & Gurevitch, M. (1973). Uses and gratifications research. *Public Opinion Quarterly, 37*(4), 509–523. https://doi.org/10.1086/268109

Khan, M. L. (2017). Social media engagement: What motivates user participation and consumption on YouTube? *Computers in Human Behavior, 66*, 236–247. https://doi.org/10.1016/j.chb.2016.09.024. ResearchGate+3SCIRP+3ScienceDirect+3

Lee, S., Kim, H., & Sundar, S. S. (2016). Customizing the Facebook news feed: Effects of user control on perceived credibility and user engagement. *Journal of Computer-Mediated Communication, 21*(1), 17–33. https://doi.org/10.1111/jcc4.12150

Lyndon, A., Bonds-Raacke, J., & Cratty, A. D. (2011). College students' Facebook stalking of ex-partners. *Cyberpsychology, Behavior, and Social Networking, 14*(12), 711–716. https://doi.org/10.1089/cyber.2010.0588

Manasijević, D., Zivković, D., Arsić, S., & Milosević, I. (2016). Exploring students' purposes of usage and educational usage of Facebook. *Computers in Human Behavior, 60*, 441–450. https://doi.org/10.1016/j.chb.2016.02.087. DergiPark+3ACM DigitalLibrary+3ResearchGate+3.

Morse, J. M. (2003). Principles of mixed methods and multi-method research design. In A. Tashakkori & C. Teddlie (Eds.), *Handbook of mixed methods in social & behavioral research* (pp. 189–208). Sage Publications.SCIRP+1Google Scholar+1.
Muntinga, D. G., Moorman, M., & Smit, E. G. (2011). Introducing COBRAs: Exploring motivations for brand-related social media use. *International Journal of Advertising, 30*(1), 13–46. https://doi.org/10.2501/IJA-30-1-013-046. ResearchGate+4PMC+4SCIRP+4.
Paul, M. P. (2014). A commentary on social media research from the perspective of a sport communication journal editor. *Communication & Sport, 2*(2), 127–132. https://doi.org/10.1177/2167479514527428
Petrič, G., & Pinter, A. (2011). Trust in social networking sites: An analysis of user perceptions. First Monday, 16(1). https://doi.org/10.5210/fm.v16i1.2971
Petrosyan, A. (2024, May 22). *Global number of online users worldwide 2023, by subregion.* Statista. Retrieved January 20, 2025, from https://www.statista.com/statistics/249562/number-of-worldwide-internet-users-by-region/
Rubin, A. M. (1993). Audience activity and media use. *Communication Monographs, 60*(1), 98–105. https://doi.org/10.1080/03637759309376300. Taylor & Francis Online.
Sendurur, E., Sendurur, P., & Yilmaz, R. (2015). Examination of the social network sites usage patterns of pre-service teachers. *Computers in Human Behavior, 51*, 188–194. https://doi.org/10.1016/j.chb.2015.04.055. ScienceDirect+2ResearchGate+2Scite+2.
Sheldon, P., & Bryant, K. (2016). Instagram: Motives for its use and relationship to narcissism and contextual age. *Computers in Human Behavior, 58*, 89–97. https://doi.org/10.1016/j.chb.2015.12.059. ACM Digital Library+4Academia+4ResearchGate+4.
Siddharta, A. (2024, June 4). *Penetration rate of social media in Malaysia 2016–2024.* Statista. Retrieved January 20, 2025, from https://shorturl.at/tLCf8
Sumner, E. M., Ruge-Jones, L., & Alcorn, D. (2018). A functional approach to the Facebook Like button: An exploration of meaning, interpersonal functionality, and potential alternative response buttons. *New Media & Society, 20*(6), 2132–2150. https://doi.org/10.1177/1461444817717511. Oxford Academic+3ResearchGate+3ORCA+3
Teng, C. E., & Joo, T. M. (2021). Analyzing the usage of social media: A study on elderly in Malaysia. *International journal of humanities and social sciences, 11*(3), 737–743. https://doi.org/10.20431/2349-0381.0809010
Thompson, J. B. (2018). Mediated interaction in the digital age. *Theory, Culture & Society, 35*(5–6), 31–53. https://doi.org/10.1177/0263276418808592
Treem, J. W., Leonardi, P. M., & van den Hooff, B. (2020). Computer-mediated communication in organizations: Theoretical developments and future research. *Journal of Communication, 70*(4), 486–501. https://doi.org/10.1093/joc/jqaa014
Valenzuela, S., Park, N., & Kee, K. F. (2009). Is there social capital in a social network site?: Facebook use and college students' life satisfaction, trust, and participation. *Journal of Computer-Mediated Communication, 14*(4), 875–901. https://doi.org/10.1111/j.1083-6101.2009.01474.x
van Dijck, J. (2013). The culture of connectivity: A critical history of social media. Oxford University Press. WorldCat+2library.auf-florence.org+2Google Books+2
Wu, L., Wang, Y., & Evans, N. J. (2020). Social media engagement and real-time marketing: Using netnography to examine the Starbucks #RedCupContest. *Psychology & Marketing, 37*(7), 918–930. https://doi.org/10.1002/mar.21342
Zawawi, D. (2008). Cultural dimensions among Malaysian employees. *International Journal of Economics and Management, 2*(2), 409–426.

University Social Responsibility in Malaysian Higher Education: A Qualitative Study of Implementation, Initiatives, and Outcomes

Jamilah Ahmad and Dayang Nurfatini Awang

Abstract The economic, political, and social changes driven by 21st-century globalization have impacted universities worldwide. Universities have emerged as pivotal agents of social, economic, and cultural progress, expanding their mission beyond academic excellence to address pressing societal challenges through diverse social responsibility initiatives. Over the years, the discourse on University Social Responsibility (USR) has predominantly revolved around developed countries, leaving a gap in understanding its development and implementation in developing nations. This study explores the implementation of USR in Malaysian higher education, with a focus on the initiatives, outcomes, and framework of USR programs. Semi-structured interviews with Malaysian university leaders reveal that USR practices are shaped by collaborative engagement, transformative projects, and sustainability objectives. Although the specific initiatives vary across universities, they share a unified goal: enhancing community well-being and advancing environmental sustainability. This research enriches the growing discourse on USR by underscoring the vital role of universities in driving sustainable development and fostering social progress. The findings provide actionable insights for higher education institutions seeking to amplify their social impact while aligning with global sustainability priorities. (176 words).

Keywords Globalization · University social responsibility · Sustainability

J. Ahmad · D. N. Awang (✉)
Universiti Sains Malaysia, George Town, Malaysia
e-mail: dayangnurfatini@student.usm.my

J. Ahmad
e-mail: jahmad@usm.my

S. O. Idowu et al. (eds.), *Competitiveness and Sustainability in the Digitization Era*, Springer Proceedings in Business and Economics,
https://doi.org/10.1007/978-3-031-91778-3_9

1 Introduction

Globalization continues to be a defining phenomenon of the twenty-first century. This global trend has reshaped economies, cultures, and societies, resulting in positive and negative consequences (Stobierski 2021). It is characterized by increased connectivity and interdependence among nations, individuals, and businesses through theintegration of economic, political, social, and cultural systems across borders, resulting in increased flows of goods, services, capital, people, and ideas (Takefman 2023). While globalization has provided numerous benefits on a global scale, it has also introduced significant challenges, particularly in terms of social and environmental implications (Feng et al. 2021). These challenges include increased competition, resource exploitation, and growing inequalities, all of which worsen sustainability issues (Zhang et al. 2022). The numerous and far-reaching negative impacts of human activities necessitate a comprehensive approach to address these complex crises and build a more sustainable future (Willamo et al. 2018).

Global awareness of environmental, social, and economic challenges has intensified in recent years, with issues such as climate change, resource depletion, social inequality, and economic instability becoming increasingly urgent (Javanmardi et. al. 2023). This heightened awareness has sparked a renewed interest in the theme of Social Responsibility (SR), underscoring the critical role organizations play in shaping societal and environmental outcomes through their decisions and actions (Calculli et al. 2021; Sierra and Suárez-Collado 2021). Awad and Martín-Rojas (2024) emphasize that the demand for greater accountability and ethical behaviour is increasingly evident across sectors—large and small, public and private. This call for collaborative action highlights the need to develop sustainable solutions that ensure the well-being of current and future generations.

Universities, as key stakeholders, are integral to the evolving discourse on social responsibility, prompting essential discussions about their role in enhancing societal well-being and promoting environmental sustainability (Ismail and Shujaat 2019). As a developing nation, Malaysia emphasizes SR to tackle significant social and environmental challenges. CSR including USR, is a practical approach for Malaysia to address these issues and progress toward becoming a fully developed nation (Sharma and Sharma 2019). USR enables universities to act as catalysts for global transformation by generating knowledge, providing evidence-based solutions, and fostering innovation to overcome barriers to Sustainable Development Goals attainment (Ashida 2022). However, the pursuit of sustainable development within Malaysian HEIs encounters numerous challenges, including restricted opportunities for collaboration, insufficient access to resources, time constraints, and a lack of robust institutional support (Zhao and Cheah 2023). As a result, Malaysian university outreach efforts have primarily occurred through occasional community service projects organized by universities and students, as well as through the independent efforts of individual lecturers or student bodies (Zakariya 2014). While some higher education institutions actively pursue the university's Third Mission by engaging with and contributing to their communities, others show a lack of interest or involvement in such activities.

Given these challenges, the implementation of social responsibility initiatives aimed at promoting sustainability in Malaysian institutions has emerged as a significant field of study that requires additional investigation (Chan and Hasan 2018; Senin et al. 2019). This research seeks to address this gap by focusing on three primary objectives:

1. To understand the strategies for the implementation of USR initiatives in Malaysian universities.
2. To analyse the scope of USR initiatives undertaken by Malaysian universities in addressing societal and environmental challenges.
3. To evaluate the impacts and outcomes of USR initiatives in Malaysian universities.
4. To propose a comprehensive USR framework tailored to the unique socio-economic and cultural context of Malaysia.

2 Literature Review

Social Responsibility (SR) entered modern discourse with Howard R. Bowen's book Social Responsibilities of the Businessman, which earned him the title "Father of Corporate Social Responsibility". At the time, SR was more commonly used than Corporate Social Responsibility (CSR), as corporations had not yet solidified their dominant role in the business sector (Carroll 1991). Building on Bowen's ideas, scholars later characterized SR as a commitment to considering the broader social effects of business decisions and looking beyond immediate economic interests (Davis and Blomstrom 1968). Over time, SR evolved to encompass social, environmental, and economic dimensions, reflecting the growing emphasis on sustainability and the triple bottom line (Latapí Agudelo 2019). Initially, the concept of "social responsibility" was primarily associated with businesses and their efforts to promote societal well-being (Ramos-Monge et al. 2017). The focus was on how corporations, particularly large multinational companies, could leverage CSR to address pressing issues such as environmental impact mitigation (Knudson 2018), equitable labor practices (Asemah et al. 2013), and philanthropic contributions for social benefit. Simultaneously, CSR evolved into a strategic tool, enabling businesses to gain competitive advantages, foster innovation, and enhance their reputation among key stakeholders, including customers, employees, business partners, government agencies, and non-profit organizations (Nimani et al. 2022). This progression positioned CSR as a near-universal expectation for businesses globally, highlighting the critical role of organizations in driving positive societal and environmental change (Hwang et al. 2020). As CSR gained traction across industries, universities began facing similar pressures to adopt socially responsible practices within their operations. Carroll (2016) highlighted the increasing influence of CSR initiatives across sectors, emphasizing that universities are also expected to embrace these practices.

Universities, originating from the Latin phrase *"universitas magistrorum et scholarium"* (Fulford and Locke 2023), emerged in the twelfth and thirteenth centuries as communities dedicated to advancing knowledge in the arts and sciences (Alemu 2018). Their mission expanded in the mid-nineteenth century with Alexander von Humboldt's academic revolution, which integrated research as a central pursuit of academia (Do 2023). By the late twentieth century, globalization, technological advancements, and sustainability concerns further reshaped higher education, introducing the concept of the Third Mission. This mission encompasses "all activities involving the generation, application, and utilization of university knowledge, capabilities, and resources beyond academia" (Compagnucci and Spigarelli 2020, p. 5) and includes the development of innovative solutions to drive broader societal progress (Naranjo Africano et al. 2023). The institutionalization of the Third Mission signifies a broader understanding of universities' role, extending beyond traditional teaching and research to include significant involvement in societal university social responsibility (Haj Teib 2024). As cited in Hall and Tandon (2021), the evolving interaction between universities and their communities illustrates how higher education institutions are transforming into more diverse, inclusive, and active establishments with strong ties to their local and global communities. Therefore, the Third Mission is now regarded as equally important as teaching and research (Vefago et al. 2020).

University Social Responsibility (USR), introduced in the early 2000s, extends the traditional mission of universities by addressing economic, social, and environmental challenges in society (Sharma and Sharma 2019). USR embodies a collaborative approach, aligning the university's Third Mission with the needs of communities (Cosenz 2022). It fosters partnerships among diverse stakeholders, including businesses, government agencies, non-profit organizations, and local communities, to drive societal progress and sustainable development. Through USR, universities are increasingly recognized as pivotal players in promoting social responsibility, contributing to the common good, and advancing environmental sustainability. As claimed by Kumari et al. (2023), USR highlights the critical role of universities in addressing complex real-world challenges—economic, social, and environmental—in an integrated manner. Ultimately, these efforts are now integral to their institutional missions and strategic priorities (Lo et al. 2017). By embedding USR into their core operations, universities redefine their role beyond academic excellence, positioning themselves as catalysts for societal transformation. This transformation necessitates continuous adaptation to balance educational objectives with commitments to community engagement and sustainability (Taliento 2022).

USR is a key concept shaping the contemporary landscape of higher education, promoting educational progress and community wellbeing through research, teaching, and community involvement (Shaari et al. 2018). However, the interpretation and implementation of USR vary globally, shaped by universities' differing priorities and contexts. In developed countries, USR initiatives often aim at long—term institutional goals, such as improving governance and advancing academic curricula (Huang and Do 2021). Developing nations, however, favour short-term, tangible programs designed to address immediate community needs, frequently leveraging philanthropy to enhance institutional prestige (Alzyoud and Bani-Hani 2015). As evidence, philanthropic responsibilities take precedence as the primary focus for Malaysian universities, with the majority of their USR initiatives directed toward promoting the welfare of others, including charitable donations, volunteer work, and community involvement (Ahmad et al. 2024). Besides that, economic issues dominate HEIs' practical and theoretical USR efforts, followed by social and environmental concerns. USR also supports national priorities. For example, in the Philippines, the Asian Institute of Management offers courses in social entrepreneurship to address economic challenges (Abu Osman 2023), while in the UAE, Khalifa University has developed renewable energy solutions, positioning the country as a global leader in this sector (Bojarajan et al. 2024).

In Malaysia, the focus on social responsibility gained momentum after the Prime Minister's 2006 mandate requiring publicly listed companies to report their CSR activities (Keong et al. 2017). This directive prompted organizations, regardless of size or sector, to move beyond legal compliance and address evolving economic, social, and environmental challenges (Ahmad and Saad 2013). Within the higher education sector, most Malaysian universities have embraced social responsibility initiatives, reflecting a growing commitment to addressing societal needs (Ahmad 2012). This commitment was further institutionalized through the National Education Blueprint 2015–2025, which formalized the integration of USR into the strategic framework for higher education. The Blueprint's main agenda is to transition academia from working in isolation towards the quadruple helix model, in which academia collaborates with industry, government, and local communities to incubate, develop, and commercialize ideas. This collaborative approach aligns closely with USR principles, which emphasize holistic student development through ethical, social, and community-oriented initiatives.

According to Mohd Hassan (2017), the adoption of USR in Malaysian public universities is informed by five key global best-practice guidelines. These include the UN Global Compact, the Global Reporting Initiative (GRI), the OECD guidelines, the Principles for Global Corporate Responsibility, and Social Accountability 8000. Carroll's (2004) revised pyramid of global CSR and performance also provides a foundational framework. Furthermore, Burke and Logsdon (1996) identified five strategic dimensions critical for enhancing value creation through CSR initiatives: centrality, specificity, proactivity, voluntarism, and visibility. Centrality emphasizes aligning CSR initiatives with the institution's core mission and objectives. Specificity highlights the development of unique, tailored initiatives such as knowledge or technology transfer that differentiate institutions. Proactivity involves anticipating and addressing societal needs ahead of time, ensuring relevance and responsiveness. Voluntarism underscores that CSR efforts should arise from internal motivations rather than external pressures. Finally, visibility ensures stakeholder awareness and recognition of CSR initiatives, amplifying their impact. Together, these dimensions underscore the strategic importance of aligning CSR efforts with institutional goals, thereby maximizing their effectiveness and societal value. These guidelines cover a broad spectrum of CSR practices relevant to developing nations, offering Malaysian universities a roadmap to align their social responsibility strategies with global standards. Following this, numerous university-community engagement projects have been undertaken in a variety of multidisciplinary ways to achieve sustainable development in Malaysia (Hasan et al. 2023).

Research by Othman and Othman (2014) highlights distinct priorities in the social responsibility practices of Malaysian public and private universities. Public universities often focus on enhancing the well-being of their staff and students, such as providing greater opportunities for career advancement and upgrading teaching and learning facilities. In contrast, private universities prioritize external stakeholders and institutional prospects, exemplified by initiatives such as educational outreach programs for primary and secondary school students. These differences reflect the influence of organizational structures, policies, and decision-making frameworks on USR efforts in Malaysia (Rahman et al. 2019). Despite these differences, both public and private universities play critical roles in advancing societal development and uniquely contribute to USR initiatives in Malaysia.

In addition, recent developments in Malaysia found that USR has increasingly aligned with the Sustainable Development Goals (SDGs) as the country strives to achieve sustainable development by 2030. As significant pillars of society, universities play an essential role in the pursuit of sustainable development in the modern era. They have the potential to become active agents of economic growth and sustainability through various means, such as (1) promoting public dialogue; (2) disseminating scientific and technological advancements; (3) fostering cooperation between legislators, corporate executives, university officials, and the public; and (4) propelling socioeconomic progress (Qazi et al. 2021).

As cited in the Times Higher Education (THE) Impact Rankings, many Malaysian universities have been recognized for their efforts toward Agenda 2030 through research, stewardship, outreach, and teaching (THE Impact Ranking 2023). For example, Universiti Sains Malaysia (USM) secured the top spot in Asia and remained among the top five globally in the THE Impact Rankings 2023. Meanwhile, Univer siti Teknologi Malaysia (UTM) ranked first worldwide in SDG 7 (Affordable and Clean Energy) (Dermawan 2023). Universiti Malaya also demonstrated significant progress in sustainability, ranking 66th globally in the QS rankings and excelling in promoting social equity and conducting SDG-aligned research (Idris 2023). These achievements highlight the pivotal role of Malaysian universities in advancing the global sustainability agenda through their USR initiatives. As Malaysia continues to champion sustainable development, the role of universities in fostering innovation, equity, and sustainability will remain indispensable. This underscores the need for ongoing research and dialogue to further enhance USR frameworks and strengthen their alignment with national and global goals in Malaysia.

3 Methodology

To address the three research questions of this study, a total of 10 in-depth semi-structured interviews were conducted between March to May 2024 with university leaders from institutions featured in the Times Higher Education (THE) Impact Rankings 2024. The THE Impact Rankings are widely regarded as a comprehensive benchmark for evaluating sustainability efforts in higher education. It is the only global ranking system that assesses universities based on their contributions to the United Nations' Sustainable Development Goals (SDGs) through research, stewardship, outreach, and teaching (Times Higher Education, n.d.).

Purposive sampling was employed to select participants, focusing on individuals holding key leadership roles, such as Directors or Deputy Directors of Sustainability or Centers for University-Industry Collaboration. These leaders play a critical role in planning, implementing, and managing USR initiatives. Their expertise and strategic positions ensured the credibility of the data collected and provided valuable insights into the decision-making processes and organizational priorities that shape USR efforts (Ma et al. 2021). Table 1 lists the 10 Malaysian public universities included in this study, based on their representation in the THE Impact Rankings 2023. The selection of these institutions ensures that the findings reflect best practices and diverse approaches to USR within the context of Malaysian higher education.

The semi-structured in-depth interviews were conducted online using Cisco WebEx Meetings, with scheduling coordinated to accommodate participant availability. This virtual format enabled efficient and cost-effective engagement with universities across Malaysia. All interviews were recorded using audio recorders and the WebEx recording feature, with prior consent obtained from participants. In addition to the recordings', detailed notes were taken to ensure comprehensive data collection. The interviews followed a structured approach, guided by a pre-designed interview protocol outlined in Table 2. The primary and probing questions were specifically crafted to elicit participants' insights on the implementation, initiatives,

Table 1 The 10 Malaysian public universities

No	Name of University	Type
1	Universiti Sains Malaysia	Research University
2	Universiti Malaya	Research University
3	Universiti Teknologi Malaysia	Research University
4	Universiti Teknologi MARA	Comprehensive University
5	Universiti Malaysia Pahang Sultan Abdullah	Focused University
6	Universiti Malaysia Perlis	Focused University
7	Universiti Malaysia Sarawak	Comprehensive University
8	Universiti Utara Malaysia	Focused University
9	Universiti Malaysia Kelantan	Focused University
10	Universiti Teknikal Malaysia Melaka	Focused University

Table 2 Semi-structured interview questions

No	Questions	Probing questions
1	How is USR implemented in the university?	• What are the key frameworks and policies that guide the implementation of USR initiatives in the university?
2	What are the top 3 USR initiatives carried out at the university?	• How does your university prioritize or select USR initiatives?
3	What are the significant outcomes of USR initiatives conducted by the university?	• What do you perceive as the primary goals or objectives of USR in the context of your university?

and outcomes of USR within Malaysian universities. This approach ensured that the data collected was both focused and thorough, addressing the study's objectives comprehensively.

To analyse the collected data systematically, this study employed **thematic analysis** as the primary analytical method. Thematic analysis is a widely used qualitative technique that allows researchers to identify, organize, and interpret patterns or themes within the data, which are subsequently used to address the research objectives (Nowell et al. 2017). Braun and Clarke (2012) delineate six sequential steps in thematic analysis: (1) familiarisation with the data (2) developing initial codes, (3) constructing themes, (4) reviewing themes, (5) defining and naming themes, and (6) writing the report.

4 Results and Discussion

This study explores the implementation of University Social Responsibility (USR) in Malaysian higher education, with a particular focus on the initiatives, outcomes, and frameworks that guide and shape USR practices.

The findings reveal that **USR implementation** in Malaysia is not an ad hoc effort but follows a structured and strategic approach designed to ensure relevance, effectiveness, and sustainability. This systematic process comprises five key phases: initiation, planning, implementation, monitoring, and reporting. Each phase plays a pivotal role in aligning USR initiatives with institutional goals and societal needs, ensuring a comprehensive and impactful approach.

Additionally, the findings highlight that **USR initiatives** in Malaysia are concentrated in four main areas: economic, legal, philanthropic, and high-impact programs. These categories reflect a holistic approach that not only addresses immediate community needs but also fosters long-term societal transformation. Furthermore, the **outcomes** of USR initiatives are found to be sustainability-driven, underscoring their alignment with Malaysia's commitment to achieving sustainable development goals by 2030.

Based on these findings, a **USR framework** is proposed to provide practical guidelines for Malaysian universities to enhance their social responsibility efforts. This framework integrates strategic processes with actionable initiatives, offering a roadmap to optimize the role of universities as catalysts for sustainable development and societal progress. The following sections provide a detailed analysis of the themes derived from the interviews.

5 USR Implementation in Malaysia

This section explores the findings related to the first research objective: understanding the implementation of USR in Malaysia. Based on insights gathered from in-depth interviews, the study identifies a five-stage, strategic approach to USR implementation, encompassing initiation, planning, implementation, monitoring, and reporting. Each stage plays a critical role in ensuring the relevance, impact, and sustainability of USR initiatives, aligning them with local and global development goals.

Beginning with initiation, participants describe this step as identifying the background, issues, and needs of the community in tailoring USR initiatives. These steps are essential for gathering preliminary data, understanding the needs of the community, and identifying potential areas for intervention. This phase is crucial for understanding the institution's unique strengths and challenges, ensuring that subsequent actions are aligned with both the university's mission and societal demands. Profiling sets the foundation for effective collaboration and tailored interventions, reflecting a proactive approach to addressing community issues.

Our lecturers will go to the community to discuss together about the problem and the process happens continuously. P5

It always starts with community engagement. We want to know what are the challenges and constraints that the community have, so the problem statement must be from the community. And we when we define or ideate, one of the processes, we will think of the strategy. P7

The second step of USR is planning which involves bringing together multiple stakeholders to strategize USR initiatives. Participants noted that the Penta Helix Collaboration model is widely recognized in Malaysia as an effective framework for fostering innovation and sustainable development. This model emphasizes the engagement of five key sectors: government, industry, academia, civil society, and individuals. This collaboration ensures a diverse range of expertise, resources, and perspectives are harnessed, making USR initiatives more inclusive and impactful. Participants noted that collaboration with these sectors helps universities overcome significant challenges, particularly financial constraints, which often hinder the implementation of USR initiatives (Abdullah 2017). Therefore, the Penta Helix approach reflects Malaysia's recognition of the interconnected nature of societal challenges and the need for collective action.

Community program needs to have collaboration involving agencies from NGOs, government or industry. So, we are together, not just the university. So, we get a third party together to contribute to the community. P8

The third step is implementation describes the actual execution of USR activities. Participants shared that these initiatives vary in scope and duration, with some being short-term and others long-term projects. The specific aims and available budgets for each program often dictate the nature of the projects. While certain initiatives focus exclusively on local outreach, others extend to global communities, ensuring inclusivity and broad-reaching impact.

Monitoring is the fourth phase and involves assessing the effectiveness and impact of USR initiatives. This stage focuses on evaluating key outcomes, such as improvements in community livelihoods and environmental sustainability, to ensure that the initiatives meet their intended goals. Participants stressed the importance of continuous assessment to measure progress and make necessary adjustments.

When we do a high-impact community project, we will measure the community's well-being index. We want to see if there are any positive changes or improvements after the implementation of the community project. P6

Last but not least, the final phase, reporting involves documenting and communicating the activities, outcomes, and impacts of USR initiatives. Participants highlighted that transparent reporting is essential for demonstrating accountability, aligning with national and international standards, and enhancing university visibility. Regular reporting not only ensures stakeholder confidence but also positions universities as credible leaders in social responsibility.

In conclusion, each stage of USR implementation in Malaysia plays an integral role: profiling ensures relevance, planning fosters collaboration and strategic alignment, implementation drives tangible action, monitoring evaluates impact, and reporting guarantees transparency and accountability. Together, these stages provide a structured framework for Malaysian universities to lead in sustainable development, emphasizing relevance, collaboration, tangible action, accountability, and transparency. This structured framework ensures that USR initiatives are impactful, sustainable, and aligned with both local needs and global development goals.

6 USR Initiatives in Malaysia

This section explores the findings related to the second research objective: analyzing the scope of USR initiatives in Malaysia. Insights from the in-depth interviews reveal that Malaysian universities typically implement USR initiatives across four main scopes: economic responsibilities, legal responsibilities, philanthropic responsibilities, and high-impact initiatives. Each scope reflects a distinct area of focus, collectively contributing to the broader mission of USR in addressing societal and developmental challenges. This multidimensional approach ensures that USR initiatives address a wide spectrum of challenges while utilizing the unique capabilities of universities.

Firstly, economic responsibility involves the efficient management of resources, revenue generation, and making financially responsible decisions to support social and community initiatives. Participants highlighted that universities strive to balance financial sustainability with their commitment to societal well-being by reinvesting revenue and leveraging partnerships to fund impactful programs. These efforts not only support community projects but also strengthen the financial stability of the universities themselves.

The solar-powered bus stop is an effort by Uni D to obtain funding through strategic partnerships with the private sector to install solar-powered bus stops at eight bus stops within the campus. So, students can charge their phones and notebooks while waiting for the bus. P4

Secondly, legal responsibility refers to the university's adherence to federal, state, and local regulations to ensure fair and lawful operations. Compliance with legal frameworks ensures that USR initiatives maintain integrity and align with governance standards. Participants emphasized that legal responsibilities serve as a foundation for ethical decision—making, safeguarding the credibility and legitimacy of USR efforts.

USR in University E consists of activities that is permitted and allowed by our legislation. P5

Thirdly, philanthropic responsibilities reflect the voluntary contributions of university members toward the greater good. As one participant articulated, the overarching objective is to "protect the environment, promote economic equity, and ultimately achieve social justice" (P1, U1). These initiatives often involve sharing resources, expertise, and influence to benefit individuals and communities. Activities such as community service, educational outreach, and social impact programs fall within this scope. Participants noted that philanthropic efforts are instrumental in enhancing community well-being and fostering goodwill between universities and their surrounding communities.

Lastly, high-impact initiatives aim to deliver sustainable and measurable benefits for both the community and the university in the long run. These initiatives are typically categorized into two formats: knowledge transfer and technology transfer. Knowledge transfer involves the dissemination of academic and professional expertise to empower communities, improve livelihoods, and address pressing societal challenges. For example, the participants informed that universities often conduct workshops or training programs to enhance financial literacy, agricultural practices, and health awareness in underprivileged communities. Meanwhile, technology transfer focuses on applying university-led research and technological innovation to solve real-world problems. For instance, the participants highlighted projects such as the installation of solar energy systems in rural areas to address energy poverty while promoting environmental sustainability.

7 USR Outcomes in Malaysia

This section addresses the third research objective: evaluating the impacts and outcomes of USR in Malaysia. The findings reveal that USR initiatives in Malaysian universities are predominantly sustainability-driven, underscoring their alignment with the United Nations Sustainable Development Goals (SDGs).

The SDGs offer a global framework for addressing critical environmental, social, and economic challenges, including climate change, poverty alleviation, and access to quality education. By integrating these goals into their USR initiatives, Malaysian universities contribute to global sustainability efforts while simultaneously enhancing their international rankings and reputation. Participants emphasized that aligning USR initiatives with the SDGs is not merely aspirational but a strategic priority. This alignment ensures that the universities' programs are impactful, globally relevant, and aligned with national and international development agendas.

We formulate the framework for Uni C Sustainability Blueprint, focusing on sustainability effort which is the guidance is on SDG of course. P3

Regardless of the projects we undertake, we must make the SDGs a primary criterion. That is crucial. P5

By embedding the SDGs into their USR frameworks, Malaysian universities demonstrate their commitment to addressing multifaceted societal challenges while ensuring measurable outcomes. For example, USR initiatives often tackle specific SDG targets, such as reducing inequalities, improving health and well-being, and promoting sustainable energy solutions. These efforts extend the universities' role beyond academic excellence to becoming active agents of global change and local impact.

In conclusion, Malaysian universities' USR initiatives reflect a strong commitment to sustainability, driven by alignment with the United Nations' SDGs. By integrating SDG—focused projects and practices, these institutions contribute meaningfully to addressing global challenges while enhancing their international standing and local impact.

8 USR Framework in Malaysia

This study introduces a USR framework that reflects the unique characteristics of the Malaysian context. As training grounds for future leaders and global stakeholders, universities have a crucial role in equipping individuals with the knowledge, skills, and mindsets needed to tackle sustainable development challenges and

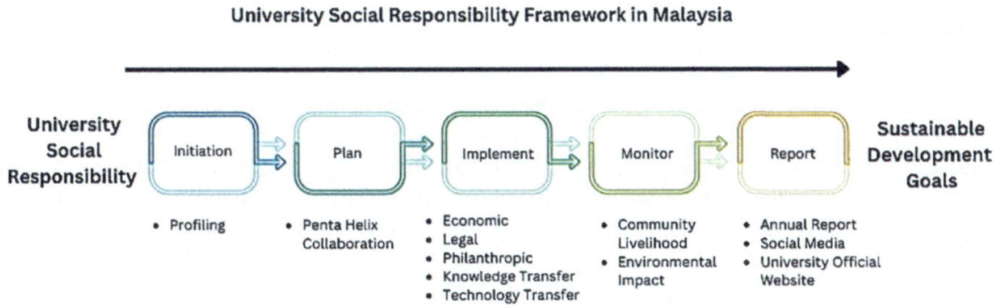

Fig. 1 USR framework in Malaysia

meet the United Nations' 17 SDGs by 2030 (Nejati, 2011). The framework highlights a systematic process that progresses through five interconnected phases: Initiation, Plan, Implement, Monitor, and Report, ultimately aligning these efforts with the SDGs. This structured approach underscores the importance of strategic planning, stakeholder engagement, and measurable outcomes in achieving sustainable development objectives. Furthermore, the framework's direct alignment with the SDGs ensures that Malaysian USR initiatives are globally relevant while addressing local challenges. This dual focus enhances the credibility and impact of Malaysian universities on both national and international stages (Fig. 1).

9 Conclusion

In conclusion, this study underscores the proactive initiatives of Malaysian universities in embedding sustainability and societal impact into their institutional frameworks. Theoretically, it enriches the body of knowledge on the implementation of USR in developing countries, highlighting its unique dimensions. For instance, the Penta Helix Collaboration model reflects Malaysia's pluralistic culture, emphasizing collective efforts and stakeholder synergy to achieve sustainable development goals. Methodologically, the qualitative research design adopted provides in-depth and novel insights into the practice of USR in Malaysia, addressing a critical gap in existing literature. Practically, the proposed USR framework offers valuable guidance for university leaders, administrators, and policymakers in effectively conceptualizing and implementing USR initiatives. As a recommendation for future research, the exploration of quantitative methods or comparative studies across different regional and cultural contexts could further validate and expand the findings.

Acknowledgements The authors would like to extend appreciation to the Ministry of Higher Education Malaysia for the Fundamental Research Grant Scheme with Project Code FRGS/1/2024/SS05/USM/01/1. This article is one of the stated tangible outputs.

References

Abdullah, D. (2017). Public universities and budget cuts in Malaysia. *International Higher Education*, (91), 15–17. https://doi.org/10.6017/ihe.2017.91.10129

Ahmad, J., Saad, S., Krishnan, M., Stancu, A., & Mogoş, O. (2024). Exploring the University Social Responsibility Initiatives and Sustainable Development in Malaysia: A Carroll Model Approach. *European Journal of Interdisciplinary Studies, 16*(1), 70–90. https://doi.org/10.24818/ejis.2024.06

Ahmad, J. (2012). Can a university act as a corporate social responsibility (CSR) driver? An analysis. Social Responsibility Journal, 8(1), 77–86. https://doi.org/10.1108/17471111211196584

Ahmad, J., & Saad, S. (2013). Beyond theory and practice: A Malaysian case study. In *Education and Corporate Social Responsibility International Perspectives*, 267–296. https://doi.org/10.1108/s2043-0523(2013)0000004014

Awad, J., & Martín-Rojas, R. (2024). Enhancing social responsibility and resilience through entrepreneurship and digital environment. *Corporate Social Responsibility and Environmental Management, 31*(3), 1688–1704. https://doi.org/10.1002/csr.2655

Ashida, A. (2022). The role of higher education in achieving the sustainable development goals. In Sustainable Development Disciplines for Humanity: Breaking Down the 5Ps— People, Planet, Prosperity, Peace, and Partnerships. Singapore: Springer Nature Singapore. 71–84. https://doi.org/10.1007/978-981-19-4859-6_5

Asemah, E. S., Okpanachi, R. A., & Edegoh, L. O. (2013). Business advantages of corporate social responsibility practice: Communication, 18(0), 45–54. A critical review. *New Media and Mass Communication, 18*(0), 45–54. https://doi.org/10.4314/afrrev.v7i4.12

Alemu, S. K. (2018, December). Meaning, idea and history of university/higher education: Brief literature review. In *FIRE: Forum for International Research in Education* ,4 (3) https://doi.org/10.32865/fire20184312

Alzyoud, S. A., & Bani-Hani, K. (2015). Social responsibility in higher education institutions: Application case from the Middle East. *European Scientific Journal, 11*(8), 122–129.

Abu Osman, N. A. (2023). Private higher learning institutions have vital role in national agenda. *New Straits Times*. https://www.nst.com.my/opinion/columnists/2023/05/905698/private-higher-learning-institutions-have-vital-role-national

Burke, L., & Logsdon, J. M. (1996). How corporate social responsibility pays off. *Long range planning, 29*(4), 495–502. https://doi.org/10.1016/0024-6301(96)00041-6

Braun, V., & Clarke, V. (2012). *Thematic analysis*. American Psychological Association. https://doi.org/10.1007/978-1-4614-5583-7_311

Bojarajan, A. K., Al Omari, S. A. B., Al-Marzouqi, A. H., Alshamsi, D., Sherif, M., Kabeer, S., & Sangaraju, S. (2024). A holistic overview of sustainable energy technologies and thermal management in UAE: the path to net zero emissions. *International Journal of Thermofluids, 23*, 100758. https://doi.org/10.1016/j.ijft.2024.100758

Calculli, C., D'Uggento, A. M., Labarile, A., & Ribecco, N. (2021). Evaluating people's awareness about climate changes and environmental issues: A case study. Journal of Cleaner Production, 324, 129244. https://doi.org/10.1016/j.jclepro.2021.129244

Carroll, A. B. (1991). The pyramid of corporate social responsibility: Toward the moral management of organisational stakeholders. *Business Horizons*, 34 (4), 39–48. https://doi.org/10.1016/0007-6813(91)90005-g

Carroll, A. B. (2004). Managing ethically with global stakeholders: A present and future challenge. *Academy of Management Perspectives, 18*(2), 114–120. https://doi.org/10.5465/ame.2004.13836269

Carroll, A. B. (2016). Carroll's pyramid of CSR: Taking another look. *International Journal of Corporate Social Responsibility, 1*(1), 1–8. https://doi.org/10.1186/s40991-016-0004-6

Chan, T. J., & Mohd Hasan, N. A. (2018). Corporate social responsibility practices from the employees' perspective: A case of Malaysian higher education institution. *International journal of Academic research in business and social sciences*, *8*(4), 131–153. https://doi.org/10.6007/ijarbss/v8-i4/4003

Compagnucci, L., & Spigarelli, F. (2020). The Third Mission of the university: A systematic literature review on potentials and constraints. *Technological Forecasting and Social Change*, *161*, 120284. https://doi.org/10.1016/j.techfore.2020.120284

Cosenz, F. (2022). University's "third mission" assessment through outcome-based dynamic performance management. In *Managing Sustainable Performance and Governance in Higher Education Institutions: A Dynamic Performance Management Approach* (pp. 133–167). Cham: Springer International Publishing. https://doi.org/10.1007/978-3-030-99317-7_4

Do, T (2023). Humboldt's philosophy of university education and implication for autonomous education in Vietnam today. Perspectives of Science and Education, 62 (2), 549–561. https://doi.org/10.32744/pse.2023.2.32

Davis, K., & Blomstrom, R. L. (1968). Business and its environment. https://doi.org/10.5465/amj.1968.4297423

Dermawan, A. (2023, June 2). *The Impact Rankings 2023: USM maintains No. 4 position in the world*. *New Straits Times*. https://www.nst.com.my/news/2023/06/impact-rankings-usm-maintains

Feng, Y., Kerner, A., & Sumner, J. L. (2021). Quitting globalization: trade-related job losses, nationalism, and resistance to FDI in the United States. *Political Science Research and Methods*, *9*(2), 292–311. https://doi.org/10.1017/psrm.2019.30

Fulford, A., & Locke, D. (2023). Being universitas: community and being present in times of pandemic. *Ethics and Education*, *18*(1), 51–66. https://doi.org/10.1080/17449642.2023.2188718

Hwang, J., Kim, J. J., & Lee, S. (2020). The importance of philanthropic corporate social responsibility and its impact on attitude and behavioral intentions: The moderating role of the barista disability status. *Sustainability*, *12*(15), 6235. https://doi.org/10.3390/su12156235

Haj Taieb, S. (2024). Measuring the third mission of European Universities: A systematic literature review. *Societyand Economy*, *46*(2), 147–167. https://doi.org/10.1556/204.2023.00030

Hall, B. L., & Tandon, R. (2021). *Socially responsible higher education: International perspectives on knowledge democracy* (p. 332). Brill. https://doi.org/10.1163/9789004459076

Hasan, S. I., Bakar, A. A., Radi, N. A. M., Mansor, M. A., Hamzah, Z. L., & Nordin, A. S. A. (2023). The Positive Impact of University-Community Engagement Projects: A Case Study in the Context of Universiti Malaya. *Journal of Research Management and Governance*, *5*(1), 30–49. https://doi.org/10.22452/jrmg.vol5no1.3

Huang, Y. F., & Do, M. H. (2021). Review of empirical research on university social responsibility. *International Journal of Educational Management*, *35*(3), 549–563. https://doi.org/10.1108/ijem-10-2020-0449

Ismail, Z., & Shujaat, N. (2019). CSR in universities: a case study on internal stakeholder perception of university social responsibility. *Advances in Social Sciences Research Journal*, *6*(1). https://doi.org/10.14738/assrj.61.5256

Idris, M. A. (2023, October 20). *Building holistic sustainability commitment in Malaysian universities*. *Malay Mail*. https://www.malaymail.com/news/what-you-think/2023/10/20/building-holistic-sustainability-commitment-in-malaysian-universities-mohd-azree-idris/97398

Javanmardi, E., Liu, S., & Xie, N. (2023). Exploring the challenges to sustainable development from the perspective of grey systems theory. *Systems*, *11*(2), 70.https://doi.org/10.3390/systems11020070

Keong, L. B., Ramakrishnan, S., & Hishan, S. S. (2017). The review of corporate social responsibility (CSR) literature in the new millennium. *Advanced Science Letters*, *23*(9), 9271–9274. https://doi.org/10.1166/asl.2017.10068

Kumari, S. K., Hariharasuthan, M., Parthasarathi, G., Pavitha, S., Pavithra, D., & Kumaran, R. S. (2023). Higher Education's Role in Fostering Societal Well-being: A Study on University Social Responsibility and its Implications. European Economic Letters (EEL), 13(4), 141–151.

Knudson, H. (2018). Making the business case: The effects of corporate social responsibility on SME competitiveness. *Kolk, A. (2008)'Corporate Governance: Exploring', Business Strategy and the Environment.*

Lo, C.WH., Pang, R.X., Egri, C.P., Li, P.HY. (2017). University Social Responsibility: Conceptualization and an Assessment Framework. In: Shek, D., Hollister, R. (eds) University Social Responsibility and Quality of Life. Quality of Life in Asia, vol 8. Springer, Singapore. https://doi.org/10.1007/978-981-10-3877-8_4

Latapí Agudelo, M. A., Jóhannsdóttir, L., & Davídsdóttir, B. (2019). A literature review of the history and evolution of corporate social responsibility. *International journal of corporate social responsibility, 4*(1), 1–23. https://doi.org/10.1186/s40991-018-0039-y

Ma, S., Seidl, D., & McNulty, T. (2021). Challenges and practices of interviewing business elites. Strategic Organization, 19(1), 81–96. https://doi.org/10.1177/1476127020980969

Mohd Hasan, N. A. (2017). Managing standards in corporate social responsibility online: A case study of a Malaysian Higher Learning Institution. *International Journal of Economic Research, 14(*14), 259–274.

Nejati, M., Shafaei, A., Salamzadeh, Y., & Daraei, M. (2011). Corporate social responsibility and universities: A study of top 10 world universities' websites. *African Journal of Business Management, 5*(2), 440–447. https://ssrn.com/abstract=1868688

Naranjo-Africano, G., Vega-Jurado, J., & Manjarres-Henríquez, L. (2023). Barriers to Third Mission: organizational and individual antecedents. Journal of Innovation and Entrepreneurship, 12(1), 1–23. https://doi.org/10.1186/s13731-023-00300-4

Nowell, L. S., Norris, J. M., White, D. E., & Moules, N. J. (2017). Thematic analysis: Striving to meet the trustworthiness criteria. *International journal of qualitative methods, 16*(1), https://doi.org/10.1177/1609406917733847

Nimani, A., Zeqiraj, V., & Spahija, D. (2022). The importance of corporate social responsibility for companies: The developing market study. *Journal of Governance and Regulation,11*(4), 312–320. https://doi.org/10.22495/jgrv11i4siart11

Othman, R., & Othman, R. (2014). Higher education institutions and social performance: Evidence from public and private universities. *International Journal of Business & Society, 15*(1), 1–18.

Qazi, Z., Qazi, W., Raza, S. A., & Yousufi, S. Q. (2021). The antecedents affecting university reputation and student satisfaction: a study in higher education context. *Corporate Reputation Review*, 1–19. https://doi.org/10.1057/s41299-021-00126-4

Rahman, A. A., Castka, P., & Love, T. (2019). Corporate social responsibility in higher education: A study of the institutionalisation of CSR in Malaysian public universities. *Corporate Social Responsibility and Environmental Management, 26*(4), 916–928. https://doi.org/10.1002/csr.1731

Ramos-Monge, E. L., Llinas-Audet, X., & Barrena-Martinez, J. (2017). Universities as corporate entities: The role of social responsibility in their strategic management. *Corporate Governnce and Strategic Decision Making*, 199–215. https://doi.org/10.5772/intechopen.69931

Sharma, D., & Sharma, R. (2019). A review literature on university social responsibility initiatives in the global context. *Journal of Emerging Technologies and Innovative Research, 6(*6), 27–35.

Senin, M. A., Halim, H., & Ali, A. A. E. R. (2019). Corporate Social Responsibility (CSR) for Education in Malaysia: A Systematic Li terature Review. *International Journal of Psychosocial Rehabilitation, 23*(3). 631–637. https://doi.org/10.37200/ijpr/v23i3/pr190352

Sierra, J., & Suárez-Collado, Á. (2021). Understanding economic, social, and environmental sustainability challenges in the global south. Sustainability, 13(13), 7201. https://doi.org/10.3390/su13137201

Shaari, R., Sarip, A., Rajab, A., & Wan Zakaria, W. Z. (2018). The impact of university social responsibility towards producing good citizenship: Evidence Malaysia. *International Journal of Organizational Leadership*, 7, 374–382. https://doi.org/10.33844/ijol.2018.60183

Stobierski, T. (2021, April 15). Effects of globalization on the environment. Business Insights Blog. Retrieved January 12, 2025, from https://online.hbs.edu/blog/post/globalization-effects-on-environment#:~:text=Increased%20greenhouse%20gas%20emissions%2C%20ocean,reduce%20biodiversity%20around%20the%20globe

Taliento, M. (2022). The Triple Mission of the Modern University: Component Interplay and Performance Analysis from Italy. *World, 3*(3), 489–512. https://doi.org/10.3390/world3030027

Takefman, B. (2023). The effects of globalization on economic development. *FDI Insights, Opinions.*

Vefago, Y. B., Trierweiller, A. C., & de Paula, L. B. (2020). The third mission of universities: the entrepreneurial university. Brazilian Journal of Operations & Production Management, 17(4), 1–9. https://doi.org/10.14488/bjopm.2020.042

Willamo, R., Helenius, L., Holmström, C., Haapanen, L., Sandström, V., Huotari, E., ... & Kolehmainen, L. (2018). Learning how to understand complexity and deal with sustainability challenges–A framework for a comprehensive approach and its application in university education. *Ecological Modelling, 370*, 1–13. https://doi.org/10.1016/j.ecolmodel.2017.12.011

Zhang, Y., Tian, K., Li, X., Jiang, X., & Yang, C. (2022). From globalization to regionalization? Assessing its potential environmental and economic effects. *Applied Energy, 310*, 118642. https://doi.org/10.1016/j.apenergy.2022.118642

Zhao, S., & Cheah, K. S. (2023). The challenges of Malaysian private universities in reaching sustainable education toward responsible consumption. *Cleaner and Responsible Consumption, 10*, 100130. https://doi.org/10.1016/j.clrc.2023.100130

Zakariya, H. (2014). Community engagement in Malaysian higher education: An overview. In *Proceedings of SOCIOINT14-International Conference on Social Sciences and Humanities* (pp. 612–616).

Strategic Evaluation of Blue Economy Components with Grey Theory: A Sustainability Perspective

Gülay Demir, Prasenjit Chatterjee, and Ercan Özen

Abstract Blue economy refers to the sustainable use of ocean resources for economic growth, improved livelihoods, and ocean ecosystem health, making it vital for regions with extensive coastlines and rich marine resources. This study employs a grey decision-making trial and evaluation laboratory (DEMATEL) method to evaluate eight critical criteria influencing blue economy. The analysis reveals that environmental sustainability holds the highest relative importance with a value of 2.0094, emphasizing the need for preserving marine ecosystems. Legal and regulatory framework and Economic growth follow closely with values of 1.6916 and 1.8119, respectively, indicating their essential roles in supporting successful blue economy projects. In terms of influence, the Legal and Regulatory Framework emerges as the most impactful criterion, with a value of 0.4549, suggesting that effective legal measures significantly shape other areas of blue economy. Conversely, Investment and Financing Opportunities are identified as the most affected criterion, with a value of -0.3974, indicating their heavy dependence on legal frameworks and technological advancements. These findings highlight the necessity of a balanced approach that integrates environmental, economic, and legal factors for successful blue economy initiatives. The practical implications provide valuable insights for resource allocation, regulatory compliance, and strategic planning, suggesting that future research could benefit from broader geographical analyses and advanced decision-making techniques.

Keywords Blue economy · Grey theory · Grey numbers · DEMATEL

G. Demir
Vocational School of Health Services, Sivas Cumhuriyet University, Sivas, Türkiye
e-mail: gulaydemir@cumhuriyet.edu.tr

P. Chatterjee
Department of Mechanical Engineering, MCKV Institute of Engineering, Howrah, West Bengal, India

E. Özen (✉)
Faculty of Applied Sciences, University of Uşak, Uşak, Türkiye
e-mail: ercan.ozen@usak.edu.tr

S. O. Idowu et al. (eds.), *Competitiveness and Sustainability in the Digitization Era*, Springer Proceedings in Business and Economics,
https://doi.org/10.1007/978-3-031-91778-3_10

1 Introduction

The concept of blue economy is a development model that seeks to balance economic growth and environmental protection by sustainably using ocean and marine resources (Silver et al. 2015). It aims to maximize economic potential of sectors like maritime transport, fisheries, marine biotechnology, coastal tourism, and offshore renewable energy while protecting the ecological health of seas and oceans (Smith-Godfrey 2016). Blue economy is particularly significant in terms of environmental conservation, biodiversity sustainability, and combating climate change (Voyer et al. 2018). One of the United Nations' Sustainable Development Goals (SDGs), 'Life Below Water' (SDG 14), highlights that blue economy is a global priority (UN 2015). Blue economy integrates environmentally sustainable practices, combining investments in renewable ocean energy with traditional activities such as sustainable fisheries and eco-friendly coastal tourism (Pauli 2010). This economic approach not only offers potential for lasting financial growth but also requires a commitment to protecting marine ecosystems and resources. Sustainable management within the blue economy framework yields both economic and environmental rewards, promoting biodiversity and helping to mitigate the impacts of climate change on marine ecosystems (Mulazzani and Malorgio 2017). However, achieving a balanced blue economy involves substantial challenges, particularly in coordinating decision-making processes among stakeholders who often have different goals and priorities. These stakeholders include government agencies, private businesses, local communities, environmental organizations, and international bodies (Bennett et al. 2019). Government agencies may emphasize regulatory measures to uphold environmental standards, while local communities are typically focused on preserving their livelihoods through sustainable practices. Meanwhile, the private sector generally prioritizes economic growth, aiming for profitable returns and market stability. In contrast, environmental organizations are dedicated to protecting ecosystems and reducing marine pollution (Kittinger et al. 2014). These differing objectives of these groups contribute to a challenging decision-making environment within blue economy initiatives, often necessitating negotiation and alignment of interests. Effective governance and multi-criteria decision-making frameworks are essential to balancing these interests, supporting an economically sustainable yet ecologically mindful blue economy that provides benefits for current and future generations. Decision-making in blue economy sectors becomes complex due to the challenges arising from these diverse priorities. For instance, increasing fishing activities may bring economic benefits but could also threaten long-term sustainability by having negative impacts on marine ecosystems (Hilborn et al. 2020). Similarly, coastal tourism can boost the regional economy, but overcrowding and pollution may negatively affect marine life (Honey and Krantz 2007). In this context, striking a balance between environmental protection and economic growth is crucial. Strategic decisions in blue economy are typically complex processes, requiring consideration of uncertainties and multiple criteria. In such situations, methods like fuzzy logic or grey system theory can assist decision-makers in managing these uncertainties and balancing various criteria.

The objective of this paper is to assess the critical factors influencing blue economy through a grey decision-making trial and evaluation laboratory (DEMATEL) approach, focusing on environmental, economic, and regulatory elements that contribute to sustainable ocean resource utilization. By evaluating criteria such as environmental sustainability, legal frameworks, and economic growth, this study aims to identify the interdependencies and impact of these factors on successful blue economy projects. The findings are intended to guide strategic planning and resource allocation efforts, supporting a balanced approach that strengthens both economic opportunities and ocean ecosystem health.

Grey system theory was developed to improve decision-making processes in complex systems where uncertainties and incomplete data are present. One of the main reasons for choosing grey system theory in this study is its superior ability to handle limited and incomplete data sets. Grey system theory enables effective decision-making in situations where uncertain and incomplete information is available and provides a flexible structure that can be easily integrated with different decision-making processes (Fu et al. 2012; Li and Qi 2024). Grey system theory plays a crucial role in resolving uncertainties caused by inappropriate decisions made by individuals (Fu et al. 2012). The theory can be used in discrete data situations where unclear and incomplete information is frequently encountered and offers optimal solutions in such data sets (Ju-Long 1982; Julong 1989). In this context, grey system theory is particularly suitable for working with small samples, which is a significant advantage in improving the accuracy of current judgments (Liu and Qiao 2014). The effectiveness of the theory in providing analytical results in situations with insufficient data makes it even more attractive (Kun-lin 2004). Another key reason for choosing grey system theory in this study is its ability to represent data with grey numbers when the data level is partially incomplete. Grey numbers represent ranges of uncertain data, playing a vital role in addressing issues related to incomplete information. This feature allows reliable results to be obtained in strategic decision-making processes in the analysis of blue economy components in Turkey, where data is limited. Due to its ability to handle such uncertainties, grey system theory stands out as an ideal method for analysis in this study. DEMATEL method has been chosen for this study due to its ability to handle complex interrelationships among multiple criteria and to identify both the influence and dependence among these criteria. In the context of blue economy, where criteria like environmental sustainability, regulatory frameworks, and economic growth are interdependent, DEMATEL is particularly suited for mapping these interconnections and determining the extent to which one criterion affects others.

1.1 Components of Blue Economy

Blue economy is a comprehensive concept that aims to sustainably manage the economic opportunities offered by the oceans and seas. In the literature, the components of blue economy are detailed on the axis of economic potential and environmental sustainability and are given in Fig. 1.

- Fisheries and Aquaculture:

Fisheries are one of the oldest and most fundamental sectors of blue economy. However, overfishing poses a significant threat to the sustainability of marine ecosystems. As a result, sustainable fisheries policies focus on the conservation of fish stocks (FAO 2020). Aquaculture, on the other hand, is a rapidly growing sector that holds strategic importance for food security and economic development. This sector supports the more sustainable use of marine resources (Bostock et al. 2010).

- Sea Transport:

More than 80% of global trade is conducted through maritime transport, which plays a strategic role in the global economy. However, this sector is associated with marine pollution and carbon emissions. Sustainable maritime transport will be achieved through the development and implementation of lower-carbon emission technologies (Buhaug et al. 2009).

- Coastal Tourism:

While marine tourism offers significant potential for economic growth, excessive tourism creates substantial environmental pressure on coastal ecosystems (Honey and Krantz 2007). Sustainable coastal tourism practices aim to minimize environmental impacts and benefit local communities. The concepts of ecotourism and green tourism, in particular, allow for more sustainable management of coastal tourism (Telfer and Sharpley 2015).

- Offshore Energy:

Renewable energy sources, especially offshore wind energy, are key components of blue economy. This sector offers significant opportunities in the transition to clean energy, but it requires the use of technologies that do not harm marine ecosystems (IRENA 2020). Renewable energy projects also have great potential for energy independence and economic growth.

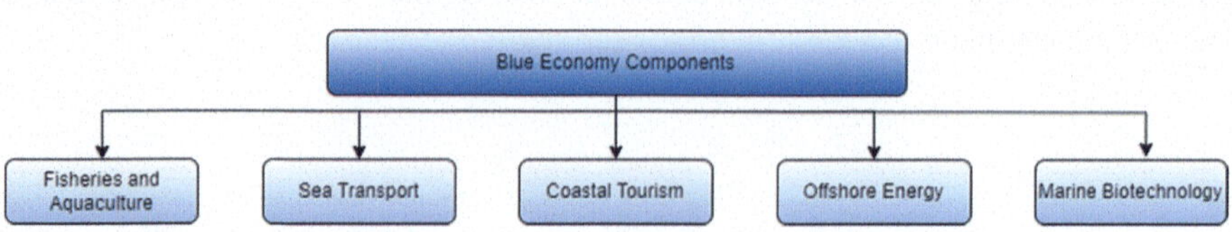

Fig. 1 Components of blue economy

- Marine Biotechnology:

Marine biotechnology is a rapidly growing sector that involves using biological materials from marine ecosystems for the development of pharmaceuticals, biofuels, and other industrial products. This field presents significant opportunities for biodiversity conservation and sustainable use (Leal et al. 2016).

2 Literature Review

The literature review is organized into two sections. The first section examines research on blue economy, with a focus on sustainable ocean resource utilization. This concept aims to balance economic growth and ecosystem health, contributing to both environmental and economic sustainability. The second section focuses on studies related to grey DEMATEL method, a tool commonly used in multi-criteria decision-making (MCDM) environments. This method is particularly effective for analyzing interactions between factors in complex systems. This section presents the applications of grey DEMATEL method across various scenarios, and reviews its areas of application in the literature.

2.1 Studies on Blue Economy

The concept of blue economy emphasizes the sustainable use of ocean resources for economic growth, improved livelihoods, and ecosystem health. It seeks to balance economic activities with environmental protection, making it a crucial area of study in contemporary environmental economics. Summaries of some important blue economy studies are as follows:

Dey et al. (2024) addressed the critical issue of microplastic pollution in coastal and marine ecosystems, focusing on its significant economic repercussions for the blue economy. The study explained that the ocean acted as a sink for microplastics (MPs), introduced through rivers, runoff, industrial effluents, and direct waste discharge. This pollution threatened marine organisms and led to indirect economic losses, particularly affecting sectors like coastal tourism that relied on a clean environment. High cleanup costs associated with marine debris were highlighted, emphasizing the need for effective management strategies to mitigate the economic challenges posed by microplastic pollution.

Hossain et al. (2024) investigated the interplay between greenhouse gas (GHG) emissions, trade, and economic growth in 25 nations bordering the Indian Ocean. Their findings indicated that while GHG emissions and economic growth positively influenced the blue economy, trade had a detrimental effect. The research called for governments to integrate ocean-based solutions into their national climate pledges to achieve the SDGs, particularly SDG 14, which focuses on life below water.

This highlighted the importance of aligning economic growth with environmental sustainability within the blue economy framework.

Geng et al. (2024) examined the relationship between economic, environmental, and social indicators and inclusive growth across 19 Asian nations. Their analysis revealed varying impacts based on income categories, with fisheries and aquaculture playing a vital role in fostering inclusive growth. The study emphasized the need for improved management of these sectors and the diversification of economic activities to reduce ecological footprints and enhance sustainable practices. This finding contributed to the understanding of how blue economy can serve as a catalyst for inclusive growth in Asia.

Matovu et al. (2024) discussed the challenges posed by sand mining in Kerala, India, and its implications for the blue economy. They highlighted the strain on livelihood-ecological systems caused by increased sand demand, which was exacerbated by inadequate regulatory frameworks. The study advocated for the development of comprehensive guidelines for sustainable sand mining and presented a novel framework based on Ecosystem Service Assessment to guide risk assessments. The research emphasized the need for integrated governance systems to promote sustainability in resource management, illustrating the interconnections within the blue economy.

Yuan et al. (2024) analyzed the social aspects of blue economy, highlighting labor issues and social justice. They argued that blue economy initiatives must address social challenges to avoid exploitation, proposing principles to integrate social justice into policies to ensure equitable benefits for all stakeholders.

Widiaty et al. (2024) explored the integration of sustainability education in curriculum design through the lens of blue economy. Fuzzy Analytic Hierarchy Process (Fuzzy AHP) was adopted to evaluate the effectiveness of green curricula and propose a framework for a blue curriculum. The importance of fostering ocean literacy skills among students was highlighted, preparing future generations to engage effectively with blue economy principles. The need for educational models that encompass both terrestrial and marine environmental concerns was also discussed, aligning with SD agenda.

Shao et al. (2024) presented an innovative methodology for selecting sites for wave power plants (WPPs) on Hainan Island, China. By combining geographic information system (GIS), MCDM, and artificial neural network (ANN) models, the study identifies optimal locations for WPP deployment, considering environmental, technical, economic, and social factors. The research not only contributes to the theoretical understanding of renewable energy deployment in coastal areas but also provides practical insights for stakeholders in blue economy seeking to harness wave energy sustainably.

2.2 Studies on Grey DEMATEL Method

Within the literature review, key findings and methodological contributions of studies applying grey DEMATEL method have been summarized. These studies demonstrate the flexibility and effectiveness of grey DEMATEL method as a tool for analyzing complex problems across various industries:

Debnath et al. (2024) examined the challenges of adopting sustainable production practices in Bangladesh's apparel manufacturing industry. Using grey DEMATEL method, key obstacles such as "slow return on investment", "lack of proper waste management systems", and "reluctance to adopt advanced manufacturing processes" were identified. The interrelations among these challenges were analyzed, and a sensitivity analysis was conducted to test the robustness of the findings. This study offers strategic recommendations to help the industry achieve SDGs.

Nguyen et al. (2024) explored the complexities of innovation capabilities in Vietnam's IT sector. Using grey DEMATEL and Delphi methods, the study analyzed interrelationships among critical factors supporting innovation, such as "visionary leadership" and "a culture that encourages risk-taking." The research emphasizes the importance of visionary leadership in strengthening the innovation ecosystem within IT firms, providing practical recommendations for emerging markets.

Koley et al. (2025) analyzed the primary barriers faced by Transportation Network Companies (TNCs) in developing countries using grey DEMATEL method. The study highlighted the restrictive impact of government policies and regulatory disparities on TNCs, and sensitivity analysis was conducted to validate the reliability of results. This analysis offers strategic insights for managers and policymakers.

Akhtar et al. (2024) proposed a hybrid approach integrating grey DEMATEL and cloud model theory to examine fault interactions in production processes. The study reveals both the prominence and interrelations of these faults, aiding in the development of preventive strategies to enhance production efficiency.

Tarei et al. (2024) analyzed challenges in humanitarian logistics (HL) in Assam region of India, particularly for disaster relief operations. Using grey DEMATEL, the study identified cause-effect relationships for critical factors such as "outdated IT infrastructure," "complex geographical conditions," and "failure of early warning systems." This study provides valuable insights into improving logistics management during disasters.

Sharma and Gupta (2024) examined strategies for achieving sustainable competitive advantage in India's Industry 5.0 era. Using grey DEMATEL, they assessed the impact of strategies like "optimization with AI and IoT", offering a roadmap for aligning industrial advancement with global sustainability goals.

Zhang et al. (2024) analyzed operational risk factors in automated container terminals using grey DEMATEL method. Key issues such as "lack of supervision", "communication network failures", and "power supply disruptions" were evaluated. This study provides strategic recommendations for effective risk management in port operations.

3 Materials and Method

MCDM refers to a method that enables decision-makers to evaluate multiple criteria in order to make a choice. It is often used in complex decision problems where different criteria may conflict with one another or have different priorities. MCDM aims to systematically address these issues to determine the most optimal decision. MCDM methods rank alternatives by considering the weights of the criteria and how well each alternative performs against these criteria. Fuzzy logic is a theory developed to handle uncertainty and imprecise information. In real-life decision problems, precise information is often lacking, and subjective judgments or uncertainties may exist. At this point, Fuzzy MCDM (FMCDM) comes into play. FMCDM is used to solve decision problems involving uncertainty and vagueness. It incorporates fuzzy logic into classical MCDM methods, creating more flexible and realistic decision models. The importance assigned by decision-makers to each criterion and the performance of alternatives with respect to each criterion are not expressed in exact numbers. Instead, they are represented within a range (typically between 0 and 1). For example, the suitability of an alternative for a criterion could be 0.7, meaning it is largely but not completely suitable. Fuzzy membership functions express how well an alternative fits a criterion using fuzzy numbers. This allows for a better representation of uncertainty in evaluating alternatives. While MCDM works with precise and clear data, FMCDM takes into account uncertainties and subjective judgments, offering a more flexible approach.

The concept of grey numbers was developed to express the characteristic behaviors of grey systems (Deng 1985). Grey system theory can assist in solving problems related to uncertainty and incomplete information in cases of discrete data (Ju-Long 1982; Julong 1989). One of the primary advantages of this theory is its ability to handle limited data under uncertainty, making it particularly suitable for small samples (Liu and Qiao 2014). This theory can be easily integrated with other decision-making processes to enhance the accuracy of judgments (Tseng 2009).

Grey system theory primarily focuses on building relational analyses and models by applying prediction and decision-making techniques to systems with incomplete and uncertain data sets (Hsieh et al. 2006). The key advantage of grey theory is its ability to handle incomplete information and ambiguous problems with high precision. It serves as an effective tool for analysis, especially in cases where data availability is limited (Kun-lin 2004). In situations where the level of information about the data is partially incomplete, the relevant information can be represented using grey numbers, allowing for flexible and robust analysis.

3.1 Grey System Theory

The grey system theory was proposed by Deng to solve uncertainties in situations involving discrete data and incomplete information. Grey system analysis is carried out with grey numbers, grey equations and/or grey matrices (Deng 1985). When it comes to grey numbers, neither black nor white concepts may come to mind once in a while, their values cannot be clearly expressed in numbers, but they are known to take values in which range. Grey number is $(\otimes x)$, $\otimes x \in \left[\underline{\otimes} x, \overline{\otimes} x\right]$ with x being a real number where, $\underline{\otimes} x$ and $\overline{\otimes} x$ refer to the lower and upper limits of the number of $\otimes x$ greys, respectively. $\otimes x_1$ and $\otimes x_2$ are used for basic mathematical operations that can be done with grey numbers.

$$\otimes x_1 + \otimes x_2 = \left[\underline{x_1} + \underline{x_2}, \overline{x_1} + \overline{x_2}\right] \tag{1}$$

$$\otimes x_1 - \otimes x_2 = \left[\underline{x_1} - \overline{x_2}, \overline{x_1} - \underline{x_2}\right] \tag{2}$$

$$\otimes x_1 . \otimes x_2 = \left[\min\left(\underline{x_1}.\underline{x_2}, \underline{x_1}.\overline{x_2}, \overline{x_1}.\underline{x_2}, \overline{x_1}.\overline{x_2}\right), max\left(\underline{x_1}.\underline{x_2}, \underline{x_1}.\overline{x_2}, \overline{x_1}.\underline{x_2}, \overline{x_1}.\overline{x_2}\right)\right] \tag{3}$$

$$\otimes x_1 : \otimes x_2 = \left[\underline{x_1}, \overline{x_1}\right].\left[\frac{1}{\underline{x_2}}, \frac{1}{\overline{x_2}}\right] \tag{4}$$

$$k \in \mathcal{R}^+, k . \otimes x = \left[k.\underline{x}, k.\overline{x}\right] \tag{5}$$

3.2 *Grey DEMATEL Method*

Application steps of grey DEMATEL method, which integrates grey numbers and DEMATEL method, are given below (Khan et al. 2024; Nguyen et al. 2024):

Step 1. Determining the evaluation scale of grey relationships.

Let "*n*" be the number of criteria used in the study and "*k*" as the number of decision-makers selected for the study. Each decision maker is tasked with evaluating the direct influence of criterion "*i*" on criterion "*j*" using an integer scale ranging from 0 to 4. This scale is defined by descriptors that depict the level of impact, namely, "no influence", "low influence", "medium influence", "high influence", and "very high influence". The evaluation is conducted across a set of "*n*" pre-identified criteria. Table 1 presents the linguistic terms and the corresponding grey numbers (Tseng 2009).

Consequently, a comprehensive set of "*k*" initial relationship matrices was developed using the evaluations of the decision-makers influences.

Step 2. Generating the corresponding grey matrix for each initial relationship matrix.

Using the values obtained in Table 1 and Step 1, an upper range and a lower range of values are obtained with the corresponding Grey matrices Eq. (6) (Rajesh and Ravi 2015a; 2015b).

Table 1 Grey linguistic expression scale

Linguistic variables	Interval grey number
No influence	[0, 0]
Low influence	[0, 1]
Medium influence	[1, 2]
High influence	[2, 3]
Very high influence	[3, 4]

$$\otimes z_{ij}^{l} = \left(\underline{\otimes} G_{ij}^{l}, \overline{\otimes} G_{ij}^{l}\right) \tag{6}$$

where $1 \leq l \leq k; 1 \leq i \leq n; 1 \leq j \leq n.$

Step 3. Obtaining the average of grey relation matrices.

Using the "k" grey relation matrices, the average grey relational matrix $\left[\otimes \check{G}_{ij}\right]$ is obtained by Eq. (7).

$$\left[\otimes \check{G}_{ij}\right] = \left(\frac{\sum \underline{\otimes} G_{ij}^{l}}{k}, \frac{\sum \overline{\otimes} G_{ij}^{l}}{k}\right) \tag{7}$$

Step 4. Calculation of crisp matrices using average grey matrices.

Crips matrices are obtained using the three-step procedure in Eqs. (8–13) (Rajesh et al. 2015a; 2015b)

Step 4.1. Obtaining lower and upper normalized values.

$$\underline{\otimes} \dot{G}_{ij} = \left(\underline{\otimes} \check{G}_{ij} - j^{min} \underline{\otimes} \check{G}_{ij}\right) / \Delta_{min}^{max} \tag{8}$$

where $\underline{\otimes} \dot{G}_{ij}$ represents the normalized lower limit value of the grey number $\underline{\otimes} \check{G}_{ij}$.

$$\overline{\otimes} \dot{G}_{ij} = \left(\overline{\otimes} \check{G}_{ij} - j^{min} \overline{\otimes} \check{G}_{ij}\right) / \Delta_{min}^{max} \tag{9}$$

where $\overline{\otimes} \dot{G}_{ij}$ represents the normalized upper limit value of the grey number $\overline{\otimes} \check{G}_{ij}$

$$\Delta_{min}^{max} = j^{max} \overline{\otimes} \check{G}_{ij} - j^{min} \underline{\otimes} \check{G}_{ij} \tag{10}$$

Step 4.2. Calculation of the total normalized crips value.

$$X_{ij} = \left(\frac{\underline{\otimes} \dot{G}_{ij}\left(1 - \underline{\otimes} \dot{G}_{ij}\right) + \left(\overline{\otimes} \dot{G}_{ij} * \overline{\otimes} \dot{G}_{ij}\right)}{\left(1 - \underline{\otimes} \dot{G}_{ij} + \overline{\otimes} \dot{G}_{ij}\right)}\right) \tag{11}$$

Step 4.3. Calculation final net values.

$$X_{ij}^{*} = \left(min \underline{\otimes} \dot{G}_{ij} + \left(X_{ij} * \Delta_{min}^{max}\right)\right) \tag{12}$$

$$X = \left[X_{ij}^{*}\right] \tag{13}$$

Step 5. Obtaining normalized direct-relation matrix.

The normalized direct relationship matrix "*N*" is obtained through Eqs. (14–15). All elements in this matrix are between 1 and 0.

$$L = \frac{1}{1 \le i \le n^{max} \sum_{j=1}^{n} X_{ij}^{*}} \tag{14}$$

$$N = L * X \tag{15}$$

where *N* is normalized direct relation matrix; *L* is the normalization factor, and *X* is the initial crisp relationship matrix.

Step 6. Determining the total relationship matrix "*S*" using Eq. (16)

$$S = N(I - N)^{-1} \tag{16}$$

where *I* represents a unit matrix.

Step 7. Obtaining causal parameters

R denotes the sum of rows and *C* denotes the sum of columns. Using Eqs. (17–18), it can be computed as follows:

$$R_i = \sum_{j=1}^{n} s_{ij} \tag{17}$$

$$C_j = \sum_{i=1}^{n} s_{ij} \tag{18}$$

Step 8. Calculation of criterion weights.

Equations (19–20) are employed for computing the weight coefficients of the criteria.

$$\omega_i = \sqrt{(R_i + C_i)^2 + (R_i - C_i)^2} \tag{19}$$

$$w_i = \frac{\omega_i}{\sum_{i=1}^{n} \omega_i} \tag{20}$$

Step 9. Generating the causal diagram.

Using the values obtained through Eqs. (19–20), causal diagram is set up.

4 Case Study

People with the necessary expertise and experience were brought together to assess the various criteria for blue economy projects. Table 2 shows the composition of the decision-making group with representatives from each area of expertise.

By clearly defining the roles and responsibilities of each expert, it is ensured that the decision-making process is carried out in a comprehensive and effective manner.

4.1 Defining and Explaining the Criteria

The criteria used in blue economy projects were explained in detail by the decision-making group and given in Table 3.

These criteria aim to comprehensively assess and prioritize blue economy projects. The decision-making group will identify the most appropriate project based on these criteria.

4.2 Data Collection and Analysis

Three different expert opinions were used separately and grey direct relationship matrices were formed with the grey numbers in Table 1. These matrices are given in Table 4.

The combined Grey direct relationship matrix obtained by averaging the Grey direct relationship matrices created by the experts with Eq. (7) is given in Table 5.

Table 2 Structure of the decision-making group

Expert group	Role	Responsibilities
E1	Environmental Expert	- Evaluation of environmental sustainability criteria - Strategies for the protection of marine ecosystems and sustainable use of natural resources - Conservation of marine biodiversity, combating pollution, and maintaining ecosystem health
E2	Economic Analysis Expert	- Assessments on economic growth and financial sustainability - Analysis of investment strategies and the economic returns of blue economy projects - Preparation of reports on job creation potential and national income growth
E3	Social Impact Expert	- Evaluation of the social impacts of blue economy projects - Development of strategies for community welfare, workforce training, and social development - Promotion of social sustainability and community participation

Table 3 Criteria used in blue economy projects

Criterion	Description
Social Impacts (C1)	Assesses the effects of blue economy projects on society, including impacts on local living standards, workforce training, and social welfare
Energy Efficiency (C2)	Evaluates energy efficiency and the optimization of resource use in renewable energy projects such as offshore wind and wave energy
Legal and Regulatory Framework (C3)	Covers legal regulations for the sustainable management of marine resources, international cooperation, and combating illegal fishing
Technological Innovations (C4)	Involves the development of maritime technologies and technological innovations in renewable energy and biotechnology projects
Environmental Sustainability (C5)	Includes the conservation of marine ecosystems, sustainable fisheries, biodiversity protection, and pollution control
Economic Growth (C6)	Encompasses the contribution of blue economy investments to the national economy, job creation potential, and increases in national income
Investment and Financing Opportunities (C7)	Assesses financing options for blue economy projects, investment incentives, and public–private partnerships
International Cooperation (C8)	Covers global and regional cooperation efforts, international agreements, joint marine management projects, and international standards

Using Eqs. (8–13), a final relationship matrix X was obtained. Normalized direct-relation matrix was obtained with the normalization factor calculated as 0.0640 and Eq. (14). Equations (17–18) is used for row and column sum. The criteria weights and order of importance calculated using the Eqs. (19–20) are also given in Table 6.

As shown in Table 6, C3, C5, C6 and C8 with positive (R–C) values are in the group that affects the criteria. C1, C2, C4 and C7 criteria with negative (R–C) values are included in the affected group.

In the last step of the method, using (R + C) and (R–C) values, interactions between the criteria are determined with the help of the effect diagram, as shown in Fig. 2.

(R + C) values represent the relative importance of each criterion. Considering (R + C) values, it is seen that the C5 criterion has the highest value. This criterion is followed by C6 and C3 criteria.

Considering the affecting criteria, it is seen that the criterion with the highest (R–C) value is C3. This criterion is followed by C6 and C8 criteria, respectively. Therefore, it is possible to say that these three criteria with the highest (R–C) values have the most influence on the other criteria.

Table 4 Grey direct relationship matrix for expert-1–2-3

Criteria	C1	C2	C3	C4	C5	C6	C7	C8
C1	[0,0],[0,0],[0,0]	[1,2],[1,2],[1,2]	[1,2],[1,2],[3,4]	[1,2],[1,2],[1,2]	[2,3],[3,4],[0,1]	[0,1],[2,3],[1,2]	[0,1],[0,1],[1,2]	[0,1],[0,1],[2,3]
C2	[0,1],[1,2],[1,2]	[0,0],[0,0],[0,0]	[0,1],[0,1],[1,2]	[2,3],[2,3],[2,3]	[2,3],[1,2],[1,2]	[2,3],[3,4],[0,1]	[1,2],[0,1],[1,2]	[0,1],[0,1],[2,3]
C3	[3,4],[3,4],[3,4]	[2,3],[2,3],[2,3]	[0,0],[0,0],[0,0]	[2,3],[2,3],[3,4]	[3,4],[2,3],[2,3]	[2,3],[0,1],[2,3]	[1,2],[0,1],[3,4]	[1,2],[0,1],[1,2]
C4	[1,2],[0,1],[0,1]	[2,3],[2,3],[0,1]	[2,3],[2,3],[0,1]	[0,0],[0,0],[0,0]	[2,3],[1,2],[1,2]	[1,2],[1,2],[1,2]	[0,1],[1,2],[1,2]	[0,1],[0,1],[2,3]
C5	[2,3],[1,2],[2,3]	[3,4],[3,4],[2,3]	[0,1],[0,1],[1,2]	[2,3],[2,3],[1,2]	[0,0],[0,0],[0,0]	[3,4],[3,4],[1,2]	[3,4],[1,2],[3,4]	[0,1],[2,3],[2,3]
C6	[2,3],[0,1],[2,3]	[0,1],[0,1],[1,2]	[1,2],[1,2],[1,2]	[2,3],[2,3],[1,2]	[3,4],[3,4],[1,2]	[0,0],[0,0],[0,0]	[3,4],[2,3],[3,4]	[3,4],[0,1],[3,4]
C7	[0,1],[1,2],[2,3]	[0,1],[0,1],[2,3]	[1,2],[1,2],[0,1]	[0,1],[0,1],[1,2]	[0,1],[1,2],[3,4]	[0,1],[0,1],[1,2]	[0,0],[0,0],[0,0]	[2,3],[0,1],[0,1]
C8	[0,1],[1,2],[3,4]	[0,1],[0,1],[1,2]	[0,1],[0,1],[0,1]	[3,4],[3,4],[1,2]	[0,1],[1,2],[1,2]	[0,1],[2,3],[2,3]	[3,4],[2,3],[2,3]	[0,0],[0,0],[0,0]

Table 5 Combined grey direct relationship matrix

Criteria	C1	C2	C3	C4	C5
C1	[0.000,0.000]	[0.667,1.667]	[2.000,3.000]	[0.667,1.667]	[1.667,2.667]
C2	[0.667,1.667]	[0.000,0.000]	[0.667,1.667]	[1.667,2.667]	[1.333,2.333]
C3	[3.000.4.000]	[2.000,3.000]	[0.000,0.000]	[1.667,2.667]	[2.333,3.333]
C4	[0.333,1.333]	[1.000,2.000]	[1.667,2.667]	[0.000,0.000]	[1.333,2.333]
C5	[1.667,2.667]	[2.333,3.333]	[0.333,1.333]	[1.333,2.667]	[0.000,0.000]
C6	[1.333,2.333]	[0.333,1.333]	[1.333,2.333]	[1.333,2.333]	[2.333,3.333]
C7	[1.000,2.000]	[0.667,1.667]	[0.333,1.333]	[0.667,1.667]	[1.333,2.333]
C8	[1.333,2.333]	[1.000,2.000]	[0.000,1.000]	[1.667,2.667]	[0.667,1.667]
Criteria	**C6**	**C7**	**C8**		
C1	[1.000,2.000]	[0.333,1.333]	[0.667,1.667]		
C2	[1.667,2.667]	[0.667,1.667]	[0.667,1.667]		
C3	[1.333,2.333]	[1.333,2.333]	[0.667,1.667]		
C4	[1.000,2.000]	[0.667,1.667]	[0.667,1.667]		
C5	[2.333,3.333]	[2.333,3.333]	[1.333,2.333]		
C6	[0.000,0.000]	[2.667,3.667]	[2.000,3.000]		
C7	[0.333,1.333]	[0.000,0.000]	[0.667,1.667]		
C8	[1.333,2.333]	[2.333,3.333]	[0.000,0.000]		

Table 6 Row and column totals of the total relationship matrix

Criteria	R	C	R + C	R–C	Weights	Rank
C1	0.6633	0.8060	1.4693	-0.1428	0.1147	5
C2	0.6869	0.7332	1.4201	-0.0463	0.1104	7
C3	1.0732	0.6184	1.6916	0.4549	0.1362	3
C4	0.6292	0.8710	1.5002	-0.2419	0.1181	4
C5	1.0400	0.9694	2.0094	0.0707	0.1563	1
C6	1.0000	0.8119	1.8119	0.1881	0.1416	2
C7	0.5012	0.8986	1.3999	-0.3974	0.1131	6
C8	0.7597	0.6450	1.4047	0.1147	0.1096	8

When the affected criteria are considered, it is seen that C7 criterion with the smallest (R–C) value is the most affected criterion by the other criteria. This criterion is followed by C4 and C1 criteria.

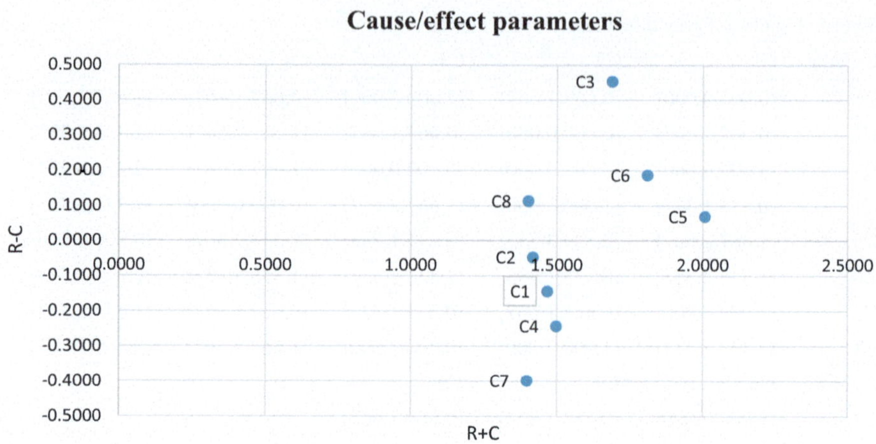

Fig. 2 Effect diagram

5 Discussion, Practical and Managerial Implications

The analysis of (R + C) and (R–C) values provide significant insights into the relative importance and influence of various criteria in blue economy projects. These findings contribute to a deeper understanding of the factors that affect the success of these projects, facilitating more informed decisions and strategic directions for stakeholders involved in such initiatives.

- (R + C) Values and Relative Importance of Criteria

(R + C) values represent the total importance of each criterion. Upon examining these values, it is clear that the highest value is assigned to environmental sustainability (C5). Environmental sustainability plays a central role in the success of blue economy projects, as it involves protecting marine ecosystems, maintaining biodiversity, and adopting sustainable practices such as responsible fishing and pollution control. These aspects minimize the environmental impact of blue economy initiatives while ensuring their long-term viability. Consequently, environmental sustainability (C5) holds the highest importance among all criteria.

The second highest values go to economic growth (C6) and the legal and regulatory framework (C3). Economic growth is critical for the success of blue economy projects, as they not only aim to preserve environmental resources but also have the potential to generate significant economic benefits. The blue economy can substantially contribute to national economies through the sustainable use of marine resources. Thus, economic growth (C6) is of high importance. Similarly, the legal and regulatory framework (C3) plays a crucial role in the effective implementation and sustainability of these projects. A strong legal foundation, including environmental protection laws, marine resource management, and international cooperation, is essential for ensuring that blue economy projects are carried out effectively and sustainably.

- (R–C) Values and Influence of Criteria

(R–C) values reflect how much influence a criterion has on others. The legal and regulatory framework (C3) emerges as the most influential factor. This indicates that the success of blue economy projects largely depends on legal and regulatory structures. Measures such as international agreements, environmental policies, and cross-border cooperation have a profound impact on the overall effectiveness of blue economy projects. Without a solid legal foundation, other factors such as environmental sustainability, economic growth, or international cooperation would struggle to achieve their potential. Hence, the legal and regulatory framework (C3) holds significant influence over the other criteria.

Following this, economic growth (C6) and international cooperation (C8) are the next most influential criteria. Economic growth drives investment and financial support, making it an essential factor in the scaling and success of blue economy projects. International cooperation, on the other hand, fosters global support for these projects, ensuring access to resources, expertise, and cross-border partnerships. These two criteria highlight the importance of the synergy between economic opportunities and international collaboration, which is crucial for the long-term success and scalability of blue economy ventures.

- Most Affected Criteria

The criterion most affected by others, as indicated by the smallest (R–C) values, is investment and financing opportunities (C7). This criterion is highly responsive to other factors, indicating that access to capital and financial mechanisms is strongly influenced by regulatory frameworks, technological innovations, and economic conditions. Without adequate financial support, blue economy projects cannot reach their full potential. Therefore, C7 is deeply impacted by the success or failure of other criteria.

Next in line are technological innovations (C4) and social impacts (C1). Technological innovations play a significant role in enhancing the efficiency of blue economy projects, offering new solutions for environmental challenges, resource management, and sustainable production methods. Technological advancements can help reduce pollution, improve resource utilization, and create more effective solutions for marine conservation. C1 is also an important criterion, as blue economy projects must consider their effects on local communities, such as job creation, social welfare, and equity. These social elements contribute to the broader acceptance and success of blue economy projects.

This analysis highlights that the success of blue economy projects depends not only on environmental sustainability but also on the interaction of legal, economic, and social factors. While the legal and regulatory framework has the most significant influence on the success of these projects, economic growth and international cooperation are also critical for ensuring their effective implementation. Furthermore, factors such as financial mechanisms, technological innovations, and social impacts must be carefully considered to ensure the sustainable and effective development of blue economy projects.

5.1 Practical Implications

For practitioners, these findings offer valuable guidance for resource allocation and project prioritization in blue economy ventures. Integrating environmental sustainability (C5) into the core of project planning not only addresses ecological concerns but also aligns with international regulations and environmental standards. Focusing on environmental sustainability can help projects gain more funding and support by aligning with the increasing environmental awareness of project stakeholders and investors. Moreover, such projects could attract financing opportunities offered by international funding institutions dedicated to green investments. This highlights that environmentally friendly practices create value not only for the environment but also for investors.

Supporting technological advancements (C4) is also crucial for the successful implementation of blue economy projects. Technological innovations make projects more efficient and sustainable, reducing costs, increasing operational efficiency, and minimizing environmental impacts. Strengthening technological infrastructure can also make these projects more attractive to investors, thus facilitating the acquisition of necessary financial resources.

Encouraging economic growth (C6) plays a strategic role in promoting the long-term sustainability of blue economy initiatives. Economic growth not only provides a solid financial foundation for these projects but also brings social benefits, such as job creation, strengthening of local economies, and improvements in public health. By emphasizing economic growth, blue economy initiatives become more appealing to local and international investors, attracting the support necessary for their development and sustainability.

The dependence of investment and financing opportunities (C7) on other criteria indicates that a comprehensive approach is needed to secure funding for these projects. Investors consider not only financial returns but also the environmental, social, and legal aspects of the projects. In this regard, ensuring robust legal frameworks (C3) and international cooperation (C8) is crucial for making blue economy projects financially attractive. International cooperation can provide broader access to global networks and resources. Moreover, the support of governments and policymakers through enabling regulations can help strengthen the foundation of such projects and increase their potential to attract more investment.

These findings emphasize that blue economy projects should focus not only on ensuring environmental sustainability but also on promoting economic growth, enhancing investment opportunities, and advancing technology. This multifaceted approach offers a crucial foundation for project managers, practitioners, and policymakers to develop strategies that will enable blue economy initiatives to be managed successfully and sustainably.

5.2 Managerial Implications

From a managerial perspective, focusing on both influential and affected criteria contributes not only to the sustainability of blue economy projects but also ensures their long-term success. Understanding the interactions among various criteria provides managers with a holistic view, enabling them to base their strategic decisions on these interconnections. In this context, the significant impact of legal and regulatory frameworks (C3) on blue economy projects is critical. Maritime resource management is closely tied to international regulations and laws. Managers must prioritize compliance with these frameworks to ensure the legal validity and international recognition of their projects. This not only prevents legal issues but also builds trust, enhancing the legitimacy of the project among potential investors and stakeholders.

International cooperation (C8) is another key factor that strengthens the success potential of blue economy projects. Globally, collaboration and knowledge sharing, particularly in areas such as marine resources and environmental management, play a crucial role. International cooperation enables projects to be shaped around a shared vision, allowing access to various technologies, knowledge, and financial resources. This kind of collaboration accelerates project execution as different parties contribute their expertise, and it helps ensure the sustainability of the project in the long term by gaining broader international support.

Environmental sustainability (C5) also plays a central role in project design. Environmental impact is increasingly becoming a global concern, not just at local or regional levels. Projects focused on the blue economy must prioritize environmental sustainability to protect ecosystems while fostering the long-term economic benefits of marine resources. Managers should integrate sustainability goals into their business models, ensuring that their projects meet both public expectations and regulatory requirements. This creates a strong case for continued investment in sustainable initiatives and encourages innovation.

Furthermore, investment in environmental sustainability should not be seen merely as a regulatory requirement but as a value-creating factor. By protecting marine resources, blue economy projects can simultaneously promote economic growth. Therefore, investing in sustainability is a critical step in ensuring the long-term viability of marine-based ventures. By focusing on eco-friendly solutions, projects can attract investor interest, offering a competitive market advantage through innovation and efficient resource management.

Additionally, the influence of criteria like legal frameworks, international cooperation, and sustainability indicates the interconnectedness of various factors. Investment opportunities (C7) are highly dependent on other criteria, such as legal support and technological advancements. Managers must therefore ensure that legal frameworks are robust and supportive, and that international collaboration efforts are maximized to make blue economy projects financially viable and appealing to stakeholders.

Ultimately, managing blue economy projects requires a comprehensive, multi-dimensional approach. Managers should not focus solely on economic success but also integrate environmental and social impacts into their strategies. By addressing both dominant and reactive factors, projects will not only achieve economic success but will also provide environmental benefits and social advantages. This approach strengthens the long-term impact and resilience of blue economy initiatives, ensuring their sustainability and broad-based support at both local and global levels.

6 Results, Limitations, and Future Directions

In this study, the criteria used in blue economy projects were analyzed in depth using grey number-based fuzzy multi-criteria decision-making methods. The analysis revealed both the relative importance of these criteria and their interrelationships, offering valuable insights into which factors are most critical for the success of blue economy projects. Environmental sustainability emerged as the most crucial criterion for blue economy projects, while the legal and regulatory framework and economic growth were identified as having the greatest influence on other areas. In contrast, investment and financing opportunities were found to be the most affected by other criteria, highlighting the importance of financial resources and investment opportunities for the success of these projects.

Environmental sustainability should be seen not only as a regulatory requirement but also as a value-creating factor essential for the long-term viability of blue economy projects. The integration of eco-friendly practices contributes to ecosystem preservation and the efficient use of resources, minimizing the environmental impact of these projects. This not only provides ecological benefits but also enhances alignment with international regulations, opening up funding opportunities.

The influence of the legal and regulatory framework emphasizes the need for blue economy projects to be developed in compliance with both local and international laws. These frameworks are critical in boosting investor confidence and reducing legal risks. Therefore, the success of blue economy projects depends on a robust legal foundation and regulatory compliance. At this point, international cooperation becomes crucial for ensuring these projects are effective and sustainable on a global scale.

Economic growth is another essential factor for the sustainability of blue economy projects. The economic efficiency of these projects attracts investors and provides opportunities for funding. Additionally, the economic benefits, such as job creation and local development, should be considered, as they contribute significantly to the success of blue economy ventures at both local and global levels.

Investment and financing opportunities are identified as the most dependent criterion, which highlights the critical role of securing financial resources for the success of blue economy projects. Projects that are attractive to investors, supported by a strong legal framework, environmental sustainability goals, and economic growth prospects, are more likely to secure funding. In this context, the accessibility of financing options not only impacts the success of individual projects but also their potential to create broader environmental and social benefits.

International cooperation and technological innovations play a pivotal role in the long-term success of blue economy projects. International collaboration fosters knowledge sharing, joint research, and technology transfer, which helps make projects more efficient and effective. Moreover, technological innovations have the potential to reduce the environmental impact of blue economy projects while also lowering costs and improving efficiency.

In conclusion, the success of blue economy projects can only be ensured by addressing the key criteria—environmental sustainability, economic growth, legal compliance, and investment opportunities—through a balanced approach. These projects require a holistic approach that aims to provide economic benefits while preserving ecosystems, ensuring legal compliance, and fostering local development. International cooperation and technological innovations further strengthen this process and guarantee the long-term success of blue economy initiatives.

6.1 Limitations

This study has some limitations. First, although the criteria used in the analysis were widely accepted in the literature and determined based on the opinions of professionals, they may not cover all the criteria involved in blue economy projects. The blue economy is a multifaceted and dynamic field, and projects may vary across different geographic, cultural, and sectoral contexts. Therefore, the criteria addressed in this study may not represent all aspects of blue economy projects. For instance, while environmental sustainability may be a critical criterion in some regions, economic growth or the legal framework may be more prominent in others. As a result, the criteria evaluated in this study may not fully encompass the range of considerations necessary for every blue economy initiative.

Second, while the adopted grey DEMATEL used in this study is a robust approach that accounts for uncertainties and subjectivity, the results are based on expert opinions. This means that the subjectivity inherent in the individual perspectives may affect the analysis. Different expert groups might provide different evaluations of the importance and interaction of the criteria, leading to potential variations in the results. In a multidisciplinary field like blue economy, experts from diverse backgrounds (e.g., economics, law, environment, technology) may offer distinct viewpoints, which could influence the final assessment. This factor highlights a potential limitation in the accuracy and reliability of the results.

Additionally, the criteria used in this study were evaluated within a specific geographic and socio-economic context. However, blue economy projects interact with socio-economic conditions, legal frameworks, and cultural differences that vary across regions. Changes in socio-economic conditions, such as rising income levels or increased environmental awareness, can alter the relative importance of the criteria. Differing legal frameworks in various regions may affect the interaction of criteria, particularly in areas like environmental sustainability and investment opportunities. Thus, the findings of this study are limited to the specific context in which they were assessed, and their applicability to other regions or socio-economic environments should be carefully considered before generalizing.

Finally, it is important to note that the criteria used in this study may evolve over time. Blue economy projects are influenced by external factors such as technological advancements, new legal regulations, and shifting market conditions. Therefore, the results of this study reflect the situation at a particular point in time, and future analyses may yield different outcomes due to these dynamic factors. Changes in the global or local context may lead to shifts in the criteria's relevance and interaction, requiring continuous reassessment. Thus, the findings of this study should be potentially revised as new developments occur in the field of blue economy.

6.2 Future Directions

Future research can be enriched by examining the criteria used in blue economy projects within a broader regional context. Such investigations can provide deeper insights into the challenges and opportunities faced by different geographic regions. For example, environmental factors such as sustainable fisheries, marine biodiversity conservation, and combating marine pollution are likely to have varying priorities across regions. These differences are influenced not only by local conditions but also by national regulations and economic development levels. In this context, regional needs and resources must be considered when designing strategies to increase the success rates of blue economy projects. Comparative studies of regulations, national policies, and investment environments across different regions can offer valuable insights for decision-makers, helping identify which criteria are more dominant and which strategies are likely to be more effective.

Researches exploring how technological innovations and environmental sustainability contribute to long-term economic growth will be crucial. In particular, understanding how to achieve economic development while meeting sustainability goals is critical for both developed and developing countries. Questions such as how technological innovations can be scaled, how new technologies can mitigate environmental damage, and how these innovations can be integrated into economic growth models are key areas for future research. Studies that link the success of blue economy projects to both environmental sustainability and economic growth will provide a better understanding of how investments in such projects can generate long-term benefits.

More advanced decision-making methods can also improve the quality of analyses. Given that the interactions between criteria and uncertainties may change over time, dynamic models that account for these changes are necessary for a more comprehensive evaluation. Moreover, in a time when decision-makers need more comprehensive and multifaceted analyses, comparisons using different grey number-based MCDM methods can provide additional insights for making more robust decisions in blue economy projects.

Lastly, future studies that evaluate financing and investment opportunities within blue economy projects will be critical. Investments in these projects must be sustainable not only from a financial perspective but also in terms of their environmental impacts. Defining the necessary policies and strategies to make sustainable investments attractive is crucial. Strengthening public–private partnerships, particularly in terms of increasing financial resources, is necessary to fully realize the potential of the blue economy. Expanding international financing opportunities and directing these funds toward blue economy projects will enable these projects to scale and thrive.

Such studies will not only enhance the success rates of blue economy projects but also ensure that these projects are executed in alignment with both environmental and economic goals, providing long-term benefits and resilience.

References

Akhtar, M. J., Naseem, A., & Ahsan, F. (2024). A novel hybrid approach to explore the interaction among faults in production process with extended FMEA model using DEMATEL and cloud model theory. *Engineering Failure Analysis*, 157, 107876.

Bennett, N. J., Cisneros-Montemayor, A. M., Blythe, J., Silver, J. J., Singh, G. G., Andrews, N., & Voyer, M. (2019). Towards a sustainable and equitable blue economy. *Nature Sustainability*, 2(11), 991–993.

Bostock, J., Lane, A., Hough, C., & Yamamoto, K. (2010). The status and future of aquaculture in the European Union. *Aquaculture International*, 18(2), 203–220.

Buhaug, O., Corbett, J. J., Endresen, Ø., Eyring, V., Faber, J., Hanayama, S., ... & Winebrake, J. J. (2009). Second IMO GHG study 2009. International Maritime Organization (IMO) London, UK.

Debnath, B., Taha, M. R., Siraj, M. T., Jahin, M. F., Ovi, S. I., Bari, A. M., & Raihan, A. (2024). A grey approach to assess the challenges to adopting sustainable production practices in the apparel manufacturing industry: Implications for sustainability. *Results in Engineering*, 22, 102006.

Deng, J.L. (1985). Grey Control Systems, Press of Huazhong University of Science and Technology, Wuhan.

Dey, U., Chell, S., Mondal, M., Das, K., Raj, D., Pandey, G., ... & Verma, S. (2024). Potential Threat of Microplastic Pollution on Coastal-Marine Ecosystem–An Emerging Economic Setback and Question to Blue Economy? *Earth Systems and Environment*, 1–29.

FAO. (2020). The State of World Fisheries and Aquaculture 2020. Food and Agriculture Organization of the United Nations.

Fu, X., Zhu, Q., Sarkis, J. (2012). Evaluating green supplier development programs at a telecommunications systems provider. *Int J Prod Econ* 140(1):357–367

Geng, B., Wu, D., Zhang, C., Xie, W., Mahmood, M. A., & Ali, Q. (2024). How Can the Blue Economy Contribute to Inclusive Growth and Ecosystem Resources in Asia? A Comparative Analysis. *Sustainability*, *16*(1), 429.

Hilborn, R., Amoroso, R. O., Anderson, C. M., Baum, J. K., Branch, T. A., Costello, C., & Ye, Y. (2020). Effective fisheries management instrumental in improving fish stock status. *Proceedings of the National Academy of Sciences*, 117(4), 2218–2224.

Honey, M., & Krantz, D. (2007). Global trends in coastal tourism. Center on Ecotourism and Sustainable Development (CESD).

Hossain, M. A., Islam, M. N., Fatima, S., Kibria, M. G., Ullah, E., & Hossain, M. E. (2024). Pathway toward sustainable blue economy: Consideration of greenhouse gas emissions, trade, and economic growth in 25 nations bordering the Indian ocean. *Journal of Cleaner Production, 437*, 140708.

Hsieh, M.F., Wang, R.T. ve Lu, I.C. (2006). Applying Grey Relation Analysis to Establish The Financial Distress Prediction Model for Electronic in Taiwan, JCIS, http://www.atlantis-press.com

IRENA. (2020). Offshore renewable energy: Increasing sustainability and security. International Renewable Energy Agency.

Ju-Long, D. (1982). Control problems of grey systems, Systems & Control Letters, 1(5), 288–294.

Julong, D. (1989). Introduction to grey system theory. *The Journal of grey system, 1*(1), 1–24.

Khan, S., Haleem, A., & Khan, M. I. (2024). Enablers to implement circular initiatives in the supply chain: a grey DEMATEL method. *Global Business Review*, 25(1), 68–84.

Kittinger, J. N., Finkbeiner, E. M., Ban, N. C., Broad, K., Carr, M. H., Cinner, J. E., & Crowder, L. B. (2014). A practical approach for putting people in ecosystem-based ocean planning. *Frontiers in Ecology and the Environment*, 12(8), 448–456.

Koley, S., Barua, M. K., & Bisi, A. (2025). Inhibitors in ridesharing firms from developing Nations: A novel Integrated MCDM–Text Mining approach using Large-Scale data. *Transportation Research Part E: Logistics and Transportation Review*, 193, 103832.

Kun-lin Wen. (2004). The grey system analysis and its application in gas breakdown and var compensator finding (Invited Paper) International Journal of Computational Cognition, 2(1), pp. 21–44

Leal, M. C., Puga, J., Serôdio, J., Gomes, N. C., & Calado, R. (2016). Trends in the discovery of new marine natural products from invertebrates over the last two decades—where and what are we bioprospecting? *PLoS ONE*, 11(1), e0147988.

Li, C., Qi, Q. (2024). A novel hybrid grey system forecasting model based on seasonal fluctuation characteristics for electricity consumption in primary industry. *Energy*, 287, 129585.

Liu, J., Qiao, J.Z. (2014). A grey rough set model for evaluation and selection of software cost estimation methods. *Grey Syst Theor Appl* 4(1):3–12

Matovu, B., Brouwer, F., Bleischwitz, R., Aljanabi, F., & Alkoyak-Yildiz, M. (2024). Resource nexus perspectives in the Blue Economy of India: The case of sand mining in Kerala. *Environmental Science & Policy, 151*, 103617.

Mulazzani, L., & Malorgio, G. (2017). Blue growth and ecosystem services. Marine Policy, 85, 17–24.

Nguyen, P. H., Nguyen, L. A. T., Nguyen, T. H. T., & Vu, T. G. (2024). Exploring complexities of innovation capability in Vietnam's IT firms: Insights from an integrated MCDM model-based grey theory. *Journal of Open Innovation: Technology, Market, and Complexity*, 100328.

Pauli, G. (2010). The Blue Economy: 10 years, 100 innovations, 100 million jobs. Paradigm Publications.

Rajesh, R., & Ravi, V. (2015a). Supplier selection in resilient supply chains: A grey relational analysis approach. *Journal of Cleaner Production*, 86, 343–359.

Rajesh, R., & Ravi, V. (2015b). Modeling enablers of supply chain risk mitigation in electronic supply chains: A Grey-DEMATEL approach. *Computers and Industrial Engineering*, 87, 126–139.

Shao, M., Han, Z., Sun, J., Gao, H., Zhang, S., & Zhao, Y. (2024). A novel framework for wave power plant site selection and wave forecasting based on GIS, MCDM, and ANN methods: A case study in Hainan Island, Southern China. *Energy Conversion and Management, 299*, 117816.

Sharma, R., & Gupta, H. (2024). Harmonizing sustainability in industry 5.0 era: Transformative strategies for cleaner production and sustainable competitive advantage. *Journal of Cleaner Production*, 445, 141118.

Silver, J. J., Gray, N. J., Campbell, L. M., Fairbanks, L. W., & Gruby, R. L. (2015). Blue economy and competing discourses in international oceans governance. *The Journal of Environment & Development*, 24(2), 135–160.

Smith-Godfrey, S. (2016). Defining the blue economy. Maritime Affairs: *Journal of the National Maritime Foundation of India*, 12(1), 58–64.

Tarei, P. K., Gumte, K. M., Patnaik, J., & Oktari, R. S. (2024). Analysing barriers to humanitarian logistics for distributing relief aid in pre-and post-disaster situations. *International Journal of Disaster Risk Reduction*, 104, 104388.

Telfer, D. J., & Sharpley, R. (2015). Tourism and Development in the Developing World. Routledge.

Tseng, M.L. (2009). A causal and effect decision making model of service quality expectation using grey-fuzzy DEMATEL approach. *Expert Syst Appl* 36(4):7738–7748

UN. (2015). Sustainable Development Goal 14: Life Below Water. United Nations.

Voyer, M., Quirk, G., McIlgorm, A., & Azmi, K. (2018). Shades of blue: what do compete interpretations of the blue economy mean for oceans governance? *Journal of Environmental Policy & Planning*, 20(5), 595–616.

Widiaty, I., Achdiani, Y., Widaningsih, L., Handayani, M. N., & Kurniasari, M. H. (2024). Fuzzy AHP for Performance Analysis: Mapping Green Curriculum and Developing Blue Curriculum Framework. *Journal of Engineering Science and Technology*, 19(4), 80–88.

Yuan, H., Choukroune, L., & Failler, P. (2024). Centring justice for labour in the new blue economy: Principles for applying emerging evidence and theoretical critiques to policy and practice. *Marine Policy*, 168, 106327.

Zhang, C., Liu, S., Hu, H., Xue, J., & Gou, Y. (2024). A hybrid SgDT framework for risk analysis of container-handling operations at automated container terminals. *Ocean & Coastal Management*, 257, 107321.

Integration and Economic Sustainability: The Impact of Foreign Economic Activity

Nabiyeva Akbayan, Temirlan Erlanuly Baigon, Saparbayeva Saule, and Ercan Özen

Abstract This article explores foreign economic activity, including international commerce, investment cooperation, scientific and technological collaboration, and monetary-financial interactions. It examines these activities' relationships and effects on national economic growth. The research also examines theoretical methods, phases, and elements affecting foreign economic activity and assesses Kazakhstan's experiences managing and maximizing international economic contacts. The research analyzes foreign economic activity using many methodologies. International commerce, investment cooperation, and scientific and technological collaboration are studied using a broad scientific method. A system approach is used to study how diverse foreign economic activities affect national economic growth. Additionally, a comparative analysis compares the international economic practices and outcomes of various countries, including Kazakhstan, in managing economic contacts. Foreign economic activity boosts commerce, investment, and technology, boosting national economic development. The study shows that successful international trade and investment cooperation management boosts output, jobs, and economic stability. Scientific and technical collaboration boosts innovation and competitiveness. The results also demonstrate that strong regulatory frameworks and international financial standards optimize foreign economic activities. The results show that economic, political, technical, and regulatory issues affect foreign economic activity and a country's global market integration and economic resilience. Trade, investment, and technical collaboration are interrelated, and foreign economic

N. Akbayan · T. E. Baigon
L N Gymilev, Eurasian National University, Astana, Kazakhstan
e-mail: akbayanmn@gmail.com

T. E. Baigon
e-mail: baigontemirlan@gmail.com

S. Saule
The L. N. Gumilyov, Eurasian National University, Astana, Kazakhstan
e-mail: saulet71@gmail.com

E. Özen (✉)
Faculty of Applied Sciences, University of Uşak, Uşak, Türkiye
e-mail: ercan.ozen@usak.edu.tr

S. O. Idowu et al. (eds.), *Competitiveness and Sustainability in the Digitization Era*,
Springer Proceedings in Business and Economics,
https://doi.org/10.1007/978-3-031-91778-3_11

activity shapes national economic progress. It shows that good management and regulatory compliance boost international economic activity. The research shows that economic, political, technical, and regulatory issues affect international economic activity. This boosts a nation's economic integration and resilience. International viewpoints frequently emphasize trade and investment as economic development drivers, although regulatory compliance and technical innovation are becoming more important. Foreign economic activity must be understood using theoretical and empirical data to maximize its advantages and sustain economic growth, according to the results.

Keywords Foreign Economic Activity · International Trade · Economic Integration · Investment Cooperation · Scientific and Technical Cooperation · Monetary-Financial Relations

1 Introduction

The study of foreign economic activity (FEA) is crucial due to its significant impact on national economies. With increasing globalization, understanding how FEA influences economic growth, stability, and competitiveness is essential. Despite extensive research on individual aspects of FEA, there is a lack of comprehensive studies integrating trade, investments, and scientific cooperation, alongside the regulatory frameworks governing these activities. This topic remains relevant due to the ongoing need for effective management and regulatory compliance to maximize FEA benefits. The object of this research is FEA, focusing on its impact on economic development and stability. The goal is to demonstrate that thorough management and adherence to regulatory frameworks significantly enhance FEA's positive effects. This study addresses a gap in the existing body of knowledge by providing a comprehensive methodology that combines analysis of trade, investment, and regulations with empirical data to evaluate their collective impact on economic results. This study aims to fill these gaps by providing an integrated approach to FEA, combining theoretical insights with empirical data. The hypothesis is that effective management and accurate accounting of FEA, supported by robust regulatory frameworks, significantly enhance economic growth, competitiveness, and stability. Using descriptive, statistical, comparative, and case study methods, data is sourced from national economic databases, international trade reports, and financial statements, analyzed with statistical tools and financial reporting software. This research offers a comprehensive framework for understanding FEA's multifaceted nature and its impact on national economies, providing actionable insights for policymakers and stakeholders to optimize strategies and achieve sustained economic growth. By addressing existing gaps, this study contributes valuable knowledge to the field of economic studies.

2 Literature Review

The study of foreign economic activity (FEA) encompasses a broad range of factors, including international trade, investment cooperation, and regulatory compliance. Alami et al. (2023) underscore the significance of financial power dynamics in shaping international economic interactions, arguing for the need to understand these dynamics to optimize national economic strategies. Okenna (2020) highlights the role of international trade in enhancing the economic stability of developing nations through market diversification and production optimization. Jia (2023) focuses on the impact of digital innovations, such as live-streaming trade platforms, on reshaping foreign trade, while Galeeva et al. (2018) address the modern challenges of global investment cooperation, albeit from a perspective that needs updating to reflect recent geopolitical and technological developments. Similarly, Goldstein et al. (2021) emphasize the critical role of scientific and technological cooperation in fostering innovation and resilience in national economies, but there remains a lack of integration between these factors and their collective impact on regulatory frameworks.

Siregar and Nuryanah (2019) explore the role of financial reporting quality and audit efficiency in optimizing investment strategies, arguing for the importance of adherence to international standards such as IFRS 21. However, more research is needed to understand how these standards interact with national regulations and economic growth strategies. Yu and Wang (2023) provide insights into the impact of geopolitical risks on international investment flows, yet further investigation is required to examine how nations can develop robust regulatory frameworks to mitigate these risks.

Despite extensive research on the individual components of FEA, there remains a gap in the literature regarding the integration of trade, investment, scientific cooperation, and regulatory frameworks. This study aims to address this gap by providing a comprehensive framework that combines these elements to better understand their collective impact on national economic growth. By doing so, it offers valuable insights for policymakers seeking to enhance the effectiveness of FEA management.

3 Research

In today's globalized economy, as economic and technological advancements accelerate, an increasing number of countries engage in international relations through foreign economic activity. This includes trade, joint ventures, and investments, driven by the desire to expand market reach, fulfill import needs, and achieve profitability. The international division of labor optimizes production and facilitates exchange among nations, crucial for global market competitiveness.

Foreign economic activity significantly impacts national economic development, enhancing enterprise competitiveness globally. Managing it requires deep expertise

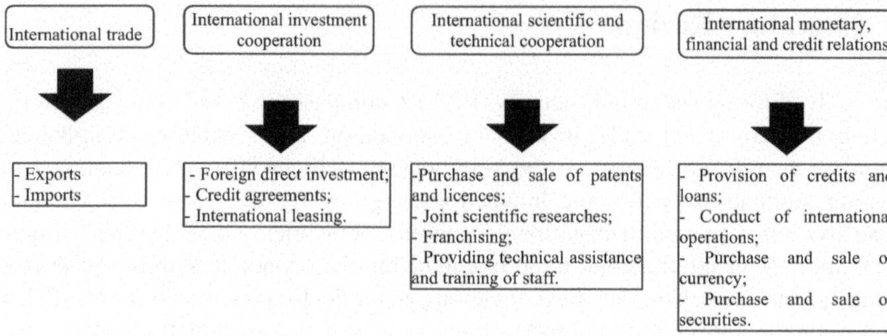

Fig. 1 Classification of forms of foreign economic activity (*Source* compiled by the authors)

in accounting legislation, international trade rules, currency regulations, and customs laws to accurately reflect transactions. Challenges arise from dealing with foreign partners, diverse currencies, and specific regulatory frameworks (Alami et al. 2023).

These activities profoundly influence economic growth rates, pricing, regional development, and living standards. Enterprises of all ownership types now participate in foreign markets, reflecting the broad scope of foreign economic transactions, pivotal for economic relationships globally.

The classification outlined in Fig. 1 encompasses the primary four forms of foreign economic activity. It's crucial to emphasize that for any nation worldwide, foreign economic activity is heavily influenced by the level of development in foreign trade and international investment cooperation. The underlying reason for this is that the advancement of these areas enables countries to expand their markets, gain access to novel technologies and resources, enhance labor productivity, improve competitiveness, and integrate into the global economy.

The level of a country's foreign economic activity hinges significantly on the development of foreign trade and international investment cooperation. These developments enable countries to expand markets, access new technologies and resources, enhance labor productivity, improve competitiveness, and integrate into the global economy.

Foreign trade encompasses the export and import of goods. International investment cooperation involves various operations: placing funds in foreign financial assets like securities, investing in tangible and intangible assets abroad for entrepreneurial profit. This cooperation fosters new enterprises, expands production, introduces technologies, and boosts international trade, thereby increasing demand for goods and services, and consequently, exports and imports (Galeeva et al. 2018).

A useful measure to understand the role of trade in a nation's economic development is the export-to-GDP ratio. This metric provides insights into a country's trade openness and economic reliance on exports, offering a basis for comparing trade dynamics across nations.

The relationship between foreign economic activity (FEA) and economic sustainability is a complex and multi-faceted issue that continues to shape global and regional economies. In an increasingly interconnected world, countries rely on trade, foreign direct investment (FDI), and exports to bolster their economic growth, diversify industries, and integrate into global markets. However, this reliance on international economic activities also presents challenges, particularly for developing nations navigating the balance between dependency on external factors and fostering sustainable, resilient economies (Tasinda et al. 2022).

Our analysis of foreign direct investment highlights a critical dimension of FEA: its dual role as a catalyst for development and a potential source of vulnerability. As noted, FDI often enables host nations to surpass domestic saving limitations, promoting capital formation and economic development. For resource-rich countries like Kazakhstan, foreign investments in sectors such as energy and mining have spurred significant growth. Yet, this benefit is tempered by the risks of overreliance on resource-based industries, which can lead to economic instability amid fluctuating global commodity prices.

In this context, the export-to-GDP ratio serves as a key metric to assess the trade openness and economic dependency of nations on international trade. By analyzing data from 2022 and 2023 for selected countries, including Kazakhstan, Malaysia, Poland, and Russia, this article aims to explore how export-to-GDP ratios reflect broader trends in FEA and their implications for economic sustainability. Understanding these dynamics provides valuable insights into the opportunities and risks of global economic engagement and its role in shaping the economic resilience of nations.

Export-to-GDP ratio (exports as a percentage of GDP) is a measure of a country's trade openness and dependency on exports relative to its total economic output. It is calculated using the formula below (formula 1):

$$E/GDP = \frac{TE}{GDP} * 100 \quad (1)$$

where, E/GDP—Export to GDP ratio;

TE—Total Exports;

GDP—Gross Domestic Product.

The export-to-GDP ratio is a critical indicator for assessing a nation's economic sustainability. Increased foreign trade provides access to new markets and inputs for domestic industries, boosting exports, diversifying the economic base, and enhancing resilience against global shocks (Das 2020).

Table 1 provides data for four countries—Kazakhstan, Malaysia, Poland, and Russia—for the year 2022 GDP, exports, and the export-to-GDP ratio. Kazakhstan's ratio indicates a moderate reliance on exports, with trade contributing significantly to its economic output. Malaysia's economy shows a very high reliance on exports, reflecting its role as an export-driven economy. Poland also exhibits a strong export dependency, with trade forming a significant part of its GDP. Russia's ratio is much lower compared to the others, reflecting its large domestic market relative to its export volume.

Table 1 Export to GDP Ratio for 2022

Country	GDP (Billion USD)	Exports	Export to GDP ratio
Kazakhstan	225,5	94,1	41,7%
Malaysia	406,3	352,5	86,8%
Poland	688,1	433,7	63,0%
Russia	2,240,4	635,1	28,3%

Compiled by the authors

Table 2 updates the data for the same countries in 2023, reflecting changes in GDP, exports, and export-to-GDP ratios. Kazakhstan's export-to-GDP ratio decreased from 41.7% in 2022 to 34.5%, showing a reduced reliance on exports due to either lower exports or a higher GDP growth rate. Malaysia's export dependency slightly decreased from 86.8% in 2022 to 78.3%, although it remains highly reliant on trade. Poland's ratio fell from 63% in 2022 to 57.8%, reflecting reduced export dependency as its GDP grew. Russia's export-to-GDP ratio dropped from 28.3% in 2022 to 23%, indicating a continued shift toward a more domestic-focused economy or a significant decrease in exports.

Both Kazakhstan and Malaysia have experienced declines in their export-to-GDP ratios, signaling reduced export reliance. However, Malaysia remains highly dependent on exports compared to Kazakhstan. A similar decline in export reliance in Poland suggests a trend toward domestic market strengthening or diversification.

The sharpest drop in export-to-GDP ratio among the four countries in Russia highlights either decreased exports or a shift toward internal economic stabilization amidst external challenges. The analysis of export-to-GDP ratios and foreign economic activity underscores the delicate balance between harnessing opportunities for economic growth and managing the associated risks. For Kazakhstan, as well as for other developing economies, foreign economic activity serves as a double-edged sword—offering a pathway to greater integration into the global economy while exposing vulnerabilities tied to overreliance on specific sectors or external factors.

As outlined, Kazakhstan has significant potential to maximize the benefits of FEA through a phased approach that addresses short-term, medium-term, and long-term objectives. Streamlining trade procedures, diversifying its economic base, and

Table 2 Export to GDP Ratio for 2023

Country	GDP (Billion USD)	Exports	Export to GDP ratio
Kazakhstan	261,4	90,2	34,5%
Malaysia	399,6	312,9	78,3%
Poland	811,2	469,3	57,8%
Russia	2,021,4	465,4	23,0%

Compiled by the authors

fostering innovation are critical steps toward reducing dependency on resource-based industries and building economic resilience.

By learning from the experiences of peer countries like Malaysia and Poland, which demonstrate varying degrees of trade reliance and economic diversification, Kazakhstan can chart a course toward a more sustainable and robust economy. Furthermore, strategic investments in innovation and value-added industries will enable the nation to mitigate the risks associated with commodity price volatility, ensuring greater stability in its foreign economic engagements.

The data-driven insights into export-to-GDP ratios highlight the broader dynamics of foreign economic activity and its implications for economic sustainability. For Kazakhstan, the path forward involves leveraging global economic integration while implementing targeted policies that address current challenges. With thoughtful planning and strategic reforms, FEA can evolve from a source of vulnerability into a pillar of sustained economic growth and resilience, fostering long-term prosperity for the nation.

The stakeholders in international investment cooperation include investors, recipient countries, and government entities. Investments can take several forms: direct investments into foreign companies' capital, joint ventures, real estate acquisitions; portfolio investments in foreign company securities; loans to foreign entities; and other forms like licensing, franchising, and contract manufacturing. In table 3 we presented the 4 main objectives of investment cooperation.

Countries collaborate internationally by pooling investments and efforts to achieve mutual goals, such as expanding, modernizing, or reconstructing enterprises across borders. This international investment cooperation is crucial for enhancing trade, production, and technological development globally, serving as a key driver of the world economy.

International scientific and technical cooperation involves various forms of interaction among entities in different countries within the scientific and technical sectors (Goldstein et al. 2021). Its objectives include accelerating scientific and technical

Table 3 Goals of international investment cooperation

Objectives of investment cooperation	Facilitating the implementation of investment projects for the production of goods and services with high added value
	Establishment of advanced processing industries in the territories of the countries
	Compensation of deficiencies and missing stages in the production chains of enterprises in order to increase their competitiveness in the international market
	Creation of new jobs that provide for the upgrading of qualification levels and acquisition of new professional skills for local residents

Compiled by the authors

progress, enhancing economic competitiveness, and broadening access to knowledge and technology. Table 4 below details further forms of international scientific and technical cooperation.

International scientific and technical cooperation has remained crucial even as time passed. Countries actively participating in these processes experience higher economic growth and improved living standards. Collaborative efforts enable countries to tackle complex scientific challenges more swiftly, introduce novel technologies, share expertise, and share advanced achievements across various fields.

International monetary, financial, and credit relations encompass a range of operations that facilitate timely international settlements for counterparties from different countries. These operations include currency purchases and sales, lending on foreign trade transactions, foreign exchange transactions to mitigate currency risks, and independent operations in global financial currency markets aimed at extracting business profits from exchange rate differences and variations in interest rates on securities and loans. In essence, international monetary, financial, and credit relations are an indispensable component of global trade, which represents the economic connections between actors from various countries, manifesting in the exchange of currencies, credit, and other financial instruments. This form of Financial Engineering Analysis (FEA) serves several essential functions presented below:

- provides international settlements—currency and credit instruments are used to pay for goods, services and other assets in international trade,
- finances international trade and investment—loans and other financial instruments allow companies and states to finance their activities on the international market,
- regulate the foreign exchange market—the National Bank coordinates its actions to ensure stable exchange rates,
- manage foreign exchange reserves—countries accumulate foreign exchange reserves to protect their economies from external shocks.

In summary, based on the aforementioned interpretations, special attention is currently being paid to foreign economic activity. International economic activity plays a pivotal role in the development of contemporary economies and involves a

Table 4 Forms of international scientific and technical cooperation

Forms	Significance
Exchange of scientific information	Publications in scientific journals, participation in conferences and seminars, exchange of information
Joint scientific research	Implementation of joint projects, participation in international programs
Personnel training	Exchange of students, internships, advanced training
Creation of joint ventures	Creation of scientific-technical companies, joint laboratories and research centers

Note—Compiled by the authors on the basis of source

diverse range of economic, legal, and organizational relationships between nations that emerge during trade. The primary forms of foreign economic activity include:

- foreign trade activity,
- international scientific and technical co-operation,
- international investment co-operation,
- international currency—financial and credit relations.

These forms of international economic activity facilitate access to novel markets, augment turnover, entice foreign investment into the nation's economic framework, generate novel employment opportunities, introduce innovative technologies, and enhance labor productivity. It is crucial to acknowledge that companies engaged in international business operations are subject to all applicable legal regulations. A well-organized accounting system for foreign economic activities can serve as a pivotal catalyst for a country's economic expansion and lead to a substantial augmentation of its prosperity.

The role of export–import operations in the global economy is steadily expanding, exerting a substantial influence on the development of enterprises and states. Accounting for this activity presents unique challenges, stemming from the intricate interactions between international entities, currency exchange variations, regulatory and legal frameworks adopted by diverse countries, and other pertinent factors.

In international trade and export/import transactions, foreign exchange accounting holds paramount importance. Given the cross-border nature of these transactions, it is crucial to account for exchange rate variations and currency conversions when recording financial events. This practice ensures accurate financial reporting and enables enterprises to effectively assess the risks associated with currency fluctuations. As stipulated in paragraph 2 of Article 6 of the Law of RK "On currency regulation and currency control" dated July 2, 2018, No. 167-VI, currency transactions involving residents and non-residents are conducted in either national or foreign currency.

It is noteworthy that the international movement of funds encompasses two primary functions:

- firstly, it contributes to increasing the economic benefits for both parties to the transaction. For exporting countries, this means profitable investment, while it represents an additional source of income for importing countries;
- secondly, it promotes the development of social infrastructure by increasing demand in the labour market and enabling access to vital goods such as medical products.

To ensure the transparency and legality of currency transactions, the government exercises stringent control over the receipt of foreign currency proceeds. The sources of foreign currency funds must be substantiated by the requisite documentation. Transactions resulting in the acquisition of currency must adhere to the current legislation and be devoid of questionable nature. International accounting standards also mandate the accounting for currency in international operations. Compliance

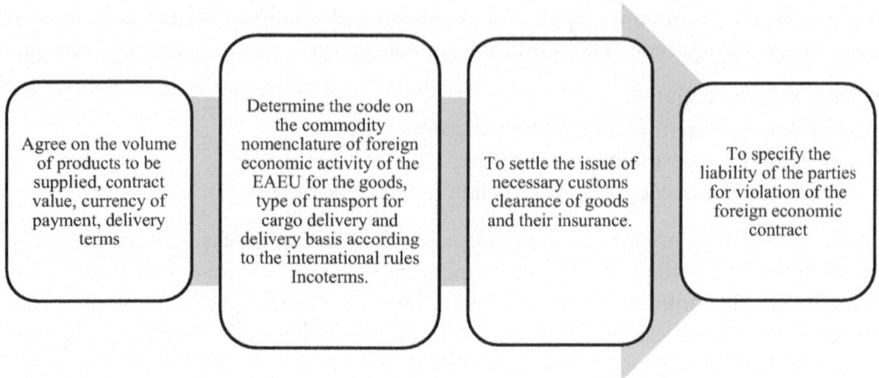

Fig. 2 Terms of a foreign trade contract (*Source* compiled by the authors)

with these standards ensures uniformity and comparability of financial statements of enterprises, which is crucial for investors, creditors, and other stakeholders.

The accounting of export and import transactions holds immense significance for companies, as it enables them to effectively manage their financial resources, analyze performance, and adhere to pertinent regulatory requirements. The initial phase in the accounting process of foreign trade transactions involves the meticulous implementation of the purchase and sale contract. An external trade agreement serves as a comprehensive framework that outlines the provisions for establishing, modifying, or revoking mutual obligations and rights between two or more parties involved in global trade and their international business partners. Figure 2 presents a comprehensive list of factors that must be carefully considered before drafting an international trade agreement.

The commencement of any interaction with international trading partners entails the formulation of the fundamental terms of an external trade agreement. These terms encompass the preamble, the price, the quantity, the quality of the goods, payment modalities, fundamental delivery conditions stipulated by Incoterms, delivery conditions, packaging requirements, conditions of transfer and acceptance of the goods, force majeure clauses, legal addresses of the contracting parties, and postal and payment details.

These paragraphs serve as the foundational document for the contract, but the list of conditions is not infallible. The Contracting Parties possess the exclusive right to incorporate additional sections, modify substantive sections, or rephrase them in a manner that prioritizes the interests of both parties within the international treaty framework.

In the realm of recording export and import transactions, the fundamental principles of accounting are applied. The primary principle is the recognition of income and expenses on a transaction-by-transaction basis. This principle stipulates that economic benefits should be recognized in the period in which they are actually realized, rather than in the period of anticipation of future economic gains. The second crucial principle is the principle of permanence, which implies that the organization will maintain its operations in the long term. This principle instills confidence in all external stakeholders regarding the company's long-term sustainability and reliability.

International Financial Reporting Standard 21 "The Effects of Changes in Foreign Exchange Rates" characterizes exchange rate differences as positive or negative when the same number of units of one currency are translated at different exchange rates. Positive exchange rates boost currency, negative lower it. IFRS 21 shows monetary and non-monetary components. Employee benefits, dividends, and goods payments are money. Non-monetary items lack rights. Currency disparities do not affect deficit losses. Recognition of deficit losses is in accordance with the provisions of International Financial Reporting Standards 2 "Inventories", according to which inventories should be valued at the lower of cost or expected average market selling price (Jia 2023).

For the effective organization and regulation of foreign economic activity the system of goods classification known as Codes of Commodity Nomenclature of Foreign Economic Activity is used. This system represents unique ten-digit numbers for different categories of goods that move across borders. HS codes are an integral part of the international trade process. These codes allow standardization and systematization of goods according to their characteristics and properties.

This classification is necessary for the correct and efficient conduct of customs procedures, including the processing of customs declarations and the determination of rates of customs duties and taxes. In addition, codes are important for international trade statistics. By assigning an appropriate code to each commodity, it is possible to analyze trade flows, identify trends and peculiarities of foreign economic activity of different countries. This allows government agencies and business structures to make informed decisions based on trade data (Okenna 2020).

The goods that are transferred from the seller to the buyer must necessarily reach their destination. To facilitate interaction in the business community, international norms for the delivery of goods, known as Incoterms, have been approved. Incoterms is a universal document that simplifies and accelerates the process of international trade, reduces the risks of disputes and disagreements between the seller and the buyer, ensuring the transparency of transactions (Siregar and Nuryanah 2019). Incoterms 2010 categorizes trade concepts in four sections based on the allocation of responsibility between the seller and buyer for carriage and risks as shown in Table 5.

Incoterms categorize international trade terms into groups that specify responsibilities between buyers and sellers. Group "E" requires the buyer to take goods from the seller's warehouse, while in Group "F," the seller delivers goods to the buyer's chosen transport. Group "C" mandates the seller to arrange carriage without assuming risk after shipment, and Group "D" covers the seller bearing all risks until goods reach the destination. These rules streamline global trade and foster economic cooperation.

Accounting records in Kazakhstan are kept in KZT, therefore at initial recognition a foreign currency transaction is recorded in KZT at the current exchange rate at the date of the transaction. The actual cost of imported goods should be recognised in

Table 5 Base categories Incoterms—2010

Group	Designation of delivery conditions	Transportation	Contents
E	EXW	All modes of transportation	The seller is responsible for packing the products, handing them over to the buyer or to the carrier. Customs, handling and delivery are the responsibility of the buyer. The risks of the transaction are transferred at the time of delivery
F	FCA FAS FOB	Sea and inland waterway transportation	The seller executes the export documentation and ships the products to the carrier. Buyer arranges and pays for delivery and is responsible for customs procedures at import. Risks are transferred to the buyer when the goods are handed over to the carrier
C	CFR CIF CIP CPT	All modes of transportation	The seller prepares the export documents and provides delivery, but is responsible for the products only until they are shipped from his warehouse. Clearance is entirely the responsibility of the buyer
D	DAT DAP DDP	All modes of transportation	The seller prepares customs documents, arranges delivery and is responsible for the goods until the buyer receives them

Compiled by the authors on the basis of Jia (2023)

accounting accounts. Accordingly, goods are valued at their acquisition cost. The contract value of goods is stated in the invoice. Depending on the terms of delivery, it includes a certain part of overheads paid by the foreign supplier, but reimbursed to him by the importer in the price of goods. Upon receipt of the invoice, the importer, after proper verification of documents, confirms it and at the time of transfer of title to the imported goods, puts them on the books. The accounting value of purchased goods is determined as follows (formula 2):

$$RS = OFS + TP + Tcip + TR \tag{2}$$

where, RS—accounting cost;

OFS—total invoice (control) value;

TP—customs duty;

Tcip—customs duties and procedures;

TR—transport costs.

It should be emphasised that export–import transactions are considered to be completed only after the goods have actually crossed the customs border. The following costs are incurred in the purchase of imported goods:

- related to the delivery of the goods from the place of production or storage to their destination;
- associated with loading and unloading of goods from vehicles;
- the costs of insuring the goods against loss, damage or other risks during transport and storage (Tsaurai and Hlupo 2008).

The above-mentioned overheads are included in the total value of the imported goods. This stage is carried out through customs clearance, which is an important component of international trade relations. Next, consider in Table 6 a brief overview of the specifics of importing goods from the Eurasian Economic Union, including the VAT rate, payment terms, required tax and statistical reporting, and mandatory documents for import operations.

VAT calculation for taxable imports in Kazakhstan follows Tax Code Article 442. VAT applies based on the earliest accounting recognition under IFRS and local laws, or the import date into Kazakhstan. For imports, this date varies by transport mode: railroad uses border postmark date, road uses border crossing or delivery act date, air uses aircraft arrival at the first Kazakh airfield from the air waybill, and mail uses postal receipt date.

In export–import operations, recognizing the cost of goods sold aligns with the supply contract terms determining transfer of ownership to the buyer. Tenge exchange rates for accounting are recorded at advance payment or transfer of risk and benefit dates (Yadgarov et al. 2019). In international trade, sellers are exporters and buyers are importers, collectively known as counterparties. Each type of foreign economic activity involves extensive economic, production, legal, currency, and financial relations. Goods in transit are recognized upon title transfer to the buyer; for exports, costs

Table 6 Import of goods from EAEU countries

Indicators	Disclosure of information
1	2
Import VAT rate	12%
VAT payers	All importers—VAT payers and non-payers
VAT payment deadline	VAT is payable by the 20th day of the month following the reporting period
Indicators	Disclosure of information
Tax reporting form	"Statement on importation of goods and payment of indirect taxes" (FNO 328.00)
Statistical reporting	"Report on Mutual Trade 1—CU" by the 20th of the month following the tax period
Obligatory documents for import of goods	Consignment note for goods before crossing the state border
Mandatory documents for sales	Electronic invoice by the 20th day of the month following the reporting period

Compiled by the authors on the basis of Okenna (2020)

are recognized upon title transfer to the customer as per the supply contract terms, guided by INCOTERMS 2020. Understanding these terms is crucial for determining ownership transfer in international trade contracts, underscoring foreign economic activity's role in economic development and stability.

4 Conclusion

This study has underscored the pivotal role of foreign economic activity (FEA) in fostering economic growth, enhancing competitiveness, and ensuring the stability of national economies. By integrating trade, investment, and scientific cooperation with robust regulatory frameworks, the research confirms the hypothesis that meticulous management and adherence to international and national regulations significantly amplify the positive impacts of FEA. The empirical analysis, supported by comprehensive data from national economic databases and international trade reports, validates the assertion that effective FEA management leads to improved economic outcomes (Yu and Wang 2023).

The findings highlight the necessity of accurate and transparent financial reporting, which facilitates informed decision-making and fosters economic resilience. The study contributes to the scientific understanding of FEA by demonstrating the interconnectedness of various economic activities and the importance of regulatory compliance. These insights are crucial for policymakers and economic stakeholders as they navigate the complexities of global economic interactions.

In summary, this research confirms the critical importance of FEA in driving economic development and stability. It suggests that continuous refinement of regulatory measures and management practices is essential to fully harness the benefits of FEA. Future research could explore the long-term impacts of evolving global trade dynamics and the role of technological advancements in shaping FEA strategies. This study provides a solid foundation for ongoing efforts to optimize FEA for sustained economic growth and resilience.

References

Alami, I., Alves, C., Bonizzi, B., Kaltenbrunner, A., Koddenbrock, K., Kvangraven, I., Powell, J. International financial subordination: a critical research agenda // Review of International Political Economy. – 2023. – №30(4). – https://doi.org/10.1080/09692290.2022.2098359.

Das, M. Does Foreign Direct Investment (FDI) Promote Socioeconomic Development? Evidence from Advanced, Emerging-market, Developing and Transition Economies // Man and the Economy. – 2020. – №7(1). – https://doi.org/10.1515/me-2020-0001

Goldstein, I., Koijen, R. S. J., Mueller, H. M. COVID-19 and Its Impact on Financial Markets and the Real Economy // Review of Financial Studies. – 2021. – №34(11). – https://doi.org/10.1093/rfs/hhab085.

Galeeva, G. M., Paiduganova, I. V., Zagladina, E. N. Modern problems of investment cooperation development in the supply chain of the world economy // International Journal of Supply Chain Management. – 2018. – №7(6).

Jia, S. A New Approach to the Development of Foreign Trade under the Economy of Internet Live Streaming with Goods // Frontiers in Business, Economics and Management. – 2023. – №8(3). – https://doi.org/10.54097/fbem.v8i3.7866.

Okenna, N. P. The Importance of International Trade to the Economies of Developing Countries // SSRN Electronic Journal. – 2020. – https://doi.org/10.2139/ssrn.3664322.

Siregar, S. V., Nuryanah, S. Financial Reporting Quality, audit Quality, and Investment Efficiency: Evidence from Indonesia // Proceedings of EAI Conference on Management of Higher Education Research. – 2019. – https://doi.org/10.4108/eai.21-11-2018.2282299.

Tasinda, O. T., Tian, Z., Imanche, S. A., Bekoe, B. B., Raphael, F. T. The Impacts of Foreign Direct Investment Flows on the Economic Growth during the Pre-Covid-19 Era // Open Journal of Social Sciences. – 2022. –№10(4). – https://doi.org/10.4236/jss.2022.104006

Tsaurai, K., Hlupo, P. Does financial development enhance foreign trade in selected transitional economies? // Comparative Economic Research. – 2020. – №23(4). – https://doi.org/10.18778/1508-2008.23.28.

Yadgarov, Y. S., Sidorov, V. A., Sobolev, E. V. Credit and banking component of the market economy phenomenon: Methodological approach transformation to the development of digitalization and capital fictivization // Finance: Theory and Practice. – 2019. – №23(5). – https://doi.org/10.26794/2587-5671-2019-23-5-115-125.

Yu M., Wang N. The Influence of Geopolitical Risk on International Direct Investment and Its Countermeasures // Sustainability (Switzerland). – 2023. – №15(3). – https://doi.org/10.3390/su15032522.

AI-Driven Digital Transformation: Enhancing Competitiveness and Sustainability in the Modern Business Landscape

Vaikunta Pai T, B. Sunil Kamath, Virgil Popescu, and Ramona Birau

Abstract AI-driven digital transformation is redefining the modern business landscape by synergizing operational efficiency, ethical governance, and long-term sustainability. This chapter explores how AI empowers organizations to optimize processes, enhance decision-making transparency, and address global challenges such as climate change and resource scarcity. By leveraging predictive analytics, adaptive automation, and data-driven insights, AI enables businesses to innovate, build resilience against disruptions, and align with global sustainability goals. Real-world case studies highlight its transformative impact, from reducing waste and carbon emissions to fostering ethical supply chains and workforce adaptability. As businesses navigate an increasingly volatile environment, the responsible integration of AI emerges as a cornerstone for achieving competitive advantage and shaping a sustainable future, emphasizing collaboration between industries, policymakers, and researchers to unlock AI's full potential.

Keywords Artificial Intelligence (AI) · Digital Transformation · Innovation · Sustainable Growth · Business Strategy · AI-driven transformation · Sustainability · Operational efficiency · Ethical AI practices

---

V. Pai T · B. S. Kamath
Department of Information Science and Engineering, NITTE (Deemed to be University), NMAM Institute of Technology, Nitte, Karnataka, India
e-mail: vaikunthpai@gmail.com

B. S. Kamath
e-mail: sunilkamath@nitte.edu.in

V. Popescu
Faculty of Economics and Business Administration, University of Craiova, Craiova, Romania
e-mail: virgil.popescu@vilaro.ro

R. Birau (✉)
Eugeniu Carada" Doctoral School of Economic Sciences, University of Craiova, Craiova, Romania
e-mail: ramona.f.birau@gmail.com

S. O. Idowu et al. (eds.), *Competitiveness and Sustainability in the Digitization Era*, Springer Proceedings in Business and Economics,
https://doi.org/10.1007/978-3-031-91778-3_12

1 Introduction

In an era of rapid digitalization, artificial intelligence (AI) is at the forefront of transforming business operations, redefining competitive strategies, and enabling sustainable practices. This chapter, examines the pivotal role AI plays in reshaping organizational structures, fostering innovation, and achieving environmental sustainability goals. By exploring AI-driven strategies that enhance operational efficiency, personalize customer engagement, and streamline resource allocation, we delve into how AI contributes to sustained competitive advantage across industries. The chapter further discusses the integration of AI into digital strategies, emphasizing the development of organizational capabilities and culture necessary for seamless transformation. It also addresses ethical considerations and challenges, including data privacy, bias mitigation, and workforce adaptation, as businesses navigate this complex digital shift. Through an analysis of case studies and industry trends, this work provides actionable insights and forward-looking recommendations, positioning AI as a crucial catalyst for sustainable and competitive growth in an evolving global economy.

Digital transformation, powered by artificial intelligence (AI), has redefined business operations by integrating technology to enhance efficiency, customer value, and innovation. This transformation represents a holistic shift in strategies and cultures, empowering businesses to adapt to a data-driven world. AI, with its ability to learn, adapt, and derive insights from vast data, drives this transformation, enabling businesses to operate with agility and foresight. In today's competitive landscape, AI empowers companies to innovate proactively, enhancing customer experiences through personalized interactions and seamless support systems. By leveraging AI tools like chatbots and recommendation engines, businesses can boost customer satisfaction and loyalty. Furthermore, AI-driven insights support data-informed decision-making, helping companies maintain relevance and set new industry benchmarks. Significantly, AI also promotes sustainability by optimizing resource utilization, reducing waste, and fostering smarter supply chain management. These dual focuses—competitiveness and sustainability—highlight AI as a cornerstone of modern business strategies.

This chapter explores AI's transformative role in enhancing competitiveness and sustainability, focusing on foundational technologies like machine learning and automation, operational benefits, and sustainable practices. It emphasizes ethical AI use, ensuring a balance between growth and responsibility, offering actionable insights for building adaptive, resilient business models.

2 Foundations of AI-Driven Digital Transformation

2.1 Historical Evolution of Digital Transformation in Businesses

The evolution of digital transformation in businesses reflects decades of technological progress that reshaped operations, customer engagement, and competition. Initially, businesses adopted basic tools, gradually moving toward data-driven technologies like artificial intelligence (AI).

From the 1960s to 1980s, automation focused on tasks like payroll and inventory management through computers, with mainframes centralizing data processing. The late 1970s introduced Enterprise Resource Planning (ERP) systems, integrating core business functions. In the 1990s, the Internet Revolution introduced the World Wide Web and email, revolutionizing communication. This period also saw the rise of Customer Relationship Management (CRM) systems, enhancing customer-centric strategies. By the 2000s, digital transformation embraced big data analytics, cloud computing, and mobile technologies, enabling real-time interactions and mobile commerce [1].

2.1.1 Automation and Early AI (2010s): Intelligent Systems Era

- **Process Automation**: Robotic Process Automation (RPA) enabled businesses to streamline repetitive tasks, improving efficiency and reducing costs.
- **Machine Learning (ML)**: ML facilitated predictive analytics for customer segmentation, demand forecasting, and risk assessment, enhancing decision-making.
- **Social Media Analysis**: AI analyzed customer sentiment and behavior, enabling real-time marketing adjustments and improved engagement.

2.1.2 The AI-Driven Era (2020s): Advanced Intelligence

- **Advanced AI and Deep Learning**: Tools like chatbots and recommendation engines improved customer experiences.
- **AI-driven Digital Twins and IoT Integration**: It enable businesses to optimize processes and simulate real-time operations. This integration reduces costs, boosts productivity, and ensures more efficient resource utilization [2].
- **Ethical AI**: Companies increasingly focus on fairness and transparency, with regulations ensuring responsible AI applications.

2.2 Foundational Technologies Powering AI-Driven Digital Transformation

AI-driven transformation relies on core technologies, including Machine Learning (ML), Natural Language Processing (NLP), and Automation, applied across sectors as shown in Fig. 1.

- **Machine Learning Applications**: In business contexts, machine learning (ML) applications are transforming various sectors by optimizing processes and enhancing decision-making. In retail, companies like Amazon use predictive analytics to forecast demand, improve inventory management, and streamline supply chain logistics. In banking, firms like JPMorgan Chase use ML models for fraud detection, analyzing transaction patterns to identify unusual behavior and improve security. Additionally, streaming services like Netflix leverage ML to provide personalized recommendations,boosting viewer engagement and subscriber retention.
- **Natural Language Processing Enhancements**: In business contexts, natural language processing (NLP) applications are enhancing customer interactions across industries. H&M uses AI-driven chatbots for efficient customer support, speeding up responses and reducing reliance on human agents. Coca-Cola employs sentiment analysis to monitor social media and adjust marketing strategies based on customer feedback. Walmart and Target leverage NLP-powered voice assistants to facilitate product searches and orders, improving customer satisfaction and engagement through seamless shopping experiences.
- **Automation**: In various business contexts, automation technologies like Robotic Process Automation (RPA) are streamlining operations. Siemens automates invoice processing by using RPA bots to capture and enter data, reducing errors and allowing employees to focus on analytical tasks. In e-commerce, Alibaba employs

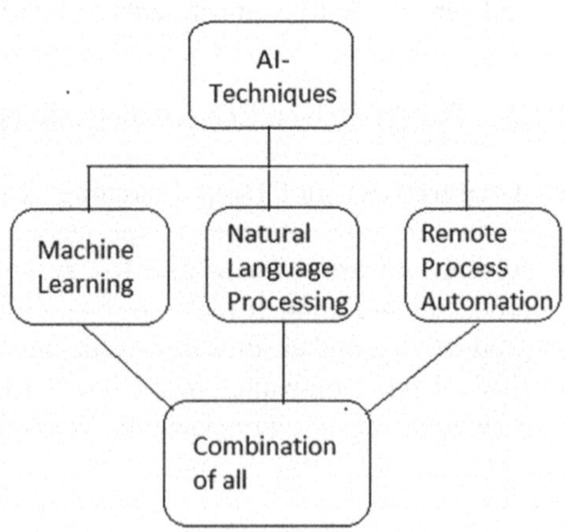

Fig. 1 Prominent AI Techniques

automated warehouses where robots manage picking, packing, and shipping, significantly reducing fulfillment times and operational costs.

2.3 AI-Driven Transformation and Alignment with Industry 4.0 Principles

Industry 4.0 emphasizes interconnected systems, automation, and real-time data analysis—are integral to modern AI-driven transformation. Through these principles, AI enhances operational efficiency, innovation, and adaptability, fundamentally reshaping the industrial landscape.

- **Interconnected Systems**: Interconnected systems emphasize the integration of devices, machinery, and software to facilitate seamless data exchange. Through AI-powered Internet of Things devices and machine-to-machine communication, companies can create an intelligent ecosystem that optimizes resources, predicts issues, and adapts to changes dynamically. Bosch uses AI in "smart factories" to analyze machine data, predict maintenance needs, and improve productivity. Similarly, Siemens' MindSphere connects industrial devices to analyze data for real-time decision-making, such as predictive maintenance in power plants, which enhances reliability and lowers operational costs. These advancements showcase the transformative role of AI in integrating systems and optimizing industrial operations.
- **Automation**: Automation under Industry 4.0 minimizes human intervention in repetitive tasks, enabling machines to operate independently with precision and speed. AI-driven systems enhance this through machine learning and robotics, allowing machines to perform complex tasks, learn from experiences, and optimize over time. BMW uses robotic arms for welding, assembly, and quality checks while leveraging AI for real-time production adjustments. Similarly, Foxconn integrates AI-powered robotic process automation (RPA) to streamline assembly, packaging, and quality assurance, reducing costs, minimizing errors, and scaling operations to meet dynamic demands. These examples highlight AI's transformative role in advancing automation.
- **Real-Time Data Analysis**: Real-time data analysis is pivotal in Industry 4.0, enabling agile manufacturing environments by offering insights into performance, quality, and logistics. AI leverages machine learning and advanced analytics for predictive maintenance, demand forecasting, and adaptive supply chains, optimizing resource allocation. For instance, GE Aviation employs AI to monitor aircraft engine health in real time, analyzing sensor data to anticipate maintenance needs and significantly reduce flight delays and unscheduled maintenance, thereby improving customer satisfaction.Nestlé utilizes AI in its supply chain management to monitor inventory levels, optimize logistics, and forecast demand. By analyzing historical data alongside real-time variables, Nestlé can dynamically adjust production schedules and distribution routes, reducing waste and improving

delivery times while aligning production with consumer demand patterns. These applications showcase AI's transformative role in enhancing decision-making and operational efficiency.

3 Enhancing Competitiveness Through AI-Driven Transformation

3.1 AI's Role in Enhancing Competitiveness Through Operational Efficiency and Customer-Centric Innovations

The strategic adoption of artificial intelligence (AI) across industries has proven to be a powerful tool for boosting competitiveness. By driving operational efficiency and supporting customer-centric innovations, AI enables businesses to not only reduce costs but also meet customer needs with heightened personalization and responsiveness. In this section, we explore the ways in which AI achieves these benefits, supported by recent research findings and case studies of companies that have leveraged AI to gain a strategic edge [3, 4].

3.1.1 Increasing Operational Efficiency

Operational efficiency is vital for organizations seeking to reduce waste and lower production costs, and AI technologies like predictive maintenance, robotic process automation (RPA), and advanced data analytics play a key role. Predictive maintenance systems analyze machinery data to foresee potential failures, as demonstrated by General Electric's Predix platform, which has achieved a 20% reduction in unscheduled maintenance. RPA automates repetitive tasks, freeing employees for more complex work; Deloitte has successfully streamlined its back-office processes through RPA, enhancing productivity and reducing costs. Additionally, AI-driven analytics optimize supply chains by providing real-time insights, as seen with Procter & Gamble's ability to adapt during the COVID-19 pandemic to meet rising demand. Research from McKinsey & Company shows that AI-driven predictive maintenance can cut machine downtime by up to 50%, while Gartner reports that RPA can reduce operational costs by up to 30%, underscoring the significant benefits of AI in improving efficiency [5, 6].

3.1.2 Driving Customer-Centric Innovations

In today's competitive market, customer-centric innovations powered by AI are crucial for brand differentiation and loyalty. AI technologies enhance personalization, customer service automation, and behavior prediction, enabling businesses to deliver tailored experiences. For instance, Netflix's AI algorithms provide personalized content recommendations, driving over 80% of its streaming activity and reducing churn rates. Similarly, H&M employs AI chatbots to assist customers with online shopping, offering 24/7 support that enhances satisfaction. Starbucks uses its "Digital Flywheel" program to analyze customer data for personalized promotions, fostering loyalty and increasing spending. Research from Accenture indicates that AI-driven personalization can boost customer engagement by 20%, and Salesforce Research shows that 84% of customers prioritize personalized experiences, highlighting the significance of AI in meeting evolving consumer demands [7].

3.2 Case Study: Leveraging AI to Transform Customer Experience at Starbucks

Starbucks, one of the world's largest coffeehouse chains, has successfully used artificial intelligence (AI) to transform its customer experience, driving both customer loyalty and business growth. Known for its high standards in customer service, Starbucks implemented AI-driven solutions to create a highly personalized experience for each customer. Through its "Digital Flywheel" program, Starbucks has turned data insights into actionable strategies, allowing it to meet customer needs with unprecedented accuracy and build a loyal customer base.

Starbucks has effectively implemented several AI solutions to enhance customer experience and operational efficiency through its "Digital Flywheel" program, which focuses on personalization, rewards, convenience, and engagement. The program utilizes AI algorithms to tailor product recommendations and offers based on individual customer preferences and behaviors. Additionally, predictive analytics helps Starbucks anticipate customer demand, optimizing inventory management and reducing waste by ensuring popular items are in stock. The mobile app enhances ordering and payment experiences, allowing customers to save preferences and reorder quickly, further improving convenience.

Despite these advancements, Starbucks faces challenges, including data privacy concerns related to the collection of personal information for customization. To address this, the company has strengthened its data security protocols and adheres to stringent regulations like GDPR. Integrating AI across various platforms also posed technical challenges, which Starbucks mitigated by investing in robust IT infrastructure and cloud computing. Furthermore, the company balances automation with a human touch by using AI for backend tasks while ensuring that in-store staff maintain direct customer interactions.

The positive impacts of these AI-driven initiatives are significant. Enhanced personalization has fostered customer loyalty, with Starbucks Rewards members accounting for nearly 50% of U.S. sales. The "Mobile Order & Pay" feature has driven digital sales, contributing to approximately 24% of total revenue in the U.S. by 2021. Additionally, AI has optimized inventory management, reducing waste and improving sustainability, while AI-powered labor allocation enhances service quality during peak hours. Ultimately, these strategies have led to increased customer lifetime value, with personalized offerings encouraging higher spending and fostering long-term relationships between Starbucks and its customers.

3.3 The Role of AI in Data-Driven Decision-Making

Artificial intelligence (AI) has become a key enabler of data-driven decision-making in business, allowing companies to analyze massive volumes of data, identify trends, and make both real-time and predictive decisions. By processing and learning from data continuously, AI provides insights that help businesses respond proactively to market shifts, optimize operations, and better meet customer needs. Real-time AI insights enable rapid adjustments, while predictive analytics allow companies to anticipate trends and potential disruptions, enhancing their competitive edge.

AI-driven data decision-making offers several key benefits for businesses. It enables real-time decision-making by analyzing data instantly, which enhances responsiveness in areas like inventory management and dynamic pricing. Predictive insights from machine learning models allow companies to anticipate future trends and consumer preferences, facilitating proactive actions in response to demand changes. Additionally, AI enhances risk management by identifying potential threats such as supply chain issues and fraud, thereby reducing uncertainty and promoting informed decision-making. Overall, these capabilities lead to improved efficiency and strategic agility in a competitive market [8].

3.3.1 Case Examples of Firms Leveraging AI for Data-Driven Decisions

Here's a table summarizing the key impacts of AI-driven data decision-making for Amazon, Walmart, Netflix, and Starbucks (Table 1).

AI-driven data decision-making enhances competitiveness by enabling proactive market adaptation, allowing companies to anticipate customer demand and adjust pricing and inventory accordingly. It facilitates personalization at scale, delivering tailored experiences that boost customer satisfaction and loyalty. Additionally, AI optimizes resource efficiency by streamlining supply chains and reducing operational costs, enabling competitive pricing without sacrificing quality. Furthermore, it aids in risk mitigation by identifying potential disruptions and market volatility, empowering businesses to take pre-emptive actions and build a more resilient foundation.

Table 1 AI-driven data decision-making for Amazon, Walmart, Netflix, and Starbucks

Company	AI Application	Key Features	Impact
Amazon	Real-Time Pricing and Inventory Management	Dynamic pricing adjustments multiple times a day, Predictive inventory management during sales events	Optimizes revenue and customer experience, Maintains competitive advantage in the e-commerce market
Walmart	Demand Forecasting and Supply Chain Optimization	Analyses sales data, weather, and local events for demand forecasting, Optimizes stock movement and transportation	Ensures product availability, reduces operational costs and enhances customer satisfaction
Netflix	Content Recommendations and Viewer Retention	Real-time personalized content recommendations, Predictive analysis for content investments	Boosts viewer engagement (over 80% of content watched), Informs investment decisions in content creation
Starbucks	Personalized Marketing and Demand Forecasting	Creates personalized offers based on customer preferences, Forecasts demand using historical data and local patterns	Builds customer loyalty, maintains smooth supply chain operations and supports competitive growth

4 Sustainability as a Core Outcome of AI-Driven Transformation

In a business context, sustainability refers to the ability of a company to operate in a manner that meets present needs without compromising the ability of future generations to meet their own needs. Sustainable business practices integrate strategies that consider not only economic growth but also environmental protection and social responsibility. By pursuing sustainability, companies strive to balance profitability with the broader goals of preserving natural resources, supporting social equity, and promoting long-term viability [9].

Dimensions of sustainability in business encompass economic, environmental, and social aspects. Economic sustainability focuses on long-term profitability and resilience through efficient resource management and responsible growth. Environmental sustainability aims to reduce the ecological footprint by minimizing waste, conserving resources, and promoting biodiversity through practices like sustainable sourcing and energy efficiency. Social sustainability emphasizes fair practices, equality, and community development, highlighting the importance of responsible labor practices, diversity, and positive contributions to society. Together, these dimensions foster a holistic approach to sustainable business practices.

Artificial intelligence (AI) provides powerful tools for companies to address these dimensions of sustainability by enabling resource optimization, reducing waste, enhancing decision-making, and promoting efficient operations. Below are examples of AI applications that help companies achieve sustainability goals across economic, environmental, and social dimensions.

AI enhances economic sustainability by improving operational efficiency, reducing costs, and optimizing resource use. Through predictive maintenance, AI monitors equipment health to anticipate failures and schedule maintenance, which minimizes downtime and repair costs. For instance, General Electric (GE) employs AI for predictive maintenance to optimize resource allocation and sustain operations. Additionally, AI-driven demand forecasting enables companies to accurately predict customer demand and manage inventory, reducing excess stock and waste. Procter & Gamble (P&G) utilizes AI-based forecasting to ensure product availability while minimizing surplus, thereby supporting cost-effective and sustainable operations.

AI plays a crucial role in enhancing environmental sustainability by promoting efficient resource use, waste reduction, and energy management. It improves energy efficiency by analyzing consumption patterns and adjusting settings, as demonstrated by Google, which reduced energy use in its data centers by up to 30% through AI-driven cooling adjustments. AI-powered waste management solutions, like those used by Zara, optimize production processes to minimize waste and support circular economy initiatives. Additionally, AI aids in sustainable sourcing by tracking materials to ensure they meet environmental standards, as seen with Unilever's commitment to responsible sourcing in its supply chain. Together, these applications help companies reduce their environmental impact and promote sustainable operations.

AI fosters social sustainability by promoting fair practices, enhancing employee well-being, and improving transparency. Workforce optimization tools, like those used by Walmart, ensure fair scheduling and balance operational needs, leading to increased job satisfaction and productivity. In hiring, AI-driven tools at IBM focus on inclusivity by assessing candidates based on objective criteria, thereby reducing bias and promoting diversity. Additionally, AI enhances supply chain transparency, as demonstrated by Nestlé, which monitors its suppliers to ensure adherence to ethical standards and fair labor practices. Together, these applications contribute to a more equitable and responsible business environment.

4.1 AI-Driven Methods for Optimizing Resources

AI-driven methods such as energy management systems and predictive maintenance are transforming industries by improving resource efficiency, lowering costs, and reducing environmental impact. These applications enable businesses to operate more sustainably and profitably by using resources precisely and proactively addressing equipment needs [10].

4.1.1 Energy Management Systems (EMS)

AI-driven energy management systems (EMS) optimize energy use in facilities by minimizing waste and lowering costs. These systems analyze real-time data from sensors and monitoring devices to detect usage patterns and make intelligent adjustments, ensuring energy is used efficiently. For example, Google employs DeepMind AI in its data centers, which analyzes data from thousands of sensors to adjust cooling systems, resulting in a 40% reduction in cooling costs and a 15% decrease in overall energy usage. Similarly, Walmart uses AI-powered EMS to manage lighting and HVAC systems across its stores, achieving annual energy cost reductions of 10–15% while aligning with sustainability goals.

4.1.2 Predictive Maintenance

Predictive maintenance leverages AI and machine learning to foresee equipment failures and schedule maintenance proactively, thereby reducing unplanned downtime and extending equipment life. By continuously monitoring equipment through sensors that track key performance indicators, AI systems can predict when maintenance is necessary. General Electric's aviation division, for instance, uses predictive maintenance for jet engines, resulting in a 30% reduction in unscheduled maintenance and lower repair costs. Siemens also benefits from this approach in its manufacturing plants, reporting a 20% decrease in maintenance costs and a 25% improvement in asset longevity.

4.1.3 Supply Chain Optimization

AI-driven supply chain optimization enhances resource efficiency by accurately forecasting demand, managing inventory levels, and streamlining logistics. By analyzing historical sales data and consumer trends, AI models help companies like Procter & Gamble (P&G) align production schedules with demand, reducing waste and excess inventory. DHL employs AI for route optimization, improving logistics efficiency and cutting emissions by 15% while lowering fuel costs by 10%. These applications not only contribute to cost savings but also minimize the environmental footprint of supply chain operations.

4.2 AI's Role in Enhancing Corporate Transparency, Accountability, and Inclusiveness

In the modern business landscape, transparency, accountability, and inclusiveness are essential for companies to meet the rising expectations of socially aware consumers, investors, and regulators. AI provides powerful tools that can help organizations monitor, report, and improve on their Environmental, Social, and Governance (ESG) performance. By facilitating more accurate data collection, analysis, and reporting, AI helps businesses align with ESG goals and build trust among stakeholders.

4.2.1 Enhancing Corporate Transparency

AI significantly enhances corporate transparency by automating data collection and facilitating accurate reporting on operations, environmental impact, and social policies. Automated Environmental, Social, and Governance (ESG) reporting systems streamline data gathering from various sources, enabling companies to report metrics more frequently and accurately. For instance, Unilever employs AI to monitor its supply chain for sustainable sourcing, tracking materials back to their origin to ensure compliance with sustainability standards. Similarly, Walmart utilizes AI to monitor energy consumption and waste reduction in its stores, providing real-time updates on its environmental impact and strengthening accountability to consumers and investors.

4.2.2 Promoting Accountability

Corporate accountability is bolstered by AI through real-time data monitoring and predictive insights, helping businesses manage risks and comply with regulations. AI systems continuously monitor compliance with environmental and labor regulations, alerting companies to potential issues. Microsoft exemplifies this by using AI to track and reduce carbon emissions, aligning with its goal to become carbon negative by 2030. The company publicly shares its emissions data, allowing stakeholders to monitor its environmental performance. Citigroup also leverages AI-driven risk assessment tools to evaluate the social and environmental impacts of its lending activities, ensuring responsible decision-making and accountability to investors and social goals.

4.2.3 Fostering Inclusiveness

AI promotes inclusiveness in the workplace by reducing bias in recruitment and enhancing accessibility for employees with disabilities. AI-powered recruitment platforms analyze candidate data based on objective criteria, helping to mitigate biases related to gender, race, and background. For example, IBM employs AI to ensure a fair hiring process by evaluating candidates solely on their skills. Accenture utilizes AI tools to forecast diversity outcomes and identify biases in communication, fostering a more inclusive work environment and supporting its diversity, equity, and inclusion (DEI) targets.

4.2.4 Aligning AI with ESG Goals: Real-World Examples

Companies are increasingly using AI to align with their ESG objectives, showcasing its potential for sustainable and ethical practices. Google employs AI to optimize energy usage in its data centers, achieving a 40% reduction in cooling costs and significantly lowering its carbon footprint. Nestlé uses AI to ensure supply chain transparency and accountability, tracking suppliers to uphold ethical labor practices. Bank of America applies AI in its recruitment process to eliminate bias, promoting diversity while also enhancing accessibility for customers with disabilities. These initiatives not only reinforce corporate responsibility but also build trust and credibility with stakeholders.

5 Challenges and Ethical Considerations in AI-Driven Transformation

5.1 Data Privacy and Security Challenges with AI Integration in Business

As businesses increasingly integrate artificial intelligence (AI) into their operations, they face new challenges in data privacy and security. AI systems require large volumes of data to function effectively, which often includes sensitive information about customers, employees, and business operations. While AI offers significant benefits, it also introduces risks related to data protection, making robust privacy and security measures essential [11].

5.1.1 Key Challenges in Data Privacy and Security with AI Integration

Integrating AI poses significant challenges in data privacy and security, primarily due to the substantial amount of personal information required for effective performance. The storage of sensitive data, such as customer preferences and biometric information, creates vulnerabilities to unauthorized access and data breaches, particularly in cloud environments lacking robust security measures. While anonymization is intended to protect privacy, there is a risk of re-identification through cross-referencing, which can inadvertently expose personally identifiable information (PII). Additionally, AI systems connected to broader IT infrastructures increase the risk of cyber attacks, where hackers may manipulate AI algorithms or introduce adversarial data to disrupt operations. Ethical concerns also arise from biased datasets, leading to discriminatory outcomes, and compliance with stringent regulations like GDPR and CCPA becomes more complex as companies navigate the challenges of transparency and data control in AI applications.

5.1.2 Examples of Recent Privacy Breaches Highlighting AI Risks

In 2020, Clearview AI faced significant backlash for scraping billions of images from social media and websites without users' consent to develop an AI-powered facial recognition system for law enforcement. This incident raised serious privacy concerns, as individuals' images were used to create a database capable of identifying them without their knowledge. The fallout resulted in several countries demanding the deletion of the collected data, emphasizing the necessity for regulations governing the use of publicly available data in AI applications.

The 2018 Facebook-Cambridge Analytica scandal further highlighted AI risks when it was revealed that Cambridge Analytica harvested data from millions of Facebook users without consent to build voter profiles for targeted political ads. This unauthorized data collection raised ethical and privacy issues, as users were unaware their data was being exploited for political manipulation. The incident prompted changes in Facebook's data policies and sparked discussions among lawmakers regarding stronger privacy protections, underlining the need for transparency in AI-driven data processing.

In 2019, Capital One experienced a major data breach affecting over 100 million customer accounts due to a hacker exploiting vulnerabilities in its cloud-based AI infrastructure. Sensitive information, including Social Security numbers and credit scores, was compromised, raising alarms about the security of cloud-based AI systems. This breach resulted in substantial regulatory fines and highlighted the critical importance of implementing robust security measures, such as enhanced authentication, encryption, and access controls, to protect sensitive data in AI environment.

5.1.3 Importance of Robust Data Protection Policies

The recent privacy breaches highlight the critical need for businesses to implement comprehensive data protection policies when integrating AI. Key measures include data minimization to collect only necessary information, ensuring compliance with privacy regulations; data encryption and access control to prevent unauthorized access; and regular audits to identify vulnerabilities. Transparency in data usage and effective consent management are essential for building consumer trust, while privacy by design ensures data protection is prioritized throughout AI development. Additionally, adopting ethical AI practices and maintaining continuous monitoring with response plans can help mitigate risks and manage any potential data breaches effectively, safeguarding sensitive information and enhancing overall security.

5.2 Issues of Bias and Fairness in AI Algorithms

AI algorithms depend on large datasets, which can carry inherent biases from historical, societal, or human errors, embedding these biases in the decision-making processes of the models. In customer-facing applications, such biases can result in unfair treatment, exclusion of certain groups, or even harm, posing significant reputational and ethical risks for businesses. Bias can manifest in various ways: historical bias perpetuates existing inequalities; sampling bias arises when training data inadequately represents all demographics; measurement bias occurs when data variables fail to accurately capture intended metrics; and algorithmic bias emerges from the structure or function of the algorithm itself, unintentionally introducing further bias into outcomes.

5.3 Case Studies of AI Bias with Significant Repercussions

See Table 2.

Measures to Mitigate AI Bias and Promote Fairness

To enhance fairness in AI systems, businesses can adopt several key measures. First, they should use diverse and representative training data to ensure all customer groups are fairly represented, reducing favoritism. Regular bias audits and model testing can help identify and address unfair patterns before deployment. Utilizing fairness and explainability tools, such as IBM's AI Fairness 360, allows companies to evaluate the impact of data changes on outcomes, promoting transparency. Establishing ethical AI guidelines ensures that fairness, accountability, and transparency are prioritized in AI development. Incorporating human oversight in decision-making processes, such as reviewing credit decisions or job applications, can further minimize bias. Finally, maintaining transparency and communication about AI decision-making processes fosters customer trust and accountability, helping to mitigate the effects of potential biases.

5.4 Workforce Impact of AI Adoption

The adoption of AI in various industries is reshaping the workforce, creating both challenges and opportunities. On one hand, AI improves efficiency by automating routine tasks, reducing costs, and increasing productivity; on the other, it leads to significant disruptions in the workforce, such as skill gaps, job displacement, and the demand for reskilling. Businesses need to take proactive steps to ensure that their workforce can adapt to these changes, and several companies are leading by example,

Table 2 Case study of AI Bias in prominent companies

Case Study	Background	Repercussions	Root Cause
Amazon's Biased Recruitment Tool	In 2018, Amazon developed an AI recruitment tool that favoured resumes from male-dominated fields, penalizing those associated with women	Discrimination: Bias against female candidates. Reputational Damage: Criticism of hiring practices. Tool Discontinuation: Wasted resources and missed innovation	The model was trained on resumes reflecting historical hiring biases and male-dominated fields
Apple Card's Gender Bias in Credit Decisions	In 2019, the Apple Card faced criticism for offering a credit limit to Steve Wozniak that was 10 times higher than his wife's, despite shared finances	Legal Scrutiny: Investigation by New York Department of Financial Services. Public Backlash: Loss of public trust. Gender Bias Allegations: Concerns over financial AI systems	The credit assessment algorithm favoured male applicants based on biased financial data points
Racial Bias in Facial Recognition Software	Studies revealed major facial recognition technologies had higher error rates for people of colour, particularly women	Privacy Risks: Misidentification and wrongful arrests. Policy Implications: Bans on facial recognition tech in cities. Company Responses: IBM exited the market	Training datasets primarily contained images of lighter-skinned, male faces, leading to underrepresentation

implementing comprehensive training programs to equip employees with AI-related skills [12].

5.4.1 Key Workforce Impacts of AI Adoption

The rise of AI has led to a significant skills gap, as there is a shortage of trained professionals in areas like data science, machine learning, AI ethics, and systems integration. This gap is critical as businesses increasingly depend on AI technologies. Additionally, job displacement is a concern, particularly in sectors such as manufacturing, finance, and customer service, where automation replaces routine tasks like data entry and assembly line work. Consequently, there is a heightened demand for reskilling and upskilling the workforce, as employees must acquire new competencies to effectively work with AI systems, understand data analytics, and utilize AI tools to boost productivity.

5.4.2 Examples of Companies Addressing AI-Related Workforce Challenges

See Table 3.

Table 3 Examples of companies addressing AI related workforce challenges

Company	Initiative	Background	Training programs	Impact
Amazon	Upskilling 2025 Initiative	Launched a $700 million initiative to train 100,000 employees in AI-related skills by 2025	Machine Learning University: Training for technical employees in AI and ML. Career Choice Program: Pre-paid tuition for high-demand fields. Amazon Technical Academy: Prepares non-technical employees for AI roles	Employees upskill for AI roles, reducing job displacement risk
AT&T	Future Ready and Nanodegree Programs	Addressing skill requirements due to AI and digital transformation	Nanodegree Programs: AI-focused training in data analysis and ML. Digital Transformation Program: Courses on AI and software development	Thousands transitioned to AI-related roles, closing internal skill gaps
Siemens	Digitalization and AI Training Programs	Implemented AI in operations, launching training for digitalization and AI	Digitalization Training Center: Hands-on AI, IoT, and digital twins training. Data Analytics and AI Curriculum: Specialized training for engineers	Workforce skilled in AI processes, minimizing job displacement
Microsoft	Global Skills Initiative	Launched to provide free digital skills training to 25 million globally, with internal training for employees	AI for Good and AI Training for Employees: Training on AI ethics and tools. Certification Programs: AI and data analytics certifications	Reduces skill gaps and enhances workforce capabilities for AI projects
IBM	SkillsBuild and AI Skills Academy	Recognized need for reskilling as AI becomes integral to business	AI Skills Academy: Specialized training in AI ethics and management. SkillsBuild Program: AI and cloud computing training for employees and learners	Equips employees with essential AI skills, improving retention and reducing skill gaps

5.5 *Regulatory Landscape Surrounding AI*

As AI technology advances and becomes increasingly integrated into business and daily life, governments worldwide are implementing regulations to manage its ethical and societal impacts. Current and emerging AI policies focus on ensuring transparency, accountability, privacy, and fairness, addressing public concerns over data security, discrimination, and autonomous decision-making. Navigating this regulatory landscape has become a critical aspect of AI-driven digital transformation for companies seeking to leverage AI responsibly and legally.

5.5.1 Current and Emerging Policies Impacting AI

Several significant regulations govern data privacy and the ethical use of AI globally. The General Data Protection Regulation (GDPR), enforced in the EU since 2018, mandates clear consent for data collection and grants individuals the right to explanations for AI-driven decisions, thereby influencing AI operations reliant on personal data. The proposed Algorithmic Accountability Act in the U.S. seeks to require companies to assess automated systems for bias and discrimination, enhancing transparency and fairness in AI decision-making. In China, AI guidelines emphasize responsible usage and user control, mandating data localization and transparency for AI interactions. The EU Artificial Intelligence Act aims to categorize AI systems by risk, imposing strict compliance requirements on high-risk applications to ensure safety and ethics. Lastly, the California Consumer Privacy Act (CCPA) mirrors GDPR by granting California residents rights over their personal data, including the right to opt-out of data sales, thereby enhancing transparency in AI applications like targeted advertising. Together, these regulations establish a framework for responsible AI development and data management.

5.5.2 How Companies Are Navigating AI Compliance Challenges

As regulations increasingly require interpretability in AI-driven decisions, companies are implementing various strategies to enhance transparency and fairness. Explainability tools are being adopted, exemplified by JPMorgan Chase, which uses these tools to analyze credit scoring algorithms for compliance with GDPR. To address bias, organizations like IBM conduct regular fairness audits using tools such as "AI Fairness 360" to identify and mitigate biases in hiring algorithms. Companies are also establishing ethical AI governance frameworks; for instance, Microsoft has created an internal framework and ethics board to oversee AI projects, ensuring alignment with regulatory standards. In response to data protection regulations like GDPR, firms are adopting privacy-enhancing technologies (PETs), such as Google's use of federated learning, to safeguard personal data without compromising AI performance. Lastly, with the EU AI Act categorizing high-risk AI systems, companies like Siemens are developing risk management protocols that include rigorous testing and real-time monitoring to ensure compliance and safety in critical applications.

5.5.3 Aligning with Industry Standards and Best Practices

In addition to complying with regulatory requirements, companies are increasingly aligning with industry standards, such as the **ISO/IEC 22989** (AI concepts and terminology) and **ISO/IEC 23053** (framework for AI trustworthiness). These standards provide best practices for transparency, fairness, and privacy in AI systems. By aligning with these standards, companies demonstrate their commitment to responsible AI use, which can improve their reputation and build consumer trust.

6 Future Directions: AI and the Evolving Business Landscape

6.1 Emerging AI Trends in Business

The field of artificial intelligence is evolving rapidly, with several emerging trends that are transforming industries and creating new opportunities. These trends include generative AI, explainable AI, and autonomous systems, which offer companies the ability to innovate, improve efficiency, and gain a competitive advantage.

Generative AI utilizes algorithms like Generative Adversarial Networks (GANs) and transformers to create new content, including images and text. Its applications span various industries, enabling personalized content creation, as seen with Adobe's integration of generative AI in Creative Cloud, NVIDIA's synthetic data for autonomous driving, and Coca-Cola's marketing initiatives with OpenAI. Explainable AI (XAI) enhances transparency in AI models, crucial for trust and regulatory compliance in sectors like healthcare and finance. Companies such as JPMorgan Chase and Siemens leverage XAI to ensure unbiased decision-making and process optimization, while Microsoft's Azure platform offers tools for model interpretability. Autonomous systems, powered by advanced machine learning and sensor technology, operate independently in fields like transportation and logistics, improving efficiency and safety. Tesla leads in autonomous driving with its Full Self-Driving software, Amazon employs robots for warehouse automation and drone deliveries, and John Deere utilizes autonomous tractors for precision agriculture, showcasing significant productivity gains across industries.

6.2 AI's Role in Supporting Long-Term Sustainability Goals

Artificial intelligence (AI) offers powerful tools for addressing global sustainability challenges and supports long-term sustainability goals, such as those outlined in the United Nations' Sustainable Development Goals (SDGs). AI can optimize resource use, reduce waste, and promote transparency and efficiency across industries. Through case studies, we can see how companies are integrating AI to make substantial contributions to sustainable growth in areas like waste reduction, carbon management, and ethical supply chains [13].

6.2.1 How AI Supports Sustainability Goals

AI significantly contributes to sustainability by optimizing resource usage to minimize waste in manufacturing, logistics, and consumer goods. It enhances carbon management through algorithms that monitor and reduce energy consumption, predict emissions, and support carbon capture, thereby lessening environmental impact. Additionally, AI promotes ethical supply chains by ensuring transparency and accountability in sourcing raw materials and delivering products, fostering fair labor practices and environmental responsibility.

6.2.2 Case Studies of AI Integration for Sustainable Growth

See Table 4.

6.3 AI-Enabled Adaptive and Resilient Business Models

In an era marked by rapid technological advancement, economic shifts, and environmental uncertainties, businesses are increasingly relying on AI to develop adaptive and resilient models capable of responding to future disruptions. AI-driven insights allow companies to anticipate changes, quickly adjust to market dynamics, and maintain operational continuity, even in volatile environments. By leveraging data, automation, and predictive analytics, AI supports flexible and scalable strategies, enabling businesses to remain competitive and responsive to evolving demands [14].

Table 4 AI Integration in prominent companies

Company	Background	AI implementation	Impact
Procter & Gamble	Global consumer goods company focused on minimizing waste and improving efficiency	Process Optimization: AI analytics monitor production, identify inefficiencies, and optimize raw material use. Inventory Management: AI-driven demand forecasting adjusts inventory levels to reduce overproduction	Reduced production waste, optimized resource use, smaller environmental footprint, and aligned with sustainability goals
Google	Aims for carbon neutrality and renewable energy usage in its operations	Energy Optimization: DeepMind AI optimizes cooling systems in data centers. Carbon Footprint Tracking: AI analyzes and tracks emissions across facilities	Reduced cooling energy usage by 30% and overall energy use by up to 15%, positioning Google as a leader in sustainable tech
IBM	Uses AI and blockchain for transparency in supply chains	Blockchain for Traceability: Tracks food product origins to ensure ethical sourcing. Supplier Assessment: AI assesses supplier compliance with standards	Increased accountability in supply chains, supporting ethical production practices and transparency for customers
Siemens	Leverages AI for circular economy initiatives and resource efficiency	Predictive Maintenance: Extends machinery life and reduces replacements. Digital Twins: Simulates product life cycles for resource optimization	Reduced waste, increased manufacturing efficiency, and supported sustainable product design
John Deere	Develops AI-driven solutions for sustainable agriculture	Precision Agriculture: Uses computer vision to apply herbicides selectively. Data Analytics for Soil Health: Optimizes planting and irrigation based on soil data	Reduced chemical and water use, improving sustainability and productivity in agriculture

6.3.1 Key Areas Where AI Supports Adaptive and Resilient Business Models

1. **Real-Time Data Analytics and Predictive Insights**: AI analyzes massive data volumes in real time, enabling companies to detect patterns, anticipate market shifts, and make proactive adjustments.
2. **Demand Forecasting and Inventory Optimization**: AI predicts consumer demand, optimizing inventory and reducing the risk of stockouts or overproduction, which is crucial for resilience in fluctuating markets.
3. **Automated Decision-Making and Process Flexibility**: Automation allows businesses to streamline operations and adapt quickly to changing conditions, whether in manufacturing, supply chain, or customer service.

Table 5 Examples of companies adopting AI driven resilient models

Company	Background	AI implementation	Impact
Walmart	One of the world's largest retailers using AI for demand forecasting and inventory management	Demand Forecasting: Analyses past sales, seasonality, local events, and weather to predict consumer demand. Automated Inventory Management: Adjusts stock levels dynamically based on forecasts	Effectively managed increased demand during COVID-19, minimizing stockouts and enhancing customer satisfaction
Rolls-Royce	Aerospace manufacturer utilizing AI for predictive maintenance to ensure engine reliability	Predictive Maintenance: Analyses sensor data to monitor engine health and predict maintenance needs. Remote Monitoring: Total Care platform provides real-time updates on engine performance	Enhanced resilience in engine services, reduced maintenance costs, and improved safety for airlines
Unilever	Multinational consumer goods company using AI for scenario planning to enhance supply chain resilience	Scenario Planning: Simulates potential disruptions to assess impacts on supply chain elements, Dynamic Adjustments: Predicts risks and proactively adjusts supply chain operations	Improved adaptability to disruptions, ensuring consistent product availability even in uncertain conditions
Netflix	Streaming service leveraging AI for content recommendations and personalization	Content Recommendations: Uses machine learning to analyse user behaviour for personalized suggestions. Production Decisions: Predictive analytics forecast show popularity for data-driven content decisions	Over 80% of content viewed comes from recommendations, enhancing user engagement and reducing churn

4. **Scenario Planning and Risk Management**: AI enables scenario planning by simulating different outcomes, allowing companies to prepare for a variety of disruptions and build resilient strategies.

6.3.2 Practical Examples of AI-Driven Adaptive and Resilient Business Models

See Table 5.

7 Conclusions

AI-driven digital transformation is reshaping industries by fostering competitiveness and sustainability through operational efficiency, innovation, and ethical practices. Key insights reveal AI's role in optimizing resources, enabling data-driven decisions, and enhancing customer-centric strategies. Notable examples include predictive maintenance by Rolls-Royce, energy efficiency improvements by Google's DeepMind, and sustainable supply chains via IBM's blockchain solutions. AI also drives economic growth, promotes sustainable innovations like John Deere's precision agriculture, and supports workforce reskilling initiatives, such as Amazon's "Upskilling 2025."

Businesses must adopt ethical AI practices to remain competitive and ensure long-term success, supported by transparent governance and workforce training. Policymakers should foster innovation through balanced regulations, promoting data privacy and public–private collaborations to address societal challenges. Researchers are encouraged to focus on advancing ethical, explainable AI solutions and transformative applications across healthcare, energy, and education. Cross-industry collaboration and scalable AI models are vital for navigating disruptions and achieving inclusive growth.

This collective effort can unleash AI's potential to deliver environmental benefits, economic resilience, and social equity, driving innovation and sustainability on a global scale. By embracing responsible AI integration, businesses, governments, and researchers can shape a transformative future, with AI contributing to a projected \$13 trillion boost to the global economy by 2030.

References

1. Vial, G. (2021). Understanding digital transformation: A review and a research agenda. *Managing digital transformation,* 13–66. https://doi.org/10.4324/9781003008637-4
2. Jagatheesaperumal, S. K., & Rahouti, M. (2023). Building digital twins of cyber physical systems with metaverse for industry 5.0 and beyond. *IT Professional, 24*(6), 34–40. https://doi.org/10.1109/MITP.2022.3225064
3. Mikalef, P., Islam, N., Parida, V., Singh, H., & Altwaijry, N. (2023). Artificial intelligence (AI) competencies for organizational performance: A B2B marketing capabilities perspective. *Journal of Business Research, 164,* 113998. https://doi.org/10.1016/j.jbusres.2023.113998
4. Dubey, R., Gunasekaran, A., & Childe, S. J. (2019). Big data analytics capability in supply chain agility: The moderating effect of organizational flexibility. *Management decision, 57*(8), 2092–2112. https://doi.org/10.1108/MD-01-2018-0119
5. Ivanov, D., & Dolgui, A. (2020). Viability of intertwined supply networks: Extending the supply chain resilience angles towards survivability. A position paper motivated by COVID-19 outbreak. *International journal of production research, 58*(10), 2904–2915. https://doi.org/10.1080/00207543.2020.1750727
6. Mohsen, B. M. (2023). Impact of artificial intelligence on supply chain management performance. *Journal of Service Science and Management, 16*(1), 44–58. https://doi.org/10.4236/jssm.2023.161004
7. Chatterjee, S., Mikalef, P., Khorana, S., & Kizgin, H. (2024). Assessing the implementation of AI integrated CRM system for B2C relationship management: Integrating contingency theory and dynamic capability view theory. *Information systems frontiers, 26*(3), 967–985. https://doi.org/10.1007/s10796-022-10261-w
8. Arias-Pérez, J., Coronado-Medina, A., & Perdomo-Charry, G. (2022). Big data analytics capability as a mediator in the impact of open innovation on firm performance. *Journal of Strategy and Management, 15*(1), 1–15. https://doi.org/10.1108/JSMA-09-2020-0262

9. Guandalini, I. (2022). Sustainability through digital transformation: A systematic literature review for research guidance. *Journal of Business Research, 148*, 456–471. https://doi.org/10.1016/j.jbusres.2022.05.003
10. Sahoo, S., Kumar, S., Sivarajah, U., Lim, W. M., Westland, J. C., & Kumar, A. (2024). Blockchain for sustainable supply chain management: Trends and ways forward. *Electronic Commerce Research, 24*(3), 1563–1618. https://doi.org/10.1007/s10660-022-09569-1
11. Jobin, A., Ienca, M., & Vayena, E. (2019). The global landscape of AI ethics guidelines. *Nature machine intelligence, 1*(9), 389–399. https://doi.org/10.1038/s42256-019-0088-2
12. Jatobá, M. N., Ferreira, J. J., Fernandes, P. O., & Teixeira, J. P. (2023). Intelligent human resources for the adoption of artificial intelligence: A systematic literature review. *Journal of Organizational Change Management, 36*(7), 1099–1124. https://doi.org/10.1108/JOCM-03-2022-0075
13. Vinuesa, R., Azizpour, H., Leite, I., Balaam, M., Dignum, V., Domisch, S., & Fuso Nerini, F. (2020). The role of artificial intelligence in achieving the Sustainable Development Goals. *Nature communications, 11*(1), 233. https://doi.org/10.1038/s41467-019-14108-y
14. Belhadi, A., Mani, V., Kamble, S. S., Khan, S. A. R., & Verma, S. (2024). Artificial intelligence-driven innovation for enhancing supply chain resilience and performance under the effect of supply chain dynamism: An empirical investigation. *Annals of Operations Research, 333*(2), 627–652. https://doi.org/10.1007/s10479-021-03956-x

The Importance of Insurance Sector Penetration for Economic Growth in China: Fresh Evidence from Quantile Cointegration and Causality Analysis

Zulfiqar Ali Imran, Muhammad Ahad, Virgil Popescu, Ramona Birau, Hira Aftab, and Mobeen Ahmad

Abstract The insurance sector is important to the economy as it plays an essential role in risk management by providing businesses and individuals with financial protection against unforeseen events. The insurance sector promotes stability and facilitates economic growth. Additionally, it mobilizes substantial investments and funds that contribute to the overall liquidity and development of financial markets. However, the relationship can demonstrate diminishing returns, as extremely high insurance penetration levels may divert resources away from productive sectors of the economy. Thus, this research aims to identify the asymmetric impact of the insurance sector at aggregated and disaggregated levels on economic growth over the distribution of quantiles. For this purpose, quarterly data from 1994Q1-2022Q4 has been used in the case of China. The quantile cointegration exhibits the presence of a long-run relationship between insurance penetration and economic growth

Z. A. Imran
Faculty of Business, Sohar University, Sohar, Oman
e-mail: zulfiqaraliimran05@gmail.com

M. Ahad
Lahore Business School, The University of Lahore, Main Campus, Lahore, Punjab, Pakistan
e-mail: m.ahad68@yahoo.com

V. Popescu
Faculty of Economics and Business Administration, University of Craiova, Craiova, Romania
e-mail: virgil.popescu@vilaro.ro

R. Birau
ugeniu Carad, Doctoral School of Economic Sciences, University of Craiova, Craiova, Romania

H. Aftab
Institute of Business and Information Technology, University of the Punjab, Lahore, Pakistan
e-mail: hira.aftab@ibitpu.edu.pk

M. Ahmad (✉)
Department of Management Sciences, COMSATS University Islamabad, Lahore Campus, Lahore, Punjab Province, Pakistan
e-mail: mobeen.cu@gmail.com

S. O. Idowu et al. (eds.), *Competitiveness and Sustainability in the Digitization Era*, Springer Proceedings in Business and Economics,
https://doi.org/10.1007/978-3-031-91778-3_13

with a verifying degree of significance across all quantiles. Similarly, the quantile regression confirms the positive impact of insurance penetration on economic growth across various data points on the distribution. Moreover, we find bidirectional causality between for various quantiles with the exception of unidirectional causality for a few quantiles. For policy perspective, policymakers should strengthen the environment that pushes competition and innovation within the insurance industry by introducing a regulatory framework that facilitates fair competition and safeguards consumer protection. Further, facilitating investment in infrastructure projects and stimulating public–private partnerships can support the insurance industry by increasing insurable assets.

Keywords Life insurance · Non-life insurance · Economic growth · Quantile cointegration · Quantile causality · China

1 Introduction

Insurance, encompassing both life and non-life insurance, is a pivotal service that plays a profound role in addressing unforeseen contingencies that individuals and businesses encounter throughout their existence. The far-reaching societal impact of insurance is underscored by the substantial cash flows that traverse the intricate web of relationships between the insured and the insurer. As described by Focarelli (2017), insurance premiums, paid to mitigate life's uncertainties, do not remain dormant in insurance reserves; rather, they serve as a crucial financial channel that mobilizes resources to the real economy and financial markets. These premiums, before they are disbursed as benefits, are strategically invested, propelling economic activity[1] (Focarelli, 2017).

In a global context, the insurance sector comprises two distinctive subsectors: life and non-life insurance, each contributing significantly to the overall insurance landscape. According to recent statistics from Sigma (3/2021), in 2020, life insurance accounted for 44% of the total insurance sector, while non-life insurance constituted the remaining 56%. Notably, the global insurance premiums market witnessed growth, with a 1.3% increase in 2020, reaching a staggering $6.3 trillion. Within this expansive market, non-life insurance premiums increased by 1.5% in the same year, with a total volume of $3.5 trillion, while life insurance premiums, despite a 4.4% decrease, remained substantial at $2.8 trillion (sigma, 3/2021).

China, a powerhouse in East Asia, has experienced remarkable economic growth over the past few decades, driven by substantial investments in infrastructure development and consumer financing. Consequently, China's insurance sector has expanded significantly, securing its position as the world's second-largest insurance market, with a staggering volume of $655 billion in 2020 (Institute, 2020). Chinese insurance companies have diversified their product offerings, venturing into the burgeoning

[1] The former is referred as premia whereas latter is called benefits.

field of insur-tech and new technologies, marking rapid growth in recent years. Notably, personal insurance, including health, life, and accident insurance, has thrived, with life insurance dominating the premia income share. Simultaneously, property insurance has gained prominence, witnessing remarkable premium income growth rates in recent years (Swiss Re Institute, 2021). Moreover, China's total insurance premium recorded a 6.2% increase from 2019 to 2020, with its global market share expanding by 0.6% during the same period (Swiss Sigma Report 3/2021).

One of the primary contributions of insurance companies to the real economy is their role in claims compensation. When individuals or enterprises face adverse events, insurance steps in to provide financial support. For individuals, this protection safeguards their income and overall wealth, which can then be directed towards consumption or investments in the real economy. Businesses, likewise, can continue their operations even in the face of disruptions caused by incidents, ensuring an uninterrupted supply of products or services to the economy. This operational resilience allows them to sustain income generation, enabling them to pay staff remuneration, dividends, and taxes. Additionally, insurance companies offer income accumulation programs akin to pensions, alleviating the burden on state social security pensions and freeing up state funds for other economic needs. The second major economic contribution of insurers is found in the financial transactions they engage in. Insurance companies, much like other enterprises, contribute to economic growth through various financial activities. These activities encompass paying salaries to personnel and intermediaries, remitting taxes to the government, distributing dividends to shareholders, and fulfilling financial obligations to lenders. Furthermore, insurance companies often partake in corporate social responsibility initiatives, making donations to society. All these financial flows, including claims payments, salaries, taxes, dividends, interest, and donations, serve as sources of income for the respective stakeholders involved. Subsequently, these funds are either spent or invested, ultimately returning to the economy, thereby contributing to its growth (Apergis and Poufinas 2020).

In examining the channels through which insurance influences economic growth, a particular focus is placed on the role of life insurance. This emphasis is due to several reasons. Firstly, from the perspective of insurance supply, life insurance and non-life insurance exhibit differing risk attitudes, resulting in distinct investment strategies. Life insurers, driven by the long-term and fixed-dollar nature of their liabilities, tend to invest in assets with similar characteristics (Haiss and Sümegi, 2008; Hickman, 1971). Consequently, a substantial portion of their investments is channeled into relatively secure instruments such as government and corporate bonds (Rejda, 2004). In contrast, general insurance claims, influenced by factors like catastrophic losses and inflation, can exhibit greater variability, necessitating liquidity in investments. Notably, the magnitude of investment activities within the insurance sector contributes significantly to the explanation of the insurance-growth nexus. Secondly, on the demand side of insurance, life insurance products offer individuals and families a means to manage income risk and foster long-term savings, a feature not commonly found in general insurance products. The long-term financial support provided by life insurers assumes a critical role in economies requiring such financing for infrastructure development. Thus, life insurance holds a unique position in facilitating economic growth through its investment strategies and long-term financial support, particularly in the context of infrastructure development. These multifaceted roles of insurance underscore its potential as a driving force in fostering economic growth (Beck and Webb, 2003).

The nature of the relationship between insurance penetration and economic growth can be non-linear through several channels. Initially, a higher insurance penetration provides stability to the economy by mitigating risks and reducing the financial burden on individuals and businesses, which can lead to higher investment and economic growth (Beck & Webb, 2003). However, this relationship can demonstrate diminishing returns, as extremely high insurance penetration levels may divert resources away from productive sectors of the economy (Cummins & Weiss, 2009). Moreover, when insurance markets are inefficient or overregulated, excessive penetration can lead to moral hazard and adverse selection problems, weakening the positive impact on economic growth (Baranoff & Sager, 2002). Thus, a U-shaped or inverted U-shaped relationship between insurance penetration and economic growth may emerge, suggesting an optimal level of insurance development that maximizes its positive contribution to economic growth (Kumar & Sehrawat, 2019). Sucha theoretical framework emphasizes the importance of striking a balance in insurance market development to attain substantial benefits for economic growth.

The dynamic interplay between economic growth and insurance penetration at aggregate and disaggregate levels serves as a compelling stimulus for researchers to unveil the precise relationship that connects these variables together. The seminal concept of Granger-causality, as posited by Granger (1969), constitutes the foundational framework for the investigation of dynamic associations within the realm of economic variables. Although Granger causality is conceptually framed in the context of conditional distribution, a majority of works have traditionally examined Granger causality through the lens of conditional mean regression models characterized by linear causal relationships. Consequently, the conventional conditional mean regression model fails to capture the subtleties of tail-dependence causal relations and nonlinear causations. Thus, this research endeavors to examine the causal nexus that exists between economic growth and insurance penetration within China during the period spanning from1994Q1 to 2022Q4, encompassing all quantiles of the distribution. To this end, we employ the Granger-causality in quantiles test, as proposed by Troster (2018), which systematically assesses causal relationships across the entire spectrum of conditional quantiles within the distribution. Our primary objective is to delineate the causal connections existing at individual quantile, thereby allowing us to discern causality's influence on both the central tendency and the extremities of the conditional distribution. Furthermore, this approach furnishes a sufficient criterion for ascertaining Granger causality when all quantiles are taken into account.

In light of the preceding discussion, this study makes a twofold contribution to the existing body of knowledge. Firstly, we enhance the existing literature by exploring the insurance-growth nexus in China at a disaggregated level. Secondly, our contribution extends to the methodological approach adopted, which enables a comprehensive understanding of the nature and magnitude of this relationship. For instance, to substantiate the presence of cointegration, indicative of a long-term association, between the insurance sector and economic growth in China, we employ a novel quantile cointegration technique as introduced by Xiao (2009). Furthermore, we employ Quantile regression to rigorously assess whether the insurance sector exerts a statistically significant positive or negative impact on economic growth in China. Additionally, we scrutinize the direction of the causal relationship by employing an advanced quantile causality analysis framework, as articulated by Troster (2018). Lastly, this study not only provides valuable insights for policymakers but also offers a set of substantive policy recommendations aimed at facilitating the attainment of China's growth targets.

The rest of the paper is organized in the following manner: the second section is a review of the literature focusing on the theoretical background and empirical basis of the insurance-growth nexus debate. The third section outlines the data and econometric techniques used in the study while highlighting the novel methodology. The fourth section reports the results of the empirical analysis, while the last section concludes the paper with a policy recommendation.

2 Review of Literature

The discussion over the linkages between economic growth and insurance penetration originated as the role of the insurance industry is highlighted in the financial sector because of its capital accumulation and investment functions. In 1955, Willett stated the words of Professor Clark that the wealth of nations can be increased by two leading factors of production i.e. capital and labor (Willett, 2016). In contrast to this, the theory of economic growth developed by Harrod and Domar in the 1940s highlighted the most influential factor for enhancing economic development is capital (Sato, 1964). In addition to the economic theory, Benston & Smith (1976) highlighted that government regulations are also an important factor that influences the intermediaries via credit allocation, licensing, price control, supervision, and commodity type. Later (Allen & Santomero, 1997) disagreed with the factors highlighted by Benston & Smith (1976) and claimed that factors like risk-sharing and participation cost are central to the theory of financial intermediation today while other factors were no longer important.

Similarly, Outreville (2013) proved that even if two countries are at the same economic level, the role of insurance in supporting economic growth would differ. The same point was expressed by Ward & Zurbruegg (2000) and they suggested that the insurance-growth nexus should be on a particular country basis while special consideration should be given to the heterogeneous nature of countries. They highlighted that it was because of the differences in culture, regulations, and religious aspects. Previous studies that investigated the insurance-growth relationships across different countries utilized linear models that assumed homogeneous slopes and intercepts while ignoring the potential heterogeneity across countries. The insurance growth nexus was explained by Kugler & Ofoghi (2005) by analyzing the data of one country along the lines of Ward & Zurbruegg (2000). They analyzed the data of the UK using a cointegration approach to explore the Insurance-growth nexus and highlighted a significant positive relationship between economic growth and insurance. Ata later stage, Adams et al. (2009) concluded the same relationship using Granger causality while utilizing the data of Sweden. Njegomir & Stojić (2010) highlighted the positive effect of insurance on the economic growth of the ex-Yugoslavia region using a country-specific fixed-effect model. Ching et al. (2010) found a long-term significant relationship between economic growth and insurance using VECM and causality approach for Malaysian data. However, Chau et al. (2013) used a co-integration and causality approach and proved that a short-term relationship exists between life insurance and economic growth while a long-term relationship holds for non-life insurance.

Furthermore, Kjosevski, (2012a) used multiple regression for Mercedonia's data from 1995–2010. He highlighted the positive effect of non-life and aggregate insurance on economic growth while the negative effect on life insurance. Horng et al. (2012)analyze data using the VAR model from 1961–2006 and prove the Insurance industry is a cause for Taiwan's economic growth. Verma & Bala (2013) use OLS technique for Indian data from 1990–2011 and proved life insurance significantly affects economic growth as well. Later using the VECM Granger approach. Ghosh (2013) reached the same conclusion only for long-term Indian data ranging from 1970–2012. Cristea et al. (2014) used a correlation approach for Romanian data ranging from 1997–2012 and explored the association between insurance and economic growth. Akinlo & Apanisile (2014) used pooled OLS, GMM, and fixed effect models for Sub-Saharan Africa on data ranging from 1986–2011 and highlighted a significant positive relationship between the insurance industry and economic growth. A bidirectional relationship between economic growth and insurance is also supported in Sub African countries. Abdul Latif Alhassan (2016) reveal that life insurance exhibits more significant long-term effect on economic growth as compared to non-life insurance, using ARDL and causality approach over the data from 1990–2010.

In addition, Ukpong & Acha (2017) used a cointegration approach and found a significant and positive relationship between life, non-life, and total insurance with economic growth in Nigeria. Wang et al. (2017) used the VECM approach for Chinese data and found a negative short-term relationship between economic growth and life insurance while positive for the long term. Further, a positive relationship was highlighted by them for the short term between non-life insurance and economic growth and insignificant in the case of the long term. Abdul L Alhassan & Fiador (2014) examined Ghana data ranging from 1990 to 2010 using the autoregressive distributed lag (ARDL) bounds approach to cointegration and found a long-run positive relationship between insurance and economic growth. Similarly, Apergis and Poufinas (2020) highlighted the importance of insurance sector growth for economic growth in the case of 27 OECD countries over the period of 2006 to 2016. The results of dynamic panel analysis predict that gross claim payments, gross operating expenses, gross premia, and insurance penetration are significantly positively related to economic growth during the pre-and post-2008-crisis periods. In contrast,

Dawd & Benlagha (2023) predicted a nonlinear relationship between the insurance sector and economic growth in 16 OECD countries from 2009 to 2020. The findings estimated an inverted U-shaped relationship between insurance premiums and economic growth, thereby supporting the fact that more finance may only be better up to a point, after which it tends to harm growth.

In addition, Dash et al. (2018) identified a causal relationship between insurance market penetration and per capita economic growth in 19 Eurozone countries for the period 1980–2014. The results observed both unidirectional and bidirectional causality between insurance market penetration and per capita economic growth as non uniformly across the Eurozone. On the other hand, in the case of demand-following and feedback hypotheses, Scharner et al. (2023) predicted that economic growth contributes to insurance sector development for a panel of 130 countries in the period between 2003 and 2016. Iyodo et al. (2020) explored the impact of non-life insurance industry performance on economic growth in Nigeria over the time period of 1988 and 2012. The findings of OLS regression showed that non-life insurance penetration had a substantially positive effect on the economic growth in Nigeria. Similarly, Asongu & Odhiambo (2020) investigated the role of insurance in economic growth on a panel of 48 African countries for the period 2004–2014. The findings of GMM suggested that Life insurance increases economic growth while the effect of non-life insurance is not significant. Increasing both life insurance and non-life insurance has negative net effects on economic growth. Recently, Osei-Bonsu et al. (2022) empirically examined the effect of the growing insurance industry on the economic growth by using 2006Q1-2018Q2 in Ghana. Findings revealed that there is a significant and positive short and long-run relationship between insurance and economic growth in Ghana, bidirectional causality between insurance and economic growth and also a long-run effect of innovations (shocks) in insurance on economic growth.

Despite extensive exploration of the insurance-growth nexus in empirical research over the past few decades, the impact of insurance on economic growth remains a subject of contention and requires further elucidation. For instance, various studies have yielded contradictory findings, with some highlighting a positive relationship between insurance and economic growth (Ward & Zurbruegg, 2000; Abdul Latif Alhassan, 2016; Anwer, et al., 2019), while others have posited an insignificant relationship (Haiss & Sümegi, 2008). Additionally, there is evidence suggesting that insurance development may follow economic growth (Ching et al., 2010), and instances of a negative relationship have also surfaced (Zouhaie, 2014). These disparate findings underscore the complexity of the insurance-growth nexus, posing significant challenges for policymakers striving to formulate informed and effective policies. Moreover, we did not find a substantial study that has explored the nonlinear relationship between the insurance sector and economic growth at lower and higher data points in the distribution. The present study enters this ongoing debate by exploring the role of insurance penetration, both at an aggregated and disaggregated level, in shaping economic growth in China. Moreover, this study also contributes to applied economic literature by accommodating the presence of asymmetry. For this purpose, quantile analysis is performed such as Quantile unit root (Galvao Jr, 2009), Quantile cointegration (Xiao, 2009), and Granger causality in quantiles (Troster, 2018).

3 Data and Methodology

To examine the nature of the causal relationship between insurance, aggregated and disaggregated levels, and economic growth across different quantiles in China, we utilize quarterly frequency data from $1994Q_1$-$2022Q_4$with a total of 116 observations. The functional forms of estimated models are as follows:

Model-1:GDP $= f$ (LIFEI).

Model-2: GDP $= f$ (NONLIFEI).

Model-3: GDP $= f$ (TOTALI).

Model1-3 describes the impact of life, nonlife, and total insurance on economic growth respectively. Here, "GDP" denotes the Gross Domestic Product per capita measured in constant 2010 US$. Similarly, "TOTALI" represents an index of insurance market activity which is comprised of four insurance activities: (1) *life insurance density* (represented by direct domestic life premiums per capita); (2) *non-life insurance density* (proxied by direct domestic non-life premiums per capita); (3) *life insurance penetration* (ratio of direct domestic life premiums divided by GDP); and (4) *non-life insurance penetration* (ratio of direct domestic non-life premiums divided by GDP). Moreover, "NONLIFEI" and "LIFEI" show the nonlife insurance and life insurance activities respectively. All data series of the insurance sector are collected from the Global Financial Development (GFD) database, World Bank (2020). However, the GDP series is extracted from the World Development Indicator (WDI) database, World Bank. All series are taken in natural log form to compute the elasticities.

3.1 *Quantile Unit Root Analysis*

This study applies traditional ADF (Dickey & Fuller, 1981) and PP (Phillips & Perron, 1988) unit root analysis to test the presence of unit roots. Further, our study applies a quantile auto regression unit root test to confirm the stationarity of each variable for the conditional mean as well as for each quantile of the conditional distribution. The quantile autoregressive (QAR) unit root is proposed by Koenker & Xiao (2004) and further generalized by Galvao Jr (2009) by incorporating covariates and a linear time trend. Suppose Y_t is a stationary time series that carries previous information $I_t^Y :=$ $(Y_{t-1}, ...Y_{t-s})' \in R^s$ and $F_Y\left(\bullet|I_t^Y\right)$ is a function for the conditional distribution of Y_t given I_t^Y. The following equation is estimated for the quantile autoregressive unit root test.

$$Q_{\tau}^{Y}(Y_t|I_t^{Y}) = \mu_1(\tau) + \mu_2(\tau)t + \alpha(\tau)Y_{t-1} + \sum_{j=1}^{P} \alpha_j(\tau)\Delta Y_{t-j} + F_u^{-1}(\tau) \quad (1)$$

In Eq. (1) the τ- quantile of $F_y(\cdot|I_t^Y)$ and the term drift are represented by $Q_\tau^Y(\cdot|I_t^Y)$ and $\mu_1(\tau)$, respectively. The linear trend and persistence parameters are denoted by t and $\alpha(\tau)$, whereas, each quantile, F_u^{-1} symbolizes the inverse of the conditional distribution of the errors. Consequently, for each quantile, a different persistence parameter $\left(\hat{\alpha}\right)$ is estimated.

3.2 *Quantile Cointegration*

To confirm the existence of a long-term relationship between each pair of variables, our study utilizes the linear cointegration test of Johansen (1991) as follows.

$$Y_t = \alpha + \beta Z_t + \sum_{j=1}^{P} \Pi_j Y_{t-j} + \sum_{j=1}^{q} \gamma_j Z_{t-j} + \mu_t$$

The substantial number of empirical applications in economics and finance confirm the change of cointegration vector over distribution; therefore, the quantile cointegration approach is employed because of its ability to accommodate linear fluctuations on the location, scale, and shapes of distribution of exogenous variables. The traditional cointegration estimation of Engle & Granger (1987) is tested where $\beta(\tau)$ there is a constant vector.

$$Y_t = \alpha + \beta' Z_t + \sum_{j=-k}^{k} \Delta Z'_{t-j}\Pi_j + \mu_t$$

and

$$Q_{\tau}^{Y}(Y_t|I_t^{Y}, I_t^{z}) = \alpha(\tau) + \beta(\tau)' Z_t + \sum_{j=-k}^{K} \Delta Z'_{t-j}\Pi_j + F_u^{-1}(\tau) \quad (2)$$

The quadratic term of the regressor is incorporated in the quantile cointegration as follows.

$$Q_{\tau}^{Y}(Y_t|I_t^{Y}, I_t^{z}) = \alpha(\tau) + \beta(\tau)' Z_t + \gamma(\tau))' Z_t^2 + \sum_{j=-k}^{k} \Delta Z'_{t-j}\Pi_j$$

$$+\sum_{j=-k}^{k} \Delta Z_{t-j}^{2'} \Gamma_j F_u^{-1}(\tau) \tag{3}$$

The test for the stability of the cointegrating coefficients in Eq. (3) is derived by Xiao (2009) where the null hypothesis variables don't cointegrate in the overall quantile (τ). Moreover, we perform 1000 Monte Carlo simulations to estimate the critical value of the statistics through estimating Eq. (3).

3.3 Granger-Causality

Granger (1969) argued that X Granger non-cause in the distribution to Y if the previous X helps to predict future Y in condition to available past Y. However, mean causality ignores the possible dependence in the conditional tails of the distribution. Therefore, Granger's non-causality in conditional quantiles is applied because it evaluates the pattern of causality in different quantiles (Troster, 2018). The estimated null hypothesis of Granger non-causality in quantiles is the follows:

$$H_0^{Z \mapsto Y} : E\{1[Y_t \leq m(I_t^Y, \theta_0(\tau))]|I_t^Y, I_t^Z\} = \tau,\ a.s. for\ all\ \tau \in \mathrm{T} \tag{4}$$

versus

$$H_0^{Z \mapsto Y} : E\{1[Y_t \leq m(I_t^Y, \theta_0(\tau))]|I_t^Y, I_t^Z\} \neq \tau,\ a.s. for\ some\ \tau \in \mathrm{T} \tag{5}$$

where $m(I_t^Y, \theta_0(\tau))$ postulates the conditional quantile $Q_\tau^Y(\cdot|I_t^Y)$, for $\tau \in \mathrm{T}$. Then, t-test statistic is calculated for decision analysis as follows:

$$S_T = \frac{1}{Tn} \sum_{j=1}^{n} \left| \psi_{\cdot j}' W \psi_{\cdot j} \right| \tag{6}$$

In the above equation, W is the $T*T$ matrix with elements $w_{t,s} = \exp\left[-0.5(I_t - I_s)^2\right]$ and $\psi_{\cdot j'}$ represents the *j-th* column of ψ.

To apply the S_T test in Eq. (6), we specify three different QAR models *m(.),* for all $\tau \in\subset [0, 1]$, under the null hypothesis of non-Granger causality in Eq. (4) as follows.

$$QAR(1): m^1\left(I_t^Y, \theta(\tau)\right) = \mu_1(\tau) + \mu_2(\tau)Y_{t-1} + \sigma_t\Phi_u^{-1}(\tau),$$
$$QAR(2): m^2\left(I_t^Y, \theta(\tau)\right) = \mu_1(\tau) + \mu_2(\tau)Y_{t-1} + \mu_3(\tau)Y_{t-2} + \sigma_t\Phi_u^{-1}(\tau),$$
$$QAR(3): m^3\left(I_t^Y, \theta(\tau)\right) = \mu_1(\tau) + \mu_2(\tau)Y_{t-1} + \mu_3(\tau)Y_{t-2} + \mu_4(\tau)Y_{t-3} + \sigma_t\Phi_u^{-1}(\tau), \quad (7)$$

We estimate the parameter $\theta(\tau) = (\mu_1(\tau), \mu_2(\tau), \mu_3(\tau), \mu_4(\tau), \sigma_t)'$ by using maximum likelihood in an equally spaced grid of quantiles and Φ_u^{-1} is the inverse of a standard normal distribution function. To verify the sign of the causal relationship between the variables, we estimate the quantile autoregressive model in Eq. (7) including lagged variables of another variable. To avoid complexity, we present the results using only the QAR(3) model with the lagged values of the other variables as follows:

$$\begin{aligned} Q_\tau^Y\left(Y_t|I_t^Y, I_t^Z\right) &= \mu_1(\tau) + \mu_2(\tau)Y_{t-1} + \mu_3(\tau)Y_{t-2} + \mu_4(\tau)Y_{t-3} \\ &+\beta(\tau)Z_{t-1} + \sigma_t\Phi_u^{-1}(\tau), \end{aligned} \quad (8)$$

4 Empirical Analysis

Table 1 shows the descriptive statistics for the data series. Notably, the Jarque–Bera normality tests, as established by Jarque and Bera (1980), decisively reject the null hypothesis of normality for all the examined series at a significance level of 1%. This observation underscores the suitability of employing quantile regression analysis, which exhibits resilience in the face of non-normal skewness during estimation. Therefore, quantile analysis is carried out to consider asymmetric aspects.

For time series analysis, it is necessary to make sure that none of the series has a unit root issue. To consider this condition, ADF (Dickey & Fuller, 1981) and PP (Phillips & Perron, 1988) unit root analyses are performed and outcomes are presented in Table 2. The results confirm that all series do not have a stationary issue

Table 1 Summary statistics

Variable	Mean	Median	Std. dev	Skewness	Kurtosis	Min	Max	Jarque–Bera
ln GDP	815.2	355.4	546.68	0.639	–0.950	179.4	1996.1	12.13*
ln LIFEI	14.698	10.941	15.133	1.204	0.836	0.381	61.428	32.744*
ln NONLIFEI	7.542	4.142	7.081	1.038	–0.237	1.050	25.383	21.596*
ln TOTALI	22.204	15.083	22.050	1.139	0.457	1.431	89.811	27.030*

Note * denotes the significance at a 1% level of significance
Source Author's Calculations

Table 2 Traditional unit root analysis

Variables	ADF Test	PP Test
	T-Stat	T-Stat
ln GDP	–2.7204	–0.6460
ln LIFEI	–1.8634	–1.7197
ln NONLIFEI	–1.9375	–1.5903
ln TOTALI	–1.9391	–2.1142
ΔGDP	–3.7354**	–3.8020**
ΔLIFEI	–3.8779**	–8.8513*
ΔNONLIFEI	–4.6674*	–5.8168*
ΔTOTALI	–5.4080*	–9.9542*

Note * and ** denote the significance at 1% and 5% levels of significance respectively
Source *Author's Calculations*

at first difference. However, none of the series is stationary at the second difference. Furthermore, quantile unit root analysis (Galvao Jr, 2009; Koenker & Xiao, 2004) is performed to check the unit root issue in the series. The reported results in Table 3 show the persistence estimate (α), t-state, and level of significance (CV095). Based the these findings series is not stationary in all quantiles at level, I*(0)*excluding life and total insurance in the extreme lower quartile ($\tau = 0.05$) for all the quantile conditional distribution. Thus, we reject the null hypothesis of unit root at the median and higher quantiles of the conditional distribution at the 5% significance level. These findings reflect that all series are also stationary at first different for all quantiles.

The stationarity of the series at first difference indicates to proceed for cointegration analysis. Therefore, Johansen linear cointegration (Johansen, 1991) is employed to check the long-run association between economic growth and life, nonlife, and total insurance. The reported results in Table 4 confirm the absence of linear cointegration between GDP, life, nonlife, and total insurance at a 5% level of significance. These findings endorse the findings of the JB normality test presented in Table 1. As per the findings of the JB test, the asymmetric/nonlinear behavior exists among all series, we proceed further to apply quantile cointegration (Xiao, 2009)that has the capacity to accommodate nonlinearities. We include two lags and two leads of $(\Delta Z_t, \Delta Z_t^2)$ in the quantile cointegrating model in Eq. (3).

In contrast to the linear cointegration, Table 5 presents the quantile cointegration estimates for Eq. (3). These findings confirm a statistically significant nonlinear cointegration between the quantiles of economic growth, life, nonlife, and total insurance sector in China at a 1% level of significance.

Further, Table 6 reports the coefficients of quantile cointegration, ß(τ) *and* γ(τ), for three models. The estimated coefficients ascertain a significant positive long-term relationship between economic growth and life insurance (model-1), nonlife insurance (model-2), and total insurance (model-3) at a 1% level significance, irrespective of different points along the economic growth distribution $\tau = 0.05$–0.95.

Table 3 Quantile unit root test

Q	ln GDP			ln LIFEI			ln NONLIFEI			ln TOTALI		
	α	t-state	CV095	α	t-state	CV095	α	t-state	CV095	α	t-state	CV095
0.05	1.0272	–1.153	–2.688	0.783	4.947*	–2.755	1.001	–0.059	–2.378	0.782	4.759*	–2.853
0.10	1.0164	0.956	–2.976	0.926	–0.550	–3.068	0.990	–0.270	–2.787	0.844	–0.666	–2.985
0.15	1.0157	1.321	–3.230	0.908	–1.614	–3.274	0.975	–0.860	–3.196	0.843	–3.230	–2.961
0.20	1.0161	1.364	–3.375	0.944	–1.550	–3.362	0.969	–1.461	–3.206	0.924	–2.688	–3.306
0.25	1.0176	1.811	–3.410	0.955	–1.654	–3.410	0.979	–1.897	–3.395	0.931	–2.664	–3.348
0.30	1.018	1.822	–3.410	0.961	–1.658	–3.410	0.981	–1.856	–3.410	0.933	–2.918	–3.408
0.35	1.012	1.064	–3.410	0.966	–1.623	–3.410	0.982	–1.844	–3.410	0.949	–2.116	–3.410
0.40	1.010	0.716	–3.410	0.960	–2.196	–3.410	0.986	–1.234	–3.410	0.953	–2.142	–3.410
0.45	1.008	0.630	–3.410	0.961	–2.501	–3.410	0.994	–0.525	–3.410	0.966	–1.939	–3.410
0.50	1.009	0.656	–3.410	0.964	–2.045	–3.410	0.994	–0.517	–3.410	0.984	–0.842	–3.410
0.55	1.007	0.494	–3.410	0.973	–1.665	–3.410	0.993	–0.543	–3.410	0.980	–0.991	–3.410
0.60	1.012	0.854	–3.410	0.980	–1.190	–3.410	0.988	–0.956	–3.410	0.990	–0.463	–3.410
0.65	1.014	0.945	–3.410	0.987	–0.625	–3.410	0.985	–1.011	–3.410	0.998	–0.079	–3.410
0.70	1.022	1.285	–3.410	0.979	–0.915	–3.410	0.978	–1.253	–3.410	0.996	–0.153	–3.410
0.75	1.026	1.347	–3.410	0.984	–0.637	–3.410	0.977	–0.836	–3.410	1.001	0.026	–3.410
0.80	1.024	1.103	–3.410	0.984	–0.337	–3.410	0.954	–1.439	–3.410	1.007	0.168	–3.410
0.85	1.020	0.754	–3.410	0.989	–0.144	–3.410	0.962	–1.054	–3.410	1.009	0.124	–3.391

(continued)

Table 3 (continued)

Q	ln GDP			ln LIFEI			ln NONLIFEI			ln TOTALI		
0.90	1.008	0.254	–3.410	1.001	–0.008	–3.410	0.902	–1.469	–3.410	0.992	–0.035	–3.266
0.95	1.035	–1.224	–3.394	1.005	–0.131	–2.839	0.964	1.344	–3.410	0.998	0.035	–2.925

Note This table presents the persistence estimates $\hat{\alpha}$ and t-statistics of the quantile unit root test proposed by Koenker and Xiao (2004) and Galvao (2009). Bold values of t-statistics denote rejection of the null hypothesis H0: $\alpha(\tau) = 1$ at the 5% significance level, where * denotes the rejection of null hypothesis H_0: $\alpha(\tau) = 1$ at the 5 percent level of significance

Source Author's Calculations

Table 4 Johansen linear cointegration

Model	Trace statistic H_0: rank = 0 (15.41)	Max eigenvalue statistic. H_0: rank = 0 (14.07)	Cointegration relations
Model-1	15.168	11.489	No
Model-2	13.922	9.579	No
Model-3	18.021	16.611	No

Note This table reports the linear cointegration test of Johansen (1991, 1995) for economic growth, life, nonlife, and total insurance in China. We selected the lag lengths of vector autoregressive models that minimize the AIC, allowing for a maximum lag length of 18 months. Numbers in parentheses next to H0: rank = 0 represent the 5% critical values of the corresponding test statistic
Source Author's Calculations

Table 5 Quantile cointegration

Model	Coefficient	$\text{Sup}_t \, \lvert V_n(T) \rvert$	CV1	CV5	CV10
Model-1	ß	**9.894****	10.236	7.476	5.827
	γ	**3.609*****	6.769	4.395	3.393
Model-2	ß	**10.622***	4.192	3.168	2.713
	γ	**1.966***	0.972	0.680	0.557
Model-3	ß	**14.666****	15.62	11.32	9.669
	γ	**3.595****	4.354	2.747	2.234

Note This table presents the results of the quantile cointegration test of Xiao (2009) for economic growth, life, nonlife, and total insurance. We test the stability of the coefficients β and γ in the quantile cointegration for each model. CV1, CV5, and CV10 are the critical values of statistical significance at 1%, 5%, and 10%, respectively. We use 1000 Monte Carlo simulations to generate the critical values. We use an equally spaced grid of 19 quantiles, [0.05;0.95], to calculate the test statistic of the quantile cointegration. We use an equally spaced grid of 5 tail quantiles, [0.05;0.25], to calculate the test statistic Bold values denote rejection of the null hypothesis at the 1%, 5%, and 10% significance levels. *, ** and *** represent the significance at 1%, 5% and 10% level of significance
Source Author's Calculations

Our findings are consistent with Answer et al. (2019) for Malaysia and Ukpon & Acha, (2017) for Nigeria. The robust and consistent positive interplay underscores the lasting impact of the insurance sector on economic growth. Further, it highlights that life, non-life, and total insurance plays a vital role in fostering economic development.

To verify the findings of quantile cointegration estimated coefficients, we apply quantile regression analysis (Koenker & Bassett Jr, 1978) and the results are presented in Table 7. The findings underscore a positive impact of life, nonlife, and total insurance on economic growth across all quantiles, i.e., from lower economic growth to higher economic growth, with a 1% significance level. However, the calculated parameters exhibit relatively higher values in quantiles above $\tau > 0.5$, suggesting that the strength of the relationship in Model-1 and Model-3, representing insurance sector activities, becomes more pronounced as we move from lower to higher

Table 6 Quantile cointegration model: estimated coefficient

Quantiles	Model-1		Model-2		Model-3	
	ß	γ	ß	γ	ß	γ
0.05	0.275*	0.059*	1.010*	−0.086*	0.459*	0.035*
0.10	0.292*	0.055*	1.046*	−0.091*	0.480*	0.030*
0.15	0.300*	0.051*	1.071*	−0.098*	0.472*	0.030*
0.20	0.319*	0.055*	1.079*	−0.099*	0.489*	0.026*
0.25	0.324*	0.051*	1.109*	−0.106*	0.504*	0.022**
0.30	0.326*	0.052*	1.121*	−0.108*	0.512*	0.021**
0.35	0.334*	0.050*	1.120*	−0.108*	0.501*	0.023**
0.40	0.342*	0.048*	1.115*	−0.108*	0.502*	0.022**
0.45	0.337*	0.050*	1.117*	−0.108*	0.485*	0.025*
0.50	0.345*	0.048*	1.116*	−0.107*	0.486*	0.024**
0.55	0.340*	0.051*	1.124*	−0.108*	0.468*	0.030*
0.60	0.320*	0.057*	1.102*	−0.105*	0.480*	0.029**
0.65	0.287*	0.069*	1.101*	−0.103*	0.465*	0.033*
0.70	0.277*	0.074*	1.109*	−0.105*	0.430*	0.040*
0.75	0.262*	0.076*	1.105*	−0.105*	0.394*	0.051*
0.80	0.262*	0.086*	1.104*	−0.105*	0.335*	0.064*
0.85	0.251*	0.090*	1.107*	−0.105*	0.361*	0.060*
0.90	0.285*	0.079*	1.114*	−0.105*	0.347*	0.062*
0.95	0.230*	0.091*	1.114*	−0.105*	0.383*	0.050*

Note This table contains estimated coefficients of the quantile cointegration. Where * denotes the significance at a 1% level of significance
Source Author's Calculation

quantiles (τ: 0.5 = > 0.95). In the case of Model-2, the magnitude of the relationship consistently exceeds that of Model-1 and Model-3; however, it demonstrates a declining trend as we progress from lower to higher quantiles, with a subsequent increase in the upper quantiles. In Fig. 1, the depicted estimated coefficients span across all quantiles, revealing that insurance at a disaggregated level exerts a more substantial influence, with non-life insurance showing a higher impact and life insurance having a comparatively lower impact on economic growth. On the other hand, total insurance demonstrates a moderate impact but exhibits an overall increasing effect on economic growth. Although we did not come across any substantial study that estimates the insurance growth nexus at a disaggregate level using a quantile approach in China, however, overall, our findings are consistent with the study of Ukpon & Acha (2017) for Nigeria, Answer et al. (2019) for Malaysia, Kjosevski (2012b) for Haiss & Sümegi (2008) and Wang et al. (2017) in Europe.

There are numerous plausible reasons for a higher impact of non-life insurance on economic growth than life insurance. For instance, non-life insurance often plays

Table 7 Estimates of quantile regression

Quantiles	Model-1	Model-2	Model-3
0.05	0.374*	0.755*	0.527*
0.10	0.402*	0.754*	0.552*
0.15	0.435*	0.754*	0.565*
0.20	0.481*	0.740*	0.571*
0.25	0.478*	0.740*	0.573*
0.30	0.481*	0.737*	0.575*
0.35	0.455*	0.734*	0.586*
0.40	0.457*	0.727*	0.589*
0.45	0.454*	0.726*	0.591*
0.50	0.456*	0.717*	0.593*
0.55	0.488*	0.711*	0.593*
0.60	0.488*	0.695*	0.596*
0.65	0.489*	0.695*	0.598*
0.70	0.488*	0.698*	0.605*
0.75	0.493*	0.738*	0.607*
0.80	0.497*	0.758*	0.607*
0.85	0.502*	0.767*	0.604*
0.90	0.507*	0.770*	0.606*
0.95	0.506*	0.776*	0.609*

Note * denotes the significance at a 1% level of significance
Source Author's Calculation

an essential role in mitigating financial risks associated with unexpected events such as accidents, natural disasters, and liability claims. These policies contribute to economic stability by reducing the financial burden on individuals and businesses, thereby positively impacting economic growth. Further, non-life insurance is coupled with commercial and industrial activities that support businesses by providing coverage for risks like property damage, theft, and liability claims. A robust non-life insurance sector can encourage entrepreneurship, investment in business, and infrastructure development, leading to increased economic activity and growth. Thus, the consistently higher coefficients for non-life insurance compared to life insurance could be ascribed to the fundamental role of non-life insurance in risk management, economic stability, and supporting various economic activities. These factors collectively contribute to a more significant and immediate impact on economic growth.

After confirming a positive relationship between economic growth and the insurance sector, we identify a direction of causality. As (Granger, 1969) argued if a long-run relationship exists, there must be a causal relationship such as X Granger cause Y or Y Granger cause X or Both Granger Cause each other. Proceeding to our quantile analysis, we apply quantile Granger causality (Troster, 2018) under the

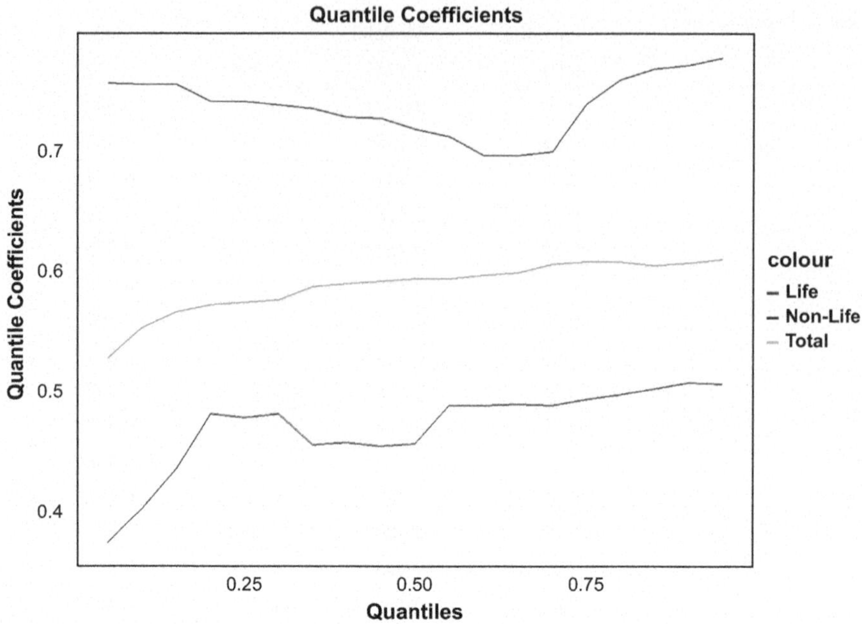

Fig. 1 Quantiles on the x-axis and quantile coefficients on the y-axis for life, non-life, and total insurance. (Source Author's Calculation)

null hypothesis of Granger non-causality in quantiles. The estimated p-values are reported in Tables 8, 9 and 10. Table 8 presents the outcomes of Granger-causality tests assessing the relationships between changes in GDP (ΔGDP) and changes in the life insurance sector (ΔLIFEI) across all quantiles, individual quantiles, and various lag lengths (1, 2, and 3). The p-values for each Granger-causality test indicate the statistical significance of causal relationships between the variables. Notably, the bidirectional Granger causality exists for overall quantiles $\tau = [0.05$ to $0.95]$ and at different quantiles and lag lengths. The significant p-values are displayed in the table without boldness, whereas, bold values indicate insignificance. The insignificant p-values establish that there is no statistically significant Granger-causal relationship between ΔGDP and ΔLIFEI. Hence, changes in GDP do not significantly predict changes in the life insurance sector and vice versa at these specific quantiles and lag structures. However, the bidirectional causality is found between economic growth and life insurance from lower quantiles to lower middle quantiles $\tau = [0.05\text{–}0.35]$. Similarly, a unidirectional causality is predicted from life insurance to economic growth at $\tau = [0.40, 0.45$, and $0.55\text{–}0.95]$ and from economic growth to life insurance at $\tau = [0.50, 0.65, 0.75, 0.85]$. Overall, we find the causality from life insurance to the economic growth is more robust at lower, middle, and upper tail. One of the plausible reasons of these findings is, when uncertain (negative tail) prevails in any economy, people tend to opt for life insurance, due to their risk averse behavior, that in turn translates into economic growth. Nevertheless, in higher economic conditions (upper tail), the insurance sector have fully developed and functional, i.e., moving national saving to rest of economic sectors, and contributes towards the economic growth.

Further, Table 9 presents the results of Granger-causality tests between changes in GDP (*ΔGDP*) and changes in the non-life insurance sector (*ΔNONLIFEI*) at all quantiles $\tau = [0.05$ to $0.95]$, at various quantiles, along with different lag lengths (1, 2, and 3). The estimated p-values indicate the significance of Granger-causality relationships at various quantiles. Particularly, the p-values are bold for several quantiles at different lag length which indicates the insignificance of the Granger causality relationship. The bold p-values imply that the change in GDP does not significantly predict the value of the non-life insurance sector or vice versa at these quantiles. However, it is important to note that there are instances of significance at all quartiles, individual quantiles, and lag lengths, which may suggest varying degrees of causal relationships in specific scenarios. For instance, the unidirectional

Table 8 Granger-causality between ΔGDP_t and $\Delta LIFEI_t$: subsampling p-values

Quantiles	ΔGDP to ΔLIFEI			ΔLIFEI to ΔGDP		
	lag = 1	Lag = 2	Lag = 3	lag = 1	Lag = 2	Lag = 3
0.05 to 0.95	0.012	0.012	0.012	0.012	0.012	0.012
0.05	0.025	0.025	0.062	0.062	0.062	0.049
0.1	0.012	0.012	0.012	0.012	0.012	0.012
0.15	0.012	0.012	0.012	0.012	0.012	0.012
0.2	0.012	0.012	0.012	0.012	0.012	0.012
0.25	0.012	0.012	0.012	0.012	0.012	0.012
0.3	0.012	0.012	0.012	0.012	0.012	0.012
0.35	0.012	0.012	0.012	0.012	0.012	0.012
0.4	**0.605**	**0.593**	**0.914**	0.012	0.012	0.012
0.45	0.012	0.012	**0.296**	0.012	0.012	0.025
0.5	0.037	0.012	0.012	**0.173**	**0.136**	**0.309**
0.55	**0.062**	0.012	0.037	0.012	0.037	0.025
0.6	0.037	0.037	0.025	0.012	0.012	0.012
0.65	0.025	0.037	0.037	0.012	0.012	0.012
0.7	0.049	0.037	**0.086**	0.012	0.012	0.012
0.75	0.012	0.012	0.012	0.012	0.012	0.012
0.8	0.012	0.012	0.025	0.012	0.012	0.012
0.85	**0.161**	**0.136**	**0.407**	0.012	0.012	0.012
0.9	**0.395**	**0.395**	0.012	0.012	0.012	0.012
0.95	**0.173**	**0.185**	**0.185**	0.049	0.049	0.037

Note The table represents the p-values Granger causality test for all quantiles and individual quantiles for different lag lengths. Bold p-values reflect the insignificance
Source Author's calculation

causality from economic growth to non-life is found at extreme lower to lower middle quantiles $\tau = [0.05–0.35]$, and non-life to economic growth is predicated for ($\tau = [0.20–0.30]$). These findings emphasize valuable insights into the dynamic relations between economic growth and the non-life insurance sector, highlighting the conditional nature of their causal relationships across different quantiles and lag structures. Similarly, bidirectional causality has been observed over the quantiles of $\tau = [0.50–0.65]$. However, at extreme upper quantiles, we don't find any causal relationship between nonlife insurance and economic growth. These findings suggest that at early phases of growth, economic agents increase nonlife insurance that subsequently, because of their risk averse behavior, hence not a condition to bear any loss, that eventually supports economic growth. However, the bidirectional and unidirectional causality disappears when economic activity is booming because of well-established systems and procedures.

Table 9 Granger-causality between ΔGDP_t and $\Delta NONLIFEI_t$: subsampling p-values

Quantile	ΔGDP to ΔNONLIFEI			ΔNONLIFEI to ΔGDP		
	lag = 1	Lag = 2	Lag = 3	lag = 1	Lag = 2	Lag = 3
0.05 to 0.95	0.012	0.012	0.012	0.012	0.025	0.012
0.05	0.025	0.025	0.062	**1.000**	**1.000**	**1.000**
0.1	0.012	0.012	0.012	**0.407**	**0.444**	**0.333**
0.15	0.012	0.012	0.012	**0.173**	0.012	0.012
0.2	0.012	0.012	0.012	0.012	0.012	0.012
0.25	0.012	0.012	0.012	0.012	0.012	0.012
0.3	0.012	0.012	0.012	0.012	0.049	0.049
0.35	0.012	0.012	0.012	0.049	**0.062**	0.049
0.4	**0.605**	**0.593**	**1.000**	0.074	**0.074**	**0.111**
0.45	0.012	0.012	**0.296**	**0.568**	**0.642**	**0.593**
0.5	0.037	0.012	0.012	0.037	0.049	**0.062**
0.55	**0.062**	0.012	0.037	0.049	0.012	0.025
0.6	0.037	0.037	0.025	0.049	0.049	0.012
0.65	0.025	0.037	0.037	0.037	**0.160**	**0.074**
0.7	0.049	0.037	**0.086**	0.037	**0.123**	**0.086**
0.75	0.012	0.012	0.012	**0.198**	**0.642**	**0.160**
0.8	0.012	0.012	**0.111**	0.012	0.037	0.037
0.85	**0.160**	**0.136**	**0.407**	**0.123**	0.049	**0.160**
0.9	**0.395**	**0.395**	0.012	**0.173**	**0.198**	**0.136**
0.95	**0.099**	**0.136**	**0.148**	**1.000**	**1.000**	**1.000**

Note The table represents the p-values Granger causality test for all quantiles and individual quantiles for different lag lengths. Bold p-values reflect the insignificance
Source *Author's calculation*

Lastly, Table 10 estimates the Granger-causality tests between changes in GDP (ΔGDP) and changes in the aggregated insurance sector (ΔTOTALI) across all quantiles $\tau = [0.05 \text{ to } 0.95]$, individual quantile and lag lengths (1, 2, and 3). The p-values reveal several significant findings. Firstly, there is evidence of feedback causality between economic growth and total insurance at quantiles equal to or below $0.35 \geq \tau$ for all lag lengths, suggesting that changes in both variables can predict changes in the other within this range which reflects the facts that insurance and growth both develops joint hands at lower stages of growth in any economy. Secondly, at quantiles 0.4 and 0.5, unidirectional causality is observed with total insurance Granger-causing economic growth and economic growth Granger-causing total insurance, respectively. Lastly, at the highest quantiles ($\tau = [0.85 \text{ and } 0.95]$), a unidirectional causality is predicted from total insurance to economic growth. Overall, the findings suggest an intricate relationship between economic growth and total insurance across different quantiles and lag structures. Overall our findings of Granger causality are in line with the study conducted by Anwar et al. (2019) that supports the existence of bidirectional causality between insurance penetration and economic growth in Malaysia.

5 Conclusion and Recommendations

This research considers the role of insurance activities at a disaggregated level and its relations with economic growth across various points of the distribution. Therefore, a bivariate analysis has been performed to evaluate the behavior of life, nonlife, and total insurance growth in quantiles for economic growth by taking time from $1994Q_1$-$2022Q_4$ for China. Starting from a quantile unit root test, findings report that all variables do not have a unit root problem at first difference. Similarly, the results of quantile cointegration confirm the existence of a long-run association between the quantiles of economic growth and aggregated-disaggregated insurance. Further, we find a positive and significant impact of life, nonlife, and total insurance sectors' development on economic growth for all quantiles. However, the magnitude of this relationship varies, starting from lower tail to higher tail distribution. The Granger causality test provides evidence in favor of bidirectional causality between the insurance sector and economic growth. Our findings suggest a positive change in the insurance sector will increase economic growth with a greater effect. In addition, the direction of a causal relationship is identified by employing Granger causality in the quantiles approach. We conclude a bidirectional causality between economic growth and life-nonlife insurance for lower to higher quantiles. Similarly, a feedback effect or bidirectional relationship is noted between total insurance and economic growth for all quantiles except the most extreme tails.

Based on the compelling results derived from our analysis, policymakers should consider several key policy recommendations to utilize the potential of the insurance sector for raising economic growth and stability. First and most important,

Table 10 Granger-causality between ΔGDP_t and $\Delta TOTALI_t$: subsampling p-values

Quantiles	ΔGDP **to** ΔTOTALI			ΔTOTALI **to** ΔGDP		
	lag = 1	Lag = 2	Lag = 3	lag = 1	Lag = 2	Lag = 3
0.05 to 0.95	0.012	0.012	0.012	0.012	0.012	0.012
0.05	0.025	0.025	**0.062**	0.012	0.012	0.012
0.1	0.012	0.012	0.012	0.012	0.012	0.012
0.15	0.012	0.012	0.012	0.012	0.012	0.012
0.2	0.012	0.012	0.012	0.012	0.012	0.012
0.25	0.012	0.012	0.012	0.012	0.012	0.012
0.3	0.012	0.012	0.012	0.012	0.012	0.012
0.35	0.012	0.012	0.012	0.012	0.012	0.012
0.4	**0.605**	**0.593**	**1.000**	0.012	0.012	0.012
0.45	0.012	0.012	**0.296**	0.012	0.012	0.012
0.5	0.037	0.012	0.012	**0.444**	**0.333**	**0.605**
0.55	**0.062**	0.012	0.037	0.012	0.012	0.012
0.6	0.037	0.037	0.025	0.012	0.012	0.012
0.65	0.025	0.037	0.037	0.012	0.012	0.012
0.7	0.049	0.037	**0.086**	0.012	0.012	0.012
0.75	0.012	0.012	0.012	0.012	0.012	0.012
0.8	0.012	0.012	0.025	0.012	0.012	0.012
0.85	**0.160**	**0.136**	**0.407**	0.012	0.012	0.012
0.9	**0.395**	**0.395**	0.012	0.012	0.012	0.012
0.95	**0.099**	**0.136**	**0.148**	0.025	0.037	0.037

Note The table represents the p-values Granger causality test for all quantiles and individual quantiles for different lag lengths. Bold p-values reflect the insignificance
Source Author's calculation

fostering an environment that pushes competition and innovation within the insurance industry should be a priority. This could imply introducing regulatory frameworks that promote and facilitate fair competition and safeguard consumer protection. Additionally, to strengthen insurance penetration, efforts should be made to enhance financial literacy and awareness about the benefits of insurance for economic gain among the public. Policymakers ought to focus on the development of both life and non-life insurance markets which could be accomplished by recognizing their distinct roles in the economy. For instance, the expansion of the non-life insurance sector should be incentivized as it has a consistent positive impact across quantiles. This could be particularly beneficial for mitigating economic risks associated with natural disasters and liability claims. Furthermore, facilitating investment in infrastructure projects and stimulating public–private partnerships can support the insurance industry by increasing insurable assets. Lastly, monitoring and periodically evaluating the effectiveness of these policies will be crucial to ensure the continued positive contribution of the insurance sector to economic growth and resilience in the long term.

Although the study provides valuable insights into the relationship between insurance and economic growth, however, several limitations should be acknowledged. Firstly, the analysis relies on quantitative data and statistical models, which may not capture the full complexity of the insurance-economy nexus. Qualitative factors, such as the regulatory environment, consumer behavior, and market dynamics, are not fully accounted for. Second, the study's findings are based on the specific time period in China. Generalizing these results to different countries or time periods should be done cautiously, as economic conditions and insurance markets vary.

References

Adams, M., Andersson, J., Andersson, L.-F., & Lindmark, M. (2009). Commercial banking, insurance and economic growth in Sweden between 1830 and 1998. *Accounting, Business and Financial History, 19*(1), 21-38.

Akinlo, T., & Apanisile, O. T. (2014). Relationship between insurance and economic growth in Sub-Saharan African: A panel data analysis. *Modern Economy, 2014.*

Alhassan, A. L. (2016). Insurance market development and economic growth: Exploring causality in 8 selected African countries. *International Journal of Social Economics.*

Alhassan, A. L., & Fiador, V. (2014). Insurance-growth nexus in Ghana: An autoregressive distributed lag bounds cointegration approach. *Review of Development Finance, 4*(2), 83-96.

Allen, F., & Santomero, A. M. (1997). The theory of financial intermediation. *Journal of banking and finance, 21*(11-12), 1461-1485.

Anwer, Z., Ahad, M., & Imran, M. (2019). Does insurance-growth nexus hold for Malaysia? *Asian-Pacific Economic Literature, 33*(2), 108-120.

Apergis, N., & Poufinas, T. (2020). The role of insurance growth in economic growth: Fresh evidence from a panel of OECD countries. The North American Journal of Economics and Finance, 53, 101217.

Asongu, S. A., & Odhiambo, N. M. (2020). Insurance policy thresholds for economic growth in Africa. *The European Journal of Development Research, 32*(3), 672–689.

Baranoff, E. G., & Sager, T. W. (2002). The relationship between insurance and economic growth in the US. Risk Management and Insurance Review, 5(1), 67-91.

Beck, T., & Webb, I. (2003). Economic, demographic, and institutional determinants of life insurance consumption across countries. The World Bank Economic Review, 17(1), 51-88.

Benston, G. J., & Smith, C. W. (1976). A transactions cost approach to the theory of financial intermediation. *Journal of finance, 31*(2), 215-231.

Chau, W., Khin, A., & Teng, K. (2013). Economic development cointegration and Malaysian life and general insurance consumption. *Australian Journal of Basic and Applied Sciences, 7*(10), 538-546.

Chen, P. F., Lee, C. C., & Lee, C. F. (2012). How does the development of the life insurance market affect economic growth? Some international evidence. *Journal of International Development, 24*(7), 865-893.

Ching, K. S., Kogid, M., & Furuoka, F. (2010). Causal relation between life insurance funds and economic growth: evidence from Malaysia. *ASEAN Economic Bulletin*, 185–199.

Cristea, M., Marcu, N., & Cârstina, S. (2014). The relationship between insurance and economic growth in Romania compared to the main results in Europe–a theoretical and empirical analysis. *Procedia Economics and Finance, 8*, 226-235.

Cummins, J. D., & Weiss, M. A. (2009). Convergence of insurance and financial markets: Hybrid and securitized risk-transfer solutions. The Journal of Risk and Insurance, 76(3), 493-545.

Dash, S., Pradhan, R. P., Maradana, R. P., Gaurav, K., Zaki, D. B., & Jayakumar, M. (2018). Insurance market penetration and economic growth in Eurozone countries: Time series evidence on causality. *Future Business Journal, 4*(1), 50–67.

Dawd, I., & Benlagha, N. (2023). Insurance and economic growth nexus: New evidence from OECD countries. *Cogent Economics & Finance, 11*(1), 2183660.

Dickey, D. A., & Fuller, W. A. (1981). Likelihood ratio statistics for autoregressive time series with a unit root. *Econometrica: journal of the Econometric Society*, 1057–1072.

Engle, R. F., & Granger, C. W. (1987). Co-integration and error correction: representation, estimation, and testing. *Econometrica*, 251–276.

Focarelli, D. (2017). Why insurance regulation is crucial for long-term investment and economic growth. In *Insurance Regulation in the European Union* (pp. 339–359): Springer.

Galvao Jr, A. F. (2009). Unit root quantile autoregression testing using covariates. *Journal of econometrics, 152*(2), 165-178.

Ghosh, A. (2013). Does life insurance activity promote economic development in India: an empirical analysis. *Journal of Asia Business Studies.*

Granger, C. W. (1969). Investigating causal relations by econometric models and cross-spectral methods. *Econometrica: journal of the Econometric Society*, 424–438.

Haiss, P., & Sümegi, K. (2008). The relationship between insurance and economic growth in Europe: A theoretical and empirical analysis. *Empirica, 35*(4), 405-431.

Hickman JC. 1971. Investment implications of the actuarial design of life insurance products. The Journal of Risk and Insurance 38(4): 571–583.

Horng, M.-S., Chang, Y.-W., & Wu, T.-Y. (2012). Does insurance demand or financial development promote economic growth? Evidence from Taiwan. *Applied Economics Letters, 19*(2), 105-111.

Institute, I. I. (2020). Insurance Handbook, World Insurance Marketplace. from https://www.iii.org/publications/insurance-handbook/economic-and-financial-data/world-insurance-marketplace

Iyodo, B., Samuel, S. E., Adewole, C., & Ola, P. O. (2020). Impact of non-life insurance penetration on the economic growth of Nigeria. *Research Journal of Finance and Accounting, 11*(2), 40–50.

Jarque, C. M., & Bera, A. K. (1980). Efficient tests for normality, homoscedasticity and serial independence of regression residuals. *Economics Letters, 6*(3), 255-259.

Johansen, S. (1991). Estimation and hypothesis testing of cointegration vectors in Gaussian vector autoregressive models. *Econometrica*, 1551–1580.

Kjosevski, J. (2012a). Impact of insurance on economic growth: The case of Republic of Macedonia. *European Journal of Business and Economics, 4.*

Kjosevski, J. (2012b). Impact of insurance on economic growth: The case of Republic of Macedonia. *European Journal of Business Economics, 4.*

Koenker, R., & Bassett Jr, G. (1978). Regression quantiles. *Econometrica: journal of the Econometric Society*, 33–50.

Koenker, R., & Xiao, Z. (2004). Unit root quantile autoregression inference. *Journal of the american statistical association, 99*(467), 775-787.

Kugler, M., & Ofoghi, R. (2005). *Does insurance promote economic growth? Evidence from the UK.* Paper presented at the Money Macro and Finance (MMF) Research Group Conference.

Kumar, S., & Sehrawat, M. (2019). Insurance development and economic growth in the United States: An empirical investigation. The Geneva Papers on Risk and Insurance-Issues and Practice, 44(3), 451-469.

Mehmood, B., Shahbaz, M., Jiao, Z. J. T. Q. R. o. E., & Finance. (2021). Do Muslim economies need insurance to grow? Answer from rigorous empirical evidence.

Nell, E. J. (1968). Aspects of Scientific Explanation and Other Essays in the Philosophy of Science. In: JSTOR.

Njegomir, V., & Stojić, D. (2010). Does insurance promote economic growth: The evidence from ex-Yugoslavia region. *Ekonomska misao i praksa*(1), 31–48.

Osei-Bonsu, A., Abotsi, A. K., & Carsamer, E. (2022). Insurance and economic growth in Ghana. *Journal of Economic and Administrative Sciences, 38*(3), 397–416.
Outreville, J. F. (2013). The relationship between insurance and economic development: 85 empirical papers for a review of the literature. *Risk Management and Insurance Review, 16*(1), 71-122.
Ozga, S. A., & Arrow, K. J. (1966). Aspects of the Theory of Risk-Bearing. . *Economica, 33*(130), 251.
Phillips, P. C., & Perron, P. (1988). Testing for a unit root in time series regression. *Biometrika, 75*(2), 335-346.
Rejda GE. 2004. Principles of Risk Management and Insurance, 10th ed. Pearson Education, Inc.: Boston, MA.
Sigma. (3/2021). World insurance: the recovery gains pace.
Sato, R. (1964). The Harrod-Domar model vs the neo-classical growth model. *The Economic Journal, 74*(294), 380-387.
Skipper, H. D. (1997). *Foreign insurers in emerging markets: Issues and concerns* (Vol. 1): International Insurance Foundation Washington, DC.
Troster, V. (2018). Testing for Granger-causality in quantiles. *Econometric Reviews, 37*(8), 850–866. https://doi.org/10.1080/07474938.2016.1172400.
Ukpong, M. S., & Acha, I. A. (2017). Insurance and economic development in Nigeria: Cointegration and causality analysis. *Scholedge International Journal of Management and Development, 4*(4), 28-39.
Verma, A., & Bala, R. (2013). The relationship between life insurance and economic growth: Evidence from India. *Global Journal of Management and Business Studies, 3*(4), 413-422.
Wang, Y., Linsen, Y., & Wenjie, P. (2017). Life Insurance Contribution, Insurance Development and Economic Growth in China. *International Journal of Business and Economic Development, 5*(2).
Ward, D., & Zurbruegg, R. (2000). Does insurance promote economic growth? Evidence from OECD countries. *Journal of Risk and Insurance*, 489–506.
Willett, A. H. (2016). *The economic theory of risk and insurance*: University of Pennsylvania Press.
World Bank. (2020). https://www.worldbank.org/en/data/datatopics/aspire/indicator/socialinsurance#:~:text=The%20ASPIRE%20database%20provides%20performance%20indicators%20of%20social,by%20those%20living%20below%20PPP%20%242.15%20a%20day
Xiao, Z. (2009). Quantile cointegrating regression. *Journal of econometrics, 150*(2), 248-260.
Zouhaie, H. (2014). Insurance and economic growth. *Journal of Economics and Sustainable Development, 5*, 102–112.

The manufacturer's authorised representative in the EU is Springer Nature Customer Service Centre GmbH, Europaplatz 3, 69115 Heidelberg, Germany. If you have any concerns regarding our products, please contact ProductSafety@springernature.com

Printed and bound by CPI Group (UK) Ltd, Croydon, CR0 4YY
01/10/2026
02225864-0012